P9-CQV-150

WINNING AT MERGERS AND ACQUISITIONS

The Guide to Market-Focused Planning and Integration

MARK N. CLEMENTE
DAVID S. GREENSPAN

JOHN WILEY & SONS, INC.
New York • Chichester • Weinheim • Brisbane • Singapore • Toronto

To my wife Anita and to our children Matt, Danny, and Marissa—
whose love and support teach me
life's most valuable lessons every day.
—M.C.

To my wife—my best friend—Rosanne Drucker,
whose love, guidance, support, and patience
make my best work possible.
—D.G.

This book is printed on acid-free paper. ♾

Published by John Wiley & Sons, Inc.

Published simultaneously in Canada.

Library of Congress Cataloging-in-Publication Data:
Clemente, Mark N.
Winning at mergers and acquisitions : the guide to market-focused planning and integration / Mark N. Clemente, David S. Greenspan.
p. cm.
Includes index.
ISBN 0-471-19056-X (cloth : alk. paper)
1. Consolidation and merger of corporations—Planning.
I. Greenspan, David S. II. Title.
HD58.8.C548 1998
658.1'6—dc21 97-38327
CIP

10 9 8 7 6

CONTENTS

FOREWORD

More than 7000 mergers, acquisitions, and corporate divestitures were completed in 1997 with a collective price tag in excess of $900 billion for just those transactions—less than half the total—in which values were announced. If commonly believed historical statistics are replicated, about a third of those deals will fail and another third won't measure up to the performances projected when the merger partners sealed their decisions to combine. That means a huge wad of shareholders' investment—in the form of cash, stock, and other types of acquisition currency—will be flushed down the drain.

"Failure" generally is equated with worst-case results at the target company—stagnation, contraction of the overall market, weakening of market position, loss of share, inability to replace obsolete products, continual defeats at the hands of competitors, drooping sales, and either declining profits or outright losses. Suboptimal performance may require more subtle judgment but is no less vexing to the acquirer who placed a big bet on the deal. The target may grow sales and earnings at less than projected rates, its market may revert to a commodity orientation from cutting-edge technology, or the acquirer may have to pour substantially more investment into the new business to keep it up to speed. Regardless of the specific manifestation, the underperformer generally falls under the broad rubric of falling short in creating shareholder value.

Mergers and acquisitions (M&A)—a key corporate growth approach—has graduated from an occasional shot in the dark to a well-established option in an operating company's basket of corporate development initiatives. Statistics aside, an inexcusably uncomfortable number of deals still don't pass muster and the biggest disasters generate intensive publicity that cloaks the entire M&A process with the stigma of being a gambler's game with a stacked deck.

In the last few years alone, the deal casualty list has included such high-priced miscues as Quaker Oats's acquisition of Snapple Beverage, Novell's acquisition of WordPerfect, and AT&T Corporation's acquisition of NCR, while Eli Lilly & Company has admitted to disappointment with its absorption of PCS. They join a long historical log of misfires such as Exxon's acquisition of Reliance Electric, Atlantic Richfield's acquisition of Anaconda, Mobil's acquisition of Montgomery Ward, and the ill-fated Sears, Roebuck diversification drive that engulfed Dean Witter and Coldwell Banker. Meanwhile, an entire acquisition-heavy corporate strategy—the conglomerate—has been demolished, and overly diversified companies formed in the 1960s literally have taken themselves apart to become slimmer, more focused, more manageable enterprises.

The bullet has been bitten by a wide variety of companies operating in diverse industries and markets, executing deals large and small. But in the majority of cases, the companies that had their fingers burned made one unpardonable mistake. They took their eyes off their markets. Conversely, the considerable, often underpublicized, volume of merger successes often can be attributed to the clear-eyed focus on the marketplace that supported the deal rationale from day one.

That is what makes this book by Mark Clemente and David Greenspan so important. Less a paradigm than a disciplinary framework of values, it synthesizes the realistic issues that must be managed in keeping a combining firm plugged into its marketplace and its customer base. It reminds executives of acquiring companies that if real value is to be created, it usually must spring from the marketplace. It provides a format for communicating the necessity of maintaining customer service and relationships throughout the combined organization during the very tumultuous and stress-filled integration period when internal turf battles can flare out of control and dominate managerial thought. And it offers useful tips for leveraging the market to maximize growth opportunities and value creation while hammering home the dire consequences for the merging company that only pays lip service to those tenets.

If there are generic elements in mergers and acquisitions they are the market and the customers. Under no conditions is M&A seamless or risk-free. But then, neither is any other corporate development format. The failure rate in new product introductions is catastrophic, and only a fraction of new technologies developed in-house can be commercialized. Joint ventures flounder for any number of reasons ranging from partner incompatibility to poor business conception. Results from partial investments in small, promising but untested firms are, not unexpectedly, inconsistent. One topflight corporate development pro once toted up the track record of initiatives launched under several different options and found that M&A was neither more nor less successful than internally generated projects.

Yet, for those acquirers who stay committed to the market, there are excellent prospects for narrowing the odds. Mergers and acquisitions in fact present the savvy buyer with unparalleled flexibility in wringing the most from the opportunities offered by an external transaction.

Deal making, as the aforementioned statistics should suggest, is widely diverse, covering a remarkably broad number of industries. Among the more high-profile, hyperactive industries are banking, insurance, health care, aerospace and defense, computers and information systems, telecommunications, entertainment, media, and utilities. Less publicized but still brisk M&A activity is underway in retailing, wholesale distribution, a wide swath of business services, and even many smokestack industries like auto parts, steel, paper, and food. Virtually no business is untouched by major merger activity.

In several of those areas, M&A activity is responding to ubiquitous, often interlocked forces—such as consolidation, globalization, advancing technology, automation, deregulation, and pressures for cost controls. Others are answering to different drummers—government spending cuts prodding consolidation in defense; deregulation prompting utility combinations; narrowed vendor lists for big-ticket assemblers (i.e., General Motors, Caterpillar) forcing components makers to get bigger; and the rise of "big box" retailers requiring consumer and commercial goods suppliers to expand.

The strategic reasons for M&A are almost infinite and acquisitions are in a unique position to fill an endless number of needs. Acquisitions are quick. When weighed against internal development, they can be cost-efficient in spite of large up-front expenditures.

They can generate value-creating returns more quickly than other formats. They bring skilled people into the organization, and the customer base throw-offs—whether adding new customers or strengthening relationships with existing buyers—can be substantial.

Acquisitions are versatile. They can be used to fill gaps in product lines, add products and technologies, fortify management capabilities, spread geographically, expand in existing markets, and enter new segments. Restaurant chains have used acquisitions to obtain new sites, pharmaceutical companies to add research capability, telecommunications firms to penetrate emerging technologically formed markets that are converging with existing operations, manufacturers to expand plant capacity, and business service providers with a broader array of skills to offer a full package to expanding clients.

In diversity, the wise acquirer can sort out the greatest opportunity by continually tuning in to its marketplace. As varied as these forces of change and acquisition rationales may be, they all inevitably loop back to product and services markets. That should be axiomatic in strategic acquisitions, but the number of chances to create value seems to be matched by the number of points where the ball can be dropped during the often arduous acquisition process. Understanding exactly where a deal can be muffed and exactly how can be useful in tying the Clemente-Greenspan market approach to rewarding acquisitions.

The very first soft spot comes in the preliminary planning stage. Remember that acquisition is a versatile vehicle that can be used to achieve any number of objectives. Choosing the specific objectives in a specific deal is critical. All follow-on actions should unfold in concert with the principal goals, and the postacquisition performance of the target should be measured on whether it achieves its objectives. In the rare instance in which the objectives are not directly connected to the market—that is, an emerging technology that will take years to develop or a business primarily designed to support internal operations and with little "merchant" trade—judge the company accordingly. In the more likely case in which market impact is envisioned, benchmark performance on how well the target or combined company hits the clearly stated objective (i.e., expansion of market share, acceleration of profitable new products, widening of sales coverage, new customers or customer niches, and so on).

Even when the strategic objective is clear, many acquirers go astray because of bad homework in the predeal analysis and search and screen zones. In many cases, this is a point of no return. The deal actually is licked before it starts. An acquirer may think it has done a thorough job evaluating the pluses and minuses of an M&A initiative and sizing up a cluster of prospective targets that can generate rewards. Yet, the same careful buyer may stop short of getting a complete handle on the market. The acquirer will painstakingly calculate the target's market share, historic sales and earnings growth rates, projections of future results including free cash flow generation and prospects for expansion of the market as a whole; evaluate the efficacy of the product line; and rank each target's performance against competitors.

Is that enough? The answer is no if the buyer hasn't probed beyond the obvious quantitative measures into key qualitative influences that can make or break a deal. Do you want to serve, or even like, the new customers being obtained? Do the target's product lines offer genuine opportunities for creating profitable new generations when present offerings run out of growth or are obsolete? Is customer service as good as claimed? Are clients happy with product quality and delivery timetables? Are payment terms customer-friendly without being too generous? Is the target's management capable of spearheading a value-adding growth plan after acquisition? In the accounting realm, are cost and other allocations masking subpar performance by supposedly star products? If there are market-related flaws in the target, do you have the skills and smarts to fix them fast and at low cost?

Assuming everything is on cue until this point, the buyer gets into another shaky area when it approaches the target and starts formal negotiations. The big threat in this stage is that the romance of the deal, impatience to get it done, and the fear of competing bidders breathing down your neck can cause the acquirer to pull away from its objective and its market assessment. The fallout can include purchasing the wrong company, paying an off-the-wall price, getting into a market at the wrong time (such as at a nonreplicable peak), painting unrealistic expectations for the acquisition, or all of the above and more.

Finally, the deal can sputter during the postacquisition integration when the potential for taking eyes off is greatest and the probability for disaster is most acute. One of the biggest mistakes committed by acquirers is placing too high a priority on cost cutting in the days and weeks immediately following deal closing. Obviously reduced costs from economies of scale, elimination of redundant functions, workforce downsizing, and blending of functions and departments are important synergistic kickers to a merger touted internally and externally as a vehicle for increasing net free cash flow. And cost reduction can produce results in a hurry.

But are these results just a temporary splash? If so, what does the combined firm do for an encore? Is the acquirer, despite protestations that it is merely cutting into the fat, really cutting down to the bone? Is it winning an early round but setting itself up for losing the battle in the marketplace?

By concentrating on cost cutting to the exclusion of almost everything else, the acquirer is blowing opportunities in the marketplace at the very time when these prospects may be the brightest. The combined company's focus is riveted internally when it needs to be reaching out to both existing and new customers. All sorts of troubles—from competitors seizing business to turning off customers miffed at not being informed about what the deal means to them—can erupt from this market inattention.

Equally important, the blurring of the external focus can defeat the very purposes of the deal including value creation. Generically, top-line growth from operations has returned to the managerial forefront in this era of low inflation and intense competition when it is extraordinarily difficult to raise prices. The typical market-centered merger is an almost ideal vehicle for increasing revenues. In fact, studies have found that far more money cascades to the bottom line from revenue growth than from cost cutting and that the revenue contribution is a continuous stream rather than a one-shot benefit.

Ironically, many of these revenue-generating opportunities are easy to implement. Acquirers must seek out the revenue enhancement programs that are the easiest to execute and hit them hard. Besides booking contributions to value and strengthening relations with customers, this approach provides a rallying point for getting people in both constituent organizations working together and serves as a clear-cut basis for rewards.

For the longer pull, the external outreach gets the combined company thinking harder on the more creative projects sketched by Clemente and Greenspan—packaging product and service lines to provide complete offerings to customers, combining the skills and products of the two firms to generate new lines, blending the strengths of the two companies to open new market niches and find new customers, and so forth.

There's also a psychological payoff to focusing on the marketplace. It takes much of the mystery out of a deal. The acquirer gets an unadorned fix on why it should do a deal and exactly how it can capture premier value. It is remarkable how a well-managed company with no fear about pushing the envelope on internal development goes absolutely ballistic about a merger. No merger is perfect. There are special risks and challenges—from analysis through integration—in any deal. But intense trepidation is anathema to good decision making. The serious acquirer that keeps the market in view knows when to abort the bad deal and to strike fast for the good deal.

A solid game plan based on the market is the blueprint for strengthening competitive advantage through the best means available. Deals don't create value. Acquirers create value.

MARTIN I. SIKORA
Editor, *Mergers & Acquisitions* Magazine, and
Lecturer, Wharton School of the University of Pennsylvania

PREFACE

The extraordinary failure rate of corporate mergers and acquisitions has been well documented. This book is designed to help reverse that onerous trend.

The vast preponderance of mergers and acquisitions today are geared to effecting strategic gain. Unfortunately, most transactions in the history of corporate combinations have been marked by the massive loss of financial and human assets. Advancement may have been the goal, but decline has—more often than not—been the actual result.

In recent years, there has been on average more than $500 billion invested by businesses annually in corporate mergers and acquisitions. Given the sheer volume and number of deals, one would suspect that companies have learned what it takes to make such transactions succeed. Evidently, they have not.

This book is an attempt to bring a pragmatic new focus to M&A decision making—one that emphasizes the best practices needed to effectively plan, implement, and actualize the benefits of strategic M&A transactions.

What has become clear in the research on which this book is based is that many managers cannot be held completely responsible for their M&A failures. The fact is, the dearth of true M&A success stories means that there has been little in the way of experiential reality from which managers can learn. The errors are being increasingly well-documented in the business literature. The home runs—given the fact that they are so few and far between—are not receiving equal treatment. As a result, there has not been much in the way of guidance.

Highlighting mistakes provides one way to learn. An equally impactive means of instructing is to highlight admirable, well-conceived and -executed efforts. In the following pages, we have attempted to do both. The successes of corporate mergers are showcased and explained. So too are the failures. Credit is given where credit is due. Criticism is offered, not to nonconstructively assail the decisions of bright, hardworking, and otherwise conscientious business executives, but with the intent of highlighting the most common and avoidable pitfalls.

By all accounts, the guidance in this book is intended to address the mistakes made by others in the past in order to help managers avoid those missteps in the future. Similarly, companies' successes are chronicled with the hope that others can replicate and build on them.

WHO WILL BENEFIT FROM THIS BOOK

Before we cite who this book is for, we'll first address who this book is *not* for.

It is not for acquisitive cost cutters: those who buy companies with the goal of stripping, rather than building up, their tangible and intangible assets. Cost cutters are concerned solely with making immediate expense reductions—usually by eliminating duplicative personnel and processes—to effect short-term increases in share price. Theirs is a near-term orientation. The cost cutter cares little about the true value inherent in an organization as embodied by its people and core capabilities. The cost cutter cares little about the target firm's future value. He or she cares only about the company's current worth and how it can be marginally and superficially increased by cost- and head-chopping.

Acquisitive cost cutters will find little value in this book and should save their money on the cover price for their next deal.

So who is this book for?

This book is for business leaders who seek to acquire or merge with companies in order to effect enduring growth. It is for managers who strive to harness the full potential of a company's corporate capabilities so as to augment that potential for the benefit of the organization that is forged as a result of the transaction. In a phrase, this book is for the "strategic buyers" of companies—the people who embrace mergers and acquisitions as an increasingly important method of effecting corporate growth and achieving competitive advantage. It is for the people who realize the tremendous gains attainable through a soundly planned and executed corporate combination, and who recognize the inherently complex series of activities that must be undertaken to make that happen.

A NEW PERSPECTIVE

There are several recurring themes that provide a new perspective on M&A planning and that constitute the foundation of the advice rendered in the ensuing chapters:

Focusing on revenue enhancement through "marketing due diligence." Strategic mergers are designed to effect corporate growth. Growth results from developing new products and services, penetrating new markets, and accessing new technologies, among other things. The common denominator of each of these "strategic synergies" is effecting top-line revenue enhancement. The vast majority of the planning guidelines offered throughout this book key on the techniques of creating near- and long-term revenue streams via the process of market-focused due diligence and integration.

(Certainly, we acknowledge the need to reduce costs when there is obvious fat that must be trimmed. But the majority of guidance ties to cultivating, not obliterating, corporate assets. The focus is on increasing financial performance via revenue enhancement, not expense containment.)

Transferring skills and capabilities. Mergers succeed when the combining companies successfully harness and build on the respective skills of each organization. Capabilities cannot be successfully transferred unless those process- and people-oriented attributes are first adequately safeguarded. Much of the counsel provided focuses on the ways to identify and protect the capabilities that are intricately woven into the fabric of a given company. Most important, we attempt to explain what must be done to effectively channel those capabilities to areas of the merged organization that will benefit most from their operational infusion.

Identifying "marketing intangible assets." Many assets resident in a target company do not show up on its balance sheet—beyond the obvious ones of patents, trademarks, and goodwill. These attributes take the form of often-overlooked intangible assets that relate directly to a company's ability to conceive, construct, and successfully commercialize products and services. These "marketing intangible assets" collectively add to the current value of a given company. They also point up distinct attributes that, when effectively protected and transferred, will ultimately augment the current and future worth of the merged firm itself. We endeavor to identify these intangibles.

Showing respect for people in M&A decision making. Too often, acquirers lose sight of the fact that an organization's most valued asset is its people. Too often, people issues take a backseat to other more financially and operationally driven areas of attention. Mergers and acquisitions continue to get a bad name precisely because of many acquirers' callous indifference to the people affected most by the corporate combinations: the employees in the merging organizations. Ample attention is given to the people-related aspects of M&A planning and integration, with a special emphasis on aligning corporate cultures. Why? First, because focusing on people is an absolutely critical way to preserve value in companies. Second, because it is the morally right thing to do. In the past, poorly planned mergers and acquisitions have seriously derailed or completely ruined the careers of thousands of loyal and valuable employees—people who, many times, would have presented the key to success to otherwise failed transactions.

THE REAL AND THE IDEAL

All target companies are different. All transactions pose different challenges and requirements. What is right for one situation may not be right for another. It is, therefore, difficult to give blanket advice covering all aspects of M&A planning. Nonetheless, we attempt to do as comprehensive a job as possible.

There are tremendous pressures during the deal planning and negotiation process. Typically, there is a period of only a few weeks or months between the time a deal is announced and when it closes. Some of the planning and investigative tactics we suggest undertaking may, in certain cases, be impossible to pursue. Time simply does not permit them. Yet it is important to understand that the guidance offered is based on a best-practices orientation. This means that the most successful acquirers have performed these tasks when it was logistically feasible and—in public company transactions—legally permissible to do so.

Your particular M&A situation, however, may not afford you the luxury of conducting as exhaustive a review as is ideal. Still, you should perform the investigative and planning activities outlined to the fullest extent possible, even if time constraints preclude you from doing as comprehensive a job as may actually be called for. In all cases, performing even a high-level review of a given operational or procedural area is more beneficial than performing no review at all.

Different M&A transactions will pose different informational requirements and timing parameters. Readers are urged to do the best they can given the time and resources available to them.

We do not profess to provide all the answers. We have, however, made a concerted effort to erect a series of helpful signposts to M&A planning that can help readers down the road to merger success—a venue that has been eminently bumpy in the past, but which can hopefully be traveled more smoothly going forward.

SOURCE OF GUIDANCE

Our firm consults with companies on strategic M&A planning and integration. Prior to forming the company, however, we collectively served as employees in a variety of marketing, sales, and business development capacities in 12 different organizations. At three different times in our respective corporate pasts, we were involved in corporate acquisitions—as "the acquired."

We have supplemented our knowledge with the knowledge of others. Credit is graciously given to the clients, business leaders, and associates who so willingly offered their experience and insights in a series of interviews. Our thanks go to the following people:

Peter S. Amico, Territory Sales Manager, Bunge Foods Group—Mr. Amico has worked in sales management for the past 21 years. Prior to joining Bunge Foods, a St. Louis–based industrial food ingredients concern, he served as a regional manager for Van den Bergh Foods and as contract sales manager for Durkee Industrial Foods. During his career, Mr. Amico has been directly involved in acquisition candidate analysis and operational due diligence.

Terence Bentley, Director of Corporate Development, Siemens Corporation—Mr. Bentley specializes in acquisitions, divestitures, and investments in networking, telecommunications, and semiconductor technologies. Prior to joining Siemens Corporation, he was a product manager with several technology companies, delivering more than 25 products to market in local area networks, data communications, and cable television network systems. He has also served as director of network research at the Yankee Group, and as a consultant to AMP, Inc.

Carolyn Chin, Vice President, Corporate Strategy, IBM—Ms. Chin is actively engaged in IBM's merger, acquisition, and corporate growth programs. Prior to becoming IBM's Vice President of Corporate Strategy, she was IBM General Manager for Electronic Commerce Services. Prior to joining IBM, Ms. Chin held a number of management, marketing, strategic planning, and business development positions at Citicorp/Citibank, AT&T, and Macy's, as well as in the U.S. departments of Housing and Urban Development (HUD) and Health, Education, and Welfare (HEW).

Paul M. Cholak, Chief Executive Officer, SHL North America—Prior to joining SHL, Mr. Cholak was managing director of Alexander & Alexander Consulting Group. He also served as chief human resource officer at Bain & Company, Zales Jewelers, Shearson Lehman Hutton, and Columbia Pictures. His career in human resource management spans more than 30 years. In addition to serving as CEO of SHL North America, Mr. Cholak is a director of Saville & Holdsworth USA.

Mufit J. Cinali, Financial Vice President, Mergers and Acquisitions, AT&T—Mr. Cinali manages transactions across AT&T including mergers, acquisitions, joint ventures, equity investments, and divestitures. Mr. Cinali joined AT&T from GE Capital after six years in corporate and new business development and business analysis. His experience also includes strategy consulting with Bain & Company and investment banking with Merrill Lynch Capital Markets. He is a member of the CFO Leadership Council and serves on the board of directors of AT&T Credit Holdings and AT&T Wireless PCS Inc.

Donald M. Curry, Vice President, Senior Markets and New Ventures, Blue Cross and Blue Shield of New Jersey—Mr. Curry has 24 years of experience in health care, marketing, and the distribution of health care products and services. During his career, Mr. Curry has held various professional responsibilities with Blue Cross of California, Continental Insurance Company, Provident Mutual Life Insurance Company, and the Life Insurance Company of North America. Mr. Curry has lectured on health care issues at the Wharton School of the University of Pennsylvania and Rutgers Graduate School of Business.

Diane C. Harris, President, Hypotenuse Enterprises, Inc.—Prior to forming Hypotenuse Enterprises, a corporate development consulting firm, Ms. Harris served for 10 years as Vice President of Corporate Development for Bausch & Lomb. She launched the company's mergers and acquisitions program, implemented a billion-dollar corporate restructuring, and completed 230 transactions accounting for half the company's growth. She serves as the president of the Association for Corporate Growth and is a director of Flowserve Corporation.

John Levinson, President, Westway Capital LLC—Mr. Levinson has over 18 years' experience analyzing and investing in technology and service companies. Prior to founding Westway Capital, he worked at Lynch & Mayer, a New York–based investment manager. For 13 years, he was a securities analyst at Goldman Sachs & Co., responsible for various technology sectors. He was named to *Institutional Investor* magazine's "All-America Research Team" for eight consecutive years—five of these years he was rated number-one in his sector.

Dudley W. Mendenhall, Managing Director–Industry Manager, Entertainment & Media Industries Group, Bank of America—Mr. Mendenhall is responsible for all commercial and investment banking activities for the Group's clients, which include major companies in television and film production, broadcasting, cable television, theater exhibition, casino gaming, and publishing. Previously, he managed the Los Angeles Corporate Finance Group in Bank of America's investment banking subsidiary, Bank America Robertson Stephens.

John L. Parodi, Manager of Engineering, Hoffmann-LaRoche Inc.—Mr. Parodi is responsible for energy management and strategic energy planning for Hoffmann-LaRoche, Inc. Prior to assuming this position, he served as a management consultant, where he worked on numerous projects involving energy industry mergers, joint ventures, and strategic alliances. He has authored and presented numerous articles and papers on the dynamics of corporate growth strategies within the rapidly changing utility industry.

Timothy W. Powell, Managing Director, T. W. Powell Company—Mr. Powell is a New York–based consultant specializing in the deployment of information and information technologies in marketing and strategy. He has authored two books and numerous articles on these and related subjects. His clients include *Fortune* 500 organizations, global professional services firms, and entrepreneurial companies.

Richard J. Rudden, President, R. J. Rudden & Associates, Inc.—Mr. Rudden is a nationally recognized management consultant within the electric, independent energy and natural gas industries. Over the last 20 years, he has been extensively engaged in a variety of strategic planning, product definition, market analysis, and organizational assignments pertaining to energy industry restructuring throughout North America, Australia, and China.

Susan W. Schoon, (former) Senior Vice President of Marketing, The Chase Manhattan Bank—Mrs. Schoon served as Senior Vice President and Retail Marketing Director for Tri-State Regional Bank before joining The Chase Manhattan Bank in 1982. Mrs. Schoon held positions on the wholesale side of Chase, running businesses that are global in nature. The positions included managing global cash, asset movement, and institutional trust. Presently, Mrs. Schoon is a consultant to major financial institutions.

We would also like to thank our editor at John Wiley & Sons, Sheck Cho, for his support during the development of this project.

In the course of our own client work and business development, we are often characterized by financial intermediaries, lawyers, and accountants as "the guys who focus on the soft stuff in mergers and acquisitions." To this categorical relegation we proudly respond, "Yes, we are."

Evidently, the "hard stuff" relates to reviewing and drafting contracts and other legal documentation, conducting valuations and calculating deal premiums, spotting financial irregularities, and going over the books to unearth various and sundry monetary and operational liabilities. The flip side—our side—relates to probing the strengths and weaknesses of the merging companies' people, products, and processes in order to identify quantifiable growth-oriented synergies and the tactics necessary to translate those concepts into actualized realities. Our goal: ensuring the viability and long-term success of the merger or acquisition at hand.

Granted, this book focuses on the so-called soft stuff in M&A planning and integration. But it is precisely the soft stuff that translates directly into hard dollars.

We hope it does so for each and every transaction in your merger and acquisition program.

MARK N. CLEMENTE
DAVID S. GREENSPAN

Part One

STRATEGIC PERSPECTIVE ON M&A PLANNING

1

"Marketing Due Diligence" in Strategic Mergers and Acquisitions

In the 1990s, seemingly not a day goes by when the business press does not report on multimillion-dollar mergers and acquisitions. Companies of all sizes and all industries worldwide are seizing the opportunities to broaden their competitiveness by forging corporate combinations with strategically synergistic partners. The goals of achieving growth, tapping into new markets, and creating unassailable strategic advantage underlie each transaction.

Corporate merger and acquisition activity continues to thrive, with the annual dollar volume of M&A transactions steadily increasing. For example, in 1994 there were approximately $350 billion in M&A deals in the United States. In 1995, that figure rose to almost $400 billion. The year 1996 saw total deal volume in the United States exceed $620 billion, a figure based on the dollar volume of known deals and projections of unannounced transactions and deal prices. And in 1997, M&A transactions totaled more than $900 billion.

Several factors are fueling the continuing explosion in merger activity. The ability of businesses to successfully achieve economies of scale, broaden geographic market coverage, and more effectively compete globally have helped create an aggressive acquisition marketplace. In addition, the search for cost reductions through M&A—particularly in such mature industries as retailing, banking, and health care—is being used to offset companies' inability to increase profits through price or production increases. In all likelihood, the merger mania of the late 1990s will carry over into the new millennium as these and other factors drive corporate growth planning.

Today's merger wave is unlike others seen throughout the 20th century. The focus of M&A today is in stark contrast to the conglomeratization mergers of the 1960s and the frenzied hostile takeovers and leveraged buyouts of the 1980s. Both eras saw dramatically more long-term failures than successes. Studies show that 60% of the cross-industry, conglomerate acquisitions that occurred between 1970 and 1982 were sold or divested by 1989.

Reports of the major LBO deals of the 1980s typically cite the downfall of those organizations, which collapsed under the weight of the heavy debt incurred in financing transactions driven by the promise of quick monetary gain rather than to ably secure long-term strategic advantage. As a means of longer-term corporate growth, mergers and acquisitions have understandably gotten a bad name. Bad numbers underscore M&A's sour reputation. History has shown that 35% to 50% of all deals ultimately fail. Why such a disastrous track record?

The simple fact is mergers and acquisitions are usually easy to envision, but incredibly complex to execute. Even when the synergies exist on paper, problems can occur almost anywhere in the prolonged M&A process. Managers today must closely oversee every phase of predeal strategic analyses and postmerger integration activities. Of particular importance is the initial due diligence process, which, when inadequately conducted, prevents merging companies from ever becoming truly integrated, market-focused organizations.

TRADITIONAL DUE DILIGENCE: STRATEGIC SHORTCOMINGS

Due diligence is the series of exploratory activities used in evaluating a target company prior to finalization of the merger or acquisition. The traditional approach to due diligence focuses on several key areas: financial, legal and regulatory, and accounting and tax. Without question, each of these areas is highly complex, and scores of business and academic textbooks have been devoted to the topics. Broad treatment of them is beyond the scope of this book. Yet it is important for readers to understand the fundamental financial and legal orientation toward due diligence investigations in order to identify its principal shortcoming.

Strategic considerations mark the focus of most M&A deals today. But as we will see, insufficient attention to strategic marketing issues is a pervasive flaw in traditional premerger due diligence.

When a merger or acquisition is first envisioned, the focus is on whether or not it makes financial sense. In due diligence, legal and accounting experts are retained to identify potential fiscal, regulatory, and tax-related liabilities of the target company. Concurrently, investment bankers are devising the financing strategy, determining where and how much capital must be raised to complete the transaction, while auditors pore over the books of the target to arrive at the most accurate valuation. Clearly, traditional due diligence is largely focused on making the numbers work. Company management will not pursue a transaction unless assurances are provided that a detailed examination of the target company's financial affairs has been conducted. In the broadest sense, the goal of due diligence is looking at and beyond the numbers to identify hidden vulnerabilities.

Due diligence in public company transactions requires analyzing a host of Securities and Exchange Commission (SEC) filings. These include Forms 8-K, 10-K, and 10-Q, as well as other documentation providing historical financial data and information on the quality of earnings. A main focus of due diligence is on identifying under- or overvalued assets and liabilities, which may take the form of property, plant, and equipment; inventory levels; marketable equity securities; work in progress; excess pension plan assets; and intangible assets such as licenses, franchises, trademarks, and patented technology.

Accountants play a central role in this phase of the due diligence process. Serving as financial experts on the team, they spearhead the process of identifying the tax consequences of given transactions, offer insights on different types of deal structures, and determine and fulfill regulatory reporting requirements. Attorneys play a critical role in the due diligence process, as well. Legal issues have a direct impact on the timing, structure, and viability of different transactions. These issues include differences in the jurisdiction of incorporation of the merger partners, whether the partners are publicly traded companies, and securities law ramifications of how the transaction is to be financed and structured.

Other M&A-related legal concerns involve antitrust considerations, a central issue in all sizable deals involving mergers of horizontal competitors. Attorneys advise on the likelihood of challenges to the proposed merger by governmental authorities—potential constraints imposed by federal antitrust laws, particularly Section 7 of the Clayton Act. This statute prohibits acquisitions "where in any line of commerce . . . in any section of the country, the effects of such acquisitions may be substantially to lessen competition or to tend to create a monopoly." Many factors combine to determine the competitive environment in a given market. However, the government primarily relies on measures of "market concentration" in evaluating mergers and acquisitions between competing, horizontally aligned companies.

Markets are considered to be either "unconcentrated," "moderately concentrated," or "highly concentrated." For instance, under the 1968 Justice Department guidelines, an industry was deemed to be highly concentrated if the four largest companies held at least 75% of the total market. Although this evaluative policy enabled companies to quickly gauge the government's stance toward a potential merger, it was deemed overly rigid. Its shortcoming lay in its inability to fully and accurately predict the level of decreased industry competitiveness in the wake of the merger of two competitors.

In 1982, the Justice Department introduced the Herfindahl-Hirschman Index (HHI). Instead of simply citing the market share levels of proposed merger partners, the HHI offers more insights on measuring the merger's impact on industry concentration and overall competitiveness. Analyzing antitrust laws obviously focuses on a basic marketing variable—market share.

This is important to note since market share is one of the few marketing-related aspects of conventional due diligence examinations.

Companies undertake due diligence to dot the legal "i's" and to make sure the accounting figures work. However, the merger partners have, in most cases, not sufficiently assessed the strategic marketing variables that lie at the heart of the deal.

When everything in the examination process checks out from a financial, legal, and regulatory standpoint, the merger partners typically plunge forward. They *assume* that the strategic benefits of the merger will necessarily fall into line along with the numbers. Statistics on the dramatic failure rate of M&A transactions suggest this is erroneous thinking.

M&A decision making now requires much closer scrutiny of strategic issues in the process of evaluating merger opportunities and individual target companies. Achieving the elusive "strategic fit" is typically marked by efforts of the merging companies to augment product lines, broaden geographic coverage, gain new distribution channels, and penetrate entirely new markets. These goals relate directly to marketing. Consequently, there is a greater need today for "marketing due diligence" in the current context of strategic mergers and acquisitions.

Marketing due diligence can be defined as *an analytical methodology that assesses target companies' sales and marketing strengths and weaknesses to ensure the success of strategic mergers and acquisitions.* By success, we mean that the deal has met the financial, operational, and strategic objectives of the companies involved. The process of marketing due diligence is critical for two main reasons:

1. It helps companies avoid the delays, missteps, and resultant multimillion-dollar losses that can result from inadequate strategic examinations of target companies and the markets in which they operate.
2. Marketing due diligence's fundamental orientation toward revenue growth—as opposed to cost reduction—is necessary to ensure the true long-term success of the transaction.

Today, strategic marketing consultants must work side by side with the investment bankers, lawyers, certified public accountants (CPAs), and others who have historically comprised the due diligence team. Corporate development officers (CDOs), too, require the input of M&A-focused marketing specialists to help in assessing the strategic attributes and potential of different M&A candidates. Even more so, financial buyers—who typically purchase a company as an investment—have sought the guidance of strategic marketing specialists to help them identify new revenue sources for their investment. It is becoming increasingly commonplace to have marketing advisers assist financial buyers in projecting and uncovering future growth initiatives that can justify more aggressive bids. By all accounts, marketing due diligence brings a different perspective and analytical eye to predeal planning and postmerger integration.

The importance of assembling a broad-based multidisciplinary team that includes marketing and sales specialists is becoming critical.

As we have seen, standard due diligence focuses in large part on a target company's financial assets and liabilities and how they meld with the acquirer's balance sheet. Some marketing-related variables are examined, but too often they are merely sketchy assessments of the target's product sales volume and margins and the general competitive environment.

Marketing due diligence, however, is based on analyzing in significantly greater depth these characteristics and numerous other attributes resident in both the acquirer's and the target's marketing systems and capabilities. For instance, marketing due diligence involves looking at not only both firms' products, but also the promotion behind them as a determinant of those products' past success. It involves examining not only both firms' markets, but also the macro- and microenvironmental trends that will affect those markets' future characteristics. It involves not only studying each firm's customer

INSIDER'S OUTLOOK

Success in M&A requires assembling a comprehensive due diligence team—one comprised of people with different skill sets and professional backgrounds. At Siemens, we have a lot of M&A specialists because we do a lot of deals. We have on-board CPAs and M&A lawyers. We have four deal-making, corporate development professionals . . . including myself. We've got a human resources M&A professional—half of her job is HR and the other half is understanding all the details involved in M&A. We've got environmental professionals. So the bottom line is that we put together a very professional team. But that team really has three people at its core. It has the operating manager . . . either the CEO or CFO of the division. The corporate developer, who is the deal expert. And the M&A lawyer. But above all you need people who understand that M&A is a growth alternative. You need people who understand why the deal is being done in the first place . . . people who recognize the corporate growth opportunities inherent in the transaction. This fact alone is why you need people on the due diligence team who truly understand marketing and product development.

—Terence Bentley, Siemens Corporation

base, but also analyzing the extent to which they have—or can be—penetrated with different product and service offerings.

Conducting financial and legal due diligence is typically the last phase of the M&A process—after the letter of intent is signed and before the transaction closes. Marketing due diligence, however, is rightfully one of the critical first steps in premerger assessments of potential merger candidates. This is because marketing due diligence generates important information that should be factored into target company valuations—which are undertaken soon after the transaction is envisioned and preliminary discussions between the would-be merger partners have commenced.

Let's now look at target company examinations and how marketing due diligence is useful in supplying information to help calculate an organization's current worth and its future potential as part of the merged company.

VALUATION PROCESS: ROLE OF MARKETING INTANGIBLE ASSETS

Valuation—determining the fair market price for a target company—is an initial, integral phase of the premerger process. Valuation is almost exclusively an arithmetic exercise, the key focus of which is assessing the target's physical assets, analyzing its current earnings performance and cash flow, and devising future projections based on current figures. The financial data studied include statistics on capital expenditure requirements, working capital requirements, and fixed and variable costs. In addition to financial information, operations-related data are collected. These include figures on the current and projected structure of the target's costs, personnel-related expenditures and current and future requirements, and labor expenditures. General industry information is also gathered to assess the impact of key trends on revenues and costs.

As predeal planning moves forward, initial financial and operational statistics are challenged, updated, and modified based on additional input generated in the target company examination process. A detailed explanation of statistical valuation methods is also beyond the scope of this book. However, a basic description of the main valuation techniques is in order. These methods include:

- *Discounted cash flow analysis.* The focus of this approach is assigning a value in today's dollars to future cash flow levels. This analysis lends insights into future financial performance, cash flow, and various balance sheet relationships. However, its shortcoming lies in its inability to accurately reflect pricing trends in the market.
- *Comparable transactions.* Not unlike real estate "comparables," management arrives at valuation figures based on the prices paid in past transactions involving companies of similar size or industry standing. A key problem of this valuation method lies in the quality and quantity of the comparative data. Information on past deals may be incomplete, inaccurate, outdated, or simply unavailable.
- *Comparable companies.* The focus here is on comparing the proposed value of the acquisition target against the prevailing market price of publicly traded companies similar to the target in terms of size, market standing, and various economic and industry-specific variables. Unfortunately, this approach largely ignores the target's expected future performance as projected by current financial or operational data.
- *Liquidation analysis.* This method keys on the value of the company's individual assets if they were to be sold at auction or in a liquidation. Liquidation analysis views a company solely from the standpoint of its current assets, in contrast to its ability to function as a future going concern.
- *Adjusted book value.* This accounting-based approach involves analyses of depreciation of assets and inventory. However, it does not factor in the company's economic value and its actual or potential earnings performance.

The valuation process focuses on identifying a company's tangible and intangible assets. Tangible assets include such items as the target's real property, machinery and equipment, and other physical attributes. The category of intangible assets includes the notion of "goodwill," which can be defined as those elements of a company's overall worth that do not appear on a balance sheet. Another definitional aspect of goodwill is that it is comprised of distinct capabilities that cannot be physically removed from the company. Some marketing-related intangibles are evaluated in the valuation process. These include such things as patents, licenses, trademarks, and customer lists.

The fact is, however, that intangible assets relative to a company's sales and marketing infrastructure can have a significant bearing on its current value, as well as its future ability to contribute significant top-line results as a part of the merged organization. Yet there is an entire realm of marketing-related intangible assets that must be pinpointed and assessed, but which are not typically viewed in traditional valuation methods—critical information necessary to supplement the conventional valuation process.

The increasing importance of the strategic marketing aspects of M&A planning requires a broadened approach to determining the value resident in the target company's sales and marketing infrastructure. Moreover, achieving long-term strategic objectives via a corporate combination requires a detailed analysis of the marketing-related variables that will affect the merged company's ability to actualize those objectives.

Thus, identifying and assessing a target company's "marketing intangible assets" is necessary to pinpoint specific growth opportunities inherent in a merger or acquisition situation, as well as to compare the attractiveness of different merger candidates.

MARKETING INTANGIBLES: WHERE THEY ARE FOUND

Marketing intangible assets reside in a target company's sales and marketing systems and capabilities. As detailed throughout this book, marketing due diligence is the process by which marketing intangible assets are discovered via the rigorous collection of qualitative and quantitative data on the target's people, products, and processes. Each area must be evaluated from the standpoint of its individual strengths, weaknesses, threats, and opportunities.

Qualitative Areas

The term "qualitative" denotes an attribute that cannot be assigned a numerical value. This is not always the case when analyzing marketing intangible assets, which can sometimes have dollar values ascribed to them for the purposes of valuation and for developing financial projections. For the purpose of this introduction to marketing due diligence, let's look briefly at the main areas of a target company where qualitative marketing-related assets reside.

In the area of *people*, and people-related variables internal and external to the target company, assets are found in:

- Marketing staff
- Sales force
- Customer base
- Distributors
- Cultural marketing orientation

Marketing staff. For instance, a high experience level, professionalism, creativity, and success rate of the marketing staff is inherently valuable. High marks and thus high worth can be assigned when affirmative answers are provided to the following questions: Is the staff an integral part of the company's operations, as opposed to being an ineffectual overhead function? Does the staff contribute to the development and execution of strategic initiatives that spark direct top-line results? Are key members of the sales and marketing team content with their positions, with little or no danger of losing them in the wake of the merger? In essence, a strong and committed marketing organization may possess much of the company's overall "intellectual property" assets.

Sales force. A well-entrenched, stable sales organization is a distinct area of value. Another aspect relates to the sales function's level of interaction with other departments, such as research and development (R&D), manufacturing, and new product development. A sales force that works closely with other corporate functions to furnish and receive market information is likely to be more successful than one that is isolated. From the standpoint of performance, the level of sales volume—collectively and by individual seller—is another indicator of value, as will be addressed in the next section on quantitative areas.

Customer base. A strong and loyal customer base is one of the most valuable intangibles a target company can possess. Companies that enjoy high customer commitment have low levels of customer turnover. Value is found in such organizations, which typically have successful programs in place to monitor and meet changing customer needs and to provide world-class customer service. Another key area of value relates to the extent to which sales are dispersed throughout the customer base. Whenever sales are concentrated with a few clients or customers, an element of vulnerability exists; major losses can be incurred if one or more of those large customers is lost postmerger. A strong and loyal customer base, where sales are spread over many different accounts, poses an element of value.

Distributors. Distributors represent a key to effective product marketing. Having smooth and solid relations with distributors (whether they are wholesalers, retailers, or other intermediaries) creates value, since products are assured of getting to market in a timely and cost-effective manner. Value can be minimized, however, when "channel conflict" exists between competing distribution arms in multiple-channel paradigms. Identifying existing and potential problems in this regard is essential in order to avoid future complications that may diminish value after or as a result of a merger or acquisition.

Cultural marketing orientation. A corporate culture marked by a broad, customer-focused marketing orientation represents a valuable intangible. Today, every person in an organization should assume marketing responsibilities to some degree. Ideally, everyone is customer-focused and employees work together to help meet customer requirements. Thus, value resides in a company where marketing is pervasive throughout the organization and is not relegated to the marketing and sales function. Cultural variables are a critical issue in determining strategic fit between merger partners, and they are discussed in great detail in Chapter 10. Yet, it is important to assess the degree to which culture fosters and enhances the process of sales and marketing throughout the entire organization.

In the realm of *products*, these external and internal factors are a source of marketing intangible assets:

- Market share
- Brand power
- New product development
- Marketplace perceptions
- Competition levels

Market share. The significance of market share in this context is not the numerical percentage held by the company under review. From a qualitative standpoint, occupying a leading position in a product market offers a host of important intangible benefits. For instance, high market share is a main driver of profitability. As was illustrated in the well-known Profit Impact of Market Strategy (PIMS) research program developed by the Strategic Planning Institute, the market share leader in a given category may be three times as profitable as the fifth-place company.

Profitability generates benefits in two basic ways.

1. Overall costs, including those for sales and marketing, are lower due to higher volumes.
2. Marketing-related advantages and cost savings may accrue from learning curve experience gains in product management and promotion.

Marketing due diligence, as you will see, determines the extent to which the company's market share is sustainable and expandable—and, consequently, a continuing source of potential value.

INSIDER'S OUTLOOK

When you are right at the very beginning of looking at a deal . . . it's a good idea to brainstorm with marketing. Go over your entire deal list and get their reactions to things. Get their input on evaluating the market or markets in which given target companies are operating. Many deals eventually fail because of "Marketing 101" type mistakes. I have seen companies make strategically sound deals, but make real marketing errors . . . such as pumping out products to the distribution network without making sure they were getting to the final customers. Marketing errors are often directly related to a lot of companies' problem acquisitions.

—Diane Harris, Hypotenuse Enterprises

Brand power. In product marketing, there are few things as valuable as a powerful brand name. A high level of name recognition—ideally coupled with positive market perceptions of product quality and value—facilitates and maximizes sales. What's more, brand name strength of given products carries over in a positive halo effect to benefit other goods and services offered by the company. Brand power is one of the few marketing intangibles assessed in the valuation category of goodwill. Yet, its broader value to the target company's overall sales and marketing processes, and, therefore, long-term profitability, often goes unrecognized.

New product development. A company that regularly introduces new products and services offers assets not found in a firm that is slow and ineffective in developing new offerings. For instance, aggressive product-driven companies are viewed in the marketplace as innovators. There is value in possessing this market perception—value that supports individual products and the organization as a whole. Moreover, strong product development capabilities typically indicate that assets reside in the strong working relationship between the corporate functions that jointly create and market new goods and services, such as R&D, engineering, manufacturing, customer service, and sales. Of course, the rate of new product introductions is not as significant as the actual success rate of those items in the market. Nonetheless, a high degree of product innovation typically illustrates progressiveness and aggressiveness—two valuable traits necessary to achieve and maintain competitiveness, thus increasing the probability of new product success.

Marketplace perceptions. The positive perceptions the market holds toward a company's products represent a fundamental marketing intangible. These may relate to product quality, value, customer service, or other variables. Positive perceptions also relate to the company as a whole. Is the company viewed as being a good corporate citizen? How is the company perceived in terms of its relations with labor unions? Has the company experienced significant public relations (PR) problems in the past? Determining the strength and ultimate value of positive market sentiment requires gauging the views of customers, shareholders, and the business community at large.

Competition levels. A weak or decreasingly intensive competitive environment represents a marketing asset in itself. For example, not having to constantly fend off competitive threats enables a company to take an offensive rather than defensive position in the market. Program planning and implementation are not hindered by the disruptions of competitors' inroads, which may necessitate countermeasures that drain important resources from ongoing initiatives. Naturally, the competitive environment is continually changing. Consequently, the search for marketing intangibles requires evaluating key market trends and their potential impact on the target's ability to maintain and bolster its competitive standing in the future.

In the area of *processes*, the following represent sources of marketing intangible assets:

- Marketing and sales planning
- Advertising and marketing communications
- Marketing information systems
- Technology applications and customer databases
- Outsourced relationships
- Organizational communication

Marketing and sales planning. Almost every company develops marketing and sales plans. The extent to which a company actually, and regularly, achieves the goals detailed in those plans represents a growth-related intangible asset. Marketing planning is just one area. Long-term corporate strategic plans, as well as short-term action plans for specific promotional or product initiatives, should also be assessed from the standpoint of their substantive foundation, practical execution, and tangible results.

Advertising and marketing communications. The bottom-line effectiveness of individual advertising, PR, direct mail, and other marketing communications programs can often be measured. From a broader standpoint, the marketing department that consistently produces creative, impactive, sales-generating marketing campaigns possesses an important intangible asset.

The extent to which products and product lines are well positioned in comparison to competitors' offerings is another key asset. Many otherwise viable products fail over time because the market does not have a clear understanding of their competitive differentiating characteristics. Of course, a product's positioning strategy may be sound while the communications execution of that strategy is not. Marketing due diligence addresses that dichotomy and determines methods of closing that gap.

Marketing information systems. Data relating to a company's markets, customers, and competitors should be regularly collected. Surprisingly, many companies do not have even the most rudimentary process of accumulating and disseminating intelligence to key sales and marketing decision makers.

The degree to which the target company gathers and applies marketing information goes well beyond the maintenance of conventional customer lists—another of the handful of marketing-related intangible assets assessed in traditional valuation and due diligence. Significant quantity and quality of marketing information is a key intangible asset. This is particularly true if that information is maintained in sophisticated, technology-based systems.

Technology applications and customer databases. Today, information technology (IT) is central to a company's operations. Yet, the degree to which IT is effectively deployed for marketing purposes—for example, in a marketing information system—often points up a valuable intangible.

The issue, however, is not whether the company uses technology for sales and marketing. The issue is how well that technology is applied to solve marketing problems and to support ongoing and future initiatives. For instance, the era of customized marketing has come upon us. The tool that enabled companies to move from mass marketing to individualized selling is the customer database—a system that tracks customers' demographic composition, geographic locations, and, most important, their buying history and patterns.

One can argue that a database is a tangible entity on which a dollar value could be placed. However, a company's customer database should not be viewed as a physical asset, but rather as a compilation of critically important information (an intangible) whose potential benefit transcends the value of the hard drives or disks it is stored on.

Outsourced relationships. A target company's roster of marketing services agencies —such as those for advertising, media buying, PR, direct mail, and sales support—is an integral, albeit external, element of its marketing infrastructure. The quality of the output of those agencies is significant. But the true intangible value lies in a corporate marketing department whose management effectively makes outsourcing decisions; that is, what functions to outsource and to what vendors they should be outsourced. By all accounts, managerial skill is needed to select and manage the work of outside advisers. There is substantial value in that ability, yet no listing on a company's balance sheet.

Organizational communication. Channels of internal communication are an important asset when they report information that directly supports the company's sales and marketing efforts. The channels, types, and media through which communications are disseminated in the target company must be assessed. The more an organization imparts sales and marketing news, such as new product introductions and selling strategies, the greater the likelihood that it functions as a customer-focused organization across all levels and locations.

Quantitative Areas

As the foregoing illustrates, much of the data collected in identifying marketing intangible assets is qualitative in nature. Some marketing intangibles, however, are discovered via statistical analyses. There are three main categories where quantitative measurements point up potential marketing intangible assets. The existence and strength of given quantitative intangible assets can be gauged by developing one or more of the following ratios:

- Marketing investment ratios
- Producivity ratios
- Efficiency ratios

Marketing investment ratios. In essence, these ratios relate to resource allocation decisions by the target company for sales and marketing programs. Marketing investment ratios range from information on general marketing expenditures (e.g., growth or decline of advertising expenditures in a given time period) to data on specific marketing resource allocation decisions (e.g., comparisons of spending on different promotional and marketing communications mix elements). How much and how well money is invested for marketing—and the return on those past investments—point up intangible assets from both a strategic and a managerial standpoint.

Productivity ratios. These ratio analyses involve measuring the success, or lack thereof, of sales and marketing programs and special initiatives such as strategic alliances and marketing tie-in programs with key stakeholders. For example, these ratios are used to pinpoint revenue gains resulting from specific advertising campaigns, sales promotion programs, direct marketing efforts, and database marketing activities.

The most frequently calculated productivity ratios relate to sales performance—both for individual sellers and for entire sales teams assigned to different corporate divisions or subsidiaries. Therefore, sales productivity can be assessed by analyzing overall sales growth (or decline), average order size by customer, sales volume by individual sellers (e.g., volume in comparison to the number of sales calls made), and other criteria.

Efficiency ratios. A number of marketing areas must be assessed in terms of their operational efficiency. One measurement relates directly to customer satisfaction. Quantitative data, for example, can be collected on warranty costs as compared to net and gross sales to identify customer sentiment toward different products and product lines. Qualitative input must also be generated via interviews with customers, and this information must be viewed against the quantitative findings.

Another example of an efficiency analysis relates to the stability of sales and marketing staff. Thus, an employee turnover ratio can provide insights into whether or not the sales and marketing function is being well managed—as well as indicate potential personnel-related problems that must be addressed as you effect postmerger integration.

In each of the qualitative and quantitative areas of investigation, data should be collected from the immediate past and, if possible, as far back as five years. Historical information must be collected and studied in order to spot positive and negative trends that will impact future initiatives, as well as to point up other relevant strengths, weaknesses, and potential threats and opportunities.

However, all marketing-related data on a target company must be assessed two ways. The target must be viewed first as an entity unto itself, then as a component of the merged company. This constitutes the fundamental orientation to growth-focused M&A planning.

On the one hand, areas of weakness in the target company may be mitigated if your company has particular strengths to offset those shortcomings. On the other hand, strengths resident in the target company's sales and marketing infrastructure represent areas that can conceivably be bolstered as the firms merge and take shape as a forceful new corporate entity.

Marketing due diligence's unique focus offers you the ability to identify strengths and weaknesses that are critical to both predeal analyses and postdeal integration and growth planning. Initially, the qualitative and quantitative data culled are valuable in assessing the target company's worth from a valuation standpoint. Going forward, this information is essential for developing forecasts, financial projections, and plans whose focus is forging growth strategies to generate near- and long-term revenues.

Without question, the emphasis on growth represents one of the most dramatic shifts in merger and acquisition planning and execution over the past 10 years. Growth through M&A is the driving force of marketing due diligence and the underlying focus of the guidance provided throughout this book.

INSIDER'S OUTLOOK

We run the due diligence process very rigorously. One of the keys is getting the appropriate experts on the team. We have people who are experienced in every aspect of a business's operations. We have experts in law, finance, tax, environmental compliance, human resources, marketing, sales, and operations. We also use outside advisors to gather specific information on subject areas we may not be totally familiar with. Over all, the due diligence team is multifunctional, multidisciplinary.

—Mufit Cinali, AT&T

REVENUE ENHANCEMENT OPPORTUNITIES

The increasing emphasis on marketing due diligence is consistent with an emerging tenet in M&A today: *Cost-reduction synergies, which are often realized through achiev-*

ing economies of scale, are becoming much less important than strategic synergies that can generate near- and long-term revenues.

The process and benefits of marketing due diligence to support growth initiatives is best illustrated by a new concept that provides a frame of reference—and represents the methodological underpinnings—of this new approach to evaluating all merger or acquisition opportunities: the "revenue enhancement opportunity" (REO).

Effecting synergies is the goal of any merger or acquisition. But what exactly are synergies? And are there different types?

Certainly, every deal offers different financial and situational benefits to the companies involved. However, whether the deal is of a strategic or financial nature, the orientation that focuses on long-term growth as opposed to short-term cost cutting requires that we view the term "synergies" in a new light. The strategic M&A perspective has spawned a new emphasis on the synergies that can lead to significant top-line revenue gains—REO synergies.

An REO can be defined as: *A newly created or strengthened product or service that is forged by the fusion of two distinct attributes of the merger partners and which generates immediate and/or long-term revenue growth.*

The process of identifying and realizing REOs is a driving focus of marketing due diligence and, consequently, is treated in detail in Chapter 3. For now, it is important to understand that REO analysis and identification is a key perspective in growth-focused M&A planning.

Marketing due diligence concentrates on delivering instant payoff, but also a filled and prioritized pipeline of revenue enhancers and growth opportunities. It aids in the process of forecasting and delivering revenue growth immediately upon finalization of the deal. But the prioritization aspect allows for the ongoing achievement of successive REO synergies—as will be discussed in detail in Chapter 3—at appropriate points in the postdeal integration timetable. Acknowledging the pipeline concept in the premerger planning stages is critical. It allows the acquirer to focus on revenue enhancers that will deliver both quick hits and incremental gains to stakeholders over the short term, while never losing sight of the revenue enhancement opportunities that will produce a steady stream of future sales. More on this later.

IDENTIFYING SOURCES OF VALUE

The search for marketing intangible assets, revenue enhancement opportunities, and other sources of value to ensure the success of strategic mergers and acquisitions requires an exhaustive review of a target company's overall infrastructure. Effectively conducting this analysis, however, requires adopting a new frame of reference, which is set forth in Part One of this book.

Part Two addresses in detail each element of a target's operations that will point up marketing-related strengths, weaknesses, threats, and opportunities. In a sense, the forthcoming guidance resembles a conventional Strengths, Weaknesses, Opportunities, Threats (SWOT) analysis—a methodology employed in conducting basic strategic planning. There is an important difference, however. In this context, the analysis is linked directly to the considerations unique to up-front, predeal planning and postmerger integration.

The focus is on analyzing:

- *Market dynamics and company performance.* Analyzing the markets in which a company operates is a standard area of any acquisition analysis. From a marketing due diligence perspective, however, market analysis takes on an important new dimension. It determines not only where the company is situated in the market, but, more importantly, how the company got there (and where it is going). In other words, it focuses on assessing how well the organization is responding to its particular marketplace threats and opportunities. Attention is paid to a target company's overall marketing effectiveness as one determinant of its current value and future potential as part of the merged company (see Chapter 4).
- *Product and service lines.* Products and services are the lifeblood of any company. It is necessary to evaluate a target company's products and services to identify the strategic fit with your own offerings and to assist you in product-related decision making in the postmerger environment.

  Various qualitative and quantitative measures are used in assessing product lines. In particular, variables such as product line strengths and vulnerabilities, product life cycle stages, and marketing communications tactics supporting individual offerings must be evaluated (see Chapter 5).
- *Customers.* Tremendous sources of value and revenue gain opportunities exist in a company's current customer base. A detailed examination of the firm's existing and prospective buyers (those with whom the company has had dealings, as well as those it is actively attempting to transform into buyers) must be conducted. The customer base should be analyzed in terms of the categories the merged firm will serve (e.g., consumer, industrial, government); composition (e.g., geographically, demographically, psychographically); and size (e.g., revenues, average purchase amounts, levels of purchase frequency, and the number of employees in an organization). When analyzing the customer base, particular attention must be paid to cross-selling opportunities that will exist vis-à-vis the merged company's product mix (see Chapter 6).
- *Employees.* A company's most valuable asset is its employees. Premerger marketing due diligence addresses such analytical areas as departmental structure, lines of reporting, staff size, geographic location, and demographic composition of the employee base. Extensively analyzing the target's employees is critical in one very important respect: determining the skills and capabilities held by employees—relative to the strategic imperatives of the merged company itself—in order to determine those people's role in the new organization going forward (see Chapter 7).
- *Management functions and processes.* Skills and capabilities reside not only in a company's people, but also in the managerial structure and procedures of its various functional units. Marketing due diligence explores the key areas of a target's management infrastructure for two compelling reasons: to determine outstanding practices and capabilities that can be imported into the new organization, and to determine the extent to which particular managerial processes can support the merged company's strategic growth initiatives (see Chapter 8).

POSTMERGER INTEGRATION: PROTECTING AND CULTIVATING SOURCES OF VALUE

The core focus of marketing due diligence is spotting sources of value inherent in a target company. And, as stated, value resides in a company's people, products, and processes.

Identifying those sources of value is the primary task in growth-focused premerger planning. The other essential responsibility is protecting and transferring value and skill sets in the postmerger environment. Whereas Part Two addresses how to identify sources of value, Part Three addresses the ways to harness and cultivate those capabilities in the future. Guidance is provided in the following areas:

• *Understanding the challenges of integration.* The obstacles to postmerger integration continue to be widely chronicled in the business literature. Employing a best-practices approach to effecting integration first requires understanding the typical roadblocks and problem areas and how to overcome them (see Chapter 9).

In addition, understanding the dynamics and attributes of different corporate cultures is critical to avoiding the well-publicized "culture clashes" that have killed many a strategically sound transaction. Evaluating the process- and personnel-related variables of an organization's culture is a crucial means of identifying the critical success factors for successful acquisition integration (see Chapter 10).

• *Aligning products and services.* In horizontal mergers, there are invariably product line overlaps that require determining which goods and services will be supported post-merger. Even in vertical mergers, there are situations where limited monetary and human resources will preclude management from supporting every product and service the combining companies offered prior to the transaction. A disciplined approach is necessary to make sound product and service line decisions relative to integrating the merging companies' offerings. Moreover, this approach must be based on evaluating the critical considerations of product management, such as branding strategies, pricing, promotion, and distribution (see Chapter 11).

• *Internal communication strategies.* A detailed employee communication program must be planned and implemented as part of the integration process. Devising and executing a communications program helps ensure that employees remain committed, motivated, and productive in the wake of the merger's close. Communications are also an essential means of effecting understanding between disparate employee bases to support the melding of corporate cultures and to provide a foundation for successful execution of the merged firm's strategic growth initiatives (see Chapter 12).

• *Training and development curricula.* Training is imperative to effect the all-important transfer of skills that will help the merged company realize the strategic gains sought. Well-designed and well-executed training and development curricula can directly support growth planning initiatives and—like communication—can facilitate integration and the alignment of corporate cultures. And, different forms of training techniques should be employed based on employees' different staff classifications and the nature of the training content itself (see Chapter 13).

• *Reward and recognition programs.* Employees who support and help facilitate the merged firm's integration program should be recognized for their contributions and rewarded for loyalty in the midst of change. Companies' failure to overtly acknowledge and reinforce such positive behavior is often a key cause of flawed or delayed integration programs and key personnel defections. Reward programs must be structured differently for employees at different levels of the organization. These initiatives must be promoted widely and monitored closely (see Chapter 14).

> **INSIDER'S OUTLOOK**
>
> [In due diligence] every team member knows what he or she is supposed to do. They know who they are going to talk to at the target company. They know how much time they are going to spend reviewing documents and visiting facilities. We use extensive checklists in order to do the most comprehensive interviews with all key managers at the target company. And we ask some very tough questions. On, say, a $100 million deal, we probably have a team of a dozen or two dozen people visiting the target company at different times. And we spend as much time as we need to get the information we want. On very complicated deals, we may spend several weeks. On less complicated deals, we'll spend a little less time.
>
> —Mufit Cinali, AT&T

• *Postmerger external communications.* The content and the timing of external communications aimed at the merged company's various stakeholders are critical. Messages must be carefully articulated based on the informational needs of different audience segments. Media must be selected to effectively reach those audiences. Media planning strategies must be devised to ensure audiences' receipt of the intended messages. Of paramount importance is communications planning aimed at the merged company's existing customers, who will likely be courted by competitors immediately upon announcement of the deal and in the weeks and months following its close (see Chapter 15).

• *Designing the merged firm's organizational structure.* The consummation of a major merger or acquisition poses the opportunity to begin competing in the marketplace as a formidable new entity. Inherent in this opportunity is the need to revamp the organizational structure of the new firm to capitalize on the human and procedural assets and resources it now has at its disposal, and to directly support the strategic drivers of the transaction itself. A number of fundamental considerations must be addressed in terms of devising new job classifications, determining the nature and number of managerial layers for ongoing oversight of company activities, and establishing the channels and flow of information to maximize operational efficiency (see Chapter 16).

SUMMARY

In the past, marketing due diligence issues were viewed as peripheral. In the context of strategic M&A today, they are central.

As the foregoing illustrates, marketing due diligence comprehensively supports each aspect of the predeal planning process:

- It provides qualitative information that can be factored into quantitative analyses of a target company's current value and future contribution as part of the merged entity. That is, it generates additional data for use in computing acquisition premiums and financial forecasts.
- It identifies strategic synergies whose foundation is revenue generation, not cost reduction.
- It helps facilitate postmerger integration, thereby enabling speedier attainment of potential sales and helping to ensure the ultimate success of the merger itself.

This last point is critical. It reinforces the widely increasing acceptance that adequate predeal planning leads to expeditious postmerger integration. Granted, integrating all corporate functions in the wake of a deal is an enormous undertaking. But of all those functions, sales and marketing is perhaps the most important.

The merged company must have its marketing organization and plans in place in order to swiftly launch growth programs upon consummation of the deal. A delayed or problem-plagued rollout can cause the merged entity to lose momentum, market share, and the backing of customers, prospects, employees, and shareholders. Even worse, the merged company can fail to realize its strategic vision.

Comprehensive predeal marketing due diligence helps expedite postmerger integration, the foundation for launching growth-focused programs that can lead to near- and long-term, top-line revenue gains. By identifying key revenue-building strategies—and planning for their swift attainment after the deal closes—the merged company can immediately begin maximizing its sales potential.

Conversely, inadequate predeal planning can severely delay the company's ability to operate at its peak marketing and sales capacity. The expression "time is money" is indeed appropriate here.

If projected sales in the postmerger environment are $10 million a month, a two-month-long marketing integration period will flow to the bottom line faster than a six-month-long integration—$40 million in accelerated income, to be exact. Clearly, the merged company has to hit the ground running from a marketing and sales standpoint. In the context of strategic mergers and acquisitions, however, the "run" is a marathon, not a sprint. Effecting expense reductions is an important, albeit short-term, consideration. Realizing and prioritizing revenue enhancement opportunities is the critical factor in ensuring the long-term viability of the deal. By ensuring that these REOs are quickly in place, you will be in a stronger position to satisfy both your short-term cash flow needs and your longer-term growth initiatives.

Marketing due diligence identifies valuable assets inherent in a target company and is focused on harnessing those assets to effect revenue growth. Insights gained regarding the target's hidden marketing strengths are critical. Equally important, however, is marketing due diligence's ability to spot marketing weaknesses that can lead to dramatic financial losses.

A well-publicized M&A failure of the mid-1990s serves as the ideal reminder of the need for extensive marketing-focused examinations of a target company and the markets in which it operates.

Late in 1994, the Quaker Oats Company acquired Snapple Beverage Corporation for $1.7 billion. Quaker, already the leader in the sports drink beverage arena with Gatorade, looked to lock up the New Age beverage market as well. Snapple was at the peak of its meteoric rise, having increased revenues 400% since 1990. At the time of the acquisition, Snapple's sales were approximately $700 million. Two years after the acquisition—and billions of dollars in losses later—Quaker, having purchased a one-product company in a saturated market, was forced to unload Snapple for a paltry $300 million!

Several key marketing-related factors combined to make this one of the most ill-fated deals in the history of corporate mergers and acquisitions.

At the time of the transaction, so-called New Age beverages like Snapple were losing their market momentum as competition was intensifying. Aggressive sales efforts were being launched by Snapple's major competitors—Fruitopia beverages by Coca-Cola; Lipton iced teas, a joint venture of PepsiCo and Unilever—as well as New Age beverage upstarts like AriZona iced tea and Mistic. In addition, Quaker Oats angered Snapple's network of bottlers by taking too long to finalize its new distribution system. This delay forced bottlers to reluctantly work in the first quarter of 1995 without a distribution plan in place, which led to irretrievable market share losses for Snapple.

Marketing due diligence's focus on spotting weaknesses and vulnerabilities from a product management standpoint would have helped Quaker Oats avoid the massive setbacks it suffered. Consider, for example, these examples relative to the three main areas of investigation—people, products, and processes (the "three Ps of Marketing Due Diligence").

- *People.* The people-related aspects of marketing due diligence include assessing a company's relationships with key stakeholders (e.g., vendors, suppliers, channel intermediaries). Marketing due diligence would have determined the critical importance of Snapple's network of bottlers, and would have forecast the negative attitudes held by them because of Quaker Oats's lack of a distribution strategy, which proved so costly to the company.
- *Products.* A complete study of a target company's products, vis-à-vis such considerations as the competitive environment, is central to effective marketing due diligence. Performing detailed marketing due diligence would have spotted the competitive inroads being made by the beverage behemoths Coca-Cola and Pepsi, a factor that would have a direct bearing on Snapple's future revenue stream, as well as fundamental marketing strategies and investments.
- *Processes.* Quickly developing new marketing communications is a key element of postmerger growth planning. In the Snapple acquisition, a change of advertising strategy was needed since the popular TV spots featuring "Wendy the Snapple Lady" were decidedly regional in their appeal. Quaker Oats's goal to bolster Snapple's sales beyond the East and West coasts required refining—but not totally revamping—its overall marketing communications approach. Interestingly, it was a full two years after the transaction was finalized that a new national ad campaign was launched. But this new ad campaign mistakenly did not include Wendy, who had become a veritable brand icon. Snapple's two most successful radio pitchmen, Howard Stern and Rush Limbaugh, also were not utilized in this campaign. Each

had regularly spread the word of Snapple for years on their national radio shows. Marketing due diligence would have identified the need to have this campaign in place much sooner to immediately reposition the product and to help keep pace with the onslaught of competitors' advertising. Additionally, it would have pointed up the value of Wendy the brand icon and the selling power of two syndicated radio stars.

It is unfair to single out Quaker Oats as having performed inadequate marketing due diligence. The absence of marketing-focused premerger examinations and swift post-merger launches of sales and marketing programs has been an expensive shortcoming in an endless number of deals.

This chapter has looked at the strategic orientation of M&A transactions today and how conventional approaches to due diligence and company valuations now require a much stronger focus on key marketing variables. The overriding goal of strategic M&A is achieving strategic advantage and enhanced competitiveness and profitability. Of course, there are various ways to do so. The next chapter explores how to determine which approach is most appropriate given your company's current standing and future strategic destination.

The focus of this book is on identifying the ways to ensure "strategic fit" with potential merger partners. We must first, however, define precisely what that amorphous, often overused term means. Ultimately, the challenge is determining what strategic fit means to your company and identifying the potential M&A partners that represent the best possible match. Nonetheless, you must first determine what it is you need before you set out to find and evaluate the M&A candidate that can potentially provide it.

2

Quest for Strategic Advantage through Mergers and Acquisitions

On paper, virtually every merger and acquisition appears to accomplish a specific financial goal. In some instances cost savings and economies of scale are driving the deal. In others, it is an increased access to capital or the belief that an undervalued company can be turned around. Yet behind most mergers today is an underlying and less tangible driver: the quest for "strategic advantage," a term often overused and rarely understood.

Public pronouncements issued by acquirers often reference the term "strategic fit" to imply the expected ease with which a target will be absorbed and cost savings will occur. Financial analysts and reporters often cite the phrase "strategic advantage" in their writings to explain the rationale behind the transaction. But with more than half of the deals of the last three decades failing to deliver their expected results, the true definitions of these terms seem to be in question. Just what do "strategic advantage" and "strategic fit" actually mean?

Understanding these concepts is central to merger and acquisition decision making. Unfortunately, what has been missing in the literature and training rooms of the global business community is a definition of strategic advantage and strategic fit in their most practical sense—a definition that focuses on the various factors that allow them to actually come to fruition. That is the goal of this chapter. By analysis of the drivers that are the motivation behind strategic M&A deals it will become clear that it is not the so often heralded cost saving issues, but rather the growth-oriented synergies and their actualization that lead to a deal's success.

There are 10 strategic drivers that are the distinct motivators behind virtually every strategic merger or acquisition (see list on pages 24 and 25). More than theoretical explanations are needed to understand and apply them. To illustrate these drivers it is helpful to examine how they influenced several of the more complex deals of the decade. Each deal's uniqueness—whether due to size, industry focus, or geographical orientation—has as its primary motivation one of the 10 strategic drivers. Yet as we will illustrate, the transactions that are motivated by at least two strategic drivers have the greatest opportunity to succeed over the long term.

To fully grasp the concept of strategic advantage, one must view M&A from a historical perspective. As many of the deals done in the 1970s, 1980s, and early 1990s have unraveled, the explanation most often cited for their failure is the lack of strategic soundness. In other words, they never delivered the long-term growth and sustained profitability that seemed so possible at first. Too much emphasis was placed on how the two companies fit together in a practical or financial sense, and not enough on whether they could truly combine to make a whole that was greater than the sum of its parts.

STRATEGIC FIT

To understand the concept of strategic fit, it is necessary to key on the word "fit." It connotes compatibility. Historically, strategic fit in an M&A context addressed the issue of combining company attributes under one roof because they were compatible. But in many cases, simply the fact that two companies have differing attributes makes them seem even more attractive. The implication is that the products, services, or qualities exclusive to one company fill a capability gap inherent in the other company and vice versa. This is a justifiable rationale for a merger or acquisition, but it is not enough. It is only the first of many considerations in the acquisition planning process that can help lead to successful results.

Unfortunately, the assumption of strategic fit as the platform for an aggressive cost-cutting approach is what drives many an acquisition strategy. On paper, the numbers look good. In theory, the two companies seem compatible. But in practice the strategy is doomed to fail. Why? In many cases, the benefits of initial cost reductions do not continue past the first year. The economies of scale fail to deliver increased efficiency over the long term. And, what at first seemed to be compatible attributes turn out to be only slight variations in products, services, or operational processes. Compatibility is important—in fact, critical. But it must be incorporated into a much broader framework that tests the complementary nature of corporate attributes beyond their inherent compatibility.

Beyond the obvious attention paid to cost reduction, the primary focus for strategic deals today must be on melding complementary, nonfinancial assets with an eye toward growth and then extending their benefits over the long term through integration. What begins as a vision of either growth or expansion must be seamlessly and continuously developed as a smoothly functioning part of the whole. Just as we do not view an arm or leg as a separate part of our bodies, but an integral part with a discrete function, a partnership between two companies should be forged based on a similar mind-set.

Let us take the human body analogy one step further, and assume that an individual's hand has the ability to firmly grasp a pencil, push a button, or hold a fork. When these discrete capabilities are combined with those of the other hand, the result is greater than simply being able to grasp *two* pencils or hold *two* forks. The new and enhanced ability of both hands working in concert to clap, push, or pull with greater force is the equivalent of two companies joining complementary assets to create something stronger, more effective, and longer lasting than what had previously existed. Each of these asset combinations is referred to as a "synergy." If the only synergy that two hands could deliver was limited to the occasional clap, we would not consider it a long-term benefit. Yet, add the ability to play the piano, and the long-term case for harmoniously integrating the efforts of two hands becomes eminently more compelling.

STRATEGIC ADVANTAGE

Within the corporate world, when two complementary capabilities are combined, leading to a third, enhanced capability, this is referred to as "strategic synergy." When recognized as such and actualized to achieve long-term growth and increased profits, it is the basis for what may rightfully be called strategic advantage. Attaining strategic advantage should be the goal of every merger and acquisition, combining the obvious compatibility issues and taking them one step further. Comprehensive in scope, strategic advantage incorporates the merged company's unique capabilities and takes them to a higher level.

True M&A-driven strategic advantage is comprised of multiple synergies that:

- Focus on growth rather than cost savings.
- Integrate easily to form the merged entity.
- Deliver benefits that materialize over the long term.

When several distinct synergies contain all three of these components, they can combine to create revenue enhancement opportunities (REOs). The essence of REOs is their focus on growth through synergy. Strategic advantage is the realization of strategic synergy.

NONSTRATEGIC ADVANTAGE

Of course, exceptions do exist—particularly when the reason for an acquisition is growth without concern for strategic advantage. For example, some companies acquire for the express purpose of becoming bigger and do not intend to integrate the smaller companies. Over time, the acquirers essentially become loosely connected conglomerates comprised of many separate pieces, so-called bolt-ons. Companies in this mode of growth often subscribe to the theory that economies of scale are the ultimate benefit of an acquisition program. Consequently, they establish corporate structures that thrive on the lack of integration.

Often, these nonintegrated smaller companies are managed separately as divisions or branches. Yet, over time, in order to successfully compete in the marketplace, each individual unit must experience its own growth, either internally or through external means such as strategic alliances, joint ventures, or R&D partnerships. Ultimately, growing pains start to emerge as one unit finds that its products or services overlap with another unit or, worse, finds itself competing directly with its own corporate brethren.

In the past, companies lacking the strategic advantage focus have fallen prey to organizational chaos. A point is reached where it is no longer feasible or profitable to monitor the multiple management teams, production facilities, or marketing efforts. Inevitably, corporate functions and processes (e.g., employee benefits, information systems, distribution networks) cost more to monitor and manage separately than under a centralized system. Hanson Industries is a case in point.

One of the world's largest conglomerates, Hanson was able to house such disparate businesses as building materials, sports equipment, chemicals, and typewriters all under one corporate roof for many years. In fact, from 1976 to 1985, shareholders enjoyed more than a 35% annualized return. Yet, over the next decade, as the pace of acquisitions quickened—with corporate management exerting little effort to integrate—the share price barely budged. In order to drive the top-line revenue growth, Hanson "de-merged" rather than integrate its core businesses.

Integration is critical to the success of any strategic merger or acquisition and will be addressed in detail in Part Three. However, the focus of this entire volume is strategic advantage where the quest for synergy, and a commitment to integration, is the rule rather than the exception.

Long after the ledger is closed on a deal, the goal of actualizing and maintaining strategic advantage must continue to be a focus. Yet, it is in the predeal planning phase, before the ledger is even opened, that the groundwork for achieving enduring strategic advantage must be laid. The first step toward achieving this goal is identifying inherent strategic synergies.

The traditional definition of "synergy" in M&A circles is *a potential cost savings that occurs when two companies combine*. The emphasis has always been on savings. However, strategic synergies are the result of combined complementary attributes that focus on growth. It is only through growth that the long-term success of major mergers and acquisitions can be achieved.

STRATEGIC DRIVERS

There are scores of reasons why companies forge unions through corporate combinations. And identifying growth synergies, rather than savings synergies, can be a confusing and arduous process fraught with uncertainty. Determining cost-reduction synergies is easy. Devising and actualizing growth-oriented synergies is hard work.

Developing industry growth projections, studying the strategic and operational findings of acquisition team members, and analyzing myriad marketing and sales variables are just a few aspects of the challenging process of identifying strategic advantage potential. The very thought of compiling this voluminous data often stands in the way of many clearly thought-out acquisitions. But having a forward-thinking map and checklist to guide you through the daunting phases of assessment and analysis is necessary in order to place a target company in perspective relative to your strategic needs.

To begin the process, you must first pinpoint the various synergies posed by a union with a given target company. An analysis of hundreds of mergers, acquisitions, joint ventures, and strategic alliances has revealed 10 basic opportunities for strategic synergy that, in one way or another, act as the strategic drivers behind the majority of deals. They are:

1. Effecting organizational growth
2. Increasing market share
3. Gaining entrée into new markets or access to new distribution channels
4. Obtaining new products

5. Keeping pace with change
6. Capitalizing on political and regulatory change
7. Pursuing innovations/discoveries in products or technology
8. Lessening competition
9. Strengthening reputation or gaining credibility
10. Responding to or capitalizing on economic scenarios

Through examining these drivers in greater detail, it is possible to get a sense of their practical application and their invaluable role in devising a successful, growth-driven acquisition strategy.

Effecting Organizational Growth

Often, a company envisions the opportunity to increase its scope and leverage simply by becoming bigger. This usually increases liquidity and access to the capital markets and broadens name or brand awareness in additional geographic markets. On its own, actualizing the strategic advantage of size can improve a company's financial performance through leveraging basic economies of scale. Yet, when combined with other strategic synergies, the advantage of size can act as the foundation and a catalyst for increased market share, production enhancements, and new market penetration that can, in turn, lead to a distinct competitive advantage.

Obviously, in every merger, the immediate result is increased size. However, after duplicative operations are eliminated, workforces downsized, and noncore operations sold or spun off, the resultant company may not necessarily be bigger. In many cases, the streamlined, merged entity is a smaller, yet more effective company with more muscle and less fat.

Increasing Market Share

Within the confines of a given product market, only so much market share can be claimed. The battle for customers over products and services is a zero-sum competition in which customer bases shift as product loyalty is strengthened or weakened. Increasing market share requires that a company seize already established customer loyalty from a competitor and then build on it to increase its own share further. Just as growing in size does not guarantee success, simply adding market share via a merger or acquisition does not make a company immediately more competitive.

During a target company analysis, one must ask the fundamental question, "Will the addition of the target's attributes to those of the acquirer spawn immediate *and* longer-term increases in market share?" One of the basic investigative areas of marketing due diligence is identifying the sources of future increases in market share. Simply adding the market share of company A to that of company B is not the solution. A synergy must then be developed that takes the sum of those numbers to a higher plane. Only a focus on steady, increasing competitiveness—which is contingent on effective integration—can help the company make that leap.

Gaining Entrée into New Markets or Access to New Distribution Channels

Many strategic acquisitions occur in defined product markets that the acquirer is currently serving. For example, buying a firm that enables you to target a broader or more responsive audience can not only give you access to a greater number of potential buyers, it can also help bring about enhanced production or distribution capabilities in new territories. As businesses have expanded throughout the last decade of this century, the fiercest battles have been fought over existing products in new markets.

Entering a market for the first time, however, is an act fraught with multiple risks. There are buyer-specific and competitive issues that need to be understood before you can successfully gain entrée to a previously unpenetrated market. Acquiring another company that already has a foothold in that segment, and that knows the ropes, can ease the process and minimize your risks.

Obtaining New Products

In the realm of new product development, companies focused on growth agonize over the "make or buy" decision. Those with available cash, depth of resources, access to technology, and strategic vision are in the best position to acquire firms in order to acquire new products. The alternative to buying a new product or capability is a complex, costly, and time-consuming period of product or service development.

Today, the key to gaining strategic advantage via new product development is commercializing those goods before the next wave of competition, which comes more quickly and more intensely every day. Some companies are tooled for it; most are not. Often, by the time a new product has cleared its beta stage, competitors and developers of knockoffs or cheaper versions are already releasing rival offerings.

Technological gains have shortened the time it takes to design, manufacture, promote, and ultimately deliver a product or service to the marketplace. Consequently, the best new product ideas will quickly be replicated by competitors. It is for this primary reason that many companies opt to buy rather than make in order to avoid extended periods of R&D that may be inordinately expensive and may not yield the desired results.

Keeping Pace with Change

A multitude of variables can act as catalysts for change within a given market, industry, or sector. Social, economic, and demographic shifts result from factors beyond a company's control and may be viewed as either opportunities or threats; and they must be acted on accordingly.

The regulatory environment, typically a slower and yet more visible agent of change, is more often the *response* to a shift in social direction rather than a *catalyst*. In other words, regulations typically change in response to socioeconomic evolution rather than vice versa. But when regulations confirm this shift, a company's external change management acumen can be sorely tested.

As change occurs, companies are often forced to modify their services and hone their products and perspectives in order to stay competitive. Sometimes employees must be retrained to effect the behavioral shift that must accompany the new strategic direction. If a massive change in the marketplace prompts a massive change in the corporate vision, the corporate culture must embrace the new vision in order to maintain focus and continue to create value. When this fails, even the most solidly grounded of businesses can run into trouble.

INSIDER'S OUTLOOK

Strategic acquisitions are those made from a position of strength rather than from a position of weakness. Experience shows that acquisitions done because they support the company's growth strategy have a reasonably good chance of working out. On the other hand, acquisitions have tended *not* to work when management thought that, by doing a deal, it will overcome one or more threats posed by changing market conditions or by fundamental errors made in the past. In short, the evidence suggests that acquisitions should not be made from a defensive posture.

—John Levinson, Westway Capital LLC

Keeping pace with change in all its many incarnations forces many companies to merge or acquire when they cannot contend with change themselves. In the 1990s, the practices of contracting for and licensing of technology and research have become commonplace. But these short-term steps must be recognized for what they are—leased capabilities. Because they are not owned and rarely integrated, they are not a reliable foundation for growth. Thus, they cannot be built on. Any advancements garnered can falter or be obviated when a newer technology presents itself, when new competitors appear, or when a licensing agreement expires.

Management must acknowledge and continually plan for social and environmental flux and anticipate the natural evolution of both their products and their markets. In some cases, a visionary leader can bring about change within an entire industry by focusing on synergies that naturally enhance his or her company's own products. This results in the rest of the market being forced to keep pace.

Acquisitions that bring into the fold progressive, marketing-oriented organizations add more than new product capabilities. They can, in some instances, revolutionize the way business is done by imbuing the acquirer's corporate culture with a growth-oriented focus that may not have existed previously.

Whether or not coping with change is the primary driver that fuels a merger or acquisition, it is an issue that every company must seriously and continuously address. How a company chooses to respond to change can tell a lot about how it will react to a takeover threat or how it will approach a target.

Change can be analyzed from the vantage points of both *reactive* companies that merge or acquire to keep pace and *proactive* companies that make visionary decisions that anticipate change or even force it.

Certainly, it was R. J. Reynolds' goal to diversify its tobacco product line when it merged with Nabisco. But half a decade later, share price and profits are still floundering. In fact, there has been more discussion about de-merging these two companies amid the legal and financial fallout from tobacco health claims then there ever was about the potential synergies a marriage like this would create. Oreos and Winstons may have looked good on paper, but, in the real world, they just do not mix.

INSIDER'S OUTLOOK

In general, I view [M&A] deals as complementary to a company's core strategic and operational initiatives. You have to have an internal game plan of how you are going to grow your business in the core markets. Only then could you supplement that game plan with targeted acquisitions that make sense in strategic terms, financial terms, and, of course, in all material contractual terms.

—Mufit Cinali, AT&T

Capitalizing on Political and Regulatory Change

As the major political parties in the United States face off each day to represent their corporate constituencies, the future ground rules of American business are forged. Whether an individual Democrat or Republican is elected to public office rarely influences broad corporate policies. But, occasionally, brief political alignments manage to push their specific agendas into the public eye. When this occurs, there is often a window of opportunity that creates a platform for M&A activity to flourish.

In the early 1990s, as the Clinton Administration led the charge for health care reform; passed the North American Free Trade Agreement (NAFTA), opening U.S. trade borders to the north and south; and rallied against tobacco use and for affirmative action, opportunities were created for companies to capitalize on the political follow-through.

Minority businesses were acquired by companies looking to prevent exclusion from government contracts. Alliances with Mexican companies were forged to gain immediate footholds in that country (and to secure cheaper labor and manufacturing facilities). And, large tobacco manufacturers looked to diversify through acquisition as pressure increased to limit the domestic distribution and use of cigarettes.

These were a few of the more visible political activities of the hundreds that were created. In fact, the Clinton Administration's health care reform initiative set in motion a detailed reevaluation of the country's entire health care delivery system, which spurred a realignment and acquisition frenzy of the entire managed care industry. For example, within three years of the Administration's announcement to revamp American health care, more than half of the hospitals in the state of New Jersey had merged—all this in response to the threat of a change in public policy that was never enacted.

The past two decades have seen increased competition in industries once heavily regulated, such as energy, telecommunications, and banking. In the age of globalization, it is more difficult for companies in those industries to claim regional control over their competition simply by acquisition. More common are scenarios in which current regulations or geographical barriers limit customer access to particular services or products, creating areas where lack of competition is virtually mandated.

The telecommunications and energy industries are clear examples in which the consumer of the service or product has been locked into using one specific provider. In fact, the most obvious industrywide deregulations are occurring right now in these two industries, first established more than 50 years ago to deliver products into our households.

More recently, phone, cable television, natural gas, and electric companies have all been grouped under the heading of utilities. Their corporate structures, as well as the delivery systems of these individual offerings, are just now being shattered by the advent of new technology and changing buyer requirements. Regulation has reined competition in, virtually eliminating it; deregulation is unleashing it again. But as regulations continue to ease and competition increases, it is more common for companies—previously restrained from entering certain businesses—to aggressively pursue entry into once-monopolized sectors.

In recent years, the energy industry has seen a form of distribution deregulation called "wheeling" change the once-oligarchic nature of the natural gas and electric power industries. Wheeling allows a utility, based in one part of the country, to pay for access to a distribution line in another territory and then sell its power to customers in that region, creating competition for prices and service.

Newly established utility partnerships, whose sole intent is to lessen competition by locking up a specific geographic area, have become increasingly tenuous. Within months, a utility from another part of the state or country can come in and undercut that partnership's pricing scheme. Additionally, as utility deregulation advances, mergers and acquisitions between gas and electric companies and between cable TV and telecommunications companies are increasing. All four of these distinct industries are likely to have lines that run into your home. As each becomes less regulated, we will see more corporate combinations among them, each vying for the dominant line that will ultimately carry all four services into the household.

Pursuing Innovations/Discoveries in Products or Technology

Today, manifest destiny seems greatest in the realms of science and technology. A company's ability to "make it faster," "do it better," and "price it cheaper" is increasingly becoming a function of its technological, rather than managerial, know-how.

Each day, we read about another breakthrough in science, medicine, or information systems. Integrating that knowledge into an existing product or process drives many of the strategic acquisitions of our day and will only increase as technological advances do. The application of technology to core processes to take advantage of time compression has accelerated the rate at which technology has played a role in the evolution of various markets. A clear line has been drawn separating those companies on the cutting edge of technology from those that have not yet realized the importance of being on that edge.

When one thinks of advances in technology, it is often within the framework of a company that is in a high-technology industry. What needs to be understood, however, is that it is the inclusion of new technologies into the products and processes of lower-tech companies and industries that is most critical. If a company's strategic objective is to attain competitive advantage, then it must harness technology in virtually every area including engineering and production, operations, human resources, and, most importantly, the functions of marketing, product management, and sales. For instance, ideal strategic synergies meld the products of one company with the services of another, creating a more efficient delivery system or adding a customer service capability to an already strong distribution network.

In strategic alliances or joint ventures in which a company is in search of some technological advantage, one company's competitive advantage may simply be another's basic technology. Thus, how that technology is developed by each partner and whether the collaboration is merely an alliance or the driver for an eventual merger are critical issues that must be addressed in the predeal planning stages.

Is it cheaper to pour money into research and development and create a new technology, buy it from a competitor, or collaborate through cost- and resource-sharing to harness it? Choosing the last option lessens the production risk but forces further collaborative issues in the event that the technology and relationship develop further, fusing the partners.

Lessening Competition

Buying one's competitor would seem like the most natural of drivers, accomplishing the dual goals of negating a competitor's market share while bolstering one's own. However, any time a firm's market standing is heightened by the fall of a competitor, issues of antitrust are immediately raised.

The process of eliminating one's competition through acquisition typically faces severe regulatory hurdles and can never be admitted on the record. But every company that has become the dominant force in its industry has acquired in this manner. Microsoft, Gillette, IBM, Campbell Soup, and Coca-Cola are just a few of the companies that have piled on market share domestically and abroad by acquiring their close competition.

Even longer is the list of companies whose acquisitive designs were squelched by conflicts with prevailing antitrust laws. Acquisitions of this nature typically take a long time to close, are very costly, and can perform short-term gymnastics on a company's stock price. But, if and when these transactions survive regulatory scrutiny and do ultimately close, they place the acquirer in a position not just to claim additional market share but—to a broad extent—to heavily influence the market itself and in some cases dominate it.

To push the potentially problematic deal through, its champions focus largely on increased efficiencies resulting from cost cutting and the elimination of duplicative operations. And, without question, synergies such as these can deliver instant and tangible results that are quickly reflected in the bottom lines of 10-Qs, 10-Ks, and even stock prices. But the focus on economies of scale, although a component of a successful acquisition, must be subjugated beneath the more relevant long-term growth-oriented synergies being discussed.

Strengthening Reputation or Gaining Credibility

There truly is a value in a company's image and it can be heightened, weakened, or transferred through acquisition. Many acquisitions are made to bring a target company's stellar reputation to the buying company. The reverse is also true, where an organization gladly agrees to be purchased by another whose reputation or credibility will create a positive halo effect that directly benefits the acquired company.

Throughout the years, revenues of many companies have seesawed as their perception in the marketplace has risen and fallen. To properly address issues regarding the most intangible of marketing intangible assets—reputation—all stakeholders and perceivers of this reputation must be identified. The community in which a company operates, whether it is the local community or the global community at large, will be the final decision maker and assessor of changes in reputation. Specific audiences include stock- or bondholders, financial analysts, customers, suppliers, distributors, and even employees.

Today, the reputation of a company, a product line, or a single product can directly influence the buying patterns of Main Street America and the financial decision making of Wall Street. Conversely, the tarnishing or lack of a good reputation can negatively influence sales and lessen corporate profitability. Reputation must be carefully and strategically monitored and nurtured.

Issues of customer service, product quality, environmental sensitivity, philanthropy, and social responsibility are but a few of the intangible components of reputation. All are important in that they reflect some type of commitment to stakeholders, and at the same time, influence competitive differentiation. One need only look at the TV commercials of Nike, Burger King, and MTV targeting the teenage market to see that they sell image not product. The durability, quality, or benefit of the product takes a backseat in their advertising to that of being accepted or "cool." Should any of these companies or their products experience a falloff in the "cool factor" then they would soon experience defections to the next "coolest" competitor. As intangible as image or reputation may be, it must never be minimized when contemplating the decision to acquire or merge.

Responding to or Capitalizing on Economic Scenarios

In periods of lower interest rates or overvalued stock markets, it is easy to be blinded by the financial successes seen around us each day. When interest rates are low, the opportunity to access cheaper capital often sparks a flurry of acquisitions by companies who could not previously afford to borrow. There are many advantages to a looser monetary policy for an acquisitive company. It can foster the refinancing of past acquisitions at lower rates while granting access to the capital markets using previously unaffordable methods.

On the other hand, when equity markets are heated up, a company's overvalued stock price can be the catalyst for fueling an acquisition program with stock as currency. But a caveat for the acquirer is this: Rising stock markets, with their attendant inflated valuations, often give a rosier impression of a target company's true value, and can mask weaknesses that lie beneath the surface. Additionally, sudden hiccups or drops in stability in these markets can substantially alter or void a transaction when stock is the currency of choice. Economic scenarios must be viewed as somewhat short-term, unpredictable, and potentially volatile and should never be viewed as the sole driver for a long-term strategic partnership.

THE NONSTRATEGIC DRIVER

The foregoing discussion of strategic drivers seems to necessitate a mention of their counterpart, the nonstrategic driver.

Many deals that are driven by favorable economic conditions are simply investments by companies that feel that a target is underachieving and believe that an infusion of cash and/or management expertise will either generate increased revenues or transform the entity into a profitable one. There may be strategic advantages that can be realized later, but the driving force behind these nonstrategic "remedy" investments is the "I can run it better" philosophy.

There are also instances in which a company is solely exploring a partnership or searching to incorporate a specific business function into the main corporate infrastructure. In such cases, the appropriate partnership would be a licensing or distribution pact, a technology exchange, or an R&D contract. It is questionable whether these can truly be termed strategic unless a long-term synthesis is desired.

Essentially, alliances that do not result in exclusive permanent partnership arrangements can only be viewed as leases, in which a specific function is borrowed from another company for a finite period of time. No holistic ownership can be felt, no empowerment can take place, and, realistically, no long-term strategic synergies can be realized when there is a time limit on a relationship.

INSIDER'S OUTLOOK

You have to articulate a vision for the merged company and stay committed to it. Many times management will invest lots of money for strategic planning and staff infrastructure development without having a clear sense of what markets they are going to serve and with what products and services. Then, they staff-up and allocate resources that are completely noncommensurate with the pace at which they could reasonably enter any of the markets they are targeting. Ultimately, they start out in a certain direction of one market, only to abandon it and then move into another one, then abandon that and move into a third market . . . never quite completing the process in any particular marketplace. Now, this is not to say you shouldn't shift gears when marketplace conditions require your doing so. But it does mean that you should take the time to craft a vision and work diligently to achieve it. Implicit in that, of course, is doing as comprehensive a job of market planning as possible.

—Rich Rudden, R. J. Rudden Associates

IDENTIFYING MULTIPLE STRATEGIC DRIVERS

Merely having an awareness of the drivers of strategic mergers and acquisitions does not assure the ultimate attainment of strategic advantage. It is only the beginning. Strategic drivers must provide the focus in formulating your acquisition strategy, be incorporated into the analysis of given target companies, and be built on throughout the rest of the predeal planning process.

In most deals, the merger partners cite growth as the number-one reason for the combination. Yet, many of these deals never focus beyond this most common and generic of drivers. The participants either are motivated by the sole vision of organizational growth or assume other drivers will follow. When those other benefits do not materialize, the blame is placed on such factors as unreceptive markets or a weakness in the economy. But that blame has been misdirected. The culprit is often the fact that management failed to identify and work toward actualizing multiple strategic drivers.

Oftentimes, once one driver is secured, others typically fall into place. But this is by no means a certainty. There must be a concerted effort to identify and realize multiple strategic drivers. Why? The more opportunities there are for attaining strategic advantage, the greater the likelihood you will successfully actualize it. If there is only one strategic reason to buy a company, then as that one reason weakens or becomes less significant over time, the acquisition will become less relevant or critical to the whole. When this occurs, more often than not it leads to flagging profits and, ultimately, divestiture.

In order for a strategic acquisition to succeed over the long term, more than one driver should motivate that company to acquire or merge with another. Indeed, there are many transactions that focus on one particular driver; the goal, however, should be to maximize your M&A investment by striving—whenever possible—to realize more than a single driver. However, it must be stressed that although each strategic driver can complement other drivers, each is unique and must be fully explored before combining it with others.

In addition to the original motivation that spawns a strategic merger or acquisition, you must delve further to understand the other drivers that influence the deal. By definition, "strategic" means beneficial on a series of levels. Additional drivers must not be viewed as secondary or less important motivators. Their actualization is as relevant to the predeal planning stage as the original driver that first prompted your pursuit of the transaction.

STRATEGIC DRIVERS: CASE STUDIES

By examining several major deals of the past decade, it will be made clear why focusing on multiple drivers significantly increases the likelihood of the success of a merger or acquisition. Beyond the obvious quest for growth, many other strategic drivers help to create the vision of strategic advantage.

In some of these deals, there truly was synergy. In others there were roadblocks or factors that may have given early warning signs that the deal was a forced situation, doomed to failure.

And then, of course, there are the deals that never happened. As mentioned earlier, antitrust law can act as the greatest stumbling block to what would otherwise seem like the perfect union of companies. Some of the most strategically sound acquisitions are never consummated because they are, in fact, too good. Their completion would create a company that would be deemed by regulators to be an impediment to future competition. Regardless of whether the transaction ultimately occurred, an analysis of the motivation for these unrealized deals lends valuable insight into the planning that is necessary to achieve strategic advantage. Let us first examine one of the most synergistically sound acquisition attempts of the decade—Rite Aid's proposed purchase of Revco.

Rite Aid/Revco: Too Good to Be True

Rite Aid Corporation's $1.8 billion attempted acquisition of Revco, D.S., in 1995 would have created the nation's largest drugstore chain. By leveraging no less than five strategic drivers, many important synergies would have been achieved by the completion of this deal:

- Rite Aid would have been able to claim a larger piece of the retail beauty products business.
- The anticipated revenue flow of $11 billion would have placed the company head-to-head with Walgreen, the industry leader.
- The new size and increased scope of operations would have helped Rite Aid attract health insurance business, a major growth vehicle in the retail drugstore industry.
- Rite Aid could have managed its inventory more efficiently using Revco's point of sale (POS) technology, in which cosmetics are reordered based on data from check-out-counter scanning devices.
- The Revlon name, prominently displayed in Rite Aid stores, would have created an image for Rite Aid of being an upscale cosmetics retailer.

Rite Aid did not just focus on the driver of effecting organizational growth. The company was motivated by multiple drivers. The company attempted to lessen competition, strengthen its reputation, gain entrée into new markets and access to new products, and capitalize on technology. All of these strategic drivers gelled with Rite Aid's strategic plan, which was to grow by acquisition in a rapidly imploding market.

When earlier in 1994 Thrift Drug merged with PayLess and Kerr Drug, Rite Aid responded by purchasing Hook/SupeRx, another drugstore chain. The acquisition increased Rite Aid's piece of the pie, but did little to widen its footprint in the marketplace. In order to truly increase market share, Rite Aid needed a bigger pie. So in 1995 the company made its play for Revco, seeking synergies that could not necessarily be gained through a purely horizontal acquisition. The potential benefits of such an acquisition were:

- Increased market share
- Product line enhancement
- Product line additions
- New industry segments
- Improved inventory management
- Economies of both scope and scale
- Increased operational efficiencies
- Access to new territories
- Cross-selling opportunities

The proposed deal was met with a long period of regulatory scrutiny and in May 1996 was abandoned altogether by Rite Aid so that it could pursue its acquisition of Thrift, another growing retail drugstore chain. The company managed to complete that deal before year-end.

The Rite Aid–Revco deal looked good on paper, but was bogged down and ultimately thwarted by issues of antitrust. The breadth of synergies and multiple drivers put forth in the planning stages would have given this merger a greater chance of success than if the sole motivator had been just effecting organizational growth.

The Megamergers

The strategic advantage of achieving organizational growth can be accomplished in many ways and for many reasons. The 1990s have been a fertile period for the "megamerger," in which two behemoths with sales in the billions combine to become an even larger corporation in search of competitive advantage. With the exception of those in the pharmaceutical industry, most megamergers have taken a vertical path, combining different industries or sectors into one semiconglomeratized larger entity. Starting with RJR Nabisco and Time Warner, whose megamergers took leaders of two discrete sectors of similar industries and combined them, the trend has continued with very mixed results.

The merger of Time Inc. and Warner Communications Inc. looked better in theory than it has turned out in reality. A host of issues have prevented Time Warner from integrating the different cultures and complex operations into a seamless, profitable company. When companies of equal size, such as Time Inc. and Warner Communications, are megamerged, there are internal issues of the dominant culture, battles of ego, and clashing of long-established relationships.

In the case of RJR Nabisco, it has long been expected that Nabisco would ultimately break away from its tobacco sibling, R. J. Reynolds. There never was and never will be a strategic fit. The arcane 1980s merger concept of "bigger is better" drove this merger, which has never been able to integrate the products, markets, or cultures of these two diverse companies.

When Time Inc. and Warner Communications combined their two companies in 1989, they created the first of the giant media conglomerates. They focused on dominating—through size and leverage—all aspects of that market from print to television to movies and now electronic media. In Time Warner's case, the blend of content and distribution was one of the first media mergers that appeared strategically sound. Yet, more than a decade later, the lack of a unified synergistic culture, a floundering stock price, unimpressive earnings, and continued reliance on debt have stood in the way of this union being termed a success.

Yet, there are exceptions to the megamerger track record of failure and a lesson for others to build on. Let's examine several deals that are considered successes because of the attention paid to the predeal planning process, the postdeal integration, and, specifically, the multiple drivers that motivated each deal from the start.

Novartis: A Prescription for Success

In 1995, Glaxo PLC's acquisition of Wellcome PLC hammered home the reality that, in the pharmaceutical industry, mass was critical in order to compete against the onslaught of generic and branded drug competition. During the previous 30 years, pharmaceutical companies kept their drug pipelines deep and their margins high. Yet, in the 1990s, health maintenance organizations (HMOs) and drug formularies forced prices and margins down, while a record number of drug patents expired, changing the complexion and direction of the pharmaceutical industry forever. The message was clear: Traditional strategies for success that had worked in the past for pharmaceutical companies could no longer be employed in the new age of health care.

In 1996, as the drug industry continued to consolidate, two Swiss competitors, Sandoz Ltd. and Ciba-Geigy Ltd., proposed a $36 billion merger to create a new company called Novartis, from the Latin for new arts or skills. Following the lead of the merging Pharmacia AB and Upjohn Company, equal to each other in size, Sandoz, the 12th-largest drug company, approached Ciba, the 10th, in an attempt to dominate the pharmaceutical and immunological markets. The combined company had initial sales of roughly $30 billion and a market value of roughly $79 billion, making it the 12th-largest corporation in the world.

Sandoz felt that to truly grow its core pharmaceuticals business, it would have to shed those pieces that did not align, such as its industrial chemicals division. Additionally, Sandoz believed that future growth must be the result of pure fusion, rooted in the philosophy that a hostile or one-sided move would defeat the synthesis of cultures and result in the domination of one company's mind-set over that of the other. This was an intellectual decision, soundly rooted in synergy with the goal of creating strategic advantage.

The combination of vast corporate resources and the broadest product range of any of the pharmaceutical competitors has made the merged company a world leader in many therapeutic areas, including immunology; inflammatory disease; central nervous system disorders; cardiovascular, endocrine, and metabolic disease; oncology; and dermatology. Additionally, the combined technology and research efforts place them in the forefront of emerging gene-, cell-, and organ-based therapies as well as xenotransplantation (the process of transplanting animal organs into humans).

The merger enhances and links the two companies' pharmaceutical and nutrition product lines, creating the largest health food producer in Europe. And in the United States, a focus on brand enhancement continues at a rapid pace. Acquired in 1994 by Sandoz, Gerber Products Company provides the perfect base from which to expand nutritional growth in the United States, by leveraging its infant food, children's nutrition, Ovaltine beverages, and health food products. This interlocking of products offers each company entrée into new markets as well as access to new products and distribution channels. Where one company is weak, the other's strength fills in, forging a bond that will lead to a successful marriage.

But why these two companies came to merge is probably less important than how, lining up multiple strategic drivers for growth and focusing on integration in the predeal planning stage. The lessons to be learned from this merger can help you approach deals in the same manner.

The confidential nature of the merger limited on-site visits and certain aspects of the traditional due diligence process. But, the homogeneity of the Swiss "consensus cultures" within each company formed the foundation for trust and a belief that postdeal integration would be easily attained. Strategic fit was a given—so much so that, instead of traditional team due diligence being implemented, an honor system due diligence initiative was agreed on as both Sandoz and Ciba made good-faith disclosures the foundation for all synergies that would develop.

The global pharmaceutical market is a highly fragmented one. And Novartis, now number two in the world, behind Glaxo, claims less than 5% of this worldwide market. Yet, because of the benign nature of the exchange, no cash or deal premium was wasted, leaving Novartis with a larger amount of cash on hand than any of its competitors, to fuel its research and development efforts. Although the focus of this book is on growth, not cost cutting, it should be noted that incorporating multiple growth drivers into the predeal planning stage can foster additional opportunities to reduce expenses.

In Novartis's case, the long-term benefit of this "fusion for growth" is the company's continued ability to finance aggressive R&D projects that will produce the next generation of cutting-edge drugs well into the 21st century. Additionally, the paring of 10,000 jobs from the combined worldwide ranks of 100,000 and a 3%-per-year cost cutting initiative continues to fuel earnings. The stock market reacted favorably to the promise of Novartis's improved earnings, sending Sandoz shares skyrocketing 30% on the day following the announcement, with Ciba rallying 20%. But the strategic benefits should have longer-lasting implications to future growth.

The fuel for this growth is twofold: broader distribution channels and a commanding position in each of the company's defined markets. Sandoz's decision to merge with Ciba was strategically a sound one. Yet, even more critical to the success of this deal was the predeal planning that structured the resultant company with cash-rich coffers. Due to the friendly nature of the merger, no premium was paid, no debt was incurred, and no new shares were issued. This liquidity will allow for new investments in the future without the restrictive burdens of financing, and will sustain the broad and aggressive marketing of existing and new products.

In time, it will become evident whether the strategic drivers that motivated the Sandoz/Ciba-Geigy merger will truly have staying power. But the fact that so many strategic drivers are present, beyond the simple quest for growth, gives this fusion more levels on which it can succeed.

INSIDER'S OUTLOOK

The purest example of a strategic acquisition is when the deal is a *natural* extension of the acquirer's enterprise—a transaction that doesn't take the company into a totally new business. Keep in mind that "business" is an amorphous word. For example, are railroad companies in the same "business" as airlines since they're both involved in transportation? I don't think so. Consequently, defining the word business is the first thing to consider when sizing up the prospects of a given transaction. Having said that, if the transaction is one where the acquirer will not be getting into another business (properly defined), there's generally going to be a much higher probability that the deal is going to work.

—John Levinson, Westway Capital LLC

Cadbury Schweppes/Dr Pepper: Avoiding the "Snapple Syndrome"

An acquisition of smaller size than Novartis but of comparable import occurred between the third- and fourth-ranked competitors in the beverage industry—Cadbury Schweppes and Dr Pepper/Seven-Up. Years later, a host of synergies have been released and revenue enhancement opportunities realized as the successful combination has created the number-one noncola soft drink company in North America. The primary strategic driver in this instance was the lessening of competition in the marketplace by acquisition.

In 1994, Dallas-based Dr Pepper/Seven-Up Group was the third-largest soft drink company in the United States behind Coke and Pepsi, with roughly 11% of the U.S. carbonated soft drink market. Its beverage lineup included the regular and diet versions of both Dr Pepper and 7-Up, as well as the Welch's soft drink line and IBC root beer and cream soda. At that time, the United Kingdom-based Cadbury Schweppes Group was a major global player in the confectionery and beverage markets, with distribution in more than 170 countries. The third-largest soft drink company in the world behind Coke and Pepsi, Cadbury Schweppes was fourth in the United States behind Dr Pepper/Seven-Up.

In its quest to dominate the market, Cadbury Schweppes first acquired A&W Brands, the largest root beer manufacturer in North America, and then took a 25.9% stake in Dr Pepper/Seven-Up, a fraction away from triggering a prohibitive poison pill. This defensive measure implemented by Dr Pepper would have forced the issuance of additional shares, diluting the value of the stock, should an unfriendly suitor attempt to own more than 26% of the company. The poison pill assured Dr Pepper that, if it was ever acquired, it would only be on its terms. A trading relationship had already been established, with Dr Pepper producing the bulk of Cadbury's soft drink concentrates in the United States, so it was no surprise that in late 1994, Dr Pepper agreed to be acquired by Cadbury for $1.7 billion.

Upon consummating the deal in 1995, the combined company instantly became the number-one noncola beverage company in North America, while controlling almost 50% of that market worldwide. Recognizing that growth in the cola arena had plateaued, Cadbury's goal was to combine Dr Pepper, 7-Up, Mott's, IBC, Schweppes, Crush, A&W, Canada Dry, Welch's, and the international beverage Oasis all under one roof, catapulting Cadbury's market share from 4.8% of the U.S. market to over 16%. The company was successful.

Seeking to avoid the costly mistakes of Quaker Oats in its acquisition of Snapple, Dr Pepper USA and Dr Pepper/Seven-Up Fountain/Food Service remained headquartered in Dallas, maintaining the same overall organizational structure to ensure the momentum of the Dr Pepper brand, which surpassed Diet Pepsi as the number-four soft drink in the United States. In fact, Cadbury Beverages North America quickly changed its corporate moniker to Dr Pepper/Cadbury North America to increase acceptance of the Cadbury name. Growth continues and the acquisition succeeds because of early implementation of promotional and marketing strategies all working to accomplish a joint goal.

Clearly, the motivation behind the acquirer's strategy and the target's eager acquiescence was to gain the competitive edge in the noncola marketplace. On a product basis alone, strategic advantage has been accomplished. Only time will tell whether the consolidation of this "Uncola" empire will produce the envisioned longer-term synergies.

But Cadbury's focus on the multiple drivers of gaining entrée to new markets, lessening its competition, and strengthening its reputation ensured that strategic advantage existed on many levels.

INSIDER'S OUTLOOK

IBM's acquisitions are not done for internal investment. We're not intent on being a holding company that's simply a portfolio of unrelated businesses. We acquire companies when we feel there is real strategic value to be gained—when those companies will fill a strategic void we have, or when we feel that an acquisition will help us decrease the cost and the time-to-market of developing an important new product ourselves.

—Carolyn Chin, IBM

Mattel/Tyco: Leveraging Size

Often the market leader of a particular product will acquire smaller competitors to increase its base and help it gain an edge over the number-two and -three rivals. The ensuing increase in size can then provide the necessary leverage with suppliers and distributors to make even greater inroads within that market.

When Mattel Inc., maker of Barbie dolls and Hot Wheels miniature cars, leapfrogged over number-two Hasbro Inc. to swallow up number-three Tyco Toys Inc., the strategy was clear. In addition to adding Tyco's Matchbox cars to its own fleet of miniature autos, Mattel added Tyco's 3% share of the $17.5 billion U.S. toy market to its own 16% share. Hasbro, the creator of GI Joe, owned almost 12% of the market at the time of the deal and went from threatening Mattel's preeminence to falling substantially behind the new stronger leader.

The expanded product line delivered more to Mattel than its new combined 19% share of the market. More critically, it increased Mattel's leverage with retailers, who now had to acquiesce and stock Mattel's slower-selling toys and games in order to gain access to its most popular ones. By leveraging this newly acquired shelf-space muscle, Mattel is now on track to increase its market share beyond current levels. By not pursuing a once-contemplated acquisition of Hasbro, Mattel avoided costly antitrust litigation. Instead, Mattel added to its already formidable industry lead in sales and profits, strengthening its reputation, lessening market competition, and gaining access to new products while expanding its distribution channels.

Primergy Corporation: A Band-Aid Merger Attempt

In May 1996, Milwaukee-based Wisconsin Energy Corporation announced a deal to merge with another Midwest utility, Northern States Power Company. As equal partners in Primergy Corporation, a potentially new $6 billion holding company, the companies sought a combination of marketing muscle, financial resources, and power generating capacity. The proximity of the two companies' service territories and energy delivery systems created an opportunity to merge all operations and pool fuel contracts with an immediate projected savings of $2 billion. The payoff to consumers was expected to be lower rates and a temporary rate freeze.

The joint goal of this merger was to become a better, more competitive company than either one envisioned for themselves on a stand-alone basis. Yet, in the energy industry, especially among natural gas and electric suppliers, reaching an agreement to create Primergy was far easier than the 12- to 18-month trek through federal and state regulatory agencies.

The two companies have many obvious similarities: Both serve growing territories in the upper Midwest, and both have clean balance sheets, experienced workforces, and low electric rates. Although the two companies have run lean, profitable, efficient operations, each has taken a different approach toward its individual successes. In 1993, Wisconsin Energy, with approximately four thousand employees, launched a sweeping restructuring program that involved a realignment of the company's organizational structure, starting with a review of most of its workflow processes and resulting in a change in job descriptions and their core functions. To that same end, Northern States, with seven thousand employees, invested $150 million in information systems equipment that automated processes and has allowed a trimming of the payroll. But the company has cut only about 250 to 300 jobs annually since 1992, and therefore has never performed the massive self-examination so critical to assessing a strategic fit of core competencies in a merger partner.

In the past, representatives of the two utilities have not agreed on the future of Wisconsin's power industry and therefore approached their nonutility businesses quite differently. Wisconsin Energy has concentrated on real estate development, venture capital, and other financing activities. Wispark Corporation, its most visible nonutility venture, has developed several southeastern Wisconsin industrial parks, which contribute healthily to the bottom line. Northern States has stayed closer to the energy business and, through its NRG Energy Inc. subsidiary, invested $100 million in two German energy concerns and an Australian power plant. Another subsidiary markets energy management services.

On the surface, a Wisconsin Energy-Northern States merger would appear to create a Midwest regional monopoly by pushing smaller utilities to consolidate and squeezing out independently owned power producers, leaving customers with fewer choices. Unfortunately for the two utilities seeking to merge, the regulators took this threat very seriously and—in the quest to maintain a competitive energy environment—responded with very specific directives that would prevent the possibility of future monopolization of the region's energy. These demands seemed too restrictive to the two companies, so they broke off the negotiations. Had the deal proceeded, this merger would have accomplished the strategic advantage of increasing competitiveness in a specific geographical region. However, in the quickly deregulating U.S. energy industry, territorial control would have proved less relevant than other strategic drivers such as diversification, gaining entrée into new markets, and capitalizing on global relationships.

In hindsight, the regulators probably did these two companies a favor. It was indeed questionable whether the two companies had enough synergies left to make this a successful long-term merger. As wheeling invades the north central states, this merger attempt may have just proved to be a short-term fix for a continuing and longer-term problem.

IBM/Lotus: Acquiring Technology

When IBM acquired Lotus Development Corporation in 1995 for $3.5 billion, many considered it a stroke of genius. For IBM, the centerpiece of the acquisition was Lotus's groupware product, Notes, which at the time was the world's leading document-sharing technology. Marketplace observers believed IBM's financial and marketing muscle could rejuvenate and help Lotus penetrate the corporate marketplace in the spreadsheet and document-sharing arena. This acquisition helped extend IBM's lead in the enterprise computing field over rival Microsoft Corporation.

Prior to the acquisition of Lotus by IBM, the market had been hesitant to fully embrace Notes, fearing that Lotus might not be able to deliver the technological support it required. There were those who felt that Lotus was too weak financially to even stay in business. However, once IBM announced the acquisition, Lotus customers knew they were now dealing with a company with deep pockets and staying power, unlike so many other technology companies. In fact, putting IBM's reputation, focus, and marketing muscle behind Notes has made a difference, quadrupling the number of Notes computing seats in the first year after the acquisition. But in that same year, Internet and intranet applications took center stage as the number-one issue in corporate computing circles.

Lotus is making money. But was IBM's prized acquisition a misplaced bet on yesterday's technology? Internet technology is advancing at a feverish pace. It is expected that groupware product technology will evolve radically in the next few years. If Lotus can complete Notes's transition to the World Wide Web before any radical Web technology makes it obsolete, then IBM will have a captive market. But, basic Internet groupware companies, such as Microsoft, are aggressively chipping away at the Lotus groupware theme. Irrespective of the competition, however, IBM boosted its technological reputation and know-how by becoming synonymous with Notes.

Its instant entry into an otherwise closed market was secured with the acquisition of Notes, and two years later, IBM—once considered weak in the groupware arena—is considered a leader. IBM is now charged with the task of fully integrating Lotus not only into its broader corporate entity, but also into the wave of advancing technology. Big Blue has already begun: Notes was recently outfitted with capabilities for Web publishing, browsing, and managed Internet access.

Creating and applying new knowledge and technology has long been critical to a company's financial success. With increasing resource requirements for technological advancement and acceleration in the rate of global technology diffusion, strategic thinking about technology must go beyond the simple development of new products or services. IBM boosted both its own market standing and the product of the company it acquired when it bought Lotus.

PaineWebber/Kidder Peabody: Strengthening Reputation

The six main ingredients that contribute to a company's public reputation are size, level of socially responsible behavior, financial performance, quality/durability of its products or services, media coverage, and advertising. And although advertising and image-building campaigns have done much to define markets and target specific audiences, in one fell swoop an acquisition can either eliminate or mask a poor reputation.

PaineWebber's 1994 acquisition of General Electric's Kidder Peabody unit is an excellent case in point. Kidder Peabody had finally shaken the fallout from its involvement in the 1987 Ivan Boesky insider-trading scandal to build itself into a premier niche investment bank rivaling the likes of Salomon Brothers, Morgan Stanley, and CS First Boston. In addition, the firm had become the market leader in derivative securities—specifically collateralized mortgage obligations (CMOs)—catering to institutions and high net-worth individuals.

PaineWebber, on the other hand, had built its reputation as a mass-market brokerage firm that asked critical financial questions of its investing public in order to help them develop sound financial planning. Their customer-focused ad campaigns—"Thank You, PaineWebber," "He Asked . . . ," and "We Invest in Relationships"—had changed the nature of how brokerage firms attracted the individual investor. Yet, the firm had little name recognition as a competitive investment bank in the institutional markets. Clearly, the two firms played to distinctly different markets.

In 1994, Kidder revealed to its parent, General Electric, that it had reported false profits to conceal losses on its government bond desk. The media ran wild with the story of Joseph Jett, whom they alleged to be a rogue bond trader, culminating in a *60 Minutes* exclusive report on Kidder management's lack of oversight on the government bond desk. The fallout from the public flowed through Kidder straight to GE. For days, articles in the press pointed a finger at GE's upper management for mishandling the situation. GE needed to shed the cloud of suspicion that hung over it, and parting with Kidder was the only answer.

A window of opportunity existed and PaineWebber quickly acquired the battered investment bank, its assets, and most of its employees for a mere $650 million, bolstering its institutional presence with more than a thousand new brokers and derivatives traders, and a sophisticated investment banking unit. The acquisition instantly gave PaineWebber entrée into new markets and access to new products and distribution channels.

Kidder, a small yet powerful competitor, was eliminated, with PaineWebber effecting organizational growth by absorbing the entire operating unit. Integrity is critical in the securities business, and PaineWebber distanced itself from the scandal by dissolving the Kidder name and quickly integrating the two firms. Years later, PaineWebber effectively competes in both individual and institutional markets, its reputation intact, while the name of Kidder Peabody is simply one from a bygone era that included the likes of EF Hutton and Drexel Burnham Lambert.

General Electric/Tungsram: Going Global

While domestic political changes have spurred M&A in the United States, under the Bush Administration the door to Europe was kicked right off its hinges as the Berlin Wall's collapse paved the way for a unified Europe. With the fall of the wall came cracks in the trade barriers of Russia and China. In fact, when eastern Europe opened its doors to foreigners, one of the first to enter was General Electric. GE moved quickly to acquire Tungsram, the previously state-owned Hungarian lightbulb manufacturer, and its 7%

market share in Europe's $2.5 billion lighting market. Combined with GE's 13% piece of that market, which had been bolstered in 1991 by acquiring Thorn EMI, Britain's largest lighting firm, Tungsram's 7% share put GE in a toe-to-toe battle with Philips Electronics N.V. as the global lighting leader.

Although GE quickly found that Hungarian production facilities were flawed, bills were unpaid, and rocks filled bulb cartons in otherwise empty warehouses, GE wanted the name recognition and the geographical presence that the Hungarian stalwart provided. As the veil of Communism fell, GE realized that a once-in-a-lifetime opportunity awaited and felt the strategic advantage of an eastern European presence outweighed any financial drawbacks.

Political barriers to expansion still exist in the United States and certainly throughout the rest of the world. Decisions to enter these markets must be carefully evaluated. The political risk in emerging markets combined with the potential for civil unrest and unstable currencies make transactions in these parts of the world extremely uncertain.

In fact, prior to the introduction of Western acquisitions in eastern Europe, emerging-market due diligence was often done after the deal was closed. In the area of post-deal integration, cultural difficulties such as managing a foreign labor force according to U.S. standards can very quickly spell the failure of a deal of this nature. Deciding whether to be the first entrant into an untapped market can be laborious and fraught with hidden risks. But the clout of being first in the door can act as a strong platform from which to build.

SUMMARY

The more popular motivation for an acquisition or merger has its genesis in the belief by one company that an absorption of another company, a service, or a product with one or more of its own will result in some longer-term success or growth by leveraging existing resources, processes, personnel, or products. Yet in the development and actualization of synergy often comes the stark reality that the stakeholders (customers, stockholders, employees, and management) are more focused on instant or short-term benefits such as cost reduction or share price increase. This often forces decisions to be made that sacrifice long-term goals in favor of realizing the tangible short-term savings generated by early reductions in overhead, staff, and basic costs. Even if the motivation for an acquisition or merger is to achieve strategic advantage, the urgency to attain—and the fear of not delivering—bottom-line dollar benefits often obfuscates what would otherwise be defined as a brilliant long-term strategic move.

So often companies will claim strategic fit because they both employ differing skill sets or sell dissimilar products. The fact that two companies are in different businesses does not necessarily make them somehow complementary or strategically a good fit. This misconception has driven many deals to failure. The key to success is being able to take the differences inherent in two companies and meld them to create an enhanced capability. The ultimate goal of all business is profit. And the pursuit of that goal is often driven through a mission for growth. Achieving growth has always been the hallmark of every strategic deal.

The concept of bigger is better heralded much of the M&A activity of the 1980s. Yet, as mentioned earlier, increasing a company's size for the sake of size alone is ill-advised if it ignores the commitment to attain strategic advantage. The series of spin-offs and divestitures that have flooded the markets throughout the 1990s are the by-products of this merger myopia. In this current period of streamlining, restructuring, and reengineering, management has been forced to reexamine and ultimately accept its mistakes as the by-products of so simple a motivator as increasing size.

Achieving strategic advantage by keying on multiple strategic drivers to release synergies is like any marriage. The goal is for the created entity to truly transcend what was first envisioned as a combination of two parties. Just as in any long-term human relationship, there must be more in common than simple attraction. If two individuals have the same backgrounds, similar goals, and aligned perceptions, then the odds of a long-lasting and successful relationship are greater. In the corporate world, if all of those issues are addressed after the union has already occurred and it is determined that none of these characteristics do indeed align, then it will be obvious that this is a deal that should not have been done.

When companies seek to merge or acquire, and can cite more than two strategic drivers as reasons to come together, then the chances of success are higher. In the next chapter, attention is paid to leveraging strategic fit to generate revenue enhancement opportunities. This lays the groundwork for the alignment of other characteristics that may help to determine long-term synergies and ensure success of the transaction. These are the true proving grounds for whether or not *theoretical* synergies can be transformed into *actual* short- and long-term revenue growth programs.

3

Essence of Strategic Mergers and Acquisitions: Focusing on Revenue Enhancement

Up to now, the vast majority of mergers and acquisitions have succeeded in one dubious respect: losing vast amounts of money and severely diminishing the combining companies' overall shareholder value.

The goal going forward is to ensure the success of corporate combinations. Central to this objective is devising ways not only to achieve short-term gains, but also to bolster overall revenue growth to effect the enduring financial viability of the merging companies.

Achieving growth through mergers and acquisitions requires planning that is focused on revenue enhancement synergies as opposed to cost-reduction measures. A revenue-driven perspective should pervade all aspects of target company examinations. Moreover, postmerger integration efforts must continually build on the quest for revenue gains over the long haul. Without the commitment to long-term growth, the potential for optimizing shareholder value cannot occur.

Cost reduction is not a building block because it does not fuel top-line growth (i.e., growth of total revenues). That is not to say that there are no important benefits to a streamlined and financially well-run company. But in order for long-term revenues to increase, it is imperative to acknowledge cost-cutting measures for what they are—a way initially to position the company in the most economical way possible. Once that is accomplished, revenues must be fueled. This can only come from growth strategies and their implementation over an extended period of time.

Everyone is familiar with the concept of the "bottom line." It is what ultimately trickles down from total revenues to create net earnings. It is often boosted in the wake of a merger by reducing expenses, usually via eliminating duplicative people and processes. But employing these measures to bolster bottom-line results is a short-lived solution and fuels neither long-term growth nor shareholder value.

In fact, for a company to grow, garner additional market share, and become dominant, it must focus on revenue enhancement or growth of the top line. To ensure that top-line growth remains the watchword of mergers and acquisitions, it is necessary to embark on a concerted effort to unearth revenue enhancement opportunities or REOs—a key aspect of the overall marketing due diligence process.

In Chapter 1 we defined REO. The definition bears repeating here. *A revenue en-*

hancement opportunity is a newly created or strengthened product or service that is formulated by the fusion of two distinct attributes of the merger partners and which generates immediate and/or long-term revenue growth.

Marketing due diligence is designed to spot weaknesses and strengths in a given target company. The REO analysis component of this investigative exercise keys on the latter: pinpointing the particular capabilities and value sources inherent in the target that can help lead to revenue growth. Yet this is by no means a one-way perspective.

Throughout this volume we will discuss the concept of the "merged-company perspective" on predeal planning. This orientation states that viewing a target company and attempting to assess its strengths and weaknesses, without addressing and considering these attributes in relation to those of your own company, will always deliver an incomplete picture.

Certainly, compatibility issues regarding the merging organizations' cultures, management styles, and structures should be addressed at the earliest possible phase of the acquisition planning process. However, once there is compatibility at the highest of levels, the complementary nature of products, services, personnel, and strategy must then be addressed at the acquirer, target, and merged-company levels. Additionally, examining features of compatibility without the focus on creating and sustaining long-term growth will place a merger or acquisition in a position to fail, even if short-term shareholder value is served in the process.

Examining the core attributes of REOs will, when collectively viewed, help provide the perspective needed to explore the REOs that are unique to a given merger or acquisition situation. Once this is accomplished, you can address the ways to identify revenue enhancement opportunities as a means of focusing on the critical success factors that will drive long-term, top-line growth.

REO SYNERGIES: OVERLAPS VERSUS OVERLAYS

Identifying REOs is a core perspective in strategic M&A planning. It is a frame of reference that can best be gained by first understanding the orientation that pervades traditional due diligence.

In standard due diligence, the attributes of the acquirer and the acquiree are compared side by side. Conventional analyses typically seek to uncover operational synergies. These lead to cost-reduction opportunities via the elimination of duplicative operations, processes, and personnel. Such expense-related areas make the deal financially beneficial—in the near term. In contrast, marketing due diligence seeks to unearth *REO synergies*, which are those sales-, marketing-, and growth-related opportunities that collectively make the deal financially beneficial—in the long term.

In general, the search for REOs begins with an exploration of the conventional internal and external issues that an acquirer faces in any M&A scenario. Factors including company ownership, product and service lines, industry trends, market penetration levels, and corporate cultures are first assessed as singular variables. From an organizational standpoint, all areas of the combining companies that are duplicative represent an *overlap*—areas that are redundant and that can be dealt with as cost-cutting opportunities.

Cost-reduction synergies are created when there are overlaps between the companies coming together. Once an overlap is identified, the weaker of the redundant attributes is eliminated. Here the postmerger benefit is represented by the numerical equation 2 + 2 = 3.

Often the identification of these overlaps sparks quantifiable savings that bolster the financial justification for the union of two companies. In public companies this is evidenced by a short-term jump in the stock price and the obligatory reports in the press of an eventual gain in shareholder value. Unfortunately, long-term shareholder value is by no means a given unless REO synergies lie at the foundation of the deal.

REO synergies result when the skills and resources of the two companies create complementary *overlays* that spawn revenue generation opportunities. An overlay occurs when two attributes combine to forge an entity whose whole is truly greater than the sum of its parts. Here the numerical analogy takes the form of the equation 2 + 2 = 5.

The overlap and overlay concepts can be best understood by envisioning two transparencies on which various parts of a face are drawn. On one of the transparencies we see two eyes, two ears, and the right half of a mouth. On the other, we see a nose, the left half of a mouth, and the same two ears. Viewed separately, each is an incomplete image. However, if we lay one transparency over the other, a face emerges with eyes, ears, a nose, and one full mouth—in other words, a complete image.

Much like the issues faced in a merger, the overlap in this image is the two sets of ears, one set of which can be discarded. In an M&A situation, the areas of the combining firms that represent overlaps are redundant and can be scaled back or eliminated. These typically include duplicative personnel, manufacturing or service delivery capabilities, or other systems and processes. As such, eliminating these overlaps represents the synergies that managers have historically referred to when discussing the financial benefits of a particular M&A transaction.

(As we will discuss in Chapter 16, immediately eliminating duplicative functions is not necessarily the most effective way to proceed. Often, redeploying personnel to other geographic locations or functional areas—or converting manufacturing sites into distribution centers—can be more cost-effective and forward-thinking than simply cutting what is initially perceived as organizational fat.)

The process of identifying REO synergies and devising the tactics to effectively actualize them is illustrated in the following examples:

- A major computer hardware and software manufacturer was exploring the acquisition of a publishing company in order to create a variety of print user-support materials. In the course of marketing due diligence, an opportunity was identified to establish a separate marketing communications function and a subscription-based editorial product line of computer publications designed for distribution to consumers and businesses worldwide. A strategic plan was developed, detailing the product concept and market positioning, staffing requirements (that took into account the disparate, yet complementary, skill bases of the two organizations' employees), operational procedures, and production timetables. Sales, marketing, and communications strategies and materials were developed to distribute and promote the new product line in domestic and international markets. The accelerated implementation of these strategies spurred immediate sales for the merged company.
- An international consulting firm that provides assessment and selection services for hiring senior-level executives sought to broaden its capabilities by performing Internet-based recruiting. Rather than develop its own Web site capability, the firm opted to ac-

quire a firm already specializing in this area. A revenue enhancement opportunity resulted in the form of a brand-new product offering. By taking the acquirer's traditional pen-and-paper method of assessing candidates and linking it with the target company's Web site development expertise, the merged firm was able to create an on-line means of soliciting candidates' qualifications data while concurrently conducting assessment and selection analyses. A whole new stream of revenues was created by melding the combining firms' disparate, yet complementary, capabilities.

- A film manufacturing company acquired a major retailer's photofinishing plants. As part of the acquisition, the manufacturer secured the rights to establish film-processing labs directly within the retailer's existing outlets, which spanned the country. Not only was the manufacturer able to gain access to the retailer's customers to develop their film, the manufacturer was able to cross-sell its other photographic products and supplies to those buyers.

REO synergy exploration begins with a comprehensive evaluation of the acquirer's own products and marketing infrastructure. A target company's marketing capabilities are then measured against that. In addition to a high-level assessment of marketing and sales variables, detailed marketing intelligence must also be gathered. Data must be culled from a wide variety of public and private sources. And to confirm the initial findings and hypotheses, face-to-face interviews with key players in the marketing process (i.e., managerial and creative executives, outside consultants, customers, and channel intermediaries) are necessary.

The marketing due diligence process brings to light challenges and opportunities that in the past went unnoticed. Today, however, these issues typically mark the difference between a deal that is only praised in a near-term mathematical sense and one that is heralded as a long-term business success.

Certainly, the basic numbers must work to satisfy all parties involved. But the calculations cannot simply speak to the short term. Identifying and planning adequately to realize REOs puts the merged entity in a position to immediately begin focusing on the market in pursuit of its long-range strategic growth objectives.

INSIDER'S OUTLOOK

Growth is the goal, and M&A is one part of growth. There's a whole spectrum of growth opportunities. Therefore, you must approach M&A as a different aspect of growth, with a different list of issues and concerns.

—Terence Bentley, Siemens Corporation

REOs AS AN ACQUISITION CRITERION

To ensure that top-line growth remains the watchword of strategic mergers and acquisitions, it is necessary to take a formal approach to discovering REOs. This helps an acquirer focus on the critical success factors that will drive long-term revenue growth and, in the process, is useful in sizing up the revenue enhancement opportunities posed by different acquisition targets. Thus, the REO analysis can become an important determinant of pursuing one organization as an M&A partner over another.

In general, an REO analysis requires you to ask two basic questions:

1. What long-term benefit or contribution can the target company make to the merged company (other than, but not excluding, operational efficiencies and cost-reduction-oriented synergies)?
2. What are the specific contributions that the acquiring company can make to enhance the attributes of the target company and, thus, ultimately benefit the merged company?

Areas to examine include, but are not limited to, management, research and development, manufacturing, and, of course, marketing and sales. Consider again the merged-company perspective. In REO planning, this is a critical consideration. Viewing a target company and attempting to assess its strengths and weaknesses without reviewing these attributes against those of the acquirer will always deliver an incomplete result. Additionally, examining features of compatibility without the focus on creating and sustaining long-term growth will place a merger or acquisition in a position to fail, even if short-term shareholder value is served in the process.

Identifying REO synergies requires an acute business development focus that takes into account financial variables, but which specifically keys on the marketing strengths and weaknesses of the merger partners. *The essence of conducting the REO analysis, however, is focusing on where strategic overlays exist.*

REO ANALYSIS: AREAS OF EXPLORATION

Before attempting to identify REOs, it is necessary to understand the areas in which they typically reside. You must key on the areas where strategic overlays may exist and which, consequently, have the greatest influence on devising revenue growth strategies:

- People
- Products
- Processes
- Markets
- Customers

Let's explore each area in order to determine where strategic overlays exist and to assess which ones can potentially lead to an increased revenue stream for the merged company.

People

There are a number of ways that divergent, yet complementary, skill sets resident in merging companies' people can lead to revenue-generating opportunities.

For example, a target company may have experts in one functional area that can be deployed to enhance an already existing capability within the acquiring company. Take the situation where a major HR consulting firm sought the capability of a small boutique consultancy that conducted surveys of employees' likes and dislikes toward the HMO serving a given client company. The acquirer's goal was to leverage this capability in order to broaden its work for health and welfare clients. This was not a product-driven REO, really, as much as it was a personnel-driven one. That is because the HMO survey product was offered by well-respected consultants who held Ph.D.'s in statistics and applied research. Although the acquiring firm could have conceivably developed its own HMO survey, it did not have the level of research-oriented technical expertise in its current ranks that the acquiring firm had.

Our earlier example of the computer company that acquired a publishing company to create user manuals is another case where the intellectual capital of people in one company was melded with the intellectual capital of people resident in another. The REO that resulted took the form of a new line of publications that linked the subject matter expertise of the acquirer (software and hardware product knowledge) with the technical expertise of the target (publishing, promoting, and circulating subscription-based periodicals).

Frequently, personnel-related REOs occur when one merger partner has the product and the other has the sales force (and usually the distribution channels to go along with selling expertise). Many M&A transactions have been conceived based on the vision of linking a highly marketable yet underperforming product with an organization that had expertise in translating a high-potential offering into significant top-line results.

Yet another personnel-related REO occurs when one merger partner has one or more well-known practitioners who are acknowledged experts in their field. Bringing these executives into the fold can enable the merged company to use them as corporate spokespeople and "door openers" in a variety of marketing, PR, and direct-selling situations. Indeed, these types of people represent an important marketing intangible asset.

INSIDER'S OUTLOOK

[It is important to look for] people who have a "nose for the customer" and know how to make money. You feel it when you're in an organization. You can see when people know how to turn ideas into something the customer will buy. These people constantly talk about the customer, and talk much less about process.

—Susan Schoon, Chase Manhattan Bank

Products

A tremendous number of strategic mergers are product-based, where companies seek to acquire items that will round out their product lines or replace goods that are sinking deeper and deeper into the dreaded decline stage of their product life cycles. But, product-driven REOs arise in other ways as well.

For instance, increased revenues can be generated when an acquirer obtains a product line that is similar to its existing one but represents goods valued in the opposite price range (e.g., a merchandiser of high-end cosmetics acquires a firm that offers similar items at the lower end of the price and quality continuum). Another common product-related REO occurs when the merging companies can effectively bundle their offerings; the classic example is where the maker of handheld electronic games and appliances acquires a battery manufacturer, thus enabling the merged firm to offer both the item and the source of energy that powers it.

The continuing transformation of the American economy from a manufacturing environment to a service environment has spawned another common type of product-driven REO. Many manufacturers today are acquiring companies that bring a complementary service capability to their traditional product offering. Consider, for example, a photocopier maker that acquires a company that provides maintenance and repair services of its machines. Not only does such an acquisition enable the acquirer to meet its warranty obligations, it also provides the ability to offer service more in the consulting vein (e.g., where the acquired firm provides fee-based consulting in such areas as computer output and document management services).

Cross-selling opportunities are another powerful source of product-driven REOs. Recall our earlier example on the film manufacturer that secured the right to establish photofinishing labs in a major retailer's stores. The product REO in that case was linked to the opportunity to market the manufacturer's film and film-processing capabilities—and the chance to gain the ability to cross-sell its ancillary photo supplies and equipment.

Processes

Many different processes within a combined company can be joined to fuel gains in revenue and profitability. For instance, a company with state-of-the-art manufacturing systems and quality-control measures can bring these valuable attributes to the production of an acquired company's goods. In such a case, the acquired firm's products may benefit from higher quality and, perhaps, a lower cost of goods sold. The resultant goods may be more alluring to buyers for their quality and generate higher profit margins as a result of the decrease in manufacturing-related costs.

R&D represents another process that can bolster a merged company's revenue streams, albeit usually in the long term. The combination of capabilities—wherein one company has the R&D expertise and the other has the ability to produce and successfully commercialize new goods and services—is a process-related REO synergy that has fueled many a strategic merger.

A process-focused REO that can lead to more immediate revenues might involve the linkage of a company known for its products with another company known for its outstanding customer service. A major telephone company merger now pending has this potential REO synergy at its core. One merger partner is renowned for its quality products and overall marketing prowess. It has suffered, however, from complaints by buyers about shoddy customer service.

Conversely, its merger partner is well-known for its world-class customer service. Joining these capabilities—strong products and marketing, combined with expertise in forging and solidifying customer relationships—can lead to massive revenue gains. The REO driver in this case is not one of products as much as it is a process: customer service.

Markets

In no area is the concept of strategic overlays more easy to illustrate than in geographical markets. In acquisition candidate evaluation, it is common to graphically depict the locales in which one company operates, then physically place on top of that map another that indicates where a potential merger partner's geographic markets lie.

Blue Cross and Blue Shield of New Jersey's combination with Blue Cross of Delaware is a classic case in which an acquisition target was identified based in large part on its geographic area of operation. This deal gave BCBS of New Jersey access not only to the marketplace in Delaware, but entrée to Pennsylvania as well.

INSIDER'S OUTLOOK

The first step involves looking at yourself and then aligning yourself with your strategic goals. "Here's where we are today and here's where we want to be three to five years from now. What do we need to do to get there?" The expansion of market is first and foremost. So you initially have to determine what market areas you want to expand to, and then determine if you can do that and still maintain and not weaken your current core structure. You must look at the opportunities within those aligning or adjoining markets—in our case our regional markets—and who are the target companies within those markets that represent possible merger, acquisition, or joint venture partners. For example, this was the thinking behind our approach to Blue Cross of Delaware. This deal fit our strategic plan, it fit our three-year goals. It aligns us with a marketplace in Delaware, which in turn aligns us with Pennsylvania and the five-county Philadelphia area, where we have licensure and operate businesses. . . . So this deal begins to complete our regional platform.

—Don Curry, Blue Cross and Blue Shield of New Jersey

Customers

A compelling strategic overlay occurs when the customers of two merging companies combine to produce a buyer base that not only increases in size but also manifests complementary compositional traits.

Customers can be analyzed in terms of any number of variables: geographic location, demographic composition, psychographic makeup, and a multitude of combinations thereof. For example, a complementary overlay occurs when the customer base of one company is primarily comprised of buyers in one geographic locale and is linked via the merger to a customer group populating another locale. Assuming the merged company is able to reach those buyers through its distribution channels, the merged company's buyer base has immediately been broadened. Of course, in the instance where direct marketers are combining, the issue of having to establish physical distribution channels to reach geographically distant buyers does not arise.

Strategic overlays also occur when customers from the combining firms may be buyers of each merger partner's products. Consider again the example of an electronic games producer who links up with a battery manufacturer. Not only can those offerings be cross-sold to the customer base, they can also be sold individually by the respective merger partners to buyers, all of whom have a need for either or both of the combining companies' offerings.

The search for REOs is predicated on identifying strategic overlays. Interestingly, however, the area of customers is one where the notion of overlap is equally important. This is because a merged company that links buyers of similar characteristics creates a situation where the organization has an immediately broader base of buyers to purchase existing and future offerings. Consequently, in the realm of customers, strategic overlays can exist side by side with overlaps, their direct counterpart.

TARGET COMPANY'S "MARKETING MIND-SET"

In Chapter 10, the characteristics of various corporate cultures are discussed in terms of their potential impact in a given merger or acquisition situation. However, in the early stages, when your focus is on growth and REO synergies, assessing the culture of the target company's sales and marketing functions will aid you in determining revenue enhancement possibilities and the likelihood of successfully actualizing them.

It is first necessary to determine the extent to which a marketing orientation pervades the target organization. Ideally, this mind-set should extend to all employees. In reality, it never truly can. But the extent to which a forward-thinking culture emphasizes a customer orientation and a competitor awareness will make a huge difference in the implementation of firmwide marketing programs.

It is also important to be able to gauge this character trait within your own organization. The ultimate compatibility of this trait for both organizations will impact the integration stage of the merger, as well as subsequent growth initiatives.

Once the organization's culture as a whole has been assessed, you should turn your attention toward characterizing the culture of the sales and marketing functions. Similar to the broader culture, you must determine the risk orientation of the target's sales and marketing team. For example, do the main players exude an aggressive or conservative mind-set toward program design and implementation?

Simply identifying this trait can offer great insight into why current initiatives are succeeding or failing. It is also important to assess how senior management views those in sales and marketing positions and how the function, as a whole, is perceived throughout the organization.

Many marketing initiatives fail because they are misdirected, others due to poor planning, and still others because the most effective people are not in the appropriate roles. This latter situation should be explicitly addressed.

Often, only an objective third party can adequately assess this aspect of the target's overall "people factor." Is the director of the marketing function from the proverbial old school? Is the marketing department orientation customer- as well as competitor-focused? Are the goals that have been established for the sales force too far-reaching or are they eminently attainable? Are they linked to the strategic plan? Asking these types of questions will open your eyes to an entirely different perspective than the traditional analysis, which is not focused on revenue growth.

A word of caution: Analyzing the attitudes toward the merger of key sales and marketing managers is also imperative for the purposes of projecting and implementing REO strategies. You will need to quickly assess the sentiments the senior members of the sales and marketing function hold toward the corporate combination.

Having advance insight into whether or not the target's senior business developers will fully and enthusiastically support the merger will aid you in your program planning and execution. Are these people whose skills and commitment you can count on post-merger? If not, this will directly impact your REO planning.

REO ANALYSIS: OTHER CONSIDERATIONS

From an REO planning standpoint, there are areas of analysis that are relatively standard for each merger or acquisition. At the same time, there are several considerations unique to the kind of company under review, as well as to the competitive environment in which it operates.

Specifically, REO planning must take into account the unique corporate attributes that result from the variables of:

- Company size
- Competition

By addressing each of these factors from the standpoint of the unique challenges it poses to devising future revenue streams, you will be able to more readily develop your own REO program.

Company Size

The size of a target company often does not affect the areas of analysis that comprise the overall marketing due diligence process. From a revenue-planning perspective, however, there are key characteristics of small to middle-market and large companies that must be understood prior to exploring specific revenue enhancement opportunities.

Small to middle-market companies. Companies with revenues in the $10 million to $50 million range are often founded by one individual, a family, or a core group of key individuals who typically control most, if not all, of the stock of the company. They often have not been in business for a prolonged period of time, yet have likely experienced sharp growth in which sales have accelerated faster than the industry as a whole. This may have been due to such factors as excessively low overhead, hands-on management, and, more often than not, a specific product, service, or innovation on which they have capitalized.

At a certain point, middle-market companies typically reach a financial impasse resulting from either erratic profits, sudden and unexpected losses, a severe demand for working capital, or increasingly limited delivery capabilities. Companies of this size have small, if existent, internal sales forces that are often supplemented by the efforts of independent manufacturers' agents or sales representatives.

On the surface, smaller companies would seem to be the easiest to analyze. The reality is, they often are not. They have their own set of unique characteristics and raise specific issues and questions that must be addressed before any REO analysis occurs. Small to midsize companies:

- Sometimes take as much time and effort to integrate as bigger ones. (Will the result justify the effort?)
- Have a distinct culture that is driven by a clear vision of its senior managers. (Is the vision malleable?)
- May often have an exciting track record of growth, but past performance does not ensure future success. (Is the acquisition focused on buying the future based on the past?)
- Have been built by a core group of people. (Will they choose to stay and, if so, what role will they play in the merged company?)
- Are typically run by people with an entrepreneurial spirit. (What is the likelihood of them continuing to stay motivated as they become employees of the merged company and lose their autonomy and sense of identity?)
- Usually attribute their success to a specialized product, service, or innovation. (Is the uniqueness of this offering sustainable in relation to current and future markets?)

These critical issues revolve around products, markets, and the individuals within the company whose unique talents have made an impact in those discrete areas. In essence, when you analyze a smaller company, you are analyzing a potentially fractious future. More than one acquirer has scooped up a smaller company with a narrow product line only to see the market dry up or quickly become saturated with competitors, making the acquisition a dismal failure.

People issues, in particular, are critical. When you buy a smaller company you are buying the individuals whose vision created it. Their buy-in, enthusiasm, and commitment is essential postmerger. Most critically, in smaller companies the assets go home each night. If for some reason they choose not to return to work the next day, you have acquired an empty shell.

Large companies. While analysis of smaller companies is fraught with issues of uncertain managerial commitment and the questionable viability of slim product lines, the analysis of larger companies carries its own set of concerns. Companies with revenues of more than $50 million have characteristics that are unique unto themselves. How they differ from smaller companies creates a perspective that should be adopted as your revenue-focused analysis is conducted.

With a large company, there is usually a more substantial past that amounts to more than a good idea spawned in somebody's garage. Large companies have advanced beyond the entrepreneurial stage, creating less reliance on a few core employees (thus, minimizing the risk that what you are purchasing will vanish into thin air upon closing). It can also be assumed that management knows how to devise, produce, and commercialize marketable goods and services. Most importantly, there will be documentation of observable growth trends that will have developed over time.

An advantage of examining the current and future revenue generation potential of larger companies is gained when they are publicly traded. The value of the shares of the company has been determined by the equity markets. Yet it is important to recognize that the stock market rewards past growth by placing a premium on share price.

Companies with successive quarters or years of exceptional growth often trade at highly inflated multiples. For example, a company with a book value of $12, annual earnings of $2 per share, and eight consecutive quarters of high-margin growth can easily trade at $50 per share. This premium may not seem extreme when compared to the company's solid track record and the price-to-earnings ratio of the market in general. But, compared to a private company, a public company's premium takes into account its potential for acquisition as well as any publicity that surrounds it.

However, if margins decline, earnings dip, or major new competitors enter the market, it may take years for the acquirer of the inflated company to recoup the original investment. Case in point: Snapple Beverage.

Quaker Oats, the manufacturer of Gatorade, negotiated to buy Snapple after years of observing it exhibit triple-digit growth, accelerating profit margins, and dominance of a niche market that it had developed. Snapple's publicly traded share price, at the time, factored in its past meteoric rise in revenues, the cache of its commercials, its popularity on the east coast (where the major stock markets are concentrated), and its potential as an acquisition target. The price Quaker Oats paid was approximately three times Snapple's annual revenues at the time of the bid. It seemed like the perfect deal.

But, within weeks of Quaker purchasing this regional purveyor of ready-to-drink iced tea, four formidable beverage rivals attacked the flavored iced tea segment—deflating Snapple's preeminence and ultimately toppling the iced tea king from its throne. Quaker's rear-view assessment of Snapple's spectacular growth guided it into paying an exorbitant premium based on its track record before the acquisition. As discussed earlier, two years after the acquisition—and billions of dollars of losses later—Quaker was forced to sell Snapple for a shockingly low $300 million after initially shelling out $1.7 billion.

Performing basic marketing due diligence and a subsequent REO analysis would have revealed the increasing troubles that Quaker would face if it proceeded with the acquisition. The moral is this: If the purpose of a merger or acquisition is to increase sales, then focusing on every real and potential threat to revenue enhancement must be a primary consideration in all phases of your predeal analysis. Many of these threats exist within the competitive environment.

Competition

There are two basic orientations that marketing planners have traditionally assumed: competitor or customer. During the REO analysis you must break the mold of focusing on just one of these areas. Awareness of both competition *and* customers in the most detailed sense is critical.

If your quest is to satisfy your customers with little concern for how your competitors are satisfying theirs, you will wake up one morning without any customers. By the same token, if your goal is simply to keep up with your competition, you may both march in lockstep away from the needs of your own buyer base.

Successful marketing planning requires balancing the needs of the customer with the dynamic forces of competition. Both must be addressed in detail during the REO analysis. Indeed, the area of competitive intelligence should be an ongoing process within your organization. You must always be aware of competing products and services in the marketplace, and how your offerings stack up in comparison.

During your marketing due diligence, identifying the key competitors—both public and private—is a critical first task. Again, this is a process that does not end. As you and others within your industry jockey for position, competitive research will be a valuable tool in helping you stay focused on an ever-changing, steadily intensifying competitive landscape.

In any candidate search, you will have compiled detailed market research that explores all aspects of competitors and potential targets. Here again the merged-company perspective applies. When sizing up competitors, envision the products that would be offered after your combination with one or more potential targets. Determine the degree to which the combined company's products hold a competitive advantage over other companies' offerings. In those cases where you do hold an advantage, see how that can be leveraged in other revenue-generating ways.

Maintaining a merged-company perspective not only allows you to view your company in relation to the competition, but allows you to anticipate other mergers and acquisitions in your industry that will directly affect you. Remember: If you are the number-three company in a given industry and the number-four and -five competitors join forces, overnight *you* may drop to number-four.

The potential for you to lose substantial market standing over the course of one day without doing anything different is, by itself, a compelling reason to maintain an aggressive competitive intelligence program. Simply tracking the changing market share levels of competitors is not enough. You must continually forecast how corporate combinations by competitors—via mergers, acquisitions, and joint ventures—can radically alter the market milieu and impact your marketing and sales strategies.

A rarely covered area of investigation is the extent that unrelated products compete with either company's products. You must determine whether or not your potential competition will come from traditional competitors or new entrants from other industries and market segments. Thinking along these lines will help you better focus your ongoing marketing efforts or even more sharply hone your corporate vision.

For example, the banking industry has taken great strides over the past decade by paying close attention to other products in other industries. Banks have moved from the traditional view of depositories—where you once kept a savings account or wrote checks—to a competitive view in which they serve comprehensive financial needs, such as college funding and retirement planning. Monitoring what were thought to be unrelated services in other industries has kept the banking segment alive and thriving. Your business is probably not much different.

INSIDER'S OUTLOOK

In mergers and acquisitions, it is not just, "We're going to combine you and us and cut $20 million out of the $200 million budget." That's fine. You're gaining efficiencies organizationally and operationally. But why are you in the marketplace? You're not in the marketplace just to save money, you're there to grow market share.

—Don Curry, Blue Cross and Blue Shield of New Jersey

FILLING THE REO PIPELINE

A REO analysis concentrates on delivering instant payoff, but also a filled pipeline of revenue enhancers. It aids in the process of forecasting and delivering revenue growth immediately on finalization of the deal. But a disciplined approach to prioritization allows for the ongoing achievement of successive REO synergies at appropriate points in the postdeal integration timetable.

Acknowledging the pipeline concept in the premerger planning stages is critical. It allows the acquirer to focus on REOs that will deliver incremental gains to stakeholders over the short term, while never losing sight of the REOs that will produce a steady stream of future sales.

Each time a revenue-enhancing overlay is identified, so is an additional opportunity to achieve top-line growth. With each new revenue-creating idea that is posited, an additional reason for the merger to succeed is brought to light. Some of these REOs can be implemented at once. Others will take time to plan more fully. Regardless, throughout the analysis period the objective is to list REOs as they are identified. Ultimately, a long list of potential REOs that can be pursued immediately on the deal's closing should be developed. It is at this point when priorities must be set.

Setting Priorities

It is important to set priorities when developing plans to actualize REO synergies. Not every opportunity should be acted on immediately. Indeed, not every one can. But, ideally, a loaded and ordered pipeline of executable REOs will allow the merged entity to remain focused on long-term results while delivering incremental successes to stakeholders over the short term.

Consider the case of two regional retailers merging their operations to create a national presence. The process of consolidating their respective customer information records into a powerful database for direct-marketing purposes was a distinct REO synergy. So, too, was the ability of the companies to establish newly revamped retail outlets under the merged company's new banner. Both actions had potential to generate revenues. Yet the database marketing project was able to yield income quickly—in contrast to the time-consuming task of store redesigns and mass media promotion to create name awareness and build store traffic. In most cases, the basic strategy should be to invest in REO synergies that will generate immediate revenues while, concurrently, planning to realize those synergies that will require more time, resources, and capital.

Prioritizing REOs first requires quantifying them. Again, it is imperative to maintain a merged-company perspective throughout this process. It is necessary to assess the synergies and areas of leverage that will be created from the combination of people, products, and processes.

By analyzing each particular variable in the target company and then comparing them against their counterparts in your own organization you will be able to gauge the effectiveness of the current systems and processes in place and determine whether they should be eliminated or improved, and, if so, by how much. These levels of improvement, once quantified and placed in the context of the combined company's capabilities and strategic imperatives, will set the stage for devising revenue enhancement activities and projections as accurately as possible.

Once the initial assessment of REO opportunities is completed, there will be some REOs that can be easily implemented and others that will be more drawn out and difficult to execute. You must determine which are the growth initiatives that can be implemented quickly to allow the revenue tap to begin flowing right away.

Identifying the steps you can take immediately after the deal's closing will help you hit the ground running and fuel short-term shareholder value. But this is where many companies stop. They combine these short-term revenue boosts with an aggressive cost-cutting initiative and, although the bottom line jumps, the long term suffers. The REOs unique to your transaction must be prioritized and stretched out to impact the bottom line both early in the process *and* over the longer term. This can only be done by ensuring that the top line continues to grow.

There will be myriad distractions that will battle effective growth, such as operational snafus, cultural divisiveness, delays in the integration program, and customer and employee defections. Indeed, the guidance to come in ensuing chapters is designed to help you avoid these problem situations. But the revenue engines must not stop after the cost cutting is implemented.

By laying out an extended and ordered list of action steps that focus solely on revenue generation and placing them in a logical, executable order, you will have the best opportunity to maintain and steadily augment shareholder value. For example, on a list of 25 REOs, the revenue generators should be categorized by affordability—placing the easiest and least expensive to perform in the first wave.

Chances are there will be a wide range of REOs that differ widely in terms of their ease and cost of execution. Some will be easy to implement. Others will be more difficult. Some will be inexpensive to launch. Others will cost significant amounts of monetary and human resources. And, still others will be capable of actualization only after executing two or three REOs from the first category has created a platform (and perhaps additional capital) for further development.

As far as time parameters are concerned, it is advisable to focus on the first three months after closing the deal to implement the quick-and-easy REOs. Your next block of initiatives should be spread out over the following year. Depending on your budget and resource constraints, it is vital to have programs in place that will extend three to five years into the future as well. This strategy ensures that the early spurt in shareholder value that occurs after the transaction's close is maintained throughout the integration phase and beyond.

SUMMARY

Today, focusing on top-line revenue growth should be the uppermost consideration in evaluating and planning strategic mergers and acquisitions.

Clearly, there is a distinct place for cost-cutting measures to streamline processes and effect certain operational efficiencies. In fact, in strategic deals, effecting near-term expense reduction synergies is a precursor to the cultivation of a long-term REO process. When this process is actualized, and both cost reductions and revenue enhancements result, true shareholder value can be ensured for years to come. But without keen attention to what you will do for an encore after cuts have been made, the financial benefits of the transaction will be extremely short-lived.

Behind the failure of hundreds of M&A transactions in the past has been management's inability to follow through on merger-related growth initiatives. Understanding the importance of follow-through is aided by envisioning a karate exhibition—one where an individual breaks boards or bricks with a chop or punch. When these people are asked how they are able to accomplish such a feat that, to most of us, seems impossible, they all respond that they do not try to punch the board to break it. They are, instead, focusing on a point several inches or feet beyond the board, with their goal to reach past the point of contact with the board. In the process, the board is broken as the hand sweeps through it on its way to that imaginary point beyond. They insist that if they focused solely on hitting the board, it would not be possible because physics would stop the hand on impact.

The same goes for one's golf swing, tennis stroke, or slap shot. Any activity that involves motion in which there is intended contact requires follow-though of momentum to efficiently actualize the movement and maximize the impact. M&A is no exception. To focus on bottom-line cost-cutting strategies *without* a long-term vision of top-line revenue growth is akin to aiming simply to hit the board *without* the intent of breaking it.

Revenue growth in mergers and acquisitions must not be an afterthought. It must drive the entire acquisition process. Certainly cost cutting is an ingredient of profitability. But, reducing expenses over an extended period of time cannot be sustained indefinitely, and too many companies have downsized themselves out of competitive existence in the quest for increased shareholder value.

However, had those organizations focused on long-term top-line growth in addition to short-term bottom-line improvements, they would have truly gained competitive advantage and increased their chances of enduring financial success.

Part Two
ANALYZING TARGET COMPANIES

4

Evaluating Market Dynamics: Starting Point of Target Company Examinations

As addressed in Part One, there are numerous ways to attain strategic advantage and effect growth through mergers and acquisitions. Any number of avenues can be taken. The key challenge is spotting the multiple drivers resident within a given target company that will take you toward your strategic destination. Once you have determined where you want to be, you must decide how to get there by mapping out a route that is based on a new orientation to evaluating M&A opportunities. That orientation is characterized by a methodology that assesses markets as a precursor to examining the acquisition candidates functioning within them.

M&A growth planning combines traditional market analysis with a broadened perspective that more fully measures a target company's current standing and future potential. Evaluating an organization in this framework is based on appraising the target as an active participant in a given market through a high-level assessment of the organization's overall market position and strategic posture. Why is this significant? Because no company is a stagnant entity. An organization is forever moving in myriad ways, impacted by the dynamics of external forces such as the local and global economies and the market in which it operates.

Of course, a company may or may not be moving in the right direction. In fact, it may not even be moving on its own if it is being pushed or pulled by stronger competitors, as opposed to creating its own market momentum. Thus, the initial phase of marketing due diligence-oriented market analysis involves analyzing market characteristics and dynamics but—more importantly—how the target company has historically functioned within the context of prevailing market forces.

This orientation is pivotal to effectively identifying a candidate's growth-oriented strengths—the basis for pinpointing marketing intangible assets, identifying opportunities for important skills transfer, and envisioning and actualizing revenue enhancement opportunities.

M&A-FOCUSED MARKET ANALYSIS: AREAS OF INVESTIGATION

Mergers and acquisitions done in the bygone days of conglomeratization required members of acquisition teams to study industries with which they were largely unfamiliar. Consequently, target company examinations first entailed understanding the fundamental issues relating to market forces and the target's quantitative standing within its given industry segment.

In strategic acquisitions, M&A candidates typically function in markets related to the acquiring organization. And, in many cases, management already has an understanding of the various market forces and trends inherent in its own, as well as the target's, industry and believes in the viability and market attractiveness of the segment in which the target competes.

Guidance on conducting basic market analysis in premerger situations might appear elementary to those to whom this book is geared. However, as the failure rate of transactions creeps higher each day, an overview of this process will help all those involved to better understand the analytical orientation uniquely designed to plan strategic acquisitions.

The process of market analysis, which involves assessing the major external variables affecting the target company, can act as the platform from which all other investigations stem. Included in this process is the identification of the target's position in the market, an assessment of the competitive environment, and a detailed analysis of industry trends and external forces that continually alter a market's landscape.

Only after studying marketplace dynamics can the target company's strategic and tactical approach to that marketplace be fully assessed. Ultimately, the goal is to gauge the target's "strategic effectiveness" as a precursor to any in-depth study of its products, its organizational composition, and its corporate processes.

The Appendix examines specific methods for collecting the information needed to support this M&A planning process. Conceptually, the information required in such an M&A-focused marketing analysis includes:

- Industry rankings and trends analysis
- Analysis of macroenvironmental forces
- Analysis of competition

Market studies will offer insight into what is currently happening in that segment, who the major players are, and what key market forces are at work. Assessments of the competitive market will help you determine current conditions, as well as provide forecasts on the competitive climate over the next three to five years. Anticipating potential M&A combinations by competitors—and projecting their impact on the overall competitive environment—is central to this phase of the premerger analytical process.

Examinations of each area of the market analysis investigation will collectively provide intelligence on the market in which the target competes.

Industry Rankings

Industry analysis involves studying all key companies operating in the segment, identifying their key similarities and differences, and evaluating the emerging trends with which all industry players contend. Your critical first step is to determine the specific industry, and industry subsegment, in which the target functions. For example, if the target is a high-tech company, you must probe deeper to determine the specific area of the high-tech industry in which it operates (e.g., hardware, software, semiconductors, Internet).

Pinpointing the appropriate industry segment is an essential component of this data accumulation phase. The most common industry grouping system is the Standard Industrial Classification (SIC) Codes, which is the U.S. government's system of defining individual industries and specific trades within them. Categories are broken down into SIC code numbers that identify industries in terms of products manufactured, business processes, or functions performed. SIC codes are the most widely referenced classification of industry groups in the United States, with the information used to identify, define, and segment market categories for a wide range of marketing and strategic planning applications.

Other industry groupings can be found in the databases produced through private-company sources. Yet, these typically employ the broad industry categories that are defined by the SIC system.

For instance, one system classifies each of the approximately seven thousand publicly traded U.S. companies into an industry group based on the business segment from which the majority of its revenues are generated, as reported by the company in its annual report. In this system, industries fall into more than 50 basic categories, which are then subdivided into another hundred or so additional industry subsegments. Other information available includes the number of companies in a given category, the total number of employees, and the average number of employees per organization.

Analyses of target companies based on their industry classification address one or more of the following criteria:

- Size
- Growth
- Profitability
- Stock performance

Size. These rankings include measures of annual revenues, reported total assets (e.g., real property, plants, and equipment), and market share (a measure of the revenues of the company, divided by the total revenues for the industry group as a whole).

Growth. These measures are based on increases (or decreases) in annual revenues, usually in comparison to the prior year's figures; in profits, that is, the increase or decrease in net income for the current year in comparison to the previous year; in earnings per share, again, for the current year compared to the previous year; or gains in total assets, calculated on a comparative basis with those of prior years.

Profitability. These calculations are based on figures depicting net income for the prior year; "profit margins" are determined by dividing net income from the past four quarters by the past four quarters' revenues; "return on equity (ROE)" is measured by dividing common stockholders' equity by net income for the prior year; and "return on assets (ROA)," which is the quotient gained by dividing net income for the prior year by total assets from the immediate past fiscal year.

> **INSIDER'S OUTLOOK**
>
> Part of the art of getting the deal done is not bringing in your [investigative] resources so early that you waste them or so late that you risk losing the deal. You've got to "peel the layers of the onion," to take the next card and keep moving but bring people in at the appropriate time. You can't bring them in so late that they can't do the work. At the same time, you don't want to bring them in so early that you pay a fortune for outside services on a deal that you're ultimately going to kill. There's a real skill in figuring out how and when to bring in the resources you need. And every deal's different.
>
> —Diane Harris, Hypotenuse Enterprises

Stock performance. This is gauged by determining the total percent return to an investor holding the company's stock. Here, stock performance is measured by changes in the stock price over the previous four quarters, plus dividends paid over that time period, divided by the closing stock price of the previous year. Another measure of stock performance is the "price-earnings ratio (P/E)," which is the latest available closing price divided by the earnings per share for the last four quarters.

An important note on industry-specific research is in order here: the vast preponderance of available data pertains to publicly traded companies. Information on private companies operating in the same segment can be remarkably scarce. Yet, the majority of companies in the United States, and many that will be under review as acquisition candidates, are not publicly traded. So, in order to gain a truly accurate picture of the industry segment under investigation, you must include private company analysis in your research.

The preceding measurement criteria will help you identify the size and general characteristics of leading companies in a particular industry segment, which is the starting point for assessing the target company. You should determine industry rankings in several other ways to gain differing and broader perspectives on leading companies' defining attributes and competitive strengths. As these measurements are determined, you will be aware of obvious links to specific companies whose individual performance can then combine with each other to forge a collective industry landscape and determine a segment's overall market attractiveness.

Evaluating Industry Trends

The size of a given market, its annual growth rate, and its historical profit margins are some of the areas typically cited in evaluations of market attractiveness. The other main focus of determining attractiveness relates to evaluating trends specific to the industry segment—forces which affect all companies operating within it. Industry trends fall into several qualitative categories, which transcend simple measures of the industry's growth or decline. The main categories include:

- Consolidation
- Convergence
- Geographic expansion

Consolidation. Industry segments that are consolidating reflect diminished competition as a result of there being fewer companies operating in that segment. Consolidation is typically driven by a change in regulatory or market forces and is manifested by many companies deciding to discontinue operations, merge, or acquire, hence lessening the number of players.

Consider, for instance, the weapons industry in the United States. The end of the Cold War prompted a sharp drop in defense spending by the federal government. Military contractors that depended on U.S. government work experienced dramatic revenue declines. Many were forced to redirect their business or in some cases shut down. It was not surprising, therefore, when one of the largest mergers in American history—the Boeing Company's $16.3 billion purchase of the McDonnell Douglas Corporation late in 1996—was traced to the Pentagon's decision to eliminate McDonnell Douglas from a multibillion-dollar competition to build the nation's next generation of jet fighters.

Prior to the announcement of the acquisition, there were only a handful of players left in the rapidly consolidating weapons industry. The government's decision to exclude McDonnell Douglas from the bidding severely weakened the company's competitive position and dimmed its future prospects. McDonnell Douglas fully realized this and was immediately amenable to Boeing's acquisitive overtures. As a result, the acquisition created a greater concentration of power held by an even smaller number of companies. If this political trend continues, it is expected that there will be even further consolidation in the weapons industry.

Convergence. Convergence occurs when companies in different industry segments begin to offer similar services and, therefore, become competitors. A prime example is the telecommunications industry, once populated solely by telephone companies offering local and long-distance service. Dramatic advances in technology over the past decade introduced hundreds of new players into the fray, such as those involving cellular phones and other forms of wireless communications.

In theory, this could have been considered an expansion of that industry. However, industry convergence began to occur as the concept of telecommunications expanded beyond the traditional local and long-distance markets. Telephone and other telecommunications providers saw new potential in the cable TV industry; cable TV operators saw new potential in alliances with media and entertainment companies; and media and entertainment companies, along with hundreds of entrepreneurial start-up companies, saw potential in the interactive communicative power of the Internet. In fact, this last group helped spark the creation of an entire new industry subsegment of Web site developers and content providers.

Companies that had never competed with each other before were now direct rivals. Industry lines blurred. Convergence in the telecommunications industry is proceeding so rapidly that even the announcement early in 1996 of US West's $11.5 billion acquisition of Continental Cablevision drew yawns of disinterest from industry observers, who viewed yet another telephone company/cable company partnership as a veritable detour for telecommunications companies speeding along the information superhighway.

Geographic expansion. Geographic expansion today often refers to the globalization of industry segments. The securities industry, for example, has truly become global with the emergence of 24-hour trading in stock markets in Sydney, Tokyo, Paris, London, and New York. Even the automotive industry—with moves by both Japanese and American companies to establish off-shore manufacturing facilities to capitalize on lower labor costs—may now be considered a global industry.

Industries may also tend to be concentrated in specific geographic regions of a given country yet, over time, begin to function in other locales. An example is retirement-community real estate developments and the attendant offerings such as home health care and nursing now being offered in the same service context. Once relegated to Florida and other Sun Belt locations, such developments are now being created in areas across the United States. As a larger and more geographically dispersed element of the American population reaches retirement age, many are choosing *not* to move south. Living longer, more active lives, many older Americans prefer to remain near their children and grandchildren rather than move to far away, warmer climes.

As several of these examples indicate, industry trends are often driven by changes to the "macroenvironment," which is defined as the collective of external forces that either directly or indirectly affect the near-term operations and long-term profitability of organizations. To best understand them, it is helpful to examine these forces in the context of premerger market analysis.

INSIDER'S OUTLOOK

[From an acquisition strategy standpoint] the way to understand where you should invest is driven by the products and markets you want to get into—and stay in—and then understanding in as much detail as possible what's happening in those markets.

—Terence Bentley, Siemens Corporation

Analysis of Macroenvironmental Forces

Strategic marketing planners should continually study macroenvironmental forces, which are external to the company and typically beyond the control of company management. In contrast to the "microenvironment" (comprising controllable factors such as an organization's relationships with its customers, suppliers, and channel intermediaries, and the interaction of units within the company itself), macroenvironmental forces may be either intensified, minimized, or neutralized, depending on the organizational dynamics resulting from the M&A transaction.

Microenvironmental forces tie directly to a company's internal infrastructure—its people, products, and processes—and are discussed in greater detail throughout the book. And, both macro- and microenvironmental forces must be understood and factored into ongoing marketing planning. However, macroenvironmental forces are of particular consequence in the market analysis phase of M&A planning due to their link to the strategic drivers of the transaction.

Macroenvironmental forces fall into the following five categories:

1. Demographics
2. Economics
3. Technology
4. Legal-regulatory issues
5. Sociocultural traits

The competitive environment is often cited in the context of a company's macroenvironment. Competitive analysis, however, merits broader treatment than other macroenvironmental variables. Consequently, competitive analysis is addressed in greater detail throughout Part Two. But first, it is recommended that you examine each of these five macroenvironmental areas vis-à-vis a marketing due diligence-focused viewpoint.

Demographics. This aspect of traditional macroenvironmental assessments involves studying the target company's customer base from the standpoint of its demographic composition such as age, gender, and nationality. Premerger market analysis, on the other hand, views the current demographic makeup of customers relative to the products and services purchased by those buyers.

INSIDER'S OUTLOOK

You have to drill down analytically in the given market you're assessing to find out what the pure grassroots demographics of the market really are. You look at the different market segments in terms of those demographics. For example, in New Jersey there are one million Medicare eligibles, there are 685,000 Medicaid eligibles, there's an insured population of about four and a half million people. There are all different segments of our state. Then you have to match up how the competition has aligned to those demographics. If we look at the Medicare population in a state and, say, there are 100,000 Medicare eligibles and we view that as a great market opportunity—but a competitor is in there with 80% of the market—that's certainly less of a market opportunity for us. So you have to align the demographics with your products and services, and then align those against the competition and existing market share that's been taken out of that market. Then that nets you out to what your market opportunity is. What will it cost for us to compete for that market opportunity in that given area? Number one, can we afford to do that? Number two, what is our profit potential? Number three, where will we be within a three- to five-year period as far as being a market share leader? Are we looking to be the number-one market share player in that region? Well, if we are and we have to displace an incumbent, then it's going to cost us a heck of a lot more than if we captured critical mass on a profitable basis and maintained a number-three position in the market.

—Don Curry, Blue Cross and Blue Shield of New Jersey

Special attention is paid toward identifying demographic changes to the customer base that will impact postmerger growth initiatives. Consider, for example, a food manufacturer targeting a regional food seller. The strategic intent of the acquisition is to penetrate the geographic market and gain access to the target's well-entrenched distribution network. Yet, the target's product line consists of a traditional array of food products typically purchased by older, middle-America-type consumers, in a geographic locale that is seeing a steady influx of younger and more ethnically diverse people.

The target's products may suffer a slump in sales if the product line is not modified to respond to this demographic shift in the population. Indeed, the offerings of the acquirer may, in fact, help effect this change.

Most references to demographic analysis specifically relate to the area of consumer marketing. Nonetheless, there are demographic shifts that also occur in the business-to-business marketplace. For example, an accounting firm specializing in serving the insurance industry might be considering the acquisition of another audit firm based in the Hartford, Connecticut, area—historically the Mecca of the American insurance industry. But, the exodus of insurance concerns from that locale, prompted by industry consolidation among other factors, points up a demographic shift of consequence to business-to-business marketers. As such, it would lessen the allure of this acquisition strategy.

Economics. Economics relate to the business conditions that impact the demand for and pricing of a company's products and services. Your market analysis must project, as closely as possible, the postmerger economic climate in which the target company's goods will be sold. For instance, some goods that are considered luxury items generally do not sell well in periods of economic decline. Of course, gloomy economic projections that will directly affect the success of a target's product offering may influence the timing of the transaction and whether to pursue it at all.

Beyond product considerations, however, economics also should address another key variable: the geographic areas in which the target operates. For example, let's assume you are considering acquiring a firm that has a strong regional presence in an area where you do not. The macroenvironmental economic assessment must ascertain how an upturn—or a downturn—in the economic prospects of that area will affect postmerger strategies and the new company's overall profitability.

Keep in mind, however, that economic considerations do not relate to whether the broad economy is currently in a recession. Nor do they relate to whether it is a good time to make an acquisition based on the general availability or cost of capital. These considerations are valid up front when you are first determining whether to engage in an external growth initiative such as an M&A transaction. But once the process of evaluating acquisition candidates has commenced, they are not really germane.

Technology. As discussed in Chapter 2, attaining new technology is one of the primary drivers of strategic mergers and acquisitions. Clearly, technology now pervades virtually all aspects of product development, manufacturing, and product and service delivery. It is from this perspective that you must view technology issues in macroenvironmental assessments. First, you must ask how changes in technology will affect production of the target company's products. Then you must address several other issues such as the impact technology changes may have on pricing strategies or how this will affect the company's distribution system.

Consider, for example, the Internet. Ten years ago, technology-related analyses would have included a study of the Internet's emergence as a ubiquitous worldwide communications medium. Without question, the advent of Internet-based communications is one of the most significant technological developments in recent history. Going forward, virtually every business will need to explore Internet applications for product delivery and promotion. The most difficult task of your macroenvironmental investigation is to spot the evolution of the next technological revolution—the applications that will impact the operations, products, and overall marketing performance of the target company and its competitors.

It is necessary to address the extent to which a target is adequately employing technology from a business processes standpoint. Yet, it is important to first view these technology trends from a broader perspective to determine how they may alter the target's current products and operations and its future direction.

Legal-regulatory issues. The review of legal and regulatory forces in the macroenvironment requires identifying new and proposed laws that will affect the merged company's operations. Such reviews key on legislative initiatives that will influence issues like product safety, price controls, advertising, and other variables that affect growth planning strategies. Major regulatory developments should be studied at the federal level, but also at the state and local levels in which the merged organization will operate.

Moreover, international issues must be studied if the merged company will operate globally or in specific foreign locales. For example, there are countries to which the U.S. government prohibits the export of American goods, directives resulting from trade sanctions and other punitive measures taken against foreign countries by the federal government.

The macroenvironmental analysis of legal issues should not be confused with the discovery of current or potential lawsuits being leveled against a target company. This falls into the domain of the attorneys conducting legal due diligence. Still, although it is not the responsibility of the professionals charged with M&A planning to spot legal complications, it is incumbent on them to understand the impact that pending or potential lawsuits may have on the provisions and timing of postmerger marketing activities. Indeed, key growth initiatives may have to be postponed, modified, or completely scrapped as a result of restraints engendered by legal actions against the target company.

INSIDER'S OUTLOOK

In M&A planning, it's imperative to be sensitive to changes in the regulatory environment. Where appropriate, it's necessary to determine what are the conditions in the regulatory environment in the markets of one of the merger partners versus that of another. You cannot assume that the regulatory environment in which they have become accustomed to working is going to be the same as the one they will be moving into after the merger.

—Rich Rudden, R. J. Rudden Associates

Sociocultural traits. Macroenvironmental factors in the sociocultural realm relate to marketplace trends that influence people's personal and business lifestyles, and, consequently, their wants and needs from a product and service standpoint. Personal lifestyle shifts are consumer-oriented issues regarding people's changing attitudes toward such things as food, clothing, and recreation. Business lifestyle variables tie to people's individual approaches to business, an integral component of almost everyone's day-to-day existence. Examples of changes in people's business lifestyles are the move toward such workplace innovations as flextime, telecommuting, and the sanctioning of casual business attire.

Sociocultural changes are significant in premerger planning in two key respects:

1. Changing social attitudes may directly impact market attitudes toward demand for a target company's products and services.
2. Socially related attitudes impact how people—including, obviously, the target company's employees—function on a day-to-day basis.

Broad sociocultural traits that may characterize an employee base must be pinpointed as part of the target company analysis. While you are undergoing the formal marketing due diligence and integration planning process, these sociocultural traits must often be viewed in the same vein as company-cultural traits.

Analysis of Competition

Analyzing the competitive environment is the most critical element of market analysis. It is necessary to study this environment and, hence, determine the involved companies' relative market standing quantitatively and qualitatively.

Quantitatively, the market should be studied in terms of an organization's rank based on the industry indexes discussed earlier. Qualitatively, the market should be gauged by studying the following aspects of that company and its competitors:

- Core traits
- Market share enhancement strategies
- Distribution power
- Research and development programs
- Marketing investment decisions

By briefly examining each of these qualitative areas of evaluation, you will have a stronger foundation when they are explored more fully in Chapters 5, 6, 7, and 8, which focus on target company analysis.

Core traits. Companies' market position may be measured in terms of the specific core traits that empower different market players. For example, competitors should be viewed from the standpoints of how well known and regarded they are, how highly they are viewed for product quality and service, and to what extent they possess such organizational strengths as capable senior managers, dedicated workers, and visionary leaders.

Market share enhancement strategies. Market share levels gauge companies' market standing from a statistical standpoint, but they also reveal particular operating strategies. The focus of companies whose market share is increasing is to steal that share away from competitors. How are they doing so? And to what extent?

Gaining market share is a costly proposition with high risks, since increases in share typically come at the expense of short-term profits. Competitors actively building market share reveal their orientation to long-term growth and a willingness to potentially incur near-term losses. Consequently, how and where companies are investing funds to augment market share is one indicator of their strategic and competitive orientation. Taken together, companies' market share strategies help characterize the competitive environment.

Distribution power. How effectively different companies are getting their products to market is a significant determinant of the competitive landscape. A high-level distribution analysis must be conducted to identify where competitors market their products geographically (a study of the physical location of markets served). Next, studying companies' network of channel intermediaries lends insight into their respective market standing in different geographic locales.

Most important is determining the extent to which given companies are dominating distribution channels. Companies in this enviable position hold tremendous power over competitors, since firms that cannot find wholesalers or retailers to carry their products are at an extreme competitive disadvantage. Firms that dominate channels also create a strong barrier to entry for market newcomers.

Research and development programs. The level of companies' spending on research and development is a measure of an industry's competitiveness. Highly dynamic industries such as biotechnology manifest high levels of R&D spending. This aspect of competitive analysis should key on trends—upward or downward—illustrating patterns of R&D investments by the companies functioning in the market under review.

Spending by American companies for R&D is again on the rise after a decline in the early 1990s. As a benchmark, industry sectors that are increasing R&D investments at a rate of 3% or more annually are exceeding the national average. Research and development programs are central to a company's product-development infrastructure. Consequently, R&D is examined in greater detail in Chapter 5.

Marketing investment decisions. Similar to investments made in R&D, companies' allocation of monetary resources for marketing programs is an indicator of market competitiveness. Information must be collected on how much organizations are spending on promotional initiatives—advertising, sales promotion, public relations, direct selling, and so on. This information is partially provided on the "selling, general and administrative (SG&A)" line item of companies' income statements.

However, additional information must be culled from advertising tracking services, trade periodicals, and other sources of competitive intelligence. The results of this research will help you to gain insights on the size and monetary allocation of industry-average sales and marketing budgets—data-gathering techniques addressed in the Appendix.

INSIDER'S OUTLOOK

It is important to constantly look at how one company compares to the others within a given industry. This lets you be on top of where the strengths are and where the weaknesses are either from an operating standpoint, from a marketing standpoint, or from a financing standpoint. This ongoing comparative analysis allows us to quickly determine how to bolster a weakness or optimize a particular strength that a company looking to acquire or be acquired may have.

—Dudley Mendenhall, Bank of America

EVALUATING THE TARGET'S "STRATEGIC EFFECTIVENESS"

By now you should have a clear understanding of the key factors that define and affect a target company's market position and standing. These include the organization's actual ranking in the market, the quantitative variables relating to the market's size and growth rate, and the marketplace and industry-specific forces impacting the organization now and in the near-term future.

Collecting this information lays the groundwork for your initial growth planning: determining whether a particular target company is effectively contending with the marketplace threats and opportunities confronting it. The goal is to assess the company's "strategic effectiveness." This critical aspect of premerger planning involves assessing the target company's strategic orientation, its marketing operations, and the execution of tactical initiatives. Our experience has shown that a company's strategic effectiveness depends on its capabilities in the following seven areas:

1. Marketing planning orientation
2. Marketing organization
3. Customer orientation
4. Marketing information systems
5. Resource allocations
6. Tactical flexibility
7. Responsiveness to macroenvironmental changes

A company may be strong in some areas of strategic effectiveness and weak in others. Consequently, assessing each category helps to identify strengths that can be bolstered after the acquisition, as well as areas of weakness that must be eliminated. Strengths are enhanced and weaknesses mitigated through an effective transfer of skills and resources between the merging organizations—the key focus of the integration guidance provided in Part Three. By addressing each of the aforementioned areas, you can develop a means of gauging the target's strategic orientation and capabilities.

Marketing Planning Orientation

A company's marketing planning orientation may range from the development of formal, comprehensive documents to simple write-ups detailing a series of promotional activities. The difference in sophistication in companies' marketing plans may be markedly pronounced in companies of similar size or industry standing.

The size of a marketing plan, of course, is hardly the most significant consideration. The *quality* of the marketing strategies detailed in the plan is. Strategies may or may not be clearly articulated. They may or may not be based on detailed and timely marketing information. They may or may not be responsive to the specific marketplace threats and opportunities confronting the organization.

Another aspect of the target's marketing planning relates to whether the company has contingency plans in place. Ideally, companies should have detailed "marketing controls" that allow them to periodically assess the ongoing implementation of marketing activities. What's more, these controls should detail *how* the company will alter its activities when market forces or competitors' moves require enacting tactical shifts.

Marketing Organization

Is marketing a strategic function driven by senior management in the companies you are assessing? Surprisingly, this is not the situation in many otherwise well-run companies. In such cases, sales and marketing are not integrated at the top of the organization. As a result, the activities of these groups are not aligned with the company's broader organizational initiatives.

The quintessential marketing organization, with the support and input of top management, is characterized by a strong level of cooperation between sales and marketing and other divisions within the company—namely (in a product manufacturing company) R&D, production, purchasing, distribution, and finance, or (in a service provider) functional disciplines, client relations, and account management. A sound marketing organization also has a comprehensive new-product development process that is adequately financed, well-structured and professionally staffed. This is addressed in greater detail in Chapter 5.

Customer Orientation

Strategic effectiveness is also characterized by management's commitment to meeting customer needs. Indeed, a customer orientation should be embraced by employees at all levels of the company. Moreover, this perspective should pervade all business decisions made by the organization. Management must continually channel its energies and resources to meet the current and changing needs of its customer segments.

Different needs by different buyers require different offerings. A true customer-oriented company continually explores its customers' needs and, where appropriate, develops new products or modifies existing ones to meet buyers' changing requirements. Keep in mind: Customers are the most important element of a company's "publics," but there are other stakeholders that cannot be extricated from the marketing equation. Suppliers, distributors, and other relevant publics must be viewed in light of their roles in developing and delivering new offerings to the company's end users. Therefore, assessing a company's customer orientation demands that you evaluate its ongoing dealings with these other relevant groups.

Marketing Information Systems

As explained in Chapter 1, an ample collection of marketing data—collected and disseminated to key decision makers on a regular basis—represents an important marketing intangible asset. A company that is not accumulating market information puts itself at a competitive disadvantage. Markets change too quickly today not to have systems in place that indicate important shifts in the competitive landscape.

Your investigation may reveal that the target company does, in fact, have binders full of market research. But how current is it? How professionally was the research conducted? By a respected research organization? Or by professionals untrained in statistically reliable data analysis? Moreover, how comprehensive is the market research? Most important, how accessible is this research repository? Other than simply being compiled, has it actively been used or leveraged?

Ideally, management should have information relative to its customers and competitors. Additionally, the company should generate information that gauges the sales and profitability of different products, market segments, and geographic territories. Information must also be collected to determine the cost-effectiveness of marketing programs and other major business development expenditures.

Resource Allocations

Is management effectively deploying its marketing and sales resources? In other words, is management devoting adequate levels of financing to the overall marketing effort as well as to major individual projects? Beyond budgetary decisions, resource allocation proficiency also ties to management's ability to respond promptly and effectively to market developments.

Today, windows of opportunity open quickly and close even more quickly. You must ascertain whether company management has demonstrated an ability to act on sudden market changes and intelligently redirect financial and human resources accordingly. Acting quickly is one thing; acting correctly is another. You must assess both aspects by studying the target's past responses to actual marketplace situations.

Tactical Flexibility

A company's ability to develop impactive strategies to meet its marketplace opportunities is an important gauge of its strategic effectiveness. Of perhaps even greater significance is the organization's agility in altering its actions in response to sudden market changes.

Competitiveness is enhanced when management is skilled at determining when given initiatives should be delayed, adjusted, or discontinued in response to dramatic market shifts. A balance, however, must be struck between staying the course in implementing well-planned marketing strategies and quickly switching direction when market forces or competitors' initiatives require doing so.

INSIDER'S OUTLOOK

In devising our acquisition plan, the goal was to take advantage of emerging opportunities in the public sector market. For example, it was clear that the government was going to force Medicaid populations into managed care. They were going to move Medicare eligibles into managed care. We needed to have that infrastructure in place in New Jersey. We basically built three different medical structures in the state to not only comply with government regulations [relative to the Health Care Financing Administration (HCFA)], but also to build out documentation to support the necessary government filings and then get approval and operate those filings.

—Don Curry, Blue Cross and Blue Shield of New Jersey

Responsiveness to Macroenvironmental Changes

Management's abilities to make strategic and tactical shifts in response to emerging changes in the macroenvironment are just as important as changes that may be necessitated by sudden marketplace alterations. Generally, the former tend not to require as quick a response. Nonetheless, a company must continually monitor major social, governmental, regulatory, and technological trends that may ultimately have to be acted on.

The target's marketing information systems should be gathering such long-term trend data. As important as collecting the data is, the issue of greater significance is when and how management acts on that information. It is important that management sees the key trends that are evolving. It is even more critical to know what actions to take to capitalize on the opportunities those trends offer or to mitigate the threats they pose.

Management may have a tendency to view long-term trends as being insignificant in terms of planning near-term tactics. The quickening pace of change, however, suggests that emerging issues may materialize sooner than anticipated. Again, assessing management's foresight requires looking at their responses to previous trend changes in hindsight.

Target companies that possess a strong level of strategic effectiveness offer intangible assets that increase the value of the company and represent strategic synergies that may translate directly into revenue enhancement opportunities. Keep in mind, however, that successes pointing up strong levels of strategic effectiveness may have been achieved through sheer good fortune (the company being in the proverbial right place at the right time) or benefiting from a universally strong economy or stock market.

Conversely, it is important to recognize that there can be many different reasons for perceived shortcomings in a target's strategic capabilities. For instance, marketing plans may have been sound, but the implementation of those plans was flawed. Or, marketing strategies were well-founded and the tactics well-executed, but inadequate monetary resources were allocated, thus rendering successful execution impossible. Additionally, you must remember that there are different gradations of failure. Shortcomings may be identified through programs that fell short of expectations, but not that far short. In such situations, radical changes in procedures or resource allocations may not be warranted as much as some careful fine-tuning of the target company's approach.

Strategic effectiveness must also be projected from the merged-company vantage point in areas that are both process- and personnel-related. Marketing planning, information systems, and some aspects of operational efficiency are processes that should be measured directly against your corresponding capabilities. The target's marketing organization, its customer orientation, and its responsiveness to market changes are people-driven attributes that should also be compared to your own.

The goal of any acquisition should be to enhance the merged company's overall productivity and profitability. Any transaction that does not have the potential to do so is, by nature, strategically flawed. Of course, strategic effectiveness and other opportunities to gain competitive advantage begin as concepts. A comprehensive approach to integration is necessary to translate those concepts into actual growth opportunities; this is the focus of Part Three.

No one would think of conducting M&A planning without performing basic market analysis. But what about studying things such as strategic effectiveness? In the thousands of acquisitions done each year, few address this aspect of a target company's infrastructure. There are two main reasons why:

1. Time does not always permit conducting the examination; when the pressure is on to consummate the transaction, management might opt to forego this phase of the target company analysis.
2. Managers might be frustrated in their attempts to gain access to the people and company information that must be evaluated in order to gauge strategic effectiveness during the negotiation stages.

Still, strategic effectiveness is an important yardstick of a target company's potential contribution to the merged company's operations. Evaluative data must be collected to the fullest extent possible. Gathering even a little information is better than gathering none.

There are many instances in which a firm's strategic effectiveness is of no interest to acquirers. Many companies buy firms with the express intent of immediately folding them into their existing operations—wherein the target's operations cease to exist on completion of the deal. In such situations the strategic effectiveness level of the acquired company is virtually inconsequential.

On the other hand, many strategic acquisitions are driven by the goal of having the acquired company function as a self-sustaining element of the corporate whole. In such cases, the acquiring firm needs to know the target is strong in terms of its strategic effectiveness. Moreover, even if the target will operate independently, the acquirer needs to know that there are strategic and tactical marketing skills inherent in the target that can ultimately be imported, as appropriate, into the parent company's infrastructure. In all cases, assessing strategic effectiveness is an important indicator of a target company's ability to help you attain the growth opportunities you seek.

"MERGED-COMPANY PERSPECTIVE"

M&A growth planning focuses all market analysis on the target company's interaction with its markets. This review requires addressing a range of criteria where the company is evaluated in terms of its mission and objectives, its operating strategies, and its tactical initiatives. But the growth planning approach to market analysis also requires a different evaluative perspective. This viewpoint primarily focuses on analyzing the target company in relation to its market; but, most importantly, *the target should be viewed not as a corporate entity unto itself, but rather as an element of the merged company.*

The growth planning focus, therefore, is comparative. A target company's strengths should be assessed with an eye toward determining how you can transfer those strengths to the merged entity. At the same time, strategic weaknesses that are unearthed must be evaluated from the standpoint of your ability to eventually eliminate them.

The merged-company perspective is both fundamentally practical and psychologically beneficial. It is valuable to immediately begin viewing a target as a potential component of a newly forged, stronger corporate entity and to start thinking about the specific ways you would translate theoretical synergies into actual gains. The more forethought given to conceptual synergies, the faster they can ultimately be actualized if and when a transaction is finalized.

It is psychologically advantageous to immediately begin thinking about the steps necessary to effect postmerger integration. This task is easier when an integration-focused view characterizes your initial analytical observations. Indeed, all aspects of growth planning are governed by the tenet that *premerger decisions must always be made with their postmerger ramifications in mind.*

The process of ranking a target by one or more quantitative criteria, assessing the macroenvironmental forces affecting the organization, and analyzing its competition should be conducted by comparing the characteristics of the target company with those of your own. Consequently, it is critical to look at each element of market analysis from the merged-company perspective:

- Industry rankings and trends
- Macroenvironmental forces
- Analysis of competition

Industry Rankings and Trends

If the target is in the same industry as you, simple arithmetic determines what the combined market share of the merged organization will be. The same is true for calculations of company size (e.g., revenues or total assets) and growth rate (e.g., net income, total assets). Somewhat more detailed arithmetic calculations must be done to project combined profitability—specifically for measures of profit margins, ROE, and ROA.

Future stock performance, as a measure of profitability, is difficult to calculate since there are myriad financial and market variables that influence changes in stock price, including the equity market's response to the announcement of cost-cutting initiatives.

From the standpoint of industry trends, suffice it to say the merged company would be contending with the same market forces that the combining firms have dealt with as separate organizations, although the merged company might serve to further industry consolidation if that, in fact, is occurring.

Macroenvironmental Forces

In this arena, the merged firm would also be subject to the same market forces. At the same time, threats might be minimized and opportunities possibly bolstered as a result of the combined firm's enhanced capabilities. For example, the external environment in which the merged company will operate can reveal immediate product opportunities. You may discover that changing demographic patterns may enhance the marketability of a new product line planned by the target company.

In terms of economic conditions, products offered by the target firm may be better suited (in comparison, perhaps, to some of your own) to prevailing economic conditions—for instance, if the target offers high-end luxury items at a time when economists are predicting a near-term surge in consumer spending.

In terms of technology, the target may offer cutting-edge products that capitalize on emerging market demand. For example, the target may be developing low-cost satellite dishes at a time when many TV viewers are moving away from cable television to quickly attain the vaunted 500-channel universe. From a regulatory standpoint, consider the case where a subsidiary of the target company has experience selling goods in a foreign market that will soon be opened up to international competition. This may be an area that represents a major new market for your products and services.

In terms of sociocultural trends, benefits might accrue if the target is viewed as an environmentally friendly company at a time when consumers favor dealing with organizations committed to ecology and the protection of natural resources.

INSIDER'S OUTLOOK

It's important to deal with the basics. I ask, "What's the world like now and where is it going, and does this acquisition fit strategically with where the market is headed?" It's one thing to know that an acquisition makes sense today. But is it going to make sense tomorrow because of something that will very likely happen in the market? You have to know if you're buying systems or products that are obsolete or which will soon become obsolete based on fundamental changes that will occur in the market. Ideally, you're acquiring something of value. But is that value sustainable over the long term?

—Carolyn Chin, IBM

Analysis of Competition

In Chapter 2, where the importance of recognizing strategic drivers was stressed, the goal of minimizing competition—without incurring the wrath of antitrust regulators—was highlighted. By acquiring a competitor, you eliminate one company from the playing field. The goal of acquiring a competitor is to make your own company more formidable in any number of respects. Greater strength may be achieved through enhanced production efficiencies, distribution channels, and overall marketing muscle.

Remember, though, that one acquisition typically begets another. Your acquisition may well prompt M&A moves by other competitors that further alter the market terrain. This fact of life in today's business world has major ramifications when projecting near-term market conditions in the wake of the transaction.

FORECASTING THE COMPETITIVE ENVIRONMENT: THE M&A PERSPECTIVE

Forecasting shifts in a market's competitive landscape is central to the work of strategic planners and senior marketing managers. Developing such projections is somewhat different in the M&A context. Specifically, marketing due diligence and growth planning focus on potential merger and acquisition activity in a given market or industry segment, insofar as it will affect the competitive environment going forward. The orientation is based on identifying possible corporate combinations that may occur between industry players in the future, as is indicated by M&A activity by key industry players in the past.

Companies considering a merger or acquisition necessarily envision what the competitive environment will look like in the wake of the deal. Yet, it is critical that management also envision what the competitive landscape will be if the company does *not* complete the transaction. In other words, management must determine what possible merger moves other acquirers may make if you, in fact, do not act first on a given transaction. A case in point is the American toy industry.

Earlier, we cited the 1996 acquisition by Mattel, the market leader, of Tyco, the number-three player. The transaction resulted in a company whose market share level significantly exceeded that of the industry's second-place company, Hasbro.

But, Mattel's strategic intent transcended simply increasing its market share. Product line considerations were among the main drivers of the deal—namely, that by acquiring Tyco, makers of the popular Matchbox cars, Mattel would gain complete market dominance of the toy car market by offering both Matchbox and Mattel's popular Hot Wheels. Another of Mattel's goals was to exercise greater clout over retailers by offering an increasingly expansive array of products that would enable the company to more strongly influence retailers' choice of the items they will stock.

At the time, everybody watching the toy market knew Mattel was about to strike a major deal, one that would radically alter the competitive environment, because earlier in the year, Mattel had sought unsuccessfully to merge with Hasbro. That transaction was never consummated, as Hasbro backed out in concern that valuable resources would be wasted if antitrust objections ultimately killed the merger (which, by all accounts, was a distinct possibility). Nonetheless, Mattel had revealed its acquisitive intent. Industry analysts knew it was only a matter of time before Mattel sought another combination. The list of potential merger partners was obvious; it would be one of the other top-five industry competitors. Additionally, Mattel had revealed its acquisitive nature years earlier with its purchase of Fisher-Price. Years before the transaction, Mattel had been allowed to review Fisher-Price's books during an acquisition courtship, but had determined that the timing was not right. Instead, Mattel signed a "stand-still" agreement that prevented it from increasing its share in the company for an extended period. During this time, Fisher-Price strengthened its market position and recorded eight solid quarters of impressive growth. Within weeks of the expiration of the stand-still agreement, Mattel swooped in, as much to garner the additional market share as to prevent any other company from acquiring this jewel.

The guidance to management is this: Any analysis of future market conditions must forecast changes in the competitive market as a result of potential M&A activity. A central task of premerger planning, therefore, is to collect as much market intelligence as possible on M&A transactions—both actual deals and those speculated on in the press and in other business circles.

There are several sources of information that identify M&A activity in different market segments. For example, *Mergers & Acquisitions* magazine each year publishes an annual roundup and analysis of the prior year's deals. The data are broken out several different ways, such as by the size of the year's major transactions, total deal volume by industry, domestic versus foreign transactions, and so forth. Companies analyzing mergers in a given industry, for example, can easily identify the most acquisitive companies in that sector, as well as the average size of the deals being done.

The publication also addresses the important trends driving M&A activity. Consider, for example, the retail business- and office-supplies segment. Recent data show a flurry of M&A activity by national companies acquiring small, regional stationers and business supplies providers. In essence, national chains are being formed to capitalize on the proliferation of home-based businesses and one- and two-person companies—the so-called SOHO (single office, home office) market. Information on this segment shows which companies are making acquisitions, in what dollar volume, and in what geographic locations. Trends and patterns are readily apparent.

Clearly, for a segment like business supplies—with extensive M&A activity continuing unabated—projecting market conditions over the next three to five years would be relatively straightforward. As stated earlier, the information available is largely on public companies. Trade publications, analysts' reports, and other sources must be scoured for information on private companies.

In a sense, analyzing the competitive environment in terms of current and potential M&A activity is another way to evaluate a target company. Any company that is not considering, or never has considered, an acquisition has failed to explore one of the primary ways that companies effect corporate growth. Does this fact point up a failing on the part of management? Maybe. Growth through the merger or acquisition process is not right for every company. But if the company has never been a potential acquirer or acquiree, there *may* be operational shortcomings that you should know about.

The notion of assessing a target company from the standpoint of its M&A orientation also relates to the company's overall strategic effectiveness. That a company has never considered or actively explored a corporate combination may represent a strategic negative. Conversely, a company that has successfully effected strategic acquisitions exhibits a distinctly positive attribute. Having made successful acquisitions points up management's ability to assess marketplace dynamics and effect growth through the complex M&A process. Unquestionably, a successful M&A track record speaks to management's strategic and organizational acumen. This is, however, only one aspect—albeit an increasingly important one—of the company's strategic effectiveness.

SUMMARY

Examining a target company as a stand-alone entity is a relatively straightforward exercise. However, strategic M&A growth planning requires adopting an analytical perspective that views an acquisition candidate not merely as represented by columns of numbers on a balance sheet, but rather as a collective of organizational and strategic attributes that will ultimately meld with your own if and when a merger or acquisition is consummated. Postmerger integration will always be significantly more efficient and expeditious when your premerger analysis takes on a merged-company orientation.

Market analysis in the context of strategic acquisitions, therefore, differs from conventional market assessments, not exclusively in terms of what information is collected but more importantly in how those data are analyzed.

Traditional market analysis looks at a company as a stand-alone organism functioning in a given environment. And, that organism, to build on the biological metaphor, is *unicellular*. On the other hand, M&A-focused market analysis views a company as a *multicellular* entity comprising a unique set of organizational, operational, and financial traits that will be augmented after its combination with your firm.

In essence, the key to M&A-focused market analysis is viewing the target as an eventual part of the merged company. It is critically important to maintain this comparative view during all phases of the information-gathering and analysis process.

Evaluating market dynamics and assessing a company's strategic capabilities require gathering extensive data from multiple sources on products, customers, and employees. The chapters in Part Two highlight the tools and techniques employed in researching acquisition candidates—the first step in launching your formal merger and acquisition program.

5

Analyzing a Target Company's Products and Product-Development Capabilities

The Cordis Corporation was one of the United States' largest makers of medical devices used in angioplasty, the increasingly popular surgical procedure designed to prevent heart attacks. In angioplasty, a doctor inserts a tiny balloon at the end of a long tube into a blood vessel in a patient's leg and maneuvers the balloon all the way up to the patient's heart. The balloon is positioned in an artery that has been clogged by fatty deposits, then inflated to push the deposits aside and clear the artery.

Johnson & Johnson does not make surgical products used in angioplasty procedures. But the Fortune 500 health products company does make a device called a "stent," which is a tiny metal scaffold that could be used in the aftermath of an angioplasty operation to keep an artery from reclosing. The synergistic nature of Cordis's products with its own was obvious to J&J. With the belief that bringing Cordis under its venerable brand name could make it the dominant player in the angioplasty market, J&J acquired Cordis for $1.8 billion in 1996. Augmenting its product line to capitalize on the growing market for angioplasty surgery was clearly at the core of J&J's acquisition strategy.

Obtaining completely new products or product lines is often the driving force behind corporate mergers and acquisitions. The Cordis-J&J union is just one example of a purely product-driven acquisition. Another, which we cited earlier, is IBM's acquisition of Lotus Development Corporation. Securing ownership of the popular Lotus Notes product was the main goal of IBM's $3.5 billion takeover. These and myriad other transactions illustrate one of the most significant benefits of mergers and acquisitions: gaining strategically significant products and services in a speedier, less costly, and less risky manner than through internal product development.

More than ever before, companies must replace their mature or declining products with new ones to stay competitive in today's market—a market that is characterized by shortened product life cycles, new technologies, industry deregulation, globalization, and the continual onslaught of new competitors. Updating and augmenting product and service offerings is also necessary to keep pace with changing customer requirements and characteristics. For example, in the past decade, many major advertising agencies acquired sales promotion, direct marketing, and public relations firms to meet clients' demands for full-service, *integrated marketing*. The maneuver was also defensive in nature. The agencies were contending with a steady decline in ad spending by clients, so their acquisitions of firms offering complementary communications services stemmed the tide of declining media commission revenues. But there was yet another factor spurring the M&A boom in this industry segment: Agencies needed to grow to serve their major clients who, through domestic and international acquisitions, were getting bigger themselves.

Obtaining established products and services via a merger or acquisition is a key way to enhance your product offering without incurring the costs and risks of developing products in-house. But even if this is not a driver of your acquisition strategy, a detailed analysis of a target company's products must necessarily be conducted. Indeed, product evaluation is one of the most fundamental and critical elements of marketing due diligence. Why? Because the lifeblood of any company is its products.

Every company exists to develop specific products for specific consumers to meet those buyers' specific needs and, through the process, generate revenues that ensure the organization can grow. More expressly, the value of a company's products—and its product development capabilities—directly correlates to the value of the company itself. In fact, the collective power of a company's product offerings represents one of the most important attributes of a company's array of tangible and intangible marketing assets.

In a related sense, the target's overall product development history and capabilities form an important component of its overall strategic effectiveness. Therefore, a company with a strong level of product development acumen possesses inherent skills and capabilities that can be transferred to the merged company—specifically from successful product developers. Consequently, as you conduct your product-related examinations, you will identify the people behind a product's success, people who can conceivably continue in a product development capacity in the merged organization, or whom you can employ in other related disciplines (e.g., sales, marketing management, R&D).

Also, keep in mind the comparative viewpoint that characterizes the merged-company perspective. By examining the way the target develops and markets products, you can identify what strengths you as acquirer can bring to the process to further enhance the acquired's product development capabilities. Additionally, this examination can help you spot weaknesses that may be mitigated by bringing your company's product development expertise to the target's product development activities (assuming that the target will ultimately function as a separate entity, as opposed to having its operations folded into your own).

Gaining a historical perspective into a target company's product development processes is important in identifying managerial strengths and weaknesses, as well as spotting opportunities for postmerger skills transfer. The first phase of your review, however, entails assessing individual products and product lines. The primary element of this review is determining the fit between the target's products and the merged firm's strategic goals.

ANALYZING PRODUCTS AND PRODUCT LINES

A host of important considerations must be addressed in determining the strategic fit of a target's product line with your own. These considerations fall into two main areas of investigation: identifying your strategic objectives and ensuring consistency with your current products.

Identifying your strategic objectives is central to determining the products you need in order either to enter new markets or to stay current with your customers' changing needs. In Chapter 2 the product-specific strategic growth synergies attainable through M&A were summarized. A quick recap is in order here. With respect to these synergies, one or more of the following may represent the underlying goal of a product-driven M&A strategy:

- *Increasing your market share* by acquiring a competitor's products.
- *Supplementing your product or service line* to better meet your customers' current or future needs.
- *Entering new product market segments* in which you are not currently operating but which are of long-term strategic significance.
- *Obtaining patents or trademarks* that may have precluded you from entering specific product markets or that can strengthen your market standing.

Ample attention has already been devoted to the business issues underlying these objectives. Therefore, analyzing existing product and service offerings will complement that research. The analysis has two phases. First, you must examine your own offerings to identify weaknesses or gaps that can be eliminated by acquiring another company's products. Second, you must evaluate the quantitative, qualitative, and operational aspects of a target company's products to see if the organization(s) under review can help you mitigate your product or service deficiencies or boost your existing strengths.

Before exploring product line analysis, it is necessary to gain a frame of reference that will guide some basic decisions in your review of an acquisition candidate's products and services.

One of the most important considerations when sizing up a target's products is ensuring consistency with your existing products. A client summed up her fundamental acquisition strategy succinctly: "Any company we look at must have the same customers as we do and must offer products and services that are compatible with ours." In short, she was referring to consistency.

There are several different, albeit interrelated, aspects of product mix consistency. A mix is consistent when its products are:

- Sold to the same end users
- Made available to the market through the same distribution channels
- Manufactured in roughly the same way

It is understandable why ensuring product mix consistency is important in mergers and acquisitions. When a target's products are sold to the same end users as yours, you can more easily market those goods to your existing customers, and market your products more readily to the target's customers. When products are sold through the same channels, you can maintain your existing distribution system and sales force. And when products are manufactured in a manner similar to yours, you can often maintain your existing production systems and facilities while realizing economies of scale and scope.

These latter two areas are relevant in situations where you plan to take on manufacturing and sales management responsibilities, as opposed to having the target company continue handling these functions on a stand-alone basis.

The common end user aspect of product consistency is often central to strategic acquisitions. In addition to the deals cited earlier, an example is the pharmaceutical giant IVAX Corporation's $570 million acquisition of its leading rival, Zenith Laboratories. Verapamil, IVAX's hypertension drug, was generating more than $150 million in annual revenues, yet was continuously being undercut by a similar product manufactured by Zenith. After the acquisition, the drugs were aggressively marketed as being usable interchangeably. Combined sales of the products skyrocketed.

Conducting your search of M&A candidates with an eye toward consistency of the merged company's product offering is an important premerger consideration that has wide-ranging postmerger ramifications.

QUANTITATIVE, QUALITATIVE, AND OPERATIONAL FACTORS

Conducting product-focused analysis involves studying your own and the target company's products from both a statistical and a nonstatistical perspective. The process begins with evaluating a given product mix and the various product lines that comprise it. By first focusing on a few basic concepts you can more easily understand how companies categorize and manage their goods and services.

Product mix refers to the entire array of products a company sells to customers. An example would be a consumer products manufacturer that markets toothpaste, toothbrushes, and mouthwash—each of which comprises an individual product line. Product lines are groups of products that are related, or consistent, in two basic respects: They are sold to the same customers and are sold through the same basic outlets (e.g., retail stores, mail order).

Product mixes and product lines differ in terms of their width and depth. Width refers to how many different product lines are offered. Depth denotes the number of variations of products within each of those product lines. Using the above example, width consists of the three individual product lines (toothpaste, toothbrushes, mouthwash), while depth might relate to the number of different flavors offered in the mouthwash product line.

Not all companies, especially middle-market ones, have overly wide or deep product mixes and lines. Indeed, there are many successful firms that market only one or two products. Nonetheless, it is important to note that any product offering will most likely be modified after you have merged with or acquired another company. Whether you offer three products or three hundred, the issues of monitoring and managing your product mix to meet changing customer needs—and your company's evolving strategic direction—are largely the same.

Quantitative Factors

Quantitative product analysis involves evaluating four aspects of a target company's product offering:

1. Market share
2. Sales and profits of individual items in the product mix or line
3. Product life cycle (PLC) stages of different products
4. Pricing strategies

Market share. This is the variable you must first assess in evaluating an acquisition candidate's current offerings. For example, are the company's products market leaders, occupying the first- or second-place position in their product segments? Or are they laggards that labor at the bottom of the pack?

Market share is a significant variable in that it is a driver of profitability. This has been documented by the well-known Profit Impact of Market Strategy (PIMS) study cited earlier, which generated information on the profit performance of businesses under different competitive conditions. The study resulted in a model of the major variables that influence a company's return on investment (ROI) and account for differences in profitability and cash flow.

One of the variables that was identified as having the most impact on ROI was competitive position as indicated by market share level. Specifically, a high level of market share tends to lead to higher profits than low market share levels. Therefore, identifying the market share levels of a target's products not only indicates the success of individual offerings, but also the extent to which they contribute to the overall profitability of the target company itself.

Sales and profits analysis. Quantitative product mix analysis also entails identifying the percentage contribution of each product to a company's sales and profits. The key focus is on spotting which products account for the majority of income on a product line-by-product line basis. If sales and profits are concentrated within one or two products in a multi-item product line, the overall line may be vulnerable. If those high-performing products begin to lose market share as a result of, say, attacks by competitors, a major source of profits will erode. Vulnerability, however, is lessened when there is a more even distribution of sales and profits across all items in the product line.

There are many examples of mergers that were based on reducing or eliminating vulnerabilities in a product or service mix. For instance, Wayne Huizenga, founder of Blockbuster Video, saw the expansion of the cable TV industry, the introduction of direct satellite TV, and the ability to potentially surf 500 channels as onerous threats to his high-flying videotape rental store chain. Consequently, he masterminded Blockbuster's acquisition by the entertainment giant Viacom before the vulnerability of his one-product/service company led to irreversible financial disaster.

In sum, a sales and profit self-analysis is necessary to unearth weaknesses that may exist in your product offering and provide insights that may, in effect, drive your overall acquisition strategy. Moreover, the self-analysis is a critical precursor to analyzing a target company's product sales and profits, which is necessary to identify whether a target can help eliminate weaknesses in your offerings or enhance existing strengths. Most important, the target company product analysis is needed to spot inherent vulnerabilities in the candidate's own product offering that can spawn long-term problems if the merger or acquisition goes through.

INSIDER'S OUTLOOK

You must take a "soup to nuts" look at all marketing activities at the target firm. Of particular importance, obviously, are the company's products. For instance, which product lines are working with which customer segments. You have to examine the concentration of revenues on a product-by-product basis. In particular, I like to see data on product line profitability and see where there are linkages between product line profitability and sales force incentives. Why is that important? Because companies must recognize that they are selling a product at a loss for a reason. For instance, an unprofitable product may be a loss leader that pulls through other products, or it's in the start-up phase of its life cycle. If they don't know why they're selling a product at a loss, then that's an issue. It sounds obvious, but we see many examples of confused sales forces selling products to boost top-line revenues without any consideration for profitability. If a company doesn't think it can make money from a product then it shouldn't be selling that product.

—Mufit Cinali, AT&T

Stage of product life cycle. The sales and profits analysis provides a snapshot of the current standing of a given product offering. But each individual item must also be viewed from the standpoint of its future potential. In this context, product life cycle (PLC) is a primary factor. The PLC concept refers to the fact that all products pass through various stages during which sales and profits rise and fall. Different marketing and financial investment strategies are required during the four basic stages of the PLC:

1. *Introduction.* The product is first entered into the market. There is limited competition, but profit margins are low because the market is not yet as large as it will eventually become and because start-up expenditures are high.
2. *Growth.* Product sales and profits increase. So too does competition as the product's popularity grows.
3. *Maturity.* Sales and profits level off and competition continues to increase. The product is offered in a wide range of distribution outlets and at different price levels.
4. *Decline.* Market size, consumer demand, sales, and profits dwindle. Management decreases its investments in marketing and distribution. If it is not able to be successfully repositioned, the product is ultimately discontinued.

Marketing due diligence must involve an accurate assessment of the PLC stages of the target company's product mix, a process that involves studying each item's sales, profit margins, market share, and pricing levels at different points in its history. Successful products may not continue to be strong sellers if they are in the latter stages of the PLC.

On the other hand, unsuccessful products may be underperforming because they are in their early PLC stages and have yet to reach their full potential. An error in pinpointing the PLC stage of an M&A candidate's products could mean the difference between identifying a good strategic fit or overpaying for a declining, low-potential asset.

Conducting a PLC analysis brings an important element of objectivity to the product evaluation process. Companies often become enamored of the past success of a certain star product to the point where it clouds their judgment of the item's future potential. On analyzing that product's PLC stage, however, it becomes apparent that they are gazing into the rear-view mirror. Again, the purchase of Snapple Beverage Corporation by Quaker Oats is the perfect case in point.

From 1986 to 1994, Snapple's sales leaped from $3 million to almost $700 million. Yet in the early 1990s, several major players—including Lipton and Coca-Cola Company's Nestea brand—began aggressively attacking the ready-to-drink iced tea market. By mid-1994, it was clear that Snapple's growth was slowing in contrast to its competitors in the maturing iced tea arena. In fact, in the following quarter operating income was down more than 70% and net profits for those first nine months of the year were down 14% in comparison to the same period in 1993.

The numbers notwithstanding, Quaker Oats went ahead and acquired Snapple. Within three months of the transaction, Snapple had been knocked from its perch as king of the iced tea segment. Immediately, questions began to be raised by industry observers as to whether Quaker Oats made the right move in acquiring Snapple. Did the company overpay? Was management dazzled by the high point of Snapple's iced tea PLC without recognizing the increased competition and decreased market growth? In short, did the company perform an adequate PLC analysis? Evidently, it did not. Three years after its $1.7 billion purchase, Quaker Oats waved the white flag and sold off Snapple in utter desperation.

Extensive PLC evaluations must be conducted for all significant products marketed by the target company. However, it is important to recognize that products rarely move so predictably through the aforementioned PLC stages. There are, in fact, a wide range of patterns that different products exhibit. For instance, it is quite possible that an item in the decline stage could suddenly exhibit renewed growth. A classic example is when the moribund product baking soda was repositioned from being a cooking ingredient to being usable as a refrigerator freshener and tooth brightener, resulting in strongly revived sales.

The important thing to remember is that the PLC is a way to chart the inevitable evolution of the target's different products. All products typically move from a period of introduction and gradual market acceptance to a period where market interest and sales necessarily decline, and competition intensifies. The other important consideration about product life cycles is that they are influenced and controlled by marketing variables. For example, the life cycle of a given product may have entered the decline stage because management failed to allocate enough promotional resources to keep it in the growth or maturity stage.

In marketing due diligence, the challenge is to identify, as well as possible, the life cycle stage of different products with an eye toward their future marketability as part of the merged company's product lineup. In essence, the merged-company perspective requires that you assess individual products from the standpoint of how they can be strengthened or revived based on the resources the merged organization can allocate to them.

Pricing strategies. Different pricing strategies are employed as products move through the various stages of their product life cycles. It is, therefore, necessary to evaluate the target's pricing strategies for the items in its product line as part of your assessment of those products' market performance.

For instance, certain pricing schemes are employed when products are first introduced into the marketplace: "Penetration" pricing is setting a low price in order to secure as much market share as possible; "meet the competition" pricing is setting prices at roughly the same levels as competitors' goods and using other variables, such as service or quality, as competitive differentiators; and "skimming" is setting particularly high prices for products when they are the first in their markets.

More important than the price levels set when products are first introduced are the pricing and related marketing strategies the target company employed as those products moved through their PLC stages. For instance, did the company monitor the marketplace effectively enough to know when to raise prices after enacting its initial penetration levels (assuming competitive market conditions and its cost structure enabled it to do so)? Did the target effectively alter other marketing mix variables (e.g., its promotion and distribution) to create compelling competitive differentiators if and when it was using a meet-the-competition pricing approach? Did the target know when to cut its prices (assuming it was necessary to do so) if and when its initial price skimming strategy no longer was appropriate in a market becoming crowded with competitors' offerings?

How a target devises its pricing level strategies is also an indicator of its overall marketing aggressiveness and its orientation to strategically positioning its products. For instance, a company that tends to charge higher than average prices for its products may be attempting to communicate high levels of quality and prestige. Conversely, organizations that typically go with lower-priced offerings may be intent on building market share at the expense of creating a highbrow image for their goods and services.

Keep in mind that assessments of a target company's pricing strategies must be done in concert with a review of its competitors' pricing moves. Pricing decisions are rarely made in a vacuum. Instead, they are often made as a direct result of competitors' pricing moves. Thus, be sure to factor in the pricing strategies of the target's competitors when evaluating the target's historical pricing decisions.

In sum, the pricing strategies the target company has adopted—and the resultant success or failure of those strategies—must be evaluated in order to assess the performance of the target's products. Those strategies represent yet another indicator of the target's overall strategic effectiveness.

Qualitative Factors

All aspects of marketing due diligence require looking beyond the numbers. In the realm of product analysis, that means not only examining a target company's product profits and losses (P&Ls), PLC stages, and pricing levels, but also the qualitative characteristics of those goods. There are several critical qualitative aspects of products that must be reviewed to effectively conduct the product analysis process:

- Brand issues: "share of mind" and brand loyalty
- Promotion
- Quality
- Customer service and warranties

Brand issues: "share of mind" and brand loyalty. You must assess the target company's products from the standpoint of their overall brand power. It is necessary to determine how those brands measure up against competitors' in terms of "share of mind" awareness, which is the degree to which the market associates that brand with its product category, and brand loyalty, which is the extent to which consumers repeatedly purchase that brand.

For instance, a striking example of the significance of share of mind is that of Microsoft. The company's dominance of the personal computer operating system market has resulted in the widespread market perception that Microsoft is the world's largest software producer. The fact is, however, IBM boasts 10 times the software sales revenues in comparison to Microsoft. Microsoft clearly dominates in terms of software consumers' share of mind.

Strong market perceptions lead to more sales and often (assuming those products and services are of high quality) to increased brand loyalty. Thus, a brand with high levels of market awareness and consumer loyalty may be more valuable, in the long run, than others whose current sales and market standing are higher.

INSIDER'S OUTLOOK

Certainly, everybody places a lot of emphasis on the value of a company's brand. But you just can't look at brand acquisition. You've got to determine what that brand means to your current, as well as your projected, customer base. A brand may have very high client recognition, but among its customers it was eroding, say, because of service issues or because of a perceived arrogance of the company by buyers. These things are not obvious if you just do an unaided awareness study. Without a doubt, the brand says a lot about the company. A company may have been on top of the world. On the other hand, it may be increasingly viewed as a "has-been." Does this brand represent a company of the past, or does it represent a company of the future? These are the things you have to find out.

—Carolyn Chin, IBM

Promotion. Many products underperform in the marketplace because of inadequate or poorly executed communications. Promotion is a critical yet often overlooked aspect of product evaluations. You must gauge the quality of the target company's advertising, direct mail, sales promotion, publicity, and so on individually and collectively, determining whether the right forms of marketing communications are being employed and whether they are integrated enough (e.g., consistent in message, timing, and execution) to be effective.

Just as share of mind is important in assessing a target product's image, so too is its "share of voice." This refers to how much a product is promoted in the marketplace. The more broadly an item is marketed, the higher its share of voice will be. Thus, the strength of promotion is a result of both creative decisions (the quality of the marketing communications themselves) and investment considerations (the amount being spent on those communications).

From an execution standpoint, a key task of marketing due diligence is to assess the target company's product promotion in comparison to your own strengths and resources in this area. That is, you or your agencies may be able to do the job better. PaineWebber's acquisition of Kidder Peabody is an appropriate example.

After years of utilizing the "Thank You, PaineWebber" campaign slogan, the firm replaced it with the more client-focused "He/She Asked" campaign. These award-winning advertisements highlighted investment issues triggered by life events (divorce, birth, death, retirement, education funding). In the spots, the PaineWebber client is better able to deal with these life events because he or she has planned for the unexpected—with the help, of course, of a PaineWebber broker. When queried how the broker knew to advise on that issue, the client responds, "He asked!"

This campaign was widely viewed as successful, in stark contrast to Kidder Peabody's eminently forgettable advertising. When Kidder was acquired by PaineWebber, Kidder's agency was immediately dropped, and the account for the newly merged financial services company went to the acquirer's agency. Thus, another area of investigation (see Chapter 8) relates to the people behind the promotion. If advertising and promotion are done in-house, the marketing staffers responsible must be evaluated. If the majority of the promotion is handled by outside agencies, you must evaluate those firms and the professionals assigned to the target's respective account teams.

Quality. Quality is a manufacturing-related variable, but it is also a perceptual phenomenon of tremendous significance when evaluating a target company's products. More and more, customers base their purchase decisions on a comparison of the quality levels of different brands. Your product analysis, therefore, must include gauging the perceived level of quality that consumers bestow on a target company's products.

A core element of the PIMS methodology relates to product quality levels and the resultant impact on sales. PIMS research indicates that high-quality products typically enjoy greater profitability than low-quality ones. Specifically, having higher product quality:

- Enables the company to charge a premium price
- Engenders higher rates of repeat purchasing
- Bolsters consumer loyalty

Determining your ability to improve a product's quality from a manufacturing standpoint is an important M&A consideration. Equally important is your ability to improve the market's perception of quality via revamped marketing communications.

Customer service and warranties. Products possess more than physical attributes. Today, the intangible, service-related aspects of products are often as important as their tangible features. Examples include customer advice, financing, delivery arrangements, parts and service, and warranties. The target company you are evaluating may offer outstanding products. But how good are the attendant services it provides? It is imperative that you evaluate the target's products as well as their customer service capabilities in the same context, since they are interrelated factors and not separate issues.

Operational Factors

Having already examined product and product line characteristics in terms of their measurable attributes, you must also review some of the key operational aspects relative to the physical production and circulation of those items in the marketplace, such as:

- Manufacturing
- Packaging
- Distribution

Manufacturing. Traditional due diligence examines a target company's manufacturing facilities particularly from the standpoint of fixed and variable costs and depreciation schedules of machinery. The marketing due diligence perspective on manufacturing, on the other hand, ties mainly to product quality specifically as a result of the target company's manufacturing processes. Thus, your review must determine the relation, if any, between a target's manufacturing practices and the levels of product defects and returns. Moreover, your assessment must spot the extent to which the target recognizes and has taken steps to heighten manufacturing efficiencies to enhance product quality.

A company's manufacturing processes may also be relevant from a promotional standpoint. For example, if the firm has an especially advanced computer-integrated manufacturing system that augments product quality or the speed with which goods are delivered to the marketplace, those attributes may merit being cited by the target's sales force in discussions with distributors, as well as in its promotional communications to the market at large.

INSIDER'S OUTLOOK

Indeed, the AT&T brand name is something we are bringing to the (negotiating) table, and there is a distinct value attached to it. How do we determine what the value of our brand is? It's through market research, lots of market research. We have been able to establish the value of our brand through what our "market pull" is. Products bearing the AT&T brand name achieve better market share than with other brand names. Consequently, the value of the AT&T brand name becomes one of the key value drivers in any transaction.

—Mufit Cinali, AT&T

Packaging. Packaging is sometimes referred to as the "fifth P of marketing" (the four Ps being product, place, price, and promotion) given its importance from a practical and perceptual standpoint and its significance in terms of consumers' likes or dislikes toward an item's physical characteristics.

Marketing due diligence should determine the extent to which a product's packaging is functionally appealing to the company's target buyers. For example, the move by a well-known ice cream company to put its product in bright multicolor containers, as opposed to conventional monochrome containers, was embraced by buyers and sparked dramatically increased sales. As each new flavor is developed, the packaging continues to drive new product revenues.

From a psychological standpoint, packaging is a marketing communication tactic. Packaging must be visually alluring so as to be noticeable on crowded retail store shelves. Marketing due diligence should assess the attractiveness of product packaging, how well it describes a product's features, and whether it contributes to consumers' recognition of the item's overall brand image and supports a product's positioning.

If, for example, promotional activities emphasize a product's prestige, you must determine whether the packaging is consistent with that desired market image. Saying a brand of perfume is upscale requires that it be contained in an attractive bottle and housed, for example, in a velvet pouch. It should not be marketed in a six-pack of pop-top cans!

In short, packaging is an alterable element of the marketing mix. Therefore, management should be regularly assessing consumers' sentiments toward packaging concepts and, where necessary, taking steps to modify packaging to meet buyers' wants. Has the target company been doing so for its long-standing items? Has the target adequately solicited customer input in designing packaging concepts for its new products? These are among the questions to be asked.

Distribution. The distribution channels employed to move goods from manufacturer to end user represent a key area of examination in the product analysis process. The first phase of analysis involves understanding the target's basic distribution strategy. Companies sell their products through either direct channels (e.g., directly to end users) or indirect channels (e.g., through wholesalers, retailers, industrial supply companies, manufacturers' agents, or a combination thereof).

Direct channels typically involve using sales representatives who are employed by the manufacturer and are utilized when the manufacturer sells specialty products requiring demonstrations or detailed explanations of product features and benefits. Indirect channels—especially multiple indirect channels—are necessary when the company's customer base is large and widely dispersed geographically.

Specifically, marketing due diligence should determine whether the target's distribution strategy is consistent with the nature of its products and the characteristics and location of its customers. Thus, you should evaluate the following variables, which relate to both distribution decisions and the activities of middlemen in the product-delivery network:

- Consistency with product positioning
- Channel intermediary performance
- Channel rivalry
- Trade relations and promotions

Consistency with product positioning. Where products are made available to end users is often determined by the market positioning of those goods. For example, upscale items such as jewelry are rarely sold in mass-market retail outlets, but rather through specialty boutiques, and usually on an exclusive distribution basis. Your review should, therefore, identify if the channels through which the target's products are sold mesh with those products' overall positioning.

Channel intermediary performance. When multiple indirect channels are used, it is necessary to gauge how well those middlemen have served the target company. Intermediaries should be measured against specific sales quotas that were established by the company on a product line-by-product line basis, as well as by specific markets served (measured in terms of geographic, socioeconomic, demographic, or other segmentation variables).

Channel rivalry. Competition among intermediaries is inevitable when multiple channels are employed. If the target distributes its products through different retail chains, for example, those outlets may be less motivated to promote the target's goods if a retailer's competitors are also in the distribution mix. Marketing due diligence must determine the degree to which channel conflict is present. You must also probe the extent of activities that the company's sales management has undertaken to study, act on, minimize, or, ideally, eliminate channel rivalry.

Trade relations and promotions. Successfully motivating channel intermediaries to carry and promote products requires formal trade relations and promotional programs. An example of such activities is a "dealer incentive program," where retailers who meet specified quotas are rewarded with bonuses like elaborate gifts or free trips to exotic locales. Today, consumer products' success is often dependent on the extent to which retailers give prominent shelf space to products and actively promote their features and benefits to buyers. Your evaluation must delve into the types, frequency, and success of trade promotions at different levels of the distribution hierarchy and for specific products.

Thus, assessing a product manufacturer's distribution strategy requires understanding the nature of its products, the positioning of those items, and their physical delivery to existing and potential customers.

The foregoing examples are more relevant for studying product merchandisers than direct marketers (e.g., a computer seller like Gateway 2000). But what of service providers? The essence of any company's distribution strategy is to make its offerings easily accessible to the largest number of target buyers. Service providers face the same challenge. Consider, for example, tax-preparation offices. These outlets need to be situated strategically throughout the company's service area to be accessible to both regular clients and walk-ins.

Of course, there are other service industries that require no physical locations at all—investment executives, for instance. These professionals do the vast majority of their work over the phone, and could rightfully be sitting in Nebraska while servicing clients in New Hampshire. Yet, even these types of companies often have regional representatives, which are necessary when certain clients who do most of their dealing with the brokers over the phone periodically require in-person meetings.

PRODUCT DEVELOPMENT HISTORY AND PROCESSES

In the target company assessment process, it is necessary to evaluate each major product and service marketed by the organization. But it is also important to gain insights and a clear understanding of how the target has historically developed and commercialized its products. You must assess the target's product development history to further appraise its current offerings and to forecast its ability to continue devising new and successful goods and services in the future.

The core elements of a company's product development history and processes include:

- Product development organization
- Research and development spending
- Degree of customer focus and input
- Pace of new product introductions and enhancements
- Product deletions
- "Core competency connection"
- Relation to corporate strategy

Product Development Organization

How a company organizes its product development function is significant since different structures have different strengths and weaknesses. For example, the company may take a "brand manager" approach, where one person has complete responsibility for one product or brand in terms of setting overall objectives and strategies and overseeing the tactical execution of product marketing activities. Yet, when this person also has responsibility for new product development, it is an arduous task to handle both assignments—and the product development function generally suffers as a consequence.

A similar problem arises when the product development structure involves "new product committees," which comprise senior executives from different corporate departments. In this scenario, new product development is also an additional chore and, as with the brand manager approach, it becomes difficult for these officers to effectively handle both existing and new product responsibilities.

The ideal structure is that of a full-time product development team. This team should comprise specialists from different areas of the company—marketing, sales, R&D, engineering, manufacturing, and finance. Beware of situations where product development is a part-time exercise for selected managers. The product development process is often ineffective when it is a duty added to managers' other responsibilities, as opposed to being the main focus of a permanent, multidisciplinary team.

Research and Development Spending

A direct relationship exists between new product introductions and spending on research and development. A company that invests heavily in R&D exhibits an emphasis on future sales growth through the introduction of a stream of new marketing offerings. R&D spending represents a significant corporate investment designed to pay important dividends in the years ahead. Evaluating a company's product development history requires determining how much that organization currently spends on R&D and how much it has spent on R&D in the past.

A comparative viewpoint should be adopted from an external and an internal perspective. Externally, you must gauge R&D spending by the target company in contrast to its marketplace peers. Internally, you must project the extent to which the merged company's financial resources can be channeled to the target organization to bolster its R&D infrastructure. If the target will ultimately operate autonomously, as opposed to being folded into your existing operations, you must quantify how much the target's competitors spend on R&D in order to identify a benchmark level. Then you need to forecast how much the merged company must allocate going forward to help the acquired firm keep pace with or exceed its competitors' investments.

Degree of Customer Focus and Input

Surprisingly, many companies conduct product development with little or no input from customers vis-à-vis initial product concepts and their ultimate designs. Consequently, a target company that only minimally secures customer input in its product development work exhibits a significant shortcoming.

Customer feedback should be obtained in all phases of creating the product or service offering. For instance, one way to view products is in terms of their purely tangible characteristics and functional features. Thus, when designing a new car, an auto manufacturer should seek customers' input when creating the instrument panel, accumulating feedback on how and where certain controls should be situated in order to be easily reached when driving.

Another, arguably more important, way to view products is as providers of a set of benefits sought by the buyer. Consider, for example, a consumer product like deodorant. From the standpoint of tangible characteristics, deodorant is simply a chemical-based compound that masks odors resulting from people's bodily fluids. From a benefit-oriented standpoint, however, deodorant may be viewed as a way for consumers to gain confidence in interpersonal dealings by eliminating offensive body odor, and hence helping them avoid rejection (a frequent claim made in advertising).

Services must also be viewed from the standpoint of the broad benefit they offer to buyers. For instance, human resource consulting services help companies in devising and managing employee benefit programs. The true value of this service to buyers, however, is not simply in plan design, but rather in the ability to help companies attract and retain key employees.

Only through procuring adequate customer input on product features and benefits can products be effectively designed and promoted in the marketplace. Therefore, you must assess the degree to which this research is done by the target company in its product development work.

Pace of New Product Introductions and Enhancements

A marketing intangible asset lies in a company's ability and orientation to regularly develop new products. Companies should continually be devising and rolling out new offerings. In addition, organizations should always be exploring ways to refine or enhance existing products through feature modifications, line extensions, or market expansions (e.g., selling existing products in new territories).

Over the past decade, major American consumer product companies developed scores of new products each year. Obviously, not every target has the financial wherewithal and product development infrastructure to create so many new offerings each year. But the pace of new product introductions is an important indicator of a company's market aggressiveness, not to mention its ability to move products from the concept stage through to successful market commercialization (an arduous and complex process).

In one sense, quantity is important since the failure rate of new products is extraordinarily high. Thus, new offerings must be regularly developed since few actually succeed in the marketplace. Of course, the quantity of product introductions is irrelevant if none of those items succeed in the marketplace. Still, there may be strategic, operational, or financial deficiencies resident in a target that is overly slow in devising and commercializing new goods and services. This represents an issue that must be probed in the course of your marketing due diligence examination.

Product Deletions

Since it is to be expected that many new products will fail in the marketplace, a target's ability to respond promptly to misguided product strategies is imperative.

The company must be able to realize when it has made mistakes and to get out before nominal losses turn into massive financial setbacks. Oftentimes, firms will keep investing in new products even when performance fails to meet expectations and when corrective measures to the marketing strategy prove ineffective. It takes honesty to realize when a product error has been made. It takes good business judgment to pull out before that error turns into a financial disaster. A target company should demonstrate that sound discretion.

"Core Competency Connection"

Some companies stray from their central capabilities when developing products; such efforts often lead to failure. For instance, a major energy utility wanted to diversify into new product and service markets, and, given the extensive land holdings on which its facilities were located, decided to move into real estate development. The move was clearly far afield from its core competencies: power generation, transmission, and distribution. The utility's total lack of knowledge of the real estate business, coupled with a severe dearth of marketing acumen, caused million-dollar losses in the venture as more savvy and aggressive real estate firms battered the utility in the marketplace.

Strategic diversification, when done right, can certainly be rewarding and profitable. It is when companies stray too far from their areas of expertise and lose the "core competency connection" that significant problems may arise. Consequently, your marketing due diligence should assess the degree to which the target's product and service launches have been consistent with its core capabilities.

Relation to Corporate Strategy

The products that a company develops should be consistent with the organization's broader corporate strategy. While this may sound obvious, companies often stray from their guiding corporate vision and develop offerings that only tangentially relate to their strategic imperatives.

For instance, organizational effectiveness work we did for an international business services firm showed that its greatest opportunities, and competitive strength, lie in its information technology capabilities. Yet, its recent product development investments showed that almost as much was being spent on training and development products as for IT-related offerings—at a time when training was a much slower growth market.

If that was the case, why did the firm allocate so many dollars to a low-potential offering, thus taking valuable resources away from product development for its high-growth IT practice area? The answer, we discovered, was a bizarre sequence of political machinations by a powerful vice chairman. Thus, evaluating a company's product development history must ascertain whether or not its new offerings have been in sync with its specific market opportunities.

SUMMARY

Conducting product-focused marketing due diligence involves identifying your overall strategic objectives, then examining and comparing a target company's product offerings from quantitative, qualitative, and operational standpoints.

Quantitatively, you must identify the sales and profits of the items in different product lines, then locate their product life cycle stage. Qualitatively, you must look at products' brand image, promotion, perceived level of quality, and customer service attributes. Operationally, you need to evaluate those aspects of manufacturing, packaging, and distribution that collectively impact a product's success in the marketplace.

A key phase of this investigation is identifying gaps or vulnerabilities in your product offering as a framework for determining which M&A candidate can best help you eliminate those weaknesses, or bolster your strengths. The findings of your comparative research will help you identify the low-potential products that can be eliminated in the postmerger environment and those products that will merit further investment to ensure continued growth.

Obviously, many M&A deals are done to eliminate duplications in order to achieve economies of scale and operational efficiencies. This is not always advisable when making product decisions. Product-focused marketing due diligence should always consider situations where you can revitalize or improve a target company's product performance through better marketing and sales management, or through applying unique skills and capabilities resident in the acquiring organization.

The goal of any merger or acquisition is expanding your market opportunities and furthering your strategic objectives. From a product standpoint, you can add new product lines to broaden your overall product mix and penetrate new markets. Or you can add individual products to supplement your existing product lines and thereby strengthen your offering to customers.

The examples cited in this chapter and elsewhere throughout the book illustrate the product-driven nature of many M&A transactions. In particular, Johnson & Johnson expanded its heart disease treatment capabilities by acquiring a company whose angioplasty devices were synergistic with its artery-opening "stent." The ad agencies that acquired PR and sales promotion shops were able to augment their service offerings and generate new revenue streams.

In each case, the products and services were complementary to each other in one all-important respect: better meeting the needs of those companies' existing and future customers.

6

Analyzing a Target Company's Customer Base

Growth-related intangible assets reside in the people, products, and processes of the target company—the primary sources of the company's value within the organization itself. Growth intangibles can also be found in areas external to the organization, such as in the positive perceptions the market holds toward the company and its products.

Chief among the external variables that determine a given organization's worth is its customer base. No business can function or exist without customers. They are the fuel that drives any company's growth engine. That is why a critical element of the marketing due diligence process is an extensive review of a target's customer base as part of the assessment of the firm's current value and its future potential as a contributor to the merged company's growth initiatives. Customers collectively represent key attributes of a target company. They are attributes that need to be evaluated in the near term and cultivated over the long term.

As an acquirer, your goal is to sell your existing products to the target company's customers and/or to sell the target's products to your own buyers. Ideally, you want to be able to develop new product and service offerings that can be sold to the combined company's customer base. Product synergies are the strategic underpinnings of many mergers and acquisitions. But such synergies can only be realized when an expanded and diversified customer base is forged by the merger. Once that is accomplished, those buyers must then be led to purchase increasing amounts of new and bundled products and services marketed by the merged firm.

In this chapter the various ways to analyze a target company's customer base in terms of both quantitative and qualitative criteria are explored. Although customers are external to the target, their evaluation and analysis is conducted largely through internal means. Company managers, salespeople, service representatives, and others are the primary people to query for their insights on the qualitative and quantitative aspects of the buyer base.

Extensive documentation must also be collected, ranging from statistics on the size and composition of the customer base to data on the amounts and frequency of sales by individual and customer group segments. Ideally, the information you seek is readily available. Sometimes it is not. But the pervasiveness of technology today means that most established and successful companies have networked, customer databases that provide ample information on their customers' demographic, psychographic (attitudinal), and geographic composition.

Still, there are many instances where the customer data you seek is not nearly as comprehensive or accessible as you would like. The critical task in these circumstances is to collect as much detailed and accurate customer information as possible. The competitive intelligence techniques discussed in the Appendix offer insights into conducting acquisition candidate research. A word of caution: Maintaining detailed, accurate information on your customers or clients is an imperative in business today. Any target company that is severely lacking in terms of customer-related data exhibits a dramatic functional and strategic weakness. This major red flag should engender healthy skepticism on your part as you examine other elements of the target's operational infrastructure.

The guidance in this chapter keys on a main area of examination: identifying the customers who have provided the target's sales in the past and are the likely source of those sales in the future. Here again the merged-company perspective must be employed to determine the marketing and sales strategies that should be devised to capitalize on the combined products and capabilities of the merged organization. Each analytical activity will be discussed in the context of immediate and long-term growth initiatives. A variety of revenue enhancement opportunities will surface in the process of examining the target's existing buyers and prospects. When the overlap-overlay viewpoint is embraced, areas of customer commonality will point up important cross-selling options for the merged organization.

ROLE OF CUSTOMER ANALYSIS IN GROWTH PLANNING

The primary focus of marketing due diligence is identifying a target company's sales and marketing strengths and weaknesses with a growth-oriented emphasis. Opportunities for growth must be capitalized on and threats that pose obstacles to revenue enhancement must be minimized or eliminated. A company's customer base poses distinct strengths and weaknesses. The importance of the target's current and potential buyers to future growth initiatives underscores the need to conduct this phase of the marketing due diligence examination immediately after an analysis of the target's product mix.

Comprehensive customer base analyses can only be conducted once the exploratory door on the target company has been fully opened during the formal due diligence process. As with product analysis, there is a certain amount of preliminary customer research that should be done as part of the acquisition candidate screening process. This data, however, may tend to be overly general. Moreover, the reliability of data from publicly available sources is always suspect.

The truly in-depth data you require resides in the target company's customer records, its databases, and its strategic and marketing plans. Only when you have been given free rein to study all of these sources can you ascertain the relevant customer base characteristics. Still, it is likely that during your initial data gathering you have already collected information and constructed hypotheses related to the target's customers. During your review of its in-house data, you will necessarily strive to confirm or disprove your initial conclusions relative to the target's buyers and prospects.

An important part of the customer analysis process involves speaking with key managers within the target company. However, obtaining data from these people may prove to be problematic. Managers may be hesitant to fully disclose every detail about their customer relationships. Why is this the case? Because these people, especially those on the front lines who have direct customer contact, may be unsure of their future status with the merged organization and may be contemplating taking customers with them if and when they leave the firm. Understandably, they will be guarded when discussing certain issues or when asked to furnish related documentation.

Regardless of whether customer information is immediately accessible from personal or impersonal sources, or whether the level of detail is as comprehensive as you would like, your investigative focus should key on what information is needed before you set out to research it. Consequently, you must first look at the process of customer base analysis, identifying the various quantitative and qualitative data that must be collected and how that information should be analyzed for growth planning purposes.

During the customer analysis, however, there is an important thing to keep in mind. Analyzing the target's customer base goes beyond the mere tallying of sales figures and pinpointing of buying patterns by customer segment. Collecting and analyzing this data is imperative, but of even greater importance is maintaining a perspective that allows you to spot qualitative trends amongst the quantitative figures.

CUSTOMER BASE ANALYSIS: A PROCESS PERSPECTIVE

A target company's customer base can be analyzed in a number of ways. It is necessary to gauge not only its measurable dimensions, but also its qualitative characteristics. Your review should encompass both numerical assessments and those that lend insight into such aspects as the attitudinal composition of the target's buyers on a product-by-product basis.

The underlying goal is to unearth information that is necessary to formulate sales, marketing, and product development strategies after the merger or acquisition is finalized. As with all other phases of marketing due diligence, the merged-company perspective must be adopted. The customer base analysis should not result in a mere snapshot of the target's existing buyers and prospects. It should generate a series of images not unlike puzzle pieces that will ultimately fit together with your own to create an enduring picture of profitability.

The customer base analysis should yield information on the source and nature of sales. For example, you must determine how many buyers there are, the products they buy, and the frequency of their purchases as well as the amounts they buy. The analysis should also provide data on the composition of the customer base from several different perspectives. You must identify where those buyers are physically located (geographic dispersion); how they are grouped in terms of such variables as their age, gender, and nationality (demographic makeup); the social strata from which they come (economic and sociocultural standing); and how, when, and why they buy goods and services (behavioral orientation). For business-to-business marketers, the variables to identify include company size in terms of revenues or employees, industry segment, and geographic locale. Advanced analyses should explore the target's customer base from a multifactor standpoint, first looking at individual variables, then at selected combinations.

Let's start by looking at the various ways to assess the target's customer base, while citing the sources from which crucial customer information is obtained. The growth planning orientation focuses on how to immediately begin using the information collected to devise strategies for sustained growth and revenue enhancement.

QUALITATIVE AREAS

Determining who the target company's buyers are and what types of goods and services they buy is a more complex task than it seems. In consumer product marketing, companies sell to a multitude of different buyers who purchase different products at different times and for different reasons. In business-to-business selling, individual buyers within customer companies often vary based on the product or service offering. These and a host of other qualitative areas must be examined. The first aspect of your customer base analysis is determining in what general categories the target company's buyers reside. Next, you should look at the physical composition of the customer base, and then its psychological or attitudinal makeup. You also need to conduct a "customer value analysis" to rank customers' buying criteria.

Category

Buyers are generally said to reside in either consumer or organizational markets. Consumer markets are those comprised of individuals or households who purchase goods and services for their own consumption. Organizational buyers include businesses and institutions that purchase products for resale or to produce other goods.

The organizational market is comprised of several subsegments. For instance, the industrial market is made up of companies that obtain goods and services to produce wares that are sold, rented, or supplied to other companies. Examples of companies functioning in the industrial market are agricultural, construction, transportation, and telecommunications concerns.

The reseller market is made up of firms that purchase goods to resell or rent to others at a profit. This subsegment market is comprised of companies that distribute products to the final buyer through selling intermediaries; wholesalers and retailers are examples of reseller organizations. (This may be a critically important component of the target's buyer base, since studies have shown that nearly 25% of all industrial marketers exclusively sell their products directly to end users, while some 75% use some type of distributor or reseller.)

Another organizational market subsegment is the government sector, which is made up of federal, state, and local governmental agencies that purchase goods and services to meet the public's needs in such areas as defense, health, education, and public welfare.

Composition

Customers next need to be analyzed in terms of their socioeconomic, geographic, demographic, behavioral, and psychographic makeup—the variables cited in traditional market segmentation analyses. In this realm, your analysis should begin with an assessment of the target's customers vis-à-vis their general socioeconomic standing. Does the company sell to affluent buyers? To lower-income buyers? Or does the firm sell its products to buyers across the entire spectrum of economic strata?

You must then determine where the target's buyers physically reside. Are they concentrated in one particular region of the country, or are they widely dispersed? This may be readily apparent if the target is a local or regional firm, in which case the physical location of its buyers may need to be studied in terms of ZIP codes or other more precise geographical units.

Demographically, you must evaluate the target's buyers in terms of their age, gender, ethnicity, religion, occupation, education level, and family size. Demographic information is important in assessing buyer composition because customer wants, preferences, and product-usage patterns are often similar among members of given demographic categories.

Customers' behavioral characteristics must also be examined. Buyers should be studied in terms of when they purchase specific goods and services, the frequency with which they do so, and the particular benefits they seek from different offerings.

Finally, the target's customers must also be evaluated in terms of their psychographic makeup—their overall lifestyles as characterized by their activities, interests, and opinions. Understanding the composition of the target company's customer base in terms of these different variables is helpful in devising growth strategies in the areas of product design, promotional approaches, and the selection of distribution channels.

INSIDER'S OUTLOOK

The Chase segmentation scheme was much more based on psychometrics, and the Chemical approach was based on behaviors with the bank. The new segmentation scheme, again, embodies the best of both worlds. When a customer walks into a branch today, our people know exactly what they're supposed to do with a person from that [psychometric or behavioral] segment. The customer information you have housed in your database represents the real critical success factor in banking today. Everybody's got pretty much the same products. Differentiating yourself in the marketplace depends on how well you are able to target and serve your customers. It's all about the ability, for instance, to know that a given customer just had a baby and that she may want to think about starting a college fund. Or that she's thinking about adding onto her home to make room for that baby . . . and "have we got a home equity loan for you."

—Susan Schoon, Chase Manhattan Bank

Buying Criteria

Of tremendous significance is determining how the target's customers make buying decisions and how they view the importance of different aspects of different product offerings. Specifically, you must conduct a "customer value analysis" to identify which of the following buying criteria are cited by customers when evaluating the target company's offerings:

- Quality
- Performance
- Features
- Price/terms
- Delivery

- Availability
- Safety

The first phase of a customer value analysis is determining which of these criteria buyers look for when considering individual products and vendors. Next, you must rank these attributes, since customers may seek one or more of them but may feel that some are more important than others. There is also a competitive component of the customer value analysis. You must gauge how the target's buyers view the relative importance of different attributes in comparison to the target's competitors' products.

Conducting a customer value analysis is critical from the merged-company perspective. First, you must understand the criteria that the target's buyers have sought in the past to ensure that you continue to offer it in the future. Second, there may be ways to enhance one or more of these value-oriented characteristics to increase sales to current buyers or to attract first-time purchasers.

Above all, you must determine whether the target's customers' values mesh with the values of your existing customers. This is a key consideration for devising cross-selling strategies for the combined company's product and service offerings and for creating broader marketing communications programs.

QUANTITATIVE AREAS

Evaluating the target's customers based on qualitative criteria is a precursor to a statistical analysis. Many times both phases of your review can be conducted concurrently. Regardless of whether this is the case, the combined data should be factored together.

As with your qualitative review, the goal of your quantitative assessment is to spot strengths that point up near- and long-term revenue enhancement opportunities, as well as weaknesses that might derail or delay the attainment of your growth objectives. Many of these strengths and weaknesses will become apparent as you pore through statistics related to more objective areas of examination. Before examining the subjective areas of appraisal, you should address more objective ways of quantifying a firm's buyer base.

Number of Customers

You must first determine the number of customers the target company has. In general, a company with more customers may appear stronger than one with fewer buyers. Yet the sheer number of customers may be a misleading indicator of the company's strength and competitive standing. You must study the target's revenue stream as it flows in from different customers. For example, a company may have 150 customers, each of which, on average, generates $1 million in revenue. Another company may have 1500 customers, each generating $10,000 annually. Obviously, the first company has fewer buyers, but those customers account for more revenue.

It is for this reason that the customer base must be gauged collectively, as well as by the size of actual accounts and on the dispersion of revenues by customer. Identifying how sales are accounted for on a customer-by-customer basis can be calculated in various ways.

First, "sales per customer" should be determined by looking at the annual revenues generated by each customer or account. Another measure relates to "average order size," where firmwide revenue is divided by the target's total number of customers. Care must be taken when generating statistics that result in average revenue, since some calculations can be extremely misleading. For instance, the *mean* average is often not an accurate indicator of an average since a particularly high or low value can distort the ultimate figure. Consider, for example, that the target firm has three major customers. One generates $11 million, and the other two generate $500,000 each. Since the mean is the arithmetic average calculated by adding the values and then dividing their sum by the number of values, the average dollar size of this target's customer accounts would be $4 million ($12,000,000 ÷ 3). Clearly, that is not an accurate picture.

In most cases where there are extremes within the sample, the better averaging method involves identifying the *median*, which is the middle case in a ranked listing of numerical observations. That is, in a set of numbers arranged from lowest to highest (or vice versa), the median is the middle number. Consider this hypothetical customer base:

Customer	*Annual Revenues*
A	$10,000
B	$200,000
C	$300,000
D	$400,000
E	$500,000
F	$500,000
G	$22,000,000

In this example, the median is $400,000, since half of the observations—the revenues for customers A, B, and C—fall above the median and the other half—the revenues for customers E, F, and G—fall below it. As you can see, the median is not affected by extreme cases, as is the case with the mean average.

Gaining insights on how a company's revenues are distributed among its customers is important in three key respects. First, it reveals which buyers are the target's biggest and most important accounts; these customers may merit specialized sales or customer service treatment after the acquisition is finalized. Second, studying the dispersion of revenues may reveal trends or opportunities that may drive future growth initiatives. For example, the analysis may reveal that major customers operate in a particular industry segment, in which you may want to invest more heavily in the future. Third, the analysis may unearth vulnerabilities. For example, a distinct weakness may exist when a target company's revenues are concentrated within a few customer companies, since the loss of one or more of those major accounts can spark immediate and irretrievable losses.

Ideally, revenues come from a relatively wide range of customers. Often, though, the infamous "80–20 rule" applies, in which roughly 80% of a company's revenues come from 20% of its customer base. Regardless of whether you have the same experiences regarding this general business formula, in most companies the majority of sales are concentrated within a few major accounts. Your task is to determine the extent to which that is the case in the target and, more importantly, how you will respond to shifts in that concentration.

Average Customer Size (Companies)

Earlier we looked at some of the ways to measure a company's size. These variables included revenues, total assets, number of employees, and so on. Gauging the size of a target company's typical customer is an important step in assessing the target's overall customer base. For example, does the target serve large Fortune 100 clients or does it serve the middle market? The revenue parameters you unearth may vary dramatically depending on whom you talk to at the target. You will need to identify what size company the target services based on one or more of the measurement criteria we have already cited.

Next, you must ask the question, "Why does the target service the sized company that it does?" Is this a strategic decision on the part of management? Or is it simply the marketplace's response to how the target company is marketing and delivering its goods and services? For example, the target may actually be striving to serve larger accounts, but may be unable to. If that is the case, it is necessary to determine why.

Profitability

Perhaps the most important measure of the value of each customer relationship is that of profitability. Profitability is measured by comparing the amount of gross revenue generated by that account against the dollars spent to service that account. For instance, professional services firms track client profitability in terms of the hours spent on a given client assignment versus the number of hours originally projected to do the work. Therefore, if an assignment was estimated to take 1000 hours for a professional billing $200 an hour (projected fees being 1000 × $200 = $200,000) the client would be profitable if the work cost the firm less than $200,000. Conversely, the client would be deemed unprofitable if the time required actually exceeded the 1000-hour figure.

Profitability is also impacted by the amount of money spent on winning a customer in the first place. For example, if $50,000 was spent in time, travel, and materials to secure the above client, that figure would have to be factored into the equation when determining the actual revenues and ultimate profit realized by the account.

Often, profitability is measured by calculating how much of all the target company's products the customer buys from the organization. Let us assume that the target is the aforementioned professional services firm offering a suite of consulting services in the areas of information technology, organizational design, and compensation consulting. In this scenario, gauging customer profitability would involve measuring the amount of sales of each service type as purchased by each client company. Hence, the firm's most profitable clients are those that purchased the greatest array of different services in the time period under study.

The 80–20 rule is also applicable in discussions of customer profitability. One can rightfully say that the companies falling in that 20% are the target firm's most profitable buyers. Profitability, however, should be measured more precisely on a case-by-case basis, as opposed to simply grouping customers into categorical buckets based on blocks of income.

Customer Satisfaction

This is largely a qualitative consideration since it connotes customer likes and dislikes. However, customer satisfaction can also be calculated statistically. For example, the "customer satisfaction ratio" factors in warranty costs in the revenues of consumer product manufacturers. In this sense, customer satisfaction is determined by subtracting warranty costs from net sales, then dividing that number by gross sales. For instance, gross sales to a given customer are $25,000, net sales are $10,000, and costs for warranties are $1000. Using this formula, the company would have a customer satisfaction ratio of 36%.

This calculation may be made on all accounts (for targets with small customer bases), or on a selected sample of accounts (for companies with larger customer bases). Naturally, it is more difficult to statistically assess customer satisfaction in a service business since there are no numbers resulting from warranty costs. Still, analyzable information may exist in the form of surveys conducted with clients that gauge their sentiments toward the target's overall service delivery and fee structure.

The growing popularity of industry measures and awards for quality has prompted more and more service firms to begin gathering feedback from clients on the quality of the firms' services. Thus, customer-service measurements for nonmanufacturing firms are much more attainable today than in the past.

INSIDER'S OUTLOOK

One of the most important things to look at is customer satisfaction survey baselines. If a target company does *not* have this type of data, I'd be worried because it shows they're not in touch with their customer base and, consequently, the possibility of customer defection may be high. You just wouldn't know. It's imperative to know if customers are satisfied with their existing service. You have to know if they're satisfied with their claims payment functionality. You have to know if they're satisfied with the bills they get—are they timely, are they accurate? You have to know if customers would consider changing carriers and why. You need some kind of customer satisfaction profile as a baseline.

—Don Curry, Blue Cross and Blue Shield of New Jersey

IDENTIFYING CUSTOMER BASE STRENGTHS AND WEAKNESSES

The underlying goal of marketing due diligence is assessing the growth-oriented strengths and weaknesses in a target company. The detailed customer base analysis that is so central to the process is acutely focused on strengths and weaknesses that exist within the collective of customers or clients the target organization serves. As with other aspects of your review, the customer base analysis focuses on spotting strong points that may lead to growth opportunities and areas of weakness that present obstacles to securing future expansion. In order to more capably gauge strengths and weaknesses, you must review both the quantitative and qualitative information you have collected in terms of the following variables:

- Distribution of customer revenues
- Patterns of revenue increases (or decreases)
- Extent of brand loyalty

- Reputation of customers
- Level of buyer's decision making authority
- Tenure of customer accounts
- Level of internal sales
- Industry concentration

Distribution of Customer Revenues

As we alluded to earlier, your analysis should determine the distribution of revenues from the target's different customer accounts. A low level of concentration of revenues among buyers (i.e., a customer base in which revenues are widely dispersed) is a discrete marketing intangible asset. This is because there is less vulnerability to the target company if one or more of those major accounts are lost. In contrast, a high level of concentration of buyers is a weakness, since the defection of one or more of those key customers will severely weaken the target's revenue stream.

Patterns of Revenue Increases (or Decreases)

You must review the pattern of sales between the target and its customers. Specifically, you should ascertain whether there has been an increase or decrease in sales in the past few years of the relationship. Steady increases represent customer satisfaction and a generally strong seller-buyer relationship.

Decreases or flat sales over a prolonged period of time illustrate potentially dissatisfied customers and possibly broader product or customer-service problems. There can be any number of reasons for a less-than-stellar sales history. Nonetheless, something is behind the numbers, and you must determine precisely what it is.

Extent of Brand Loyalty

You must attempt to gauge the extent to which brand loyalty exists amongst the target company's buyers. A high degree of loyalty means that buyers have a strong affinity to the company's products, are less sensitive to price increases, and are generally less likely to take their business elsewhere. This is a distinct strength.

However, a target's customer base that is decidedly less brand loyal, such as customers purchasing the same item or service from other providers in addition to the target company, is clearly more volatile and represents a distinct weakness. Moreover, there is a greater chance that these buyers may someday stop buying from the target company altogether, especially if products or services are altered or somehow change for the worse as a result of the merger or acquisition itself.

Reputation of Customers

Customer quality is another important yet often overlooked area of evaluation, particularly for business-to-business marketers. Are the target's customers, by and large, well-known and respected companies? Or are they small, unknown players? Few marketing communication opportunities are as desirable as being able to say your clients are leaders in their respective fields. The ability to "name-drop" is invaluable. In fact, citing the pre-eminent companies on their client list is the rhetorical focus of many firms' advertising.

If a target company has a roster of big-name clients, once acquired, those clients will become yours. Conversely, a company with small-name clients poses a weakness because you will not be able to leverage powerful customers' names for your promotional benefit. This is not a glaring shortcoming. But having an impressive customer list can be an invaluable tool in driving future revenues.

Level of Buyer's Decision Making Authority

It is important to determine who the primary buyer is within the customer organization. This is significant because the higher up that person is, the more influential he or she is. And, the more influential that person is, the greater the potential for the merged company to sell additional services or to gain introductions to other influential managers within the customer company.

Strength exists when individual customer contacts have decision making power. Weakness exists when customer contacts are lower-level functionaries. Chances are that if the target company has had difficulty in growing its relationships because of the buyers' limited authority, there is little reason to believe the merged company will necessarily have greater success in doing so.

Tenure of Customer Accounts

Customer base strengths exist when the buyers have been doing business with the target company for a long period of time. Long-term customer relationships suggest a level of comfort, confidence, and implied commitment that can carry over in the postmerger environment.

However, a company whose accounts tend to have short life spans or are transactional in nature as opposed to relationship-oriented portray a weaker, more tenuous bond. The absence of enduring relationships points up the possibility that those customers will move to other product or service providers—a vulnerability that can be exacerbated when customer relationships are not handled carefully enough in the first stages of postmerger integration.

Level of Internal Sales

Many companies sell their products and services to other units of their own company. Keep this fact in mind when evaluating targets that are subsidiaries being divested. Consequently, it is helpful to determine the percentage of sales sold to these internal customers. A weakness exists when there is a high level of internally generated revenues, since those sales are by no means guaranteed after the transaction is finalized. Spotting a high level of internal sales raises a red flag, where the question to be asked is, "To what extent is the target unable to sell to other companies in the marketplace?" Product or service deficiencies may be the reasons why a company's sales may only be sought by corporate cousins (who, by the way, typically enjoy below-market prices and hence deliver lower profits).

Industry Concentration

The target company's customer base composition in terms of industry category must be analyzed. A company that dominates its industry offers a definite strength, but also an unavoidable weakness. The strength lies in the firm's ability to claim industry leadership and to leverage that role in landing work from other firms operating in the same segment. (The fact that more and more companies insist on using firms with deep experience in their industries underscores the increasing importance of industry expertise.)

The weakness is that the target firm can get pigeonholed. For instance, we know an information systems firm that is dominant in the telecommunications industry. Yet, the company's expertise and the experience base of several of its senior consultants qualifies it to function in other segments. Unfortunately, the market's perception of the firm is that it is exclusively a consultant to telecommunications concerns. Thus far, the firm has been completely unable to shed its one-industry reputation, despite its continuing efforts to penetrate new sectors.

The process of assessing customer base strengths and weaknesses is essential for planning both near- and long-term initiatives. Strengths often point up immediate growth opportunities that should be explored and pursued. Weaknesses may point up more deep-seated problems that must be probed and ultimately mitigated before any growth initiatives are conceived and carried out. On completion of your analysis of the target's customer base, another series of activities should be conducted from the merged-company viewpoint.

COMPARING CUSTOMER INFORMATION: MERGED-COMPANY PERSPECTIVE

It has been emphasized that M&A planning requires adopting a perspective that views the target company not as an organization unto itself, but rather as an eventual element of the combined company. Again, the "overlap-overlay" orientation is particularly appropriate in the context of customer base analysis.

After you have collected quantitative and qualitative information on the target's customers and analyzed that data from the standpoint of inherent strengths and weaknesses, it is necessary to view this information from the merged-company perspective. In essence, you must compare the target's customers directly against yours so as to identify areas of commonality and dissimilarity. Consequently, the next phase of your customer analysis requires assessing four distinct areas:

- Customers served by the target (but not by your company)
- Customers served by your company (but not by the target)
- Customers not served by either your company or the target (key prospects)
- Customers served by both your company and the target

Customers Served by the Target (But Not by Your Company)

These companies represent your new customers. Your task is to review the analytical data you have accumulated on products or services purchased, buying criteria, and profitability levels to determine where new selling opportunities exist for the combined company's new product mix. For example, assume yours is a medical supply firm that acquires a company that also sells medical products—goods that are different from, yet complementary, to yours. A detailed examination of both sets of customers' buying histories must be conducted to unearth opportunities where the merged company can market new or bundled products that are directly related to those which the target has historically sold its customers. This exercise should be conducted, in the near term, with all major accounts and, over time, with smaller customers.

Customers Served by Your Company (But Not by the Target)

The reverse strategy is true in this second scenario: You must conduct a self-assessment of your own customer base (in the same areas of analysis as your target company examination), then identify which of your customers are likely buyers of the target's goods and services. It should be assumed that you have a thorough understanding of what products your customers are currently buying and insights on your customers' existing needs that are *not* being met by your current product offering. Indeed, this exercise may have already been conducted as part of your acquisition strategy development—that is, if attaining a company's product line to supplement your own was a strategic driver of the transaction. If this is not the case, however, you must address your customers' comprehensive needs as basic business strategy.

Customers Not Served by Either Your Company or the Target (Key Prospects)

This segment represents the most important element of the combined company's potential market. Your planning should focus first on the status of each major prospect. Specifically, you must determine which of these potential buyers your company has approached in the past (and the sales status of each), as well as those which the target company has solicited. Conducting this assessment should lead to strategies that can help convert these prospects into actual buyers.

For example, if your company was close to landing one of these prospects, but was unable to because of a particular shortcoming, this deficiency may be eliminated by virtue of what the target company now brings to the table. The reverse may be true. The target may not have been able to land those accounts because of an inability to offer exactly what the prospects needed, but which the merged company can now provide—such as more desirable prices, terms, product features, or delivery schedules.

Customers Served by Both Your Company and the Target

This category is arguably the most important since it points up an opportunity for new-business gains—and losses due to redundancy. New-business gains can be generated as a result of the merged company's potentially powerful new product offerings. Customer losses, however, may result from this fact of life: A large number of companies prefer to dole out different aspects of their accounts to different product or service providers, and may view the corporate combination as a violation of this policy.

Consequently, you must ascertain the degree to which major customer accounts pose great new opportunities or vulnerabilities after the acquisition is finalized. Keep in mind that losses may also result from negative perceptions held by these common customers toward your organization or the firm you acquire.

For example, several years ago a major Wall Street securities brokerage acquired a Midwestern mutual fund company. The latter company's customers were mainly affluent businesspeople and well-to-do farmers from the nation's "breadbasket." These customers obviously could have dealt with a Wall Street firm, but instead preferred to work with one in their own region. The acquiring Wall Street firm failed to acknowledge the negative sentiments the mutual fund's customers held toward New York-based financial services concerns and, after the merger, immediately changed the mutual fund's name to the parent company's moniker. Customer defections resulted and millions of dollars in assets were lost.

Had the Wall Street firm studied the target company's customer base—particularly its demographic and attitudinal composition—it would have realized that an immediate dissolution of the mutual fund's identity would be a strategic miscalculation. Ideally, the name should have been retained or, rather, phased out over time. You must be sensitive to why both your customers and the target's maintain buying relationships.

These are only two reasons existing customers might leave in the wake of the merger. There are a multitude of others, and they have to be anticipated and acted on to lessen the possibility of key customer defections.

INTEGRATING CUSTOMER INFORMATION: STRATEGIES AND APPLICATIONS

Information is objective data, and on its own has little value. It is only when that information is analyzable and actionable that it becomes useful for growth planning purposes. This is the perspective to embrace as you take on the arduous task of melding the acquired company's customer base information with that of your own. The goal is not simply to amass reams of data. The goal is to catalog relevant information that will ultimately be useful in devising and executing growth strategies.

The previous section addressed segmentation from the standpoint of customer relationships: those held by the target company, those held by yours, those held by neither firm, and those which are held by both. The last is arguably the most important segmentation criterion for launching immediate growth initiatives in the wake of the merger.

Ultimately, however, you will want to segment the combined customer base via the five primary variables used in market segmentation exercises, which we discussed earlier when studying the composition of the customer base:

- Socioeconomic
- Demographic
- Geographic
- Behavioral
- Psychographic

Socioeconomic Segmentation

A market may be grouped into segments based on its members' social and economic characteristics. Perhaps more than any other segmentation scheme, socioeconomic classifications (e.g., middle class, upper class) reflect strong similarities in terms of their members' day-to-day behaviors and lifestyles.

Demographic Segmentation

Here, customers are categorized in terms of their age, sex, religion, race, nationality, size of family, and so on. Dividing a market by its demographic makeup is the most popular segmentation strategy because demographic data are relatively easy to measure and obtain (much of the data are available through government censuses of the population). Also, wants of the buyer and product usage patterns are often very similar among members of the same demographic category.

Geographic Segmentation

In this vein, customers are classified by nation, state, region, county, city, or neighborhood. Other geographic variables are population density and climate.

Behavioral Segmentation

This segmentation criterion involves defining customer groups based on how they use a product and/or perceive its benefits. Behavioral categories may include "purchase factors," relating to when people buy a particular product, such as Christmas or Mother's Day; "benefits," or the particular attributes of a product that customers may hold to be important, such as improvement to lifestyle, health, or socioeconomic standing; "usage rates," referring to how frequently customers employ the product (which can range from occasional users to regular users to heavy users); "loyalty," gauging customers' predisposition to trying competitors' products; and "attitudes," referring to customers' emotional feelings toward the product, which can range from enthusiastic and positive to indifferent, negative, or even hostile.

Psychographic Segmentation

The customer base should be divided into groups based on lifestyle, characterized by:

- Members sharing common activities, interests, and opinions
- Personality, relating to customers' commonality in terms of the degree to which they are independent, impulsive, self-confident, thrifty, and prestige-conscious

Understanding the various ways you will ultimately want to segment the merged company's customer base is an important first step in growth planning. It is also imperative to understand the strategic applications of that information when planning the physical consolidation of the combining companies' respective customer databases.

CUSTOMER DATABASES

Today, having a customer database is not a luxury, it is an imperative. If your firm has a state-of-the-art system, your task is to incorporate relevant data from the target's customer records into your system. If your firm does not have a database, but the target company does, the reverse is necessary; you must take your customer data and incorporate it into the acquired firm's system.

INSIDER'S OUTLOOK

We are now moving closer to a world of targeted marketing, as opposed to a world of mass marketing where companies try to be everything to everybody. Being able to understand customers and their needs is key to successful marketing. The company you're examining must have that type of useful information—data which provides insights into elements such as purchasing patterns, seasonality, propensity to purchase other products, etc.

—Mufit Cinali, AT&T

If both firms have a database, obviously two systems are not needed (nor is it advisable to maintain two separate depositories of information). Therefore, you must objectively assess the power and functionality of each system and determine which one should be maintained and which should be dismantled. However, there may be beneficial features found in the weaker system that could be incorporated into the more powerful unit. Your strategy should be to select the best features from both systems.

In any case, an extensive redesign of the final database configuration will most probably be necessary since it is unlikely that the two organizations have compiled the same types of data and that the systems have identical technical characteristics. Moreover, the merged organization may have new database information requirements as dictated by its guiding strategic objectives.

It may be the case that neither of the merging companies has a database. Effecting a corporate combination represents the ideal time to develop one. If creating a merged company database is necessary, this complex and time-consuming project is one of the first activities you must undertake in order to begin launching your initial growth programs.

There are many books on how to construct a customer database, as well as the ways to conduct database marketing. A few words are in order here, however, on designing a database to ensure it has the functionality needed to plan and support strategic growth initiatives. There are seven basic purposes or benefits of a well-designed customer database. Keep these core applications in mind as you spec out your own system's infrastructure:

1. *Compile transaction data.* Above all, a database must track transaction data: purchases and inquiries. In terms of purchases, the database should track specific product or service purchases by customer, the frequency of those buys, and individual purchase amounts. Product-related inquiries should also be monitored in terms of both when they were made and the nature of the query (e.g., on what particular product or service the inquiry was placed).

2. *Attract new customers.* The transaction data compiled should help you identify your best customers—and attract new ones. By studying the characteristics of your best customers, you can construct a profile of them based on one or more of the market segmentation variables cited earlier (e.g., your most frequent buyers are people from a distinct demographic or geographic segment, or from a particular industry group). Ascertaining these characteristics enables you to compile or rent commercially available lists that are comprised of prospects who resemble your best customers.

3. *Support the process of message development.* Database information should aid in your efforts to formulate messages for marketing communications purposes. For instance, customer feedback on specific products can be used to articulate important selling points for future marketing materials. From a direct-marketing standpoint, purchase pattern information can reveal whether or not a given customer is an infrequent user, a moderate user, or a heavy user of your goods and services. Consequently, direct-marketing messages can be tailored to mirror the buyer's standing: Infrequent users would be targeted with marketing messages designed to stimulate repeat product usage; moderate users would receive communications that graciously acknowledge their purchases (and reinforce that behavior); and heavy users would be the targets of specially designed communications that reward their loyalty with discounts or special offers.

4. *Facilitate cross-selling initiatives.* Cross-selling strategies can be devised by matching the characteristics of buyers of one type of product with the characteristics of the buyers of another offering. Consider, for example, that yours is a financial services firm. Your database information may reveal that the general profile of the buyer of a given mutual fund product is a male, aged 45, with an income level exceeding $50,000. In your analysis, you may discover that buyers of a specific type of insurance product—one offered by the acquired company—have the same demographic and socioeconomic characteristics. Therein lies a cross-selling opportunity, which the merged company can attempt to exploit.

5. *Solicit customer feedback regarding specific marketing initiatives.* A database should have fields in which customer feedback on given products or marketing initiatives can be collected and analyzed. For instance, information might be compiled to address buyers' likes and dislikes toward a specific product offering, or to indicate at what point the customer would be ready to purchase the product highlighted (assuming he or she was not ready at the time of the initial solicitation). The collection and analysis of this information would be applicable in subsequent launches of the same or a related marketing initiative, or when designing similar campaigns for different offerings.

6. *Employ data for other management decision making.* A database could be constructed to collect data that has applications beyond the corporate sales and marketing functions. For example, the database may be designed to accumulate information useful to other managers in such areas as corporate development, R&D, customer service, finance, warehousing, and distribution. This is not to say that many non-marketing-related areas should be designed into that database, which will already be a highly complex information system. Yet, marketing data that is tangentially related to other corporate functions can and should be collected and distributed to other managers for benchmarking or competitive comparisons as appropriate.

7. *Generate market research.* Cited several times has been the importance of regularly collecting and disseminating market research to key corporate decision makers. A customer database is an ideal vehicle to amass actionable information on such things as customers' current and changing needs, new product features sought (by buyers of different demographic or psychographic categories), and people's attitudes relative to pricing.

A well-constructed database can also provide important information on product distribution, helping you to gauge the effectiveness of different distribution channels. For instance, by studying the addresses of your buyers, you can determine which channels are generating the most sales—an analysis that can be done based on individual markets, store chains, or individual retail outlets within those chains.

SUMMARY

One of the greatest sources of value a company gains when it merges with or acquires another is that target firm's customer base. In the growth planning process, customers must be evaluated in terms of their physical composition and their historical relationship with the target firm (e.g., their buying patterns). Above all, customers must be viewed from the standpoint of their potential as future buyers of the merged company's product and service offerings.

The target's customer base must be examined from a host of different quantitative and qualitative standpoints. Of particular importance is spotting areas of similarity and dissimilarity between the makeup of the target's buyer base and that of your own company's. Doing so points up areas of opportunity—and areas of vulnerability—which must be addressed in planning both near- and long-term growth strategies.

The process of accumulating data on the target's customer base will generate reams of voluminous information—data that must ultimately be analyzed on its own merits, but also physically melded with your own. This information should be collected with an eye toward how that data will eventually be employed for growth planning purposes. Moreover, the data collection process must be approached from the standpoint of how the information will be formally incorporated into the merged company's computerized customer database.

Chances are an entirely new computer-based system may need to be created to reflect the types and amounts of data that have historically been collected by the combining companies, as well as to support the merged company's specific business development strategies. If you are required to create a new system from scratch, it is necessary to understand the basic functions and benefits of state-of-the-art customer databases before you begin the process of constructing one that will adequately serve the merged company's strategic and tactical purposes.

Marketing due diligence requires assessing each of a target company's key publics, customers being the first and foremost among those groups. Now let's turn inward to look at the other people and groups that figure prominently in a target company's current activities: its employees.

7

Evaluating a Target Company's Employees: A Skills-Based Approach to Personnel Decision Making

Many questions surrounded the $3.5 billion acquisition of Lotus Development Corporation by IBM in June 1995. As discussed earlier, Big Blue made the move in order to acquire Lotus's phenomenally popular Lotus Notes software, which enables users to work collaboratively over computer networks. Yet the explosive interest in the Internet led many industry observers to believe that Notes might ultimately become obsolete when similar capabilities became available on-line. IBM discounted the severity of the threat. But the company did suffer serious doubts about one other critical factor: whether the creator of Lotus Notes, Ray Ozzie, would stay on after IBM took over.

Given his importance to the creation of future versions of Notes, Ozzie was viewed as the single most important asset IBM was acquiring. Without him, Lotus would not be the same company. Without him, Lotus would not be worth $3.5 billion. IBM's strategic goal to grow Lotus's user base from 3.3 to 20 million could never be realized without Ozzie's input and commitment to craft upgraded versions of the software. That is why, on the day the deal closed, IBM chairman Louis V. Gerstner personally hopped aboard a helicopter in Boston and flew to Lotus's headquarters 45 miles away in Westford, Massachusetts. His goal: to personally welcome Ozzie and his product development team to IBM and to secure their continued employment.

Months earlier, Lotus's chairman, Jim P. Manzi, and other senior Lotus executives had left the company in the wake of the IBM takeover announcement. Ozzie, however, was too valuable to lose, and Gerstner personally intervened to make sure that would not happen. Ultimately, Gerstner was successful, and Ozzie became a committed member of the Lotus team in the critical first years following the close of the transaction.

It has become somewhat of a cliché in American business: A company's most valuable asset is its people. It is, in fact, true. Today, more and more companies are being assessed based not only on their physical assets but also on their intellectual property. Intellectual property is not resident in equipment. It is resident in people. Yet, as has been seen in numerous instances, there is a tremendous danger of losing key employees in the wake of a merger or acquisition. The primary reason for this relates to the historical mind-set acquirers have maintained toward personnel: "Who do we cut?" Conversely, the growth orientation to M&A planning requires that acquirers now ask two different questions:

1. Who do we keep?
2. What do we have to do to keep them?

Though "people are a company's most valuable asset" has become a cliché, this statement's veracity does not diminish. Senior managers of acquiring companies must acknowledge the value that people alone bring to a target company—particularly those organizations in the services sector or which develop cutting-edge products derived from the creative brilliance of engineers, designers, and software programmers.

Today, managers widely agree that attracting and retaining key employees is central to a company's current and future success. The tactics involved in doing so take on even greater urgency in merger and acquisition situations. The challenge, however, begins with—but is broader than—devising reward systems to ensure that the best and the brightest stay on board after the deal is closed.

The growth-driven approach to personnel planning requires determining not so much who the people are that should stay, but rather what skill sets are necessary to help the merged company achieve its strategic objectives. You must first determine what you need in the way of critical skills before you can identify the people who can provide them. Sometimes the skills needed, and the people who possess them, are readily apparent. (It was widely known, for example, that Ray Ozzie was the father of Lotus Notes.) Most times, however, you need to probe into the target company to unearth where critical skills lie and pinpoint the people who hold those talents.

This chapter looks at the critical areas of examination in assessing a target company's employee base and in making personnel decisions that enhance the merged firm. A perspective based on analyzing the social and organizational structure of a company is presented. Once that perspective is internalized, the approach to assessing the skill sets necessary to facilitate postmerger integration is detailed to help you realize the strategic drivers of the merger. Most of the critical skills needed reside in the people currently employed by either your company or the target. Therefore, the challenge becomes identifying which people have which skills—and then determining what steps you must take to ensure those employees remain with the merged firm.

Getting on a helicopter to personally secure key people's commitment to stay on is one way of doing so. A host of other more conventional, and less costly, types of retention strategies that managers should employ are detailed herein.

SOCIAL AND ORGANIZATIONAL CONTEXT

The task of evaluating the target company's personnel begins with understanding the social and organizational context in which employees work. With the exception of people working in so-called virtual corporations, employees interact not unlike the way people interact in any social setting. They assume roles. They adhere to certain rules of behavior—social mores unique to the company.

There are different strata that different people belong to based on their titles and levels of power, roles, and responsibilities. In multilocation companies, there are often discrete regional factors that create differences in how people function on a day-to-day basis. In essence, a company is a minisociological milieu that exhibits the same dynamics as any other social context.

It is important to adopt this perspective to gain insight on how employees function within their own company context, which is the first step in determining their possible roles in the merged organization. It is impossible not to discuss issues of corporate culture when addressing the social environment of a given company. Yet, they are touched on only briefly in this chapter, since detailed guidance on understanding culture as a key integration issue is provided in Chapter 10.

Too often, management of the acquiring company has only a cursory understanding of how the target is structured. We have seen acquirers make the fatal mistake of first beginning to gather information on a target's organizational makeup and key management (beyond the senior officers) weeks after the transaction has closed. Valuable time is lost when this process is delayed until that long after the deal has been finalized.

Ideally, management should be able to begin making personnel decisions shortly after closing. Unfortunately, this is usually the point at which acquirers just start to gather data for personnel decision making. Employee uncertainty and anxiety is fostered when management delays making these key personnel decisions.

Conducting personnel research as early as possible in the acquisition candidate evaluation process is one of the most important integration measures you can take. Doing so will put you in a position to promptly make key personnel announcements and, thus, mitigate employees' concerns as you make longer-term staffing decisions.

From a social and organizational perspective, a company should be viewed in three different ways:

1. It should be studied in terms of its physical structure—the subsidiaries, divisions, and departments that comprise the corporate whole.
2. The firm should be assessed from the standpoint of its geographic structure—the cities, states, and countries in which its physical units are located.
3. The organization should be viewed in terms of its management structure—the ways power is distributed throughout the company, as well as the specific roles and responsibilities of the management of various divisions, departments, and corporate functions. (This last viewpoint is the most significant in that the greatest source of transferable skills is concentrated within the managerial ranks of a given company.)

Compiling complete organizational data lets you identify which employees are responsible for which functions, and how lines of reporting—both solid and dotted lines—are established. Detailed later in the chapter is the fact that there is a direct correlation between how power is distributed in a company and how that company is characterized from a cultural standpoint.

In analyzing the target's management structure, you should initially focus on the most senior-level officers and division managers. Your review is a top-down approach. You must first identify the "C-level" functions (i.e., CEO, CFO, COO, CIO, etc.)—starting at the corporate level, then at the major subsidiary level. Next, you must determine the heads of the various corporate functions, including R&D, engineering, purchasing, manufacturing, finance and accounting, credit, marketing, and sales. Some acquirers are even guilty of the major investigative oversight of never looking at middle managers when conducting personnel assessments.

As you accumulate information on the organization from the aforementioned three perspectives you must assemble an organization chart. This, of course, should be obtainable from the target's management. On the occasions when it is not, you must visually chart the physical aspects of the target's organizational composition. This can be based on the information you collect as a starting point for exploring the less tangible characteristics that constitute the firm's social fabric.

ANALYZING THE COMPANY'S "SOCIAL FABRIC"

Gaining an understanding of the physical, geographic, and managerial composition of the target organization is relatively simple compared to the more arduous task of deciphering the company's social context. This critical step entails evaluating the demographic composition of the employee base, as well as other sociological factors—such as the collective mission of the workers, their values, beliefs, and the social mores to which they adhere.

You cannot effectively evaluate individual employees' skills and accomplishments without fully understanding the social context in which they function. Assessing a company's social composition requires examining each of the following variables:

- Demographics
- Geographic factors
- Titles and staff classifications
- Reference groups
- Opinion leaders

For you to better understand how and why these social and organizational forces are pertinent to your examination of a target's employee base, we detail a personal experience.

We have done extensive work with a major national insurance company that grew its human resource advisory firm primarily through acquisition. Several specialized consultancies were brought into the fold over a period of 10 years. In particular, two West Coast-based compensation firms were acquired, as well as a Southeastern company that provided employee communication services. It should be noted that the acquiring firm had existing capabilities in each of these geographic areas, so its acquisition strategy was to strengthen its delivery capabilities in each of the designated practice areas. Our efforts were required to provide integration services for the client's subsequent acquisitions.

It was during the first stages of our work that we quickly discovered that little integration had actually ever occurred. The fact was these units had only marginally been integrated. They existed, years later, as separate and virtually autonomous entities despite management's contention that they had been effectively blended into the broader organization. In actuality, the firms maintained their own preacquisition identities. There was little sharing of organizational resources. There was only nominal cross-selling between units (even though management cited this as a strategic driver of each of these deals). Stated simply, the overall organization's social fabric had become a patchwork quilt.

The company's situation points up an example where severe barriers existed within the social makeup of the organization. There were more social and organizational divisions than you would see in a company that had grown internally, as opposed to externally through acquisitions. Nonetheless, this company's organizational composition highlighted the divergent social characteristics that necessarily exist within any company to some extent and which are often created and magnified by corporate acquisitions.

Each of the aforementioned variables must be examined to understand the social fabric of a company and, thus, assess the employees functioning within it. Using the insurance company client as an example of the differences that exist in a company from a social and organizational perspective, as you explore your target company's employee base with an eye toward appraising existing skills and devising integration approaches, each of these factors should be carefully examined.

Demographics

In a corporate context, demographics relate to workers' age, gender, and level of education. This is a slightly more narrow definition than in consumer marketing, where other demographic variables include such things as religion, race, and nationality—which are irrelevant, and legally unmentionable, in studying corporate social contexts.

Prior to making any acquisitions, there was a veritable cross section of employees in the acquiring firm's HR consulting subsidiary. The senior consultants ranged in age from their late 20s for junior practitioners to mid-40s and mid-50s for the senior-most consultants.

There was generally the same balance of male to female consultants as appeared in competing firms of similar size. From an educational standpoint, all professionals were considered extremely well-educated, with most having advanced degrees (MBAs and PhDs) from top-ranked colleges and universities.

The acquired firms, however, brought new demographics into the mix. For example, the new members of the compensation practice differed significantly in terms of age, where the consultants in each of these organizations tended to be older than the acquiring firm's existing professionals. The communications acquiree, however, brought professionals of a similar age demographic, but those consultants had noticeably less impressive academic and experiential credentials.

Geographic Factors

There are distinct geographic nuances that characterize the workings of companies in different parts of the country. For instance, the West Coast-based firms were much more casual organizations (e.g., every day was a business casual-dress day, as opposed to the acquirer, which had a dress-down day only once a week). These firms also had flexible work schedules that enabled workers to set their hours based on personal needs and situations. Conversely, the acquirer had rigid nine-to-five routines. The acquired firm from the Southeast also exhibited regional nuances. The firm's managers tended to "move slower," in the words of one company insider, and, by and large, took longer to make decisions and launch new initiatives.

While the West Coast firms were casual, the Southeastern organization was even more conservative than the acquirer. For instance, there were no casual-dress days, and workers often complained about management's refusal to embrace flexible hours even after many employees had vigorously lobbied management to adopt them.

Titles and Staff Classifications

In sociology, classes are defined as segments of a population that are separated in terms of economic parameters. In business, classes are categorized by titles and staff classifications. The thing to remember is that titles are used differently in every organization. Consequently, different levels of power and organizational status are ascribed to people at different staff levels.

For instance, in the Southeastern firm, an "account manager" was a relatively low-level person who supported the "engagement team leaders," who serviced major clients. In both of the West Coast firms, an "account manager" was one of the highest designations a consultant could achieve, the position being responsible for high-level, strategic interactions with the firm's most important clients. The title was the same, but the level of status was radically different. Thus, you need to know what titles people hold in order to decipher how the target organization is structured and how power is distributed throughout the firm.

Reference Groups

The groups to which a person belongs influence that individual's behavior, attitudes, and beliefs. In society, so-called reference groups include clubs, religious groups, or any type of social collective (e.g., a country club). In business, reference groups may take the form of departments or divisions within an organization that give people their identity and drive their behavior in day-to-day business activities.

Corporate reference groups exist in nearly all large-scale businesses, particularly those that are made up of different, geographically dispersed subsidiaries. People tend to identify with the group within which they work. For instance, in interviews we conducted with employees of the HR consulting firm, we asked them to describe whom they worked for, and we posed the query in rather open-ended terms. Nearly half of the people first cited the practice area or office location they were assigned to. (For instance, an employee would immediately say, "I work in the 'information technology' practice," or "I work in the Dallas office.")

These interviewees were people who had always worked with the parent company, as opposed to with one of the recently acquired units. This strong identification with a practice area or office location makes it understandable that when members of the acquired firms were asked which firm they worked for (several months after the transactions had closed), the vast majority still cited the acquired companies' names. These employees identified with the reference groups as defined by the companies from which they had come, not those of the acquirer for whom they now worked.

Any large organization is comprised of small reference groups. Your challenge in examining a target company's employee base is to spot what these groups are as a first step in determining how people view their roles in the broader organization. Why is this important? Because the strength of identity employees hold toward these subgroups must ultimately be factored into your integration program. If strong barriers exist between subgroups, it is likely that those barriers may present formidable obstacles to the success of the integration process, whose central goal is forging one corporate culture as opposed to a confederation of unrelated subcultures.

INSIDER'S OUTLOOK

Every time I've worked on an acquisition, employees have proven to be one of the most valuable assets we stood to gain. Time and again, the decision to buy a company was based on the fact that it has this particular expertise. What it usually boils down to is that the major element of that expertise resides in the people. We're in a business where the scarcest resource is intellectual capital. And it's the passion of the people and the brains of the people that represent this intellectual capital. People are what really make the difference.

—Carolyn Chin, IBM

Opinion Leaders

Reference groups tend to breed opinion leaders. These are the people to whom members of the reference group turn for guidance and who help shape members' attitudes and beliefs. In the consultancies acquired by our client, opinion leaders were not necessarily the heads of those organizations. Typically, they were senior managers who led individual units and divisions.

When their firms were being acquired, for example, the opinion leaders were turned to for emotional support as word of potential layoffs sparked widespread anxiety among the rank and file. Consequently, just as reference groups within the target must be identified, so too must the opinion leaders who head or influence the people within them. Opinion leaders can play either a constructive or a destructive role in the integration process, which is addressed later in this chapter.

The key guidance in analyzing a company's social context relates to the fact that organizational variables cause workers within the same company to function slightly differently. Even when there is a strong sense of corporate commonality, there will often be perceptible divisions between employees based on their specific standing within the company.

Moreover, there will always be corporate reference groups that must be identified and assessed as determinants of that employee behavior at different levels of the company. Your investigative task is to identify these collectives, define their key attributes, and determine whether to preserve or dismantle them as the integration process moves forward.

ASSESSING PERSONNEL NEEDS: STRATEGIC PERSPECTIVE

Effectively assessing a target's employee base requires first determining the skills needed to further the merged organization's growth objectives. A transformed organization requires transforming people: There will be new roles, new responsibilities, and new positions needed to execute growth plans. Clearly, there is no greater form of organizational change—or a greater need for organizational realignment—than in a major merger or acquisition.

The determination must be made as to what skills and competencies will be needed to support the merged company's strategies. It is necessary to do so before you begin trying to identify what skills are possessed by workers in the target firm—as well as those of your own—in the process of deciding on who will fill what roles.

Most times the acquiring firm's management will have a postmerger organization chart in mind before beginning the employee assessment process. As was previously suggested, devising an organization chart is a valuable starting point for making decisions on departmental needs and individual job functions, and defining levels of responsibility and power to be distributed among managers in the organization. The danger, however, is beginning the personnel assessment process with a rigid organizational paradigm in mind, in which the mind-set is, "Who do we have to fit into this structure?" On the contrary, it is advisable not to have an organizational structure carved in stone, but rather to adopt a flexible approach to ascertaining departmental configurations. To truly build the most effective company, the mind-set should rightfully be, "Let's determine what skills we need and how those skills should be best deployed organizationally." This approach allows the organization chart to create itself based on strategic staffing requirements.

Ensuring that people are assigned the right roles in the new firm's operational infrastructure requires taking a disciplined approach to determining how and where they will fit in. Trying to autocratically slice them into a preconceived organizational alignment may force them to flee immediately prior to or just after consummation of the transaction. This represents the loss of critical human assets that are the key ingredient to the ultimate success of the transaction.

There are three aspects of employee skills that must be evaluated when identifying the talents resident in the company:

1. Strategic skills are needed to specifically support the new organization's growth plans and objectives.
2. General business and managerial skills are the basic categories of personnel evaluation used in grading individuals' performance, but must be reviewed somewhat differently in M&A personnel planning.
3. Change adaptation skills, which relate to a person's ability to function in the volatile context that characterizes the integration process, comprise a skill set that is particularly important when selecting the managers to play prominent roles in the integration effort. This evaluation process starts by examining the most important capabilities you need—those of the skills that will help you execute your strategic growth initiatives.

Strategic Skills

Chapter 2 discussed the drivers that provide the impetus for most strategic mergers and acquisitions. Essentially, companies combine with other firms to acquire:

- Technology
- Management
- Complementary products
- New markets or distribution channels
- Production facilities
- Diversification

Each of these drivers points up specific skills that are required by both managers and, to a lesser degree, rank-and-file employees in order to realize the strategic synergies sought. By examining each driver with a skills-based focus, you can learn how each one will influence personnel evaluations and decision making.

Acquiring technology. Companies acquire technologies that are either physical (e.g., advanced manufacturing systems) or intangible (e.g., intellectual property that creates physical technologies). In both cases, your staffing requirements will immediately dictate retaining people who can understand, produce, and market that technology. IBM's acquisition of Lotus Notes was to acquire a technology product. Given the complex nature of the product vis-à-vis developing continually upgraded versions, it was crucial to retain the skills resident within Lotus—from Ray Ozzie, the developer, all the way down to his key development team members—to ensure continued success in marketing the technology offering.

Acquiring management. Sometimes companies acquire others to gain managerial expertise that is needed to move the acquiring company forward. That is, newly attained managers may complement or supplement the acquirer's existing skills or update their managerial capabilities to enter new businesses or to keep pace with rapidly changing markets. When only a select few managers are sought, it makes no sense to acquire their entire company when you can simply hire them away.

Sometimes, however, the company's capabilities and its management team are inextricably linked, and an acquisition is the only way to procure the managerial skills needed. Conceivably, IBM could have hired only Ray Ozzie, the driving force behind Lotus Notes. But he alone could not realize IBM's vision. Ozzie's entire management infrastructure was needed to help IBM achieve its ambitious sales goals for Notes.

Acquiring complementary products. Here again, the IBM-Lotus combination is an apt example. Notes was indeed complementary to IBM's network technology product and service offerings, as was Lotus's suite of office software. From a staffing standpoint, acquiring these products also required retaining the entire team of Lotus workshare and spreadsheet professionals—the software developers, product managers, customer-service representatives, and technical support personnel who collectively bring the products to market and who work with customers to provide the assistance necessary to augment the overall product offering.

Penetrating new markets or distribution channels. Companies engage in M&A often to tap into new markets or channels for their existing products. In both cases, specific expertise is needed. For instance, if the merger is designed to provide an entrée into a given geographic territory, you will need people with strong contacts and an intimate familiarity of that locale's regional nuances and the unique characteristics of its buyer base. Another example: Say you are acquiring an investment firm to gain a brokerage distribution network for your line of financial investment products. You will need people familiar with how the target's customers think and act in order to craft impactive sales and marketing strategies for the new, expanded offerings.

Acquiring production facilities. Acquisitions are often made to secure larger or more sophisticated facilities for new and existing products. From a purely logistical standpoint, personnel requirements dictate having operations people on staff who are familiar with the workings and maintenance of those facilities. Therefore, if the goal of the acquisition is to attain production facilities that update or expand your current capacity, you will need the people who can operate those installations and devise ways to effect, where possible, economies of scale and scope.

Acquiring for diversification. By definition, "diversification" means adopting that which gives variety. In business, it means getting into entirely new businesses or product areas, the goal often being to avoid having all your resources in one area and, thus, to help keep your business from being vulnerable to dramatic shifts in market conditions.

If diversification denotes difference, it is imperative that, in merger situations, you keep the company's people in place to manage the intricate workings of a business that is radically different from your own. For example, if yours is an electric utility holding company that is diversifying into energy consulting, you will most certainly need to retain the core group of managers in the acquired company to help you learn to navigate safely through those uncharted waters.

General Business and Managerial Skills

Beyond the particular skills needed to advance your organization's strategic initiatives, there are certain general competencies that your managers need to hold. Yet, even these conventional skills take on a new dimension in light of the inherent challenges of mergers and acquisitions, not to mention the merged company's specific market characteristics.

Consider, for example, the energy utility industry. As discussed earlier, specific conditions are driving massive alterations to the energy industry landscape and spawning vibrant M&A activity: deregulation and the resultant surge in competition, industry convergence, and cross-border alliances. Keep these and other types of market changes in mind when you view the following areas of competence, which represent the basic skill categories on which employees in the merged company will be evaluated when making staffing decisions:

- Technical
- Interpersonal communication
- Customer service/relationship management

- Supervisory and project management
- Business management
- Leadership

Technical skills. The technical area of competence relates to having the core talents appropriate to a position's basic responsibilities. For instance, an engineer must have strong quantitative skills, whereas an internal communications specialist must possess a commensurate degree of editorial and people skills.

In organizational realignments wrought by mergers and acquisitions, technical skills may need to be redefined in light of the specific responsibilities of positions in the merged company. Using the energy industry example, technical skills for an engineering group manager may require electrical engineering expertise—if the utility is an electric utility. But what if that utility merges with a gas company?

The ideal manager must now have a broadened technical skill base to perform in a supervisory capacity. That is, an entirely new set of technical capabilities may now be required in order to fulfill the merged company's managerial requirements.

Interpersonal communication skills. In M&A situations, interpersonal communication skills become increasingly important not only to the performance of one's job, but also for supporting the integration process. Companies meld when they each gain an understanding of each other's values, histories, and ways of doing business. That knowledge is imparted through spoken and written communications.

For example, electric utility professionals speak one "language," while gas utility professionals speak another. Getting the two camps to work together to forge a powerful energy services company requires that the new coworkers have the ability to learn and understand each other's social, organizational, and technical vernaculars.

Customer service/relationship management skills. With competition sweeping the telecommunications and energy industries, both are becoming more customer-oriented. No longer do utility company employees function in a corporate vacuum with no interaction with customers. More and more workers at different levels of the organization are and will be interacting with customers and prospects.

Consequently, workers must cultivate a service orientation, gain knowledge of customer needs and wants, and develop an awareness of how the organization will strive to address its customer requirements. Thus, skills that were historically insignificant now take on tremendous importance. Expanded customer service roles in the energy industry context are an ideal case in point.

Supervisory and project management skills. Skills in this category tie to employees' ability to assemble and coordinate teams, and to assume the task of understanding what motivates workers in order to maximize their commitment and productivity. It is incumbent on the people being tapped for supervisory roles that they have these core managerial skills, coupled with the foregoing attributes of technical and communicative expertise.

In changing industries such as the utility sector, project management takes on a new dimension as energy and telecommunications converge: Department heads must understand how management roles change when the fundamental orientation of their business is being radically altered. Leaders must learn project management for new types of initiatives being handled by combined teams of employees from once-disparate organizations. In essence, there are new games with new rules and new players. Being the captain of these teams requires even greater project management acumen than in non-M&A situations.

Business management skills. This skills category relates to such capabilities as financial and cost management, administrative management, and resource management. Department heads, more so than rank-and-file employees, must have a command of basic business management concepts and practices. This is significant since group managers may be required to gain a familiarity with how the acquired firm historically coordinated its business management processes.

General business management skills take on even more criticality in mergers involving companies in converging industry segments, such as electric and gas utilities and telephone and cable. In such cases, personnel must learn the managerial processes of businesses that, historically, offered unrelated products with different cost drivers and different administrative and resource requirements.

Leadership. An organization's leaders must embody each of the aforementioned skills competencies. Yet, leadership in and of itself is widely viewed as a capability that is innate, not taught. It is often thought that a person who can lead in one environment generally is able to lead in another environment. This is not necessarily the case in merger situations, where the leadership styles that worked in one firm may be anathema to the styles that will work in the merged company milieu.

In general, leaders must contribute to the development of the firm's intellectual capital, support the development of people via monitoring and providing feedback on workers' performance and contributions, and participate in efforts that raise their firm's market visibility. Specifically, leaders must be able to do all of those things—but in ways that are consistent with the character and culture of the merged firm. In many cases, it will take time to identify which people will make the best leaders since only over time will the combined company's character begin to emerge.

Selecting leaders is central to facilitating the integration process. Leadership, however, takes on different defining characteristics in merger situations. It is helpful to be aware of some of the "softer," yet more critical, skills that should necessarily be held by the managers who will play central roles in your integration program.

Change Adaptation Skills

Ascertaining technical job requirements and descriptions is a rather straightforward exercise. You identify what a given position's major duties are, the authority to be assigned to that spot, and the relationship between that position and other functions and departments within the company. Typical job descriptions indicate what the person should know to perform the job (from the standpoint of technical, professional, and managerial knowledge); what the person will actually be expected to do; what educational and professional background the staff member should have; and what that person can expect in terms of the position's compensation and benefits and advancement potential. That is the easy part. A more difficult challenge lies in identifying the people who, from a personality standpoint, have what it takes to help lead in the merged company environment, particularly during the trying first stages of the integration process.

Careful consideration must be given to the people who will be assigned to integration transition committees and be tapped for other important roles. Certain character traits have been shown to be the most important for surviving, and thriving, in merger situations. Consequently, you must, as best you can, gauge an individual's possession of the following qualities and the ability of that person to inspire these traits in others:

- Patience
- Ability to accept change
- Coworker relationship skills
- Willingness to learn
- Facilitation
- Teamwork

INSIDER'S OUTLOOK

The people factor is key, because in so many acquired companies the entrepreneurs control the marketplace. They know the customer. They know the field supervisor. If you bring in a guy that has not lived in the marketplace, he doesn't really know it. He's got to start all over again. It's going to take him years to acquire the knowledge that that manager or that owner has accumulated for years. That's why I say the key is the people.

—CEO of Fortune 1000 industrial management company

Patience. In virtually all mergers and acquisitions, few integration steps ever go precisely according to plan. There are always unforeseen snafus and delays. Senior managers serving as team leaders and committee heads must exhibit saintly patience. They must understand that, as organizational decisions are addressed and finalized, even the best-laid timetables are rarely perfectly met.

Ability to accept change. Integration is, in itself, the ultimate corporate change initiative. People and processes change. Compensation and benefit programs change. Office dwellers become cubicle dwellers. Some shifts are major; some are minor. Yet change is inevitable. Change is a defining characteristic of M&A situations and it necessitates assessing people's individual orientation and ability to accept that change. The personality trait of flexibility is of paramount importance for managers charged with supporting integration initiatives.

Coworker relationship skills. All employees must be able to get along with their coworkers. But this is especially crucial in M&A contexts, where managers must help people learn how to interact with new coworkers who, in the past, might have been hated rivals from competitor companies and who possess markedly different attitudes and beliefs. Getting along with new coworkers means more than just getting to know their names and being able to converse politely around the coffee machine. It means being able to understand, and accept, their different corporate mind-sets and the ways they have historically done business.

Willingness to learn. Embracing new modes of day-to-day operations requires an ability and desire to learn. This trait is similar to the flexibility needed to adapt to organizational change. Similarly, the issue is not one of cognitive capacity; rather it is one of emotional volition. Inherent in this trait is a commitment to the process of understanding new practices and processes through formal training programs, as well as through informal interactions with coworkers.

Facilitation. For senior managers, the skill of being a leader is becoming less important than that of being a facilitator. In the traditional sense, a leader is a person who wields power and issues directives to lower-level employees who, without question, carry out those instructions. A facilitator, however, is someone who, rather than issuing intractable directives, helps individuals devise their own solutions and cultivate their own vision while coordinating the efforts of the group. Increasingly, businesses are placing people with facilitation skills into key positions. Leaders are most certainly needed at the highest rungs on the corporate ladder. Facilitators, however, may be more valuable than pure leaders for positions related to implementing integration initiatives.

Teamwork. The merged company's integration coordinators must be the consummate team players—people who, by nature, are inclined to pull together to achieve their organization's goals. In mergers and acquisitions, employees are often asked to switch teams. You need people who are team players wherever they go, regardless of the color of their corporate jersey. It is one thing to be a great team player when you are leading your longtime squad to multiple winning seasons. The ultimate team player is the person who leaves the comfort of his or her past position, moves to another team, and becomes a committed member of that squad—so much so, that the new member helps them win a championship of their own.

How do you identify, assess, and measure these desirable traits? There are a number of systems available for use in gauging relevant personality characteristics. One such system is the Career Architect®, which is a multipurpose tool for assessing, planning, and managing employees' development. This system addresses more than 60 "competencies" that were established based on various longitudinal studies of job performance and which involved thousands of workers in a wide range of organizational settings. Numerous research studies over a period of decades have validated the fact that these competencies are directly related to successful job performance. Tools such as this can be quite valuable in identifying the people with the technical and change-adaptation skills needed to move the integration process forward, as well as to ultimately adopt key managerial positions in the merged organization.

Assessing a target company's employees involves evaluating workers based on their functional skills, as well as on personality traits needed to function in what, by all accounts, is a dynamic and volatile environment. However, it is important to be realistic. Nobody is perfect. People are both good and bad. Rarely will you find an individual who exhibits all the technical skills *and* the personality traits discussed. People will invariably have to be assigned roles regardless of whether they demonstrate each and every desirable technical and emotional characteristic. Your goal is to try to find and place people with as many of these sought-after skills as possible.

Preliminary personnel investigations should take place in the initial phases of target company examinations, and in the Appendix you will find research techniques you can employ to unearth information on key employees. However, it is only after the due diligence process has commenced that you typically gain full access to the data that will enable you to conduct an in-depth personnel appraisal.

Nonetheless, all employee investigations must be undertaken with a perspective focused on your current organizational needs and your long-term strategic requirements. Among the most pressing organizational imperatives is ensuring that key people stay with the merged company. So, as the first phase of your planning identifies who those people are, the next phase of work involves making sure they remain in the fold.

EMPLOYEE RETENTION STRATEGIES

Most likely there will be people in your current staff or the acquired firm who can fill the main managerial roles in the new organization, as opposed to having to go outside to recruit new talent. The challenge to management, therefore, is one not of attracting new talent, but rather of keeping the talent you already have.

Many times, management of the merged company makes staffing decisions prematurely without systematically determining who will fill what roles, what departments or corporate functions will be kept in place or dismantled, and the staffing complements for those various areas. Too often, management does not engage in the kind of exhaustive personnel-related methodology that has been described. As a consequence, valuable people—those who would likely make a major contribution to the merged firm or who are central to the integration process—are lost because of management's tendency to make decisions subjectively and without the requisite level of forethought. Here is a striking case in point.

In the acquisition of a major pharmaceutical company by another, management's first inclination was to begin cutting overhead positions. Among the people who were asked to leave in the days following the deal's closing was a senior-level manager in the acquired firm's accounting department. The acquirer already had an accounting department and saw the target's group as a duplicative area that could immediately be scrapped to lessen its overhead. A termination date was provided to the accountant and a separation plan was devised in which he was given one month to stay with the firm while he looked for a new position; if at the end of that period he had not found a new spot, the acquirer would pay him three months' severance allowance. Understandably, he immediately began looking for new work.

Soon after, management began looking at the acquired firm's various organizational processes, including its accounting systems. Management realized that the target had a radically different accounting setup, and that the voluminous data housed within it would have to be incorporated into its own systems—a process that was expected to take two or three months.

The fact was, however, that the target's system was so complex that only people who had actually used it would be able to explain its intricate workings. Management suddenly realized that accountant was needed, and reapproached him with a severance package carrying different terms: He could stay on for three months (instead of one) to aid in the transition process. Despite the animus he felt toward the acquirer for having fired him, the accountant decided to sign on for the new terms, while continuing to actively seek new employment.

The accountant was instructed to serve alongside the acquirer's accounting people to educate them on the nature and functions of the system and to facilitate melding the vastly dissimilar processes. But the stark incompatibility of the systems made management realize that the process was going to take much longer than anybody had expected. The accountant's skills and knowledge grew increasingly more valuable. So what did management do? It rescinded his termination. Management admitted the error of making a hasty decision and asked the accountant to accept a full-time position. The accountant was amazed at the new bosses' ineptitude and general insensitivity to playing him like a yo-yo. The father of two—with a healthy mortgage to boot—the accountant said he would accept the offer, but he vigorously kept job hunting.

Two weeks later, an exciting job opportunity arose and the accountant jumped at it, leaving management with no one to effect the critical bridge between the divergent accounting systems. "I'd never work for people like that after the way they treated me," the accountant said later. "They showed not only blatant insensitivity, but also a total lack of managerial acumen. I could never work with those guys as a full-time staffer."

In the final analysis, management looked foolish—not only to the departed accountant, but also to many others in the acquired firm who were staying on board.

This happens all too frequently. Management acts quickly on personnel decisions without evaluating its process-related integration requirements or identifying the skills needed to specifically address them. As a result, management loses valuable employees who could have played a critical role in moving the merged company forward.

The fact is, there will always be key people in the target organization whom you want and need to keep. The challenge is to first identify who they are, then devise ways to make sure they stay on as enthusiastic, committed employees.

Provide Monetary and Emotional Incentives

Employee retention strategies in the wake of a merger are not unlike compensation and benefit program provisions. Essentially, there are two types of rewards that can be offered to retain key employees: monetary rewards and those that satisfy people's emotions. As the saying goes, "Money talks," and dollars are the ultimate motivators. Yet, a combination of quantifiable, remunerative rewards coupled with those that appeal to people's egos represent a compelling package that will keep favored employees in the fold.

Monetary rewards. There are several basic types of monetary rewards, starting with base salary. Employees can be given immediate salary increases, or a nominal raise can be offered with the promise of additional pay hikes in the ensuing months. Bonuses are another form of monetary compensation, which may be provided as an initial up-front payment or stay-on bonus, or can be added to the employee's overall compensation package.

To a person who has never received one, a bonus is a valuable supplement to one's base pay. For those who already receive bonuses, increasing the amount will provide the necessary incentive. Ideally, bonuses should be structured as part of a broader "pay for performance" compensation scheme, where higher amounts will be rendered if the employee reaches or exceeds certain performance goals. Stock options represent another, increasingly common form of compensation, and these too can be awarded in quantities based on predetermined performance objectives.

Emotional rewards. There are several ways to reward people with qualitative, rather than quantitative, benefits. For example, employees may be given a more impressive title (with or without an increase in the scope of that person's responsibilities). Another is to reward them with a choice of office location (in multilocation companies) or to allow flexible working hours via part- or full-time telecommuting. Naming selected employees to important new committees or transition teams may also establish their sense of belonging in the new order and engender loyalty and commitment.

Keep in mind that retention strategies are necessary for employees of both the target firm and the acquiring organization. Many managers think that the only people who need assurances and special treatment are the angst-ridden employees of the acquired company. Not true. The fact is, there is often a tremendous level of anxiety exhibited by workers of your own organization—people who may feel that star players from the acquired firm will swoop in and steal their jobs.

Recall our earlier example of the consulting company that acquired several smaller firms. One of the acquired compensation firms was populated by extremely talented, nationally known consultants. The practice director from the acquiring organization privately expressed his fears to coworkers about his role in the merged organization. Would he lose his position to a newcomer? The plans were, in fact, to keep this person as the national director of the compensation practice.

Unfortunately, management never communicated this to him. This person got so nervous at the prospect of losing his leadership role that he began seeking other employment opportunities. In haste, he left to take a position with a lesser-known organization. He subsequently found out that management had no plans to unseat him. By then, it was too late, since he had signed a contract with a new firm. Management was sorry to have lost him. In retrospect, the CEO realized that someone should have assured the practice director that his position was not in jeopardy.

SUMMARY

Companies acquire other companies to secure new skills and capabilities, which reside in people. Evaluating a target company's employee base requires focusing on the skills held by key employees that need to be harnessed to ensure the ultimate success of the merger. Understanding the company's social and organizational context is necessary to fully appreciate individuals' roles, responsibilities, skills, and accomplishments.

In M&A planning, you must evaluate people not only on their skills but also on their relevant personality traits. These are the attributes that transcend the tangible measures of people's education levels, professional experience, and accomplishments and that point up a person's (especially a key manager's) ability to function amidst the organizational upheaval that typically results during the long and arduous integration process.

Personnel decisions should be based on both skill levels and an enthusiastic commitment to contribute to the merged company. If employees of the target firm demonstrate those attributes more so than their counterparts in the acquiring organization, it is the former, not the latter, who should occupy key positions. *Ideally, there should be no guarantees to workers from either side of the fence.* Your goal should be to put the best people in the jobs that will help move the merged organization forward.

You must begin the process of evaluating a target company's employees by identifying the physical composition of the firm as well as the main social and organizational variables that underlie its structural makeup. A main part of this exercise is pinpointing groups within the target company and the people who function within them as leaders and influencers. Thus, you must take a two-pronged approach to assessing the target's employee base: a social and organizational assessment to identify who those people are and then a detailed assessment of the strategic, technical, and integration-related skills needed in the merged company environment.

Time again for a reality check. You may not always have the time to conduct the type of exhaustive personnel analyses outlined in this chapter. There may be other more pressing issues that need to be addressed and which will delay the employee assessment process. Unfortunately, it is during the period right before and after closing that people in both the merging firms will suffer pangs of anxiety that may prompt them to jump ship. The challenge is to "buy time" until you can adequately size up your personnel requirements and decide which people will best fulfill them.

This is why at least a preliminary assessment of the target's key personnel is essential. You may not have the time to fully explore and analyze the physical, geographical, and managerial structure of the company. Nor will you necessarily have time to evaluate all of the key social and organizational variables. Yet some level of personnel evaluation must be conducted before or immediately after the deal has closed in order to preserve your acquired human resources.

The research techniques detailed in the Appendix should be employed to gather the high-level personnel data you require. Arming yourself with information on the key players will help you determine those with whom you need to communicate immediately. Doing so can help you gain valuable time in retaining the personnel whom you will ultimately want to stay on board. Consider this example.

A senior manager of a major systems integration firm was one of many long-time employees who considered leaving after the acquisition of that organization had been announced. The acquirer's management realized that it would be several weeks before it could make its final personnel decisions. But management knew that it might be too long a waiting period to keep people like this manager from moving on. Fortunately, the CEO and his acquisition team had scouted out who the target's key players were. The day after the deal was announced, the CEO personally called the manager to say he was aware of his standing in the firm and of his admirable past contributions.

The CEO encouraged the manager to be patient although the acquirer was weeks away from making decisions on roles and responsibilities until various issues were sorted out. The manager waited, appreciating the candor and recognition exhibited by the CEO. Ultimately, there was an important new role carved out for the manager, which he eagerly accepted. "That was a classy thing for him to do," the manager later said about the CEO's phone call. "He wasn't guaranteeing anything to me, but he showed that he knew who I was and recognized my accomplishments. That made me say to myself, 'Let me stick around and see what happens.' Had he not made that call, I might well have been out of there the next week."

Whether it is a phone call or a specially chartered helicopter trip, promptly communicating with key personnel from the target company is necessary to keep them in place—for the long haul or at least long enough for you to determine whether there are viable roles for them in the merged organization.

8

Analyzing the Target Company's Management Functions and Processes

After the M&A transaction is closed, the merged firm's organizational structure should ideally be finalized. Taking the stance of "waiting for the dust to settle" before making decisions relative to departmental structure and composition is not advisable. The dust does not settle. In time, people just become used to it and, inevitably, if you have not taken a proactive stance, you will be forced to mop up a potentially messy situation.

By analyzing the target company's management functions and each one's attendant processes from a growth-oriented perspective—versus a cost-savings orientation—you will be able to develop an organized plan for putting into place the managers and mechanisms needed to advance the long-term strategic drivers of the transaction. More immediately, a broad-based review of the target's managerial infrastructure is needed to determine which of its organizational processes should be absorbed, replaced, or preserved in the postmerger environment.

This chapter focuses on a company's core management functions, their components, and how they should be analyzed to identify sources of value. Studying these managerial units will enable you to assess each area within the target and compare them to those resident within your own. The ultimate goal: planning an effective integration program in order to support your underlying acquisition strategy.

When looking at the managerial functions and processes found in most organizations, you must start with the function most directly aligned with strategic mergers and acquisitions and with growth planning in the M&A context.

ANALYZING THE MARKETING AND SALES FUNCTIONS

The corporate function most closely related to growth planning, and the one that merits your initial review, is that of sales and marketing.

At the outset, it is necessary to determine what specific functional areas comprise the target's marketing department and how those functions are grouped to comprise the overall marketing organization. Ultimately, you must determine how the marketing organization interacts with other managerial functions within the target company. There will always be an element of conflict between marketing and other managerial departments. Your task is to determine how much conflict there is and, more importantly, the level of actual cooperation that exists between these disparate yet interrelated areas.

In general, the more closely aligned and interdependent a company's functional areas are from a product development and marketing standpoint, the greater the company's level of customer orientation. As stated, a key investigative area of marketing due diligence involves determining the extent to which the target company truly embraces a customer or marketing orientation.

First, however, it is necessary to understand the specific areas within marketing. This will help you to assess what skills are resident in the target company and which should be retained in the merged firm to support the combined company's strategic objectives.

Functional Areas of Marketing

Different functions carry different names in different companies. However, the following are basic functions that are resident in a contemporary marketing department:

- Marketing vice president or director
- Marketing manager
- Product/brand manager
- Marketing research manager
- Advertising manager
- Promotions manager
- Public relations manager
- Sales manager
- Sales administration manager
- New products manager
- Distribution manager
- Customer relations manager
- Communications/editorial services manager
- Government relations/public affairs manager
- Telemarketing manager

Marketing vice president or director. The person who heads the overall marketing effort at the company, the marketing director serves at the behest of the firm's CEO and is responsible for providing direction for the marketing function and for rendering counsel on a wide range of marketing and sales issues to various groups within the company. Each of the following job positions, or functional specialists, typically report to the marketing director.

Marketing manager. Responsible for working with the marketing director to devise marketing plans for the company, the marketing manager also coordinates such areas as marketing plan implementation, hiring other functional specialists, and monitoring marketplace developments to provide input for new product development and to forge marketing communication strategies.

Product/brand manager. The product or brand manager is responsible for a particular product or service offered by the company. Usually found in large organizations that market multiple offerings, this manager coordinates all aspects of the marketing mix relative to the specific product or service under his or her management. This includes pricing strategies, promotional initiatives, and selecting and managing distribution channels.

Marketing research manager. Responsible for collecting, analyzing, and disseminating marketing data for use in managerial decision making, the marketing research manager coordinates data collection using in-house resources and/or retained outside professionals to conduct primary and secondary research. This manager may also be responsible for managing the company's technology-based marketing information systems, including its customer database.

Advertising manager. The ad manager is responsible for coordinating all aspects of the company's advertising activities, including creative (copy writing and art direction), media planning and buying, production, and traffic. This includes devising advertising strategy for all types of advertising undertaken by the company (e.g., direct-mail, print, and broadcast media advertising), and for collateral materials (e.g., sales literature). The ad manager also serves as liaison between the company and its outside advertising agencies.

Promotions manager. This manager is responsible for developing and implementing sales promotion programs, including the creation of various tools and techniques such as coupons, samples, premiums, rebate programs, contests and sweepstakes, point-of-purchase displays, and dealer incentives.

Public relations manager. Responsible for devising the company's media relations and publicity strategies, the PR manager secures news coverage of the company and its products and develops other communication programs to present a favorable image of the organization to its external publics. Included in the PR manager's responsibilities is overseeing the work of retained PR agencies. In large consumer product companies, there are PR managers responsible for publicizing individual products or brands.

Sales manager. The sales manager is responsible for overseeing the organization's personal selling function and coordinates either all or part of the company's sales efforts. That is, the manager may be responsible for national sales activities or those for a particular region or territory. In general, the manager plans the company's sales objectives and devises tactics to achieve them. In addition, he or she organizes and directs the activities of the company's sales force, monitors external developments and market trends to develop sales programs, and enacts controls to gauge the company's overall sales performance in relation to its stated new revenue objectives.

Sales administration manager. Responsible for tracking, analyzing, and issuing data relative to sales activities, this manager is the central point for receiving information from the sales force on their day-to-day selling efforts—collecting data on such variables as the number of prospects identified, in-person meetings held, and business closed. Typically, this person develops regular progress reports for review by the sales manager and/or the marketing director. In technologically sophisticated companies, sales administration managers compile and input data in computerized tracking systems and customer databases.

New products manager. This manager is responsible for working directly with the R&D department to devise new goods and services, while helping to manage their market introduction. The new products manager monitors changing market conditions that drive customers' changing wants and needs. He or she then helps develop and test new product concepts with consumers prior to the actual research and development of those offerings.

Distribution manager. Responsible for devising strategies for delivering the company's finished goods to consumers, this manager makes decisions relative to which channels of distribution to employ and the number of outlets through which a given product will be sold. In general, the distribution manager oversees the overall process of ensuring that the company's goods are available and accessible to its buyers.

Customer relations manager. The customer relations manager is responsible for ensuring that customers' needs are met and that customer complaints are handled promptly and effectively. The manager coordinates all services the company provides to buyers after the product is sold, including product repairs, support, and general product information. This manager devises systems and procedures to maintain goodwill between the company and its buyers by answering questions, solving problems, and responding to customer requests.

Communications/editorial services manager. This manager is responsible for writing and editing communications materials directed at the company's various publics. Communications managers may coordinate internal communications, such as those disseminated through corporate newsletters and house organs. These managers may also be involved in crafting communications aimed at key external publics—customers, investors, and the community at large. With the advent of the Internet, the role of the communications manager has been expanded to include management of the corporate Web site. In addition, as use of the Internet has grown, specific departments solely responsible for electronic media have been developed.

Government relations/public affairs manager. Responsible for communication and other types of activities designed to help the company maintain a positive relationship with government, special-interest, and community groups, these managers also may get involved in monitoring governmental and legislative developments and supporting the company's lobbying efforts.

Telemarketing manager. The telemarketing manager oversees the various ways the target company communicates with its customers and prospects via the telephone. This manager may coordinate inbound and/or outbound telemarketing. With inbound telemarketing, customers dial toll-free numbers (e.g., 800 numbers) or minimum-toll numbers (e.g., 900 numbers) to order products or make inquiries. Outbound telemarketing is the proactive technique of contacting consumers to qualify their buying needs and sell them products or services. The telemarketing manager may also supervise the activities of outside telemarketing firms, which work on either a retainer or a project basis.

Types of Marketing Organizations

Once you have determined what marketing specialists the target company has, you must evaluate how they are deployed organizationally.

There are many different ways a company can organize its marketing and sales function, but there are three general types of structural paradigms. Typically, the chosen organizational structure is derived from the scope of the company's product or service line and the geographic breadth of its target markets. Following is a brief description of each type of marketing organization:

- Functional
- Product management
- Geographic

Functional. In the functional marketing organization, each of the aforementioned marketing specialists handles activities in his or her area of expertise and reports to the VP or director of marketing. The benefit of a functional organization is that each manager is an expert in his or her assigned area of responsibility, and it is easy for the marketing vice president to monitor and administer their activities. The drawback is that some products or markets are inadequately covered since no one functional specialist has responsibility for them—that is, the specialists support all products and markets, and there may be uneven attention paid to one or more of them.

Product management. The product management organization is similar to the functional organization. But in addition to having specialists in different marketing areas, there are managers assigned to specific products—thus eliminating the danger of inadequate attention paid to key products, as is often the case in a pure functional paradigm. In a product management organization, there are managers assigned to oversee all aspects of the marketing mix for given products. The benefit is that each offering receives ample attention by a person who is directly responsible for that item's market success. Additionally, the intimate familiarity the product manager has with that offering means that the company can quickly respond to changes in the marketplace that necessitate shifts in marketing strategy and budgetary allocations.

There are drawbacks, however, to this organizational structure. First, competition is fostered between product managers, who are all vying for additional resources for the products under their watch. A second drawback is that product managers are, by nature, generalists who never develop the detailed understanding of functional marketing areas that their specialist counterparts have. Third, from a sales standpoint, a product management structure assigns selling responsibility to managers based on individual offerings. As a consequence, the company's sales force may contend with competition within their own ranks as sellers attempt to market their assigned goods to the same customer companies.

Geographic. Companies that operate in many geographic markets often structure their marketing organizations to provide coverage within those locales. The geographic structure also has functional specialists. Unfortunately, severe competition is often spawned between these managers as they strive to service customers and prospects in their markets, where overlaps almost always occur. For example, salespeople are deployed in regional, zone, or district roles. Each local seller is responsible for devising plans and tactics to compete in his or her given market.

The benefit of this organizational structure is that territories are clearly defined and covered by people who live day in and day out in those areas. But the drawback is that there is often duplication of effort—and resultant competition—between sellers who are attempting to serve companies in their districts, but which are multimarket enterprises. For example, one seller may be attempting to sell to a customer whose headquarters is in that region, while a coworker is attempting to sell to another customer representative in another company location.

Interdepartmental Cooperation and Conflict: Determining the Company's Customer Orientation

As the foregoing illustrates, different marketing organizations offer different benefits and drawbacks. Ultimately, you must determine which of those structures will be appropriate for the merged organization, and you can gain insights to help aid your decision making by studying what has worked, or not worked, in the target company's past.

However, you are still at the stage where you are examining the target's marketing infrastructure and attempting to isolate a key marketing intangible asset: the level of interdepartmental cooperation that, in large part, contributes to the company's level of customer orientation.

Ideally, all corporate functions should pull together to advance the organization's strategic goals by jointly developing and delivering products that meet customers' needs. In reality, however, there are often rivalries that exist between corporate functions that hinder attainment of this goal and which, as a result, collectively lessen the organization's ability to embrace a true customer orientation.

By examining the main functional areas within a company—specifically those that tend to interact most closely with marketing—vis-à-vis their working relationship, you will be best able to assess the potential level of interdepartmental cooperation resident in your corporate combination. The greater the level of cooperation and coordination, the stronger the company's overall marketing infrastructure.

Sales management. The first area to examine is the sales management function. As you have seen, in many companies marketing and sales are structurally linked. Yet they may not always be as closely aligned as the official company organization chart may indicate.

The linkage between marketing and sales is absolutely critical. Via effective market analysis, product development, promotion, and distribution, marketing creates the foundation for sales. In fact, in a perfect world, effective marketing can take the place of sales because the product or service will sell itself. But, in the real world, the two must be inextricably linked so that one effort complements and reinforces the other.

Unfortunately, in many organizations sales and marketing have been characterized more by rivalry than by cooperation. Salespeople tend to be oriented to the near term and focused on generating immediate results via sales. Marketing people, on the other hand, tend to be more strategic and long-term-focused, intent on devising products that meet customers' needs and crafting marketing strategies that enhance the company's long-range market standing. Clearly, the first phase of gauging the level of intracompany cooperation between functional departments is examining the extent to which the overall new-business team is aligned—that is, whether they are focused on achieving similar goals and in fact work harmoniously to achieve them.

Research and development. R&D is a central component of a company's overall new product development process. Yet the interaction between R&D and marketing is often characterized by friction.

R&D staffers are many times viewed by marketers as technicians who are more focused on scientific theory and exploration than on developing offerings that will generate achievable, bottom-line business results. Conversely, R&D professionals tend to see marketing people as being concerned more with generating revenues than with allowing the time needed to devise products with the technical features and attributes customers truly need. In the best-case scenario, there is little or no animosity between R&D and marketing, and the new product development process is characterized by coordinated teamwork between these groups to identify the best ways to meet customer needs through ongoing product introductions and enhancements.

Manufacturing. This function can be at odds with marketing for a number of reasons. Manufacturing managers, who are responsible for the technical aspects of running the factory and producing goods according to rigid quality standards and timetables, frequently feel that marketers do not fully appreciate the challenges of doing so. They feel marketers are insensitive to the difficulties manufacturing managers contend with in terms of machinery breakdowns and overall facilities management. At the same time, marketers often complain about the slowness of manufacturing in producing and delivering goods to the marketplace, and about defective merchandise, poor product quality, and inadequate customer service.

Yet, so much of a company's success is dependent on a smooth working relationship between these two functions. In highly cooperative environments, marketers understand manufacturing strategies and practices (e.g., Just-in-Time production) and their relationship to producing goods at the lowest cost and highest quality. Similarly, manufacturing managers appreciate the challenges marketers face in devising and delivering product offerings that effectively meet customer needs from a functional, quality, price, and service standpoint.

Finance and accounting. Here the conflict tends to relate to monetary resources. Marketers want more of them to fund product development, marketing communications, and sales force support. Financial managers are charged with watching the budget and allocating only as many funds for marketing as are absolutely needed. Clearly, there is a constant tug-of-war.

True cooperation between finance and marketing is characterized by a high degree of understanding between the two groups. Marketers ideally have at least a fundamental understanding of financial management and the role of the finance group in budgeting fiscal resources for all business functions to ensure corporate profitability. At the same time, financial managers should appreciate the scope of monetary resources needed to successfully devise and market new offerings to keep pace with customers' evolving needs, as well as the need for flexibility in shifting budgetary resources in response to changing market conditions and competitors' initiatives.

CORE MANAGEMENT FUNCTIONS: INTERNAL VIEW

The merged-company perspective holds that the process of analyzing the core management functions of a target company begins with an examination of your own. You should ask yourself, "To what extent do my company's management functions and processes directly support my strategic vision?" Determining which of these functions do support your vision, and which do not, paints a clear picture of where your strategic gaps lie and which shortcomings need to be filled by a merger partner's capabilities.

To adequately assess your own managerial capabilities and, ultimately, those of a given target company, it is necessary to first understand the skills and capabilities resident in each management function. Although they are not always present in a given company, there are several core management functions—beyond sales and marketing—that are necessary for an organization to exist as a viable entity and that require evaluation:

- General management
- Operations
- Research and development
- Financial management
- Human resources and personnel
- Legal and tax

Some of these functions are handled by in-house staff. Others are outsourced to third-party vendors or consultants. Irrespective of where the actual responsibility lies, you must assess each area and the key processes and core capabilities that comprise it.

You will need to look at each management area from two key standpoints: the core capabilities and responsibilities of each function, and some of the main issues and considerations that will arise during the postmerger integration process. Your frame of reference is this: identifying the key sources of skills-based value that reside in each functional area.

General Management

The realm of general management comprises many management aspects that are pieces of other functions. For example, as we have seen, communication is typically a role that the public relations and the communications/editorial services departments handle. Yet, senior management is often placed in the position of having to address customers, employees, and the community in speeches and in other direct and indirect forums and media. This requires senior management to work directly with your corporate communicators. By the same token, strategic issues, such as corporate development and long-range planning, must be addressed at the highest level within an organization. Eventually, however, planning must be coordinated with a very defined administrative and tactical focus in order for plans to be effectively implemented.

A discussion of general management capabilities, including process- and skills-related traits, appears in the following sections.

Problem solving. All members of a management team must be able to anticipate potential problems, understand the threats they pose, and devise contingency plans. When analyzing a target company's management team, those employees who demonstrate an acceptance of the inevitability of problems and a willingness to solve them should be retained. This is a valuable character trait that not everyone possesses. Yet, those that do exhibit it can make a world of difference, particularly during the complication-plagued integration process.

Another very important trait linked to problem solving is a willingness to follow through. Many corporate innovations die quick deaths due to a lack of implementation thoroughness. Managers must have the inclination and ability to roll up their sleeves to make things happen. If the target's management team seems not to want to dirty its hands when it comes to implementation, factor this into your decision making relative to determining which managers to place in key operating positions.

Communication. As discussed previously, internal and external communication most often falls under the purview of public relations or corporate communications. Yet, managers who are in the public eye or who need to address their employees and other stakeholders must be able to communicate clearly and persuasively. This trait is particularly significant in the wake of any merger or acquisition, where communication emanating from the highest levels of both companies must be active and compelling. Assembling a team of managers skilled in all modes of public communication is vitally important—not only during the integration process, but also as the combined company takes form and begins moving forward in the marketplace.

Planning. You must explore the planning-related capabilities resident in your merger partner's management ranks. It is necessary to identify the people who are focused on setting realistic and attainable goals. Moreover, you must identify the managers skilled in identifying obstacles to achieving these goals—people who know what needs to be done to sidestep potential pitfalls and to achieve stated goals and objectives.

Clearly, in any organization there are planners and doers. The merged firm's management ranks must be populated with a balance of the two. For instance, there may be people who have been silent throughout planning sessions, yet who are filled with solid ideas and recommendations regarding the development of work plans and timetables. Their role is essential in the broader planning process—as much as those people capable of conceiving brilliant planning concepts.

Decision making. One quality that differentiates effective managers from less effective managers is the ability to make critical decisions when there is little or incomplete data. The fact is that businesspeople do not always have the most complete data needed to make the best, most thought-out decisions. Nonetheless, decisions must be made, and often under intense time constraints and pressures.

Decision making is both an organizational phenomenon (e.g., a consensus approach to setting managerial directives) and an individual capability. It is important to gauge how managerial decisions are made by groups and by executives within the target's management team. This is significant in two respects. First, modes of decision making are an important component of corporate culture. Second, style of decision making by individual executives (e.g., aggressiveness, conservatism, or an inability to make decisions) is a critical trait to evaluate in determining the role a given manager will play in the merged organization.

Project management. The ability to simultaneously coordinate myriad initiatives is a necessary skill of any senior manager. Project management-related skills include organizing project teams, establishing goals and objectives, setting budgets, and defining specific project tasks. A secondary aspect of project management is monitoring and moving the actual tasks to completion. As problems invariably crop up, the flexibility of a manager to shift both speed and direction becomes increasingly significant. Contrasting the flexibility of one manager versus the intransigence of another reveals more than just a character trait. It may give you insight into the reasons for success or failure of previous projects, and into the ability of given managers to handle broader management responsibilities on future initiatives.

Negotiating. The skill of negotiation is not necessarily relegated to money or finance (although it is certainly a priority in the context of corporate development). Being able to readily evaluate the benefits, as well as the pitfalls, of a given opportunity—and then balancing them to determine a value—is more of an inherent skill. Individuals can be trained in the art of negotiation, but it helps to have a nascent understanding.

During the actual negotiation phase of the transaction, you will have the opportunity to directly examine these skills of the target company's senior managers. Their capabilities can be valuable in the future as the merged firm begins forging new relationships with vendors, suppliers, and other product or service providers. Additionally, if future growth is to be driven by additional corporate combinations, managers' negotiating skills will likely assist that process.

General leadership. The age of the leader-manager has arrived. Today, truly successful managers are viewed as leaders with many diverse abilities, only one of which is general business management. An important trait is the leader-manager's ability to see the big picture and to understand the interrelationship between the task at hand and all the players involved in that exercise. The ability to lead also derives from a good perception of political right and wrong, as well as a strong sense of empathy. This allows natural leaders to place themselves in the fray and manage as they would want to be managed—a variation on the Golden Rule in a corporate setting. The leader-manager actively manages through teaching, supervision, and motivation. Since effective leader-managers are often very popular among their staff, their staff people will go above and beyond the basic requirements of their job in order to satisfy the manager's demands.

The increasing prevalence and importance of leader-managers necessitates determining which members of the target's management team hold both types of skills.

Operations

Operations refer to the day-to-day aspects of the target company's processes and procedures. The function broadly encompasses a host of departments and organizational variables that are easily viewed in a company where raw products are purchased and a finished product is manufactured and distributed in the marketplace. However, the operations function in a pure service company is just as important and, in this instance, is often referred to as the behind-the-scenes part of the company. Since no products are manufactured in this environment, the issue to examine is whether the target makes good on its service promises. It is in the operations department where those promises are backed up.

Companies that are product-focused have very different organizational and structural requirements than their service-focused counterparts. The product-focused company has very specific needs from an operations standpoint. The biggest difference is that a product-focused company actually creates tangible goods. To effectively analyze the target, you must understand the most traditional aspect of a target's operations: managing the production of these tangible goods.

Manufacturing management. In the true production environment, you must gain a deep understanding of the target's production processes. Specifically, you must carefully evaluate the machinery, facility requirements, and workforce involved in producing the product. With a focus on process and an understanding of the prevailing quality criteria, you must gauge the production team's experience and familiarity with the time and expense it takes to make individual products, and how efficiently and cost-effectively they do so.

Inventory control. A tremendous asset, or liability, exists in the form of a manufacturing company's existing inventory. Indeed, analyzing inventory levels is a critical variable studied in valuing a target company. The focus on inventory is different when the perspective is on integration and growth planning. For instance, your investigative task involves gauging the tools and techniques used to monitor and regulate inventory levels, insofar as those measures contribute to profitability levels of individual products and distribution efficiency. For instance, does the target use antiquated methods of tracking inventories? Or does it employ advanced computer-based systems for doing so?

The target's production manager will typically have responsibility for inventories of raw materials and finished products. It is necessary to assess this manager's familiarity with techniques of controlling both in-process and finished goods in order to determine the similarity or dissimilarity with your own firm's methods.

Quality control. The concept of quality must extend down from the top of the organization. If the target's core manufacturing processes do not include a commitment to quality, or if there are visible signs of a lack thereof, it is questionable whether you can easily inject a "quality mind-set" into a situation where it previously did not exist. It is imperative to ask the basic questions, such as, "Are there standards for effective control of the product's quality at all stages of its development?" and "What type and how broad are physical inspection processes?"—as well as to evaluate the extent to which formalized quality control measures, such as Total Quality Management (TQM), have been incorporated into the target's manufacturing processes.

Purchasing. A company's purchasing activities are a function of the relationship of corporate buyers and its suppliers. A knowledgeable purchaser can save a company millions of dollars if he or she employs savvy materials-buying techniques. Does the target have this capability? Is there a strategic buying plan in place, or does the target view the purchasing function as purely clerical? The experienced buyer not only employs efficient processes but also has the ability to identify necessary and less costly sources of supply. Working with manufacturing management, the buyer should be intimately familiar with the amount of raw and finished material in inventory. If there is a disconnect between these two functions, you must isolate it and ensure that there is ultimately a strong bond between them in the merged company's operational infrastructure.

Research and Development

Earlier, R&D was addressed in terms of understanding its relationship with marketing and its role in the product development process. Research and development, clearly, must be examined in great detail. The importance of R&D cannot be overstated given the increasing pace of change in domestic and global markets.

Tremendous sources of value may reside in the target's R&D processes—value that can often be transferred in total or in part into the merged organization. Even if the target's R&D processes are initially viewed as being less vital to the success of the acquisition than your own company's, there may be managers in this department who can add value to your own product development function.

Of more immediate concern is the fact that there are likely to be products already out on the market—or in the R&D pipeline—that need to be shepherded by the people who initially devised them. From a longer-term perspective, the effectiveness of the target's R&D department may well influence your "make or buy" decisions in the future.

Direction and management of R&D pipeline. As mentioned previously, the focus of many acquirers is on short-term issues. Yet, R&D is a corporate function that, by nature, is long-term in focus. Still, there must be a balance between new products whose commercialization is imminent and those whose market introduction will occur further down the road. The R&D pipeline must be filled with an equitable balance between the two. Ideally, the success of shorter-term product launches helps to fund the longer-term, more expensive ones that have blockbuster potential. Your investigative assignment is determining the extent to which this potential exists.

Management of the R&D process. Balancing the products in the pipeline is a challenge in itself. However, the R&D team must also be managed to optimize their productivity and contribution to their company. Does the director of R&D effectively oversee budgets to keep costs within predetermined ranges? Where along the product design continuum have breakdowns historically occurred? Are production schedules being met? How successful have past beta tests been? Most important, what is the success rate of actually translating new product concepts into fully commercialized offerings?

Sharing information. Research and development is a proprietary process whose day-to-day activities are typically shrouded in a veil of secrecy. Nonetheless, open information-sharing within the team is a vital characteristic of an effective R&D group, where no one manager has a monopoly on ideas and where a collective mind-set is eminently more productive than individual thinking.

If your goal is to merge the R&D departments of the combining firms, the ability and willingness of each employee to contribute to unfamiliar projects and share data are critical. Those who continue to feel their efforts are proprietary—and who will potentially be reticent postmerger—must be identified, since they will more than likely create a negative influence in the combined department. In short, collegiality and communication are as important as creativity. Make sure the members of the combined R&D team possess each of these traits.

Financial Management

A target company's financial management function is often viewed by the acquirer as being immediately expendable. Typically, this is exactly what occurs. Too many acquirers dismantle every one of the target's accounting, banking, and financial management functions only to realize that they never understood what any of them did in the first place. In many instances, there is substantial procedural overlap and a strong belief by the acquirer that financial controls must always rest within its managerial domain. In fact, it is rare to see a merger or acquisition in which, after the transaction, the keys to the financial management engine were handed over to the acquired firm's fiscal managers.

However, there may well be value inherent in the acquired company's financial function that must be recognized before the decision is made to eliminate it. For example, the target may have the better sources for short-term financing. Before making sweeping overhauls to the target's financial management function, be sure to assess the complete range of its financial capabilities.

Raising capital. Managers coordinating this function require both financial acumen and an ability to establish and maintain relationships in the banking community. If the company you are acquiring is relatively young, chances are that funds were needed for its initial start-up. If the company is more mature, there is likely to be expertise in securing funds to finance growth initiatives. Whichever is the case, before you clean house, first assess the impact of disrupting the banking relationships the target already has in place. If you can benefit from those relationships, it will make sense to retain the employees who have forged them.

More common in most financial management functions is the staff's ability to project funding needs and prepare budgets. There is a greater chance that you will identify an overlap in these capability areas with people in your own organization. But it is important that, before you use the redundancy as an excuse to close down this department, you take a careful look at which employees have the strongest levels of capital budgeting acumen and who can make the greatest contribution to the merged company going forward.

Money management. The overall ability of a company to control its bottom line stems in large part from its money management capabilities. If effective financial controls have been designed and installed, they must be maintained and managed—at least in the near term. Keep in mind that the designer of the system may no longer be the manager of it. For example, the current CFO could have inherited a system developed by a predecessor five years ago. If the system is effective and runs smoothly, that may be a function of a flawless design. But more often than not, the reason for this efficiency will be proper management of the accounting and cost control systems, and an insistence on clear and regular reporting, by current key managers whose continued contributions will be necessary.

Financial strategy. Among the resources in both your company and the target, you should locate the true financial strategists. These employees, rich in forecasting skills, typically can perform such tasks as cash flow, present value, and contribution analyses. There must be strong abilities resident in this department to analyze balance sheets, employ profit sharing techniques, and quickly read a P&L (profit and loss statement). Ultimately, all members of the merged firm's finance department should be sent to regular training classes to help them keep current on newer techniques. This is necessary to ensure that these managers continue to hold sharp analytical skills. Also, this recognition of abilities and subsequent reinforcement via regular training can act as a motivator that will further augment their individual and collective contributions.

Human Resources and Personnel

Traditionally, the human resources (HR) department was responsible for hiring employees, addressing their payroll and benefit issues, and, ultimately, retiring or terminating them. Now, in the age of reengineering and restructurings, the HR department has become linked to broader business issues while forging an intimate involvement with the employee throughout his or her entire tenure with the company. In many companies, HR has attempted to position itself as the "lifetime partner" of employees by taking a proactive role in their ongoing career development. Today, HR encompasses several functions:

- Personnel administration
- Human resource service
- Conflict resolution
- Fostering teamwork
- Recruiting, selecting, and developing employees

Personnel administration. Often lumped under basic administrative tasks, personnel has become intimately linked to HR. Information technologies have created an environment in which an employee's employment record, annual reviews, compensation, payroll, and benefits are all housed in a human resources management system (HRMS). In many companies, health benefits are administered by a staff that performs multiple functions. Yet, in others, this function has been outsourced to third-party administrators. Often, there is a training and development component to many personnel departments that helps employees understand the overall structure of the organization and more easily integrate their activities into the corporate whole. In smaller companies, one individual typically handles payroll, hiring, compensation, and benefits. In larger firms, more emphasis on specialization for employees working in these functions helps each discrete area evolve toward a model of greatest efficiency.

Human resource service. The HR department's "customers" are the very employees of the firm. HR's number-one reason for being is listening to, understanding, and acting on the needs of the workforce. Your investigative task is assessing how well the target's HR professionals serve their constituents.

Evaluating the HR function yields unique and important organizational insights. Without question, there is a wealth of information to be gained from the members of the HR department. That is because an effective HR department takes a proactive role in the lives of employees. Consequently, its staff assists in the performance appraisal process and provides constructive criticism and guidance to aid employees in furthering their personal advancement. As a result, the HR department can provide important information on many aspects of the target's culture, as well as on selected managers and employees.

During your investigation, if you are able to speak to the target's HR director, ask this point person questions about the target's culture and the various subcultures, and, in particular, ask for the names of standout employees. It is inadvisable to ask the director about organizational negatives at this early phase of the corporate courtship as it may place him or her on the defensive. Focusing on positives is much more productive at this early stage of your examination.

Conflict resolution. An increasingly important trait of HR professionals is the ability to help address and resolve differences between employees. As staffers of the company, yet agents of their fellow workers, HR people must follow both the rules of the company and a human resources code of ethics. In resolving conflicts they must never be seen as representing either side unfairly.

In all cases, dispute resolution requires having a very strong ethical foundation, because all conflicts must be resolved objectively and selflessly. To be sure, the skill of resolving employee disputes may be particularly significant in the pressure-filled weeks and months following the launch of the integration program. Pinpointing the HR staffers who possess this critical capability is one of the first personnel-related determinations you should make.

Fostering teamwork. The importance of teamwork—especially in the context of postmerger integration and aligning corporate cultures—is obvious. Today, the practice of team building, team management, and devising team rewards has increasingly fallen into the domain of corporate HR departments. Identifying and evaluating the team-building efforts of the target should be a priority. If the transaction is consummated, these programs and the individuals responsible for guiding them can be vital contributors to the integration process.

Recruiting, selecting, and developing employees. One of HR's traditional roles has been procuring talented employees. If the target's HR department has been unsuccessful in recruiting a top-notch workforce, it is imperative that you find out the reasons why. If the company has attracted only substandard candidates, then you must ascertain whether this is due to the company's reputation in the marketplace, its overall compensation structure, or a void in the firm's recruitment policies—or a combination thereof.

An experienced HR department has a formal assessment and selection process in place. An inexperienced department typically hires in an informal manner, and often on instinct rather than based on detailed skills profiles and stringent hiring criteria. The ever-increasing competition for attracting "the best and the brightest" requires a disciplined, formalized approach to recruitment, assessment, and selection.

If there is no selection process in place, more than likely the employee base is made up of people who represent the best candidates who were available at a given point in time, not necessarily because their skill sets matched a specific need in the company. Indeed, there may be square pegs who were squeezed into round holes. This is certainly not a reason to not go through with the transaction. It is simply an issue you should be aware of. In the event that the deal is consummated, you will have to approach your strategic staffing with this knowledge in mind.

Another critical HR function, and one that will be addressed in detail in Chapter 13, is training and development. As stated, HR has recently begun to play a greater role in employees' personal and career development. That a target has a comprehensive training infrastructure is a valuable attribute that can both cultivate the specific technical skills required of employees in the combined company and expedite integration.

Legal and Tax

Ever-changing laws and regulations require having legal expertise within a company's senior managerial ranks. This is particularly critical in light of changes in the regulatory environment. As regulation increases in some industries while it ebbs in others, having legal professionals who are adept at analyzing regulatory mandates is necessary to keep the organization abreast of changes that will directly influence the company's current and future growth planning initiatives.

In particular, there are four areas within the target's legal capabilities that require your review.

1. Corporate law
2. Contract law
3. Patent law
4. Tax law

INSIDER'S OUTLOOK

Whenever you're buying a business, you're buying a *complete business* . . . a complete organic entity that starts from HR, manufacturing, R&D, the distribution network, the sales rep who works out of London, the purchasing arrangements you have with XYZ suppliers, etc. All of these things change when you buy a company. For example, a lot of people don't realize that most contracts—such as those with suppliers and customers—terminate upon the sale of the entity in question. That means if I buy this company, I have to renegotiate all my purchase and sales contracts. Remember, you're buying a business and everything changes when you do.

—Terence Bentley, Siemens Corporation

Corporate law. Basic in-house legal counsel provides advice on issues such as methods of incorporation, issuance of stock, and the legality of all agreements entered into by the various agents of the company. The target's legal department may or may not have that expertise resident on staff. If so, however, take note of who the "go-to" in-house attorney is when the target is dealing with complicated issues, since he or she may be a valuable resource in the merged company as it enters into various alliances and embarks on such growth initiatives as R&D partnerships and licensing agreements.

Contract law. In-house legal staff typically are the best source for basic contract issues due to their familiarity with the procedures and requirements of the company and the industry in which it operates. Among the many other areas that they advise on are how to structure fees, establish overhead, and determine allowable general and administrative expenses. One of the few marketing-related aspects of traditional due diligence involves examining all the contracts of the target to identify if there are strategic relationships in existence (e.g., joint ventures) that represent ongoing revenue growth opportunities. These must be analyzed to determine their current life span.

Patent law. A company that has an aggressive R&D program typically requires having patent law expertise on staff. The patents that a company holds are central to future revenue growth, so they require careful review in the legal due diligence process. Indeed, a company's patents, copyrights, and trademarks are critical intangible assets that directly contribute to a company's value and the level of its products' brand equity. Assessing the expertise of the target's attorneys who specialize in this area is extremely important if the merged firm plans to launch a series of proprietary new offerings in the future. Again, all patents must be assessed to determine their expiration dates. A proprietary product that generates consistent revenue may be attacked by competing generic products when the patent expires.

Tax law. Federal, state, local, and property tax laws change constantly. Many have a direct bearing on the operations of a company, particularly one that competes in multiple jurisdictions. If your merger partner is located in a different state than that in which you operate, retaining on-staff tax law specialists will clearly benefit the merged company.

Of course, if the merged firm will begin competing in global markets, having expertise in international tax matters will be imperative and may necessitate hiring specialists in this area if none are currently employed in either of the merger partner organizations.

CORE MANAGEMENT FUNCTIONS: EXTERNAL VIEW

Assessing a target's core management functions requires evaluating its internal people and processes. Yet not every managerial function is handled by a company's in-house staffers. Many times, specific functions are coordinated by outside vendors—either in their entirety or as a supplement to the work of on-staff professionals.

It is, therefore, important that you determine where the responsibility for particular managerial activities lies. If certain functions are outsourced, it is necessary to evaluate the firms that have been retained to perform that work. Each of the foregoing managerial functions and processes may be supported, to varying degrees, by outside professionals.

Keep in mind that it is also necessary to identify which in-house staff person has had responsibility for managing the relationship with each vendor. The productivity of outside consultants oftentimes is a direct result of the ability of an executive to effectively guide and oversee the work of that retained firm. In other words, the success of an outside service provider may largely be the result of an inside staffer's ability to provide the direction and oversight needed to maximize the productivity of the vendor's output.

In general, these are the types of retained vendors and professional services firms that may merit review:

- Marketing services agencies
- Law firms
- Audit firms
- Financial advisers
- Management consultants

Marketing services agencies. This category includes advertising, public relations, direct marketing, and all other firms that may support the target company's promotional activities. Other agencies provide services that supplement the company's overall marketing and sales processes and infrastructure. These include telemarketing firms, market researchers, independent sales representatives, and manufacturer's agents. The day-to-day management of marketing services agencies may either be concentrated or be dispersed throughout the target company. For instance, some organizations may have all such support overseen by the corporate marketing director. In larger firms, outside agencies may report to the functional manager (e.g., a direct-response ad agency reports to the advertising manager, or a publicity firm reports to the head of public relations).

Law firms. The target may have on retainer, or use on a project basis, law firms that provide general or highly specialized services. Any of the aforementioned areas of legal expertise—patent, contract, tax, or corporate law—may be rendered by outside counsel.

Typically, the work of retained attorneys is overseen by the company's corporate counsel. In smaller organizations, outside attorneys may be managed by the CEO or CFO.

Audit firms. It is likely that the target employs an outside auditor, particularly if it is a public company. Retained accountants, however, may provide more than audit services. Often accountants are retained for tax planning and compliance work, in addition to traditional financial reporting. Moreover, audit firms may also be retained to help design and manage information technology systems used in a variety of accounting, tax, and internal control applications. In most cases, the work of outside audit professionals is overseen by the CFO or tax director.

Financial advisers. In addition to outside auditors and tax advisers, the target firm may retain the services of financial intermediaries (e.g., banks, investment bankers) to address a wide variety of corporate finance issues, such as raising capital and exploring other financial and investment-related options for growth. The work of financial advisers is typically coordinated by the firm's CFO, tax director, or corporate development officers (in the case of using outside advisers to plan and implement the purchase or sale of various assets of the company).

Management consultants. Management advisory services may be rendered in virtually every functional area discussed herein. General consulting may be provided in areas of business process reengineering, management information systems, organizational development, and any number of specialized areas (such as sales force automation, value management, data warehousing, etc.). The particular focus of the consulting engagement will dictate which managerial department in the target has oversight of the project team. Consulting firms are typically hired on a project basis. Still, it is not uncommon for companies to sign on for long-term consulting support that may transcend a period of months or years and that may, in effect, almost amount to a managerial function unto itself.

Each of these advisers and vendors represents a company's key relationships, all of which must be examined as part of your review of managerial activities; indeed, larger firms may use multiple outside advisers in each functional area. This examination is important for two reasons. First, it is necessary to assess past performance by understanding the outside professionals who supported particular initiatives. Second, evaluating those outside professionals is needed to determine if and how those companies can support the merged firm in the future.

SUMMARY

This chapter has been a detailed look at an organization's core management functions and the processes that typically support each one. By focusing on growth in this analysis rather than cost savings, you will more readily develop a revenue-oriented mind-set that will guide your predeal planning and postmerger implementation of key strategic initiatives. Moreover, you will have a firm understanding of the steps that must be taken to combine these specific functions during the integration process.

The primary goal of analyzing management functions is to provide a framework for determining which will be absorbed or preserved by the acquiring company. Having addressed these issues up front will save you hundreds of hours of after-the-fact research, and potentially millions of dollars in lost productivity.

If processes are not identified and analyzed up front, an environment will be created in the wake of the deal in which every small procedural problem will require drastic measures to resolve. At a time when your focus should be on expeditiously launching the merged company via a smooth integration effort, you will instead find yourself having to put out an inordinate amount of fires.

Having a firm understanding of the steps involved in melding each management function will move the integration process forward and will facilitate subsequent decision making. In fact, having a pipeline of revenue enhancement opportunities and knowing in advance what each management function must accomplish in order to actualize those opportunities will help you attain results that much quicker.

The ultimate goal should be to weave together the primary management functions into a cohesive framework that supports the merged firm's vision. By addressing these critical management functions in the target company analysis phase, you will have developed a sound blueprint for an effective structure that will help minimize problems when they do arise and maximize the opportunities that constitute the foundation of the transaction itself.

The target's managerial functions and capabilities will ultimately be either integrated or eliminated. If you are not able to gauge whether a particular process or the function itself will be appropriate in the new environment, place your focus on what needs to be accomplished strategically. If the process or the function supports your growth goals, it should be retained. If it is too quickly eliminated or misunderstood, your broader integration plan may be flawed and the result could be fatal to the success of the transaction.

Sources of value reside in all elements of a target company's managerial infrastructure. From a growth planning perspective, the message is clear: When assessing the target's management functions, identify those you can assimilate before you decide which you should eliminate.

Part Three
STRATEGIES FOR INTEGRATION

9

Understanding and Acting on the Challenges of Postmerger Integration

It has been said that mergers are like snowflakes. No two are alike.

As similar as any two deals may seem to be, they each involve a separate strategic and human dynamic that in turn makes each different. Because of these variations, the process of joining two companies and melding their people, products, and processes is a daunting and time-consuming task that must be carefully planned in light of the precise obstacles each transaction presents. Just as the realization of strategic synergies and revenue growth is so frequently assumed after corporate management has "blessed" the merger, successful integration is mistakenly assumed to be easily attainable once the transaction becomes official. This assumption could not be further from reality. The formation of a comprehensive integration plan and its attendant follow-through will ultimately determine the success or failure of the initial vision.

There are certain basic challenges to integration that arise in transactions of every nature and scope. The stark reality, however, is that virtually nothing is standard when two distinctly separate organizations are being combined into one.

Before we address the common obstacles to successful integration, we will attempt to define and understand this nebulous concept. Clearly, integration means different things to different people under different circumstances. As definitions vary, so do approaches, since only by identifying the motivation and strategic vision behind an individual merger or acquisition can you effectively devise an integration strategy and plan its successful implementation.

Integration is planned at the highest corporate level, but its implementation invariably occurs at the people level. The employee population is the fuel that drives the corporate engine. A cohesive workforce ensures that the engine runs efficiently. Much of the guidance contained herein is designed to help effect that level of interpersonal cohesion.

This chapter examines the most important keys to integration success and the various roadblocks companies encounter along the way. An awareness of the pitfalls and weaknesses inherent in basic integration assumptions will help you avoid or mitigate them. By examining various integration strategies and the factors that drive these approaches, you will be able to select the most appropriate techniques. Additionally, lessons from the costly mistakes that even the most experienced of acquirers have made will enable you to steer clear of potential problems. The challenges that are faced when attempting acquisition integration are myriad. Yet, a focus on the most pervasive obstacles will help you in ultimately applying the more detailed integration tactics outlined in later chapters.

INTEGRATION—DRIVEN BY STRATEGIC VISION

Before we explore tactics needed to effect postmerger integration, let's first try to define the term.

In mergers and acquisitions, integration is basically defined as *two companies coming together to create a whole*. But as we know, mergers and acquisitions are rarely the combinations of two equals. The company driving a merger is typically making most of the decisions, and certainly that is the case in an acquisition. So it follows that the concept of integration will be radically different depending on whether one is the acquirer or the acquired.

As stated, the growth planning approach to M&A planning is founded on the premise that the ultimate success of any merger or acquisition depends on a preacquisition decision making process that incorporates a postacquisition integration mind-set—the merged-company perspective. Having a clear understanding of the type of company that will ultimately be created is a necessary ingredient, if not the most important aspect, of preacquisition planning. The basis for defining integration and developing the integration process will therefore be determined by this understanding. When a merger or acquisition is first posited by its champion—whether CEO, CFO, COO, or CDO—the resultant vision is one in which the acquirer sets the rules, continues to run the company, and makes few concessions. Of course, there are exceptions to this mode of thinking, but they are rare. Initiating a transaction and eventually effecting integration require a leader who, more often than not, is a senior member of the acquirer's management team. The integration strategy embarked on typically flows directly from that person's preacquisition conception of the type of company that will result on the deal's completion. Once this vision has been determined and accepted by all key members of the decision making body, it will extend through the entire acquisition process. The breadth of postdeal possibilities and problems must never divert the acquisition-planning team from its predetermined path toward the intended vision and its actualization. Yet, when unforeseen obstacles appear in the process, all involved must have both the flexibility and the willingness to adapt.

ORGANIZATIONAL CONTROL

Before addressing specific integration challenges, we must first examine one of the most fundamental issues of integration: organizational control. Will the acquired company retain its autonomy or will all future decisions be made by the acquirer? Will the acquired company be left to operate as it did originally, or will its operations be markedly altered or discontinued? Early in the process, it must be determined who the controlling authority will be.

The answer for each individual merger or acquisition is different, lying somewhere between the realm of the acquired firm maintaining total autonomy and that of it being totally absorbed into the acquiring company. If the acquired company is allowed to operate autonomously, then a different set of integration issues must be addressed than for a company in which the acquirer's management intends to maintain total governance. To understand which path to choose, it is necessary to understand the two broad categories of organizational control—centralized and decentralized.

Centralized control refers to the acquiring management's objective of forging a new identity for the acquired company in the acquirer's image. In other words, the acquiring firm's management sees the purchased company as becoming "just like us." Decentralized control is the philosophical opposite. It is characterized by the acquiring management's intention to (at least in the near term) let the acquired firm maintain its original identity. Determining the mode of organizational control is the first and most fundamental decision an acquirer must make. Indeed, this philosophical approach drives discrete actions that will dictate virtually all decisions relative to the integration process.

Whichever route is chosen, it is critical that the decision be conveyed early on to the acquired company's management and employee base. This will make it easier for all involved to understand the new strategic vision and direction and the near-term managerial decisions to be made. It will also allow all the participants to respond to this new direction, which can, in turn, foster employee commitment and generate energy to move the integration planning process forward. By focusing on the particular characteristics of centralized and decentralized paradigms we can more readily see the resultant ramifications for integration planning.

Centralized Control

Often employed in fold-in or absorption acquisitions, centralized control is usually most common between two companies that have similar product or service offerings. The goal of a horizontal acquirer is to end up with one organization that continues to offer the same goods and services. Centralized control is characterized by the blurring of the line between the two combining companies with the ultimate goal of dissolving it. The quest for complete interdependence drives the integration process. In the centralized setup, complete and total integration is a critical focus.

An example of establishing centralized organizational control was illustrated in the recent combination of two large insurance companies. At the time of the transaction, the acquirer itself was a patchwork of previously acquired insurance companies and management consulting units, loosely knit into one corporate flag. However, other than changing their names, each acquired company had maintained its distinct culture, its own corporate functions, and its respective branded service offerings. In fact, the suite of consulting services and financial products that the acquirer had strung together through acquisition appeared to so closely mirror the recent acquiree's that a smooth and quick integration seemed an obvious afterthought.

Although the products and services of the two companies cleanly overlapped, their cultures were another issue. The target's employees were not so quick to shed their century-old history and empowered culture. In fact, when it became apparent that none of the acquirer's other acquisitions had been effectively integrated (but simply had had their company names changed and had new leaders appointed from the acquirer's ranks), the acquired management tried to maintain certain aspects of its own culture. For example, the target's consultants were an entrepreneurial group who had at their disposal national functions such as marketing and sales to create processes and programs that were implemented and leveraged at the local level. This environment empowered the insurance brokers and management consultants to select and request the help they needed to support their individual needs in their local markets. Many consultants were determined to preserve these business development resources.

Initially, the acquired firm's employees were told that their firm had been selected as a "merger partner" because of the unique nature of their collective workforce. In a series of internal communication videotapes, the acquirer's CEO stressed that his firm was not "buying a company, but rather its people." Hence, he was implicitly supporting whatever policies and procedures those people had employed to become the unique workforce that it was. As managerial decisions began to be made in the wake of the closing, however, fewer and fewer employees believed their new CEO's claims.

For instance, when a regionalized structure was instituted that effectively eliminated within the acquired firm the prized position of "national practice leader," it was the first indication of the acquirer's move to a centralized control structure. The action contradicted the CEO's words. Suddenly, the acquired firm's employees were confused over the control issue, not to mention their own individual fates. Key members of the acquired firm's senior management team began to resign. Those that remained had their national positions regionalized.

Other organizational and operational changes clearly indicated the move to an interdependent, centralized control structure. Many of these decisions were not readily accepted by a workforce that was used to autonomy and a consensus-driven decision making process. Hindsight showed that the goal of the acquirer was not to preserve the value inherent in the acquired firm's people. Its goal was to totally absorb the organization. Apparently, it was not the target's capabilities as much as its size and the scope of its distribution channels that comprised its true appeal.

A year after the acquisition, the integration appeared to be evolving smoothly. Having virtually doubled its workforce, the acquirer had built a more experienced and capable global distribution system that included many, but not all, of the unique qualities that made the target firm a marketplace leader. Yet, much value was lost as the independent, progressive thought leaders of the acquired firm were either indoctrinated into embracing the acquirer's mind-set or were lured away by competitors. Nonetheless, many of these valued employees might have stayed and rallied behind the acquirer's new vision had management stated up-front its plans to move to a centralized control structure.

An acquirer's past behavior is not necessarily the sole indicator of its future approaches to integration. However, if the acquirer has not been proactive about its intentions, it probably will continue that pattern.

INSIDER'S OUTLOOK

Whether or not a deal is viewed (by the investment community) as having the potential to be successful also depends on the history and experience of the company in doing the merger or acquisition. If a company has never made an acquisition before and it's a big one, there will be a lot questions about the company's ability to integrate products, leverage their customer base, integrate operations, and make the combined company work from an overall management standpoint.

—John Levinson, Westway Capital LLC

Decentralized Control

A decentralized infrastructure is typically selected when the product or service offered by the acquired company differs from that of the acquiring firm or when there are distinct strategic and marketing approaches employed by each firm. Though the hallmark of this paradigm is autonomy, it does not mean that an aggressive integration program need not be developed. On the contrary. Even more attention must be paid to integration in a decentralized environment because of the potential for divisiveness as wrought by the intentional organizational independence bestowed on the acquired unit.

Under a decentralized setup, efforts are made to preserve the culture and operations that made the acquired company an attractive acquisition in the first place. In essence, the autonomy of the acquired company is maintained. But the lack of a direct control mechanism can create a multitude of management, operational, marketing, and communication problems.

For example, companies develop their own language based on common understandings or cultural characteristics. Contrary to the ease of management that ultimately occurs in a centralized infrastructure—in which the acquirer dictates and defines all aspects of operations—in the decentralized environment, definitions must first be clarified. To a certain degree a common language must be forged before the sides can truly understand one another. The acquiring company must ensure that a common language is maintained and that the value inherent in the acquired company is not destroyed by an overzealous integration plan that strips the target company of its cultural and linguistic identity. Even if the two companies operate independently, the implementation of cross-unit promotions and other initiatives—so key to growth planning and skills transfer—cannot commence until each unit understands the other's language.

In a decentralized setup, the acquirer essentially observes from the sidelines, which makes the most tangible benefit to that acquirer one of gaining and ultimately effecting shared knowledge. However, acquirers that extend too much autonomy to companies they acquire fail to receive the maximum benefits of shared knowledge. This is often due to the acquirer's establishment of an organization in which there are no managerial links to serve as a conduit of skills transfer.

Managing the acquired company at arm's length, yet ensuring that value continues to be created and transferred, requires strong leadership and diplomatic savvy. In order to facilitate the transfer of unique skills resident in each company, a coordinated effort must be made to guide and support without tampering. How do you do so? One way is to appoint a key member of the acquisition team who has a stake in the success of the merger, such as the deal champion, to head the integration effort at the acquired company. By installing an individual who is loyal to the acquirer, yet committed to the success of the acquired company, the continuity of the acquired company can be maintained while the information flow to the acquirer will be strong throughout both the near and the long term.

Learning best practices from the acquired company in all aspects of operations and processes can give the acquirer an advantage in enhancing its current operations and in making future acquisitions. Studying the acquired business from both inside and out will ensure that value is transmitted back to the acquirer. Also, openly sharing knowledge can promote the corporate osmosis necessary to effect a centralized management structure, if that is the longer-term plan.

Symbiosis

Although it is a rare occurrence, two companies sometimes come together in the classic "merger of equals," where an even exchange of capabilities, information, and management creates the value of the newly forged organization. This scenario results in neither a centralized nor a decentralized control structure. At the same time, however, it manifests elements of both. This symbiotic relationship reflects a true partnership. And like in any partnership, a commitment to flexibility and compromise is the driving force. There is an assumption of a willingness by both sides to adopt and adapt to the new vision.

Consequently, an environment must be created that promotes the autonomy of a decentralized setup while fostering the interdependence so prevalent in the centralized approach. The symbiotic infrastructure requires an iterative integration plan that continuously reflects on changes that are made along the way and then builds on them throughout the process. Because this process is highly adaptive, the resultant company will often be very different from that which was originally envisioned. In symbiotic relationships, the integration strategy requires management that is very patient, egoless, and flexible, yet entrepreneurial, as the final result is, as yet, an unknown entity.

Regardless of whether the control structure you select is centralized, decentralized, or symbiotic, making that decision sets the arduous integration process into motion. Every day, as another merger is announced, we are treated to press conferences in which the respective CEOs triumphantly hold up their hands in a unity embrace. They know it has been a long, rocky road to the final signing of the merger documents where months of analysis, weeks of valuations, and around-the-clock negotiations have finally yielded the sought-after result.

The acquisition team can revel in its success and the intermediaries can put another feather in their deal-making caps. But, the managers charged with actually making the merger work realize that this celebratory moment marks the true beginning of the merger process, not the end. Similar to the birth of a baby, the merger celebration is one of new beginnings, not an end to anything except the birthing process. Putting management's signatures down on the dotted line is the kickoff to a complex period of organizational change that will begin quickly—and that may never end.

TWELVE KEY CHALLENGES OF INTEGRATION

Every corporate combination will pose different obstacles to integration success. History has shown, however, that there are several challenges that arise in virtually every merger situation. These challenges span all facets of the combined company, from people issues to function and process areas and ultimately extending to the product and market arenas.

As we have stressed, every corporate combination is unique. Yet, as more and more mergers and acquisitions fail, lose money, break up, and de-merge, the common mistakes have become more evident. The methods employed to cope with and ultimately overcome them often determine the long-term success or failure of the particular deal. After studying hundreds of failed acquisitions, we have identified the most common challenges to integration. If each challenge is met with a clear focus and forward-thinking tactics, the road to success will be smoother and straighter. Doubtless, because of the unique nature of every merger and acquisition, there will be many additional, peripheral challenges. However, by actively addressing the following 12 challenges, the scales will be tilted in your favor:

1. Embracing the concept of change
2. Setting priorities
3. Sharing information and effecting corporate understanding
4. Melding cultures
5. Forging a new corporate identity
6. Determining managerial roles and responsibilities
7. Effecting teamwork and cooperation
8. Combining corporate functions and internal processes
9. Aligning capabilities, services, and products
10. Measuring results
11. Acknowledging the two levels of integration
12. Maintaining flexibility

Embracing the Concept of Change

There is no greater organizational change initiative than that of a major merger or acquisition. The companies entering into such a transaction must anticipate and accept the inevitability of massive alterations that will occur in the integration process. The fact is, few merging companies adequately prepare themselves psychologically for the changes they are about to experience.

The process of coping with change is rarely construed as an easy one. However, the inability or unwillingness to acknowledge change can prevent the start of a program that is created to manage it. Whether the combination of companies occurs through a merger or an acquisition, it must be understood that typically at least half of the people involved will have their lives altered by circumstances over which they have no control. Simultaneously, while this sentiment of uncertainty permeates throughout the organization, new plans, procedures, strategies, and tactics to grow the business must be implemented.

The melding of people who have been thrust into change—in an operationally altered environment—is a daunting task. In fact, it may be mistakenly viewed as a peripheral issue contrasted against the millions of dollars spent to create a new company. But, when you buy a company, you are buying its people. The collective human resources of a company are its most valuable asset. And as with any asset, great pains must be taken to retain it, maximize it, and build on it. The death knell of an integration program is the mandate from management: "Business as usual." It is eminently unrealistic to think that such a substantial change to one's work environment could ever be termed "usual"; nothing could ever be "usual" in the context of a major merger or acquisition.

INSIDER'S OUTLOOK

People are, without question, the most important and the least considered factors in the merger/acquisition process. The more it makes sense to merge financially—that is, the more synergies there are, the more overlaps that can be eliminated to produce a stronger balance sheet—the greater are the risks on the people side. Initially, talk of merger or acquisition will raise the anxiety level at any organization. Long-term, if the "people factor" is not considered adequately, all of the great looking financial projections won't be enough to piece together the aftermath of a decimated or demoralized staff.

—Paul Cholak, SHL North America

Setting Priorities

While the time from the signing of the letter of intent to the closing of the transaction may be a short one, the impact of the deed is long-term. So much must be done to meld the organizations, but not everything can be done at once. The highest-priority activities must be acted on first. Decisions made during the compressed and pressure-filled weeks of due diligence and negotiation often do not include integration planning. Yet once the deal closes it is the number-one priority. In the realm of integration planning, however, there are critical first steps. In other words, there are priority actions within the high-priority act of integration planning.

In assessing which programs come first, a triage approach is the most practical. Stop the bleeding first; then address the areas that require deeper thought and more extensive planning. Where do you begin?

Most acquired businesses can continue to run for a short time without any input from the acquiring company. The functions that do not require day-to-day oversight can be considered secondary priorities. Training is an example of a function that falls into this category. Growth-focused integration planning requires that areas such as corporate information, marketing, and sales be addressed very quickly. These departments and the people within them are on the front lines representing the company every day to stakeholders.

Corporate image and branding issues should be addressed promptly to ensure the right messages about the merged company can begin to be communicated. Advertising programs already in the works should be evaluated and, where possible, altered. Many times, the knee-jerk reaction is to put on hold or completely stop marketing campaigns already in the works. View this instead as an opportunity to immediately begin promoting the combined firm's new image. Advertising, telemarketing, trade show appearances, speaking engagements, direct mail initiatives, and collateral material development all should be addressed, coordinated, and leveraged immediately, not discontinued. Placing marketing communications as a top priority will enable you to put the best face on the merger to external audiences while you grapple with many of the longer-term internal and operational issues.

Immediately on closing, communication programs must be deployed whose focus is key employee retention. This is discussed in great detail in Chapter 12. Focusing on the bottom line instead of people at this critical juncture can jeopardize future revenue streams and those responsible for creating them. On hearing of the merger, your top employees will begin to receive calls from headhunters or directly from your competition. If retention programs are not quickly devised, you risk losing those people. Again, protecting your vital people-related assets is of paramount importance. For the first three months, remember to keep employees, not revenues, as your top priority. Rewarding those who will stay on in the merged environment should be addressed up front. Whether through soft-dollar benefit arrangements, stay-on bonuses, salary adjustments, or stock/stock option incentives, compensating key employees *not* to leave is essential. This issue is detailed in Chapter 14.

Customer retention is also critical to maintaining the value of the acquired company. If your purchase was based on an anticipated revenue stream, making sure that revenue continues is of supreme importance. Identifying key customers is a critical phase of the marketing due diligence process. Contacting the most profitable customers and influencers should take place immediately after, if not before, the closing comes. An in-person meeting or phone call from a high-level member of the acquiring organization goes a long way toward effecting customer retention. Remember that customer contact strategies are an essential component of your first-phase external communication program.

Over the weeks and months following the transaction, follow-through will be required to reinforce all your employee and customer relationships. However, taking certain fundamental steps early in the process will allow you to focus on integrating the organization without having to contend with major disruptions in business as wrought by disruptive customer relations problems and employee defections.

INSIDER'S OUTLOOK

A key to success of the ongoing integration is that you have discussed some of the critical things up front. There has to be a plan. You have to determine such fundamental things as who is going to report to whom. Who's going to be on the board of directors? What are the differences in corporate culture going to be and how are they going to possibly conflict? But underlying it, the most important questions are, "Do we both agree on what the vision is for the merged firm? Do we agree on the tactics and strategies for how we're going to do it?" If you save all these discussions to postdeal, you can be in for some real unpleasant surprises.

—Diane Harris, Hypotenuse Enterprises

Sharing Information and Effecting Corporate Understanding

Merging companies often fail to recognize the importance of educating the combined organization's employees on their respective histories. Before you can effectively begin communicating about the future, it is necessary to communicate about the past. Employees can only understand and appreciate where they are going once they understand where each has come from.

The quest for complete oneness through M&A is a utopian vision. No more can two companies become one than two people who marry become one. But ideally, they can share the same goals, leverage their respective attributes, and achieve compatibility across a broad base of major issues. Then, acting together, they can be a stronger force in the world than previously as individuals. This analogy comes closest to how we view the integration process.

Simply placing two different groups of people under one corporate roof does not automatically make them one unified collective. They need to first meet each other, share information, and finally understand the complementary nature of their new corporate relationship. What is the company's corporate philosophy? What are the strategic intentions of senior management? Why has the company come to develop, commercialize, and invest in the products and services it does? How are the sales and production people compensated and why? These and scores of other questions will be asked by people on both sides of the merger equation.

INSIDER'S OUTLOOK

You must promote the integration process very early in the deal process. You get the right people involved at the outset of your planning. Basically, you have to understand that when you are bringing a new business into the fold, you have to integrate the *entire* business. That means you have to make sure the right professionals are involved from an integration perspective—manufacturing, MIS, sales—all the people who will ultimately own the responsibility for the business you're bringing in.

—Terence Bentley, Siemens Corporation

Fact-based financial, legal, and regulatory due diligence clearly is extremely technical in scope and does not address compatibility issues. Marketing due diligence and predeal growth planning must determine whether the two companies can fuse together into a brand-new entity.

How do you begin the process of sharing all-important corporate history information? Joint management meetings in which personal and professional ideas are shared help to start lowering the barriers that are certain to exist. For instance, when Blue Cross and Blue Shield of New Jersey announced the merger with its counterpart in Delaware, the first act of BCBS/NJ was to assemble the managers of both organizations for a celebratory weekend retreat. This allowed key executives to mingle and exchange information in a positive, unstressed environment, and the forum set the tone for future dealings between them as the formal integration program was launched.

A schedule of similar gatherings was established in which the venue alternated between New Jersey and Delaware. Sharing the language, history, and culture of both organizations laid the foundation for acceptance of the new order and helped foster an atmosphere in which employees could productively interact and, together, begin effecting corporate growth.

Of course, disseminating company-historical information must be directed at employees at all levels of the merged organization. This is a long-term process that is part of your broader employee communications efforts. Strategies for conducting postmerger internal communications programs are provided in Chapter 12.

Melding Cultures

Much is written on melding divergent corporate cultures and the ensuing compatibility issues. Cultural compatibility is one of the most significant determinants of a successful M&A transaction. Although this sentiment has been repeated thousands of times, that does not diminish the veracity of the statement nor the importance of the cultural alignment process.

Acknowledging whether cultural compatibility can exist should be a factor in determining whether to pursue a given deal. Integration can never be attained—and growth strategies never realized—if two companies are worlds apart culturally. If you determine that there will be compatibility problems, it is advisable to halt the acquisition process and walk away from the negotiations. Arguments may ensue and egos may be crushed. But, with the merger divorce rate at more than 50%, buying blind in terms of compatibility will ensure the failure of the deal.

Naturally, even if compatibility is established, smooth integration is by no means a given. Yet, once the potential for cultural alignment is ascertained, the process of melding both cultures into one cohesive whole is a matter of tactical implementation. By this we mean that aligning cultures is achieved by sharing information, bolstering similarities, and mitigating dissimilarities to the point of the latter's eventual demise. How is this done? Through effective communications and a coordinated approach to bridging the organizations' products and processes—all topics detailed in Part Three.

Forging a New Corporate Identity

When two companies come together to form a single new entity, one or both of their past identities will be shed, or substantially altered, and a new identity will emerge. This identity is the essence of the company—its spirit or soul that must be embraced by the newly combined employee base, and which is often guided by the acquiring CEO's strategic vision.

When a company is acquired and its identity is erased overnight, an identity vacuum is created. The natural response is for the acquired firm's employees to hold firmly onto their past. An acquirer must be sensitive to the fact that the acquirer has, in essence, stolen the soul of the acquired's workforce. A new identity must be articulated and promptly set forth. The longer it takes for the void to be filled, the greater the likelihood for employee confusion and resentment.

Many acquirers immediately craft a new mission statement in hopes of imparting a new identity. But simply putting forth a new mission statement will not suffice, since it represents only a theoretical framework or list of guiding principles from which the new company will operate. Just as the Bill of Rights and the Ten Commandments set the rules by which we live our lives, the merged firm's mission statement is only a platform on which to build. The merged company's corporate identity is what its employees believe and live.

In the near term, sharing information on the respective firm's histories and missions and highlighting the strategic benefits of the combined entity should be your focus. In the longer term, training classes and broadened information programs that reinforce the mission, as well as results-based compensation programs that reward integration-focused behavior, further support the efforts that will get employees to embrace the new corporate identity.

Keep in mind that creating the merged firm's corporate image is a very different issue from forging its identity. If the identity is the spirit or soul of the company, then the image is the outer skin. The image is the face that management wants external stakeholders to discern.

Putting a positive spin on the merger for all the world to see is critical. Stockholders, analysts, politicians, customers, suppliers, and distributors must feel good about the prospects for the merged company. Employing aggressive marketing communications aimed at your various stakeholder groups is critical.

The identity is truly what the company and its employees believe and live. Internally sharing the joint histories and reinforcing the benefits of a combined entity are actions that require immediate attention. Training classes that reiterate how the new combination will help individual employees are imperative. Introducing results-based compensation to reward behavior that reinforces the new vision will also help in forging the new identity.

Determining Managerial Roles and Responsibilities

The growth planning orientation on M&A planning is largely based on transferring valuable skills and capabilities held by personnel within the merging companies. This focus should pervade all aspects of personnel decision making. It is particularly important in making decisions on which people will fill key managerial positions in the merged organization. As we have seen, effective premerger analysis of the target company's employee base should identify the organization's key people and their core talents. Information gathered in this phase of your acquisition candidate research—as well as during your organizational and marketing due diligence—provides a starting point for selecting your managerial team.

Naturally, in a pure merger there are only so many positions available. But great care must be taken to make personnel decisions that put the right people in the right jobs without alienating employees whom you want to stay in the merged organization but who may be disenchanted by individual managerial designations. For example, we have often seen the scenario in which people of the acquired company are extremely loyal to a particular executive. If the acquirer feels up front that there is no role for this officer in the new company, then an important decision must be made. Should a position be created for this individual to maintain coworkers' allegiance to the merged firm? Or should the executive be terminated regardless of the possible animosity that decision may spawn?

Remember, severing a key manager of the acquired company sends an ominous message to the acquired rank and file. If maintaining the allegiance of the acquired workforce is important to you, termination of key leaders should be the action of last resort. It can lead to defections and confusion among both employees and customers, as well as a general decrease in morale within the acquired company—all of which can slow or derail the integration process. One solution is to create a figurehead role for this individual so that harmful emotional waves do not cascade through the acquired firm's employee base. Regardless of your decision on an individual manager, your focus should always be on value preservation of the acquired firm's broader employee population.

Staffing decisions must be made with an eye toward your long-term goals but also toward the near-term challenge of ensuring continuity of the merged firm's operations. Consider, for example, the combined company's financial and accounting systems. Placing someone from the acquirer in the role of CFO, controller, or financial liaison will ensure a two-way flow of critical financial data and a sharing of information on key processes.

It is important to acknowledge that the incumbent management team can best operate its own business more smoothly than a brand-new group that is unfamiliar with the acquired firm's internal processes.

Allowing the acquired company's managers to maintain responsibility for activities central to its core operations will help to accelerate integration by minimizing gaps in performance or production. Ideally, the acquiring management should audit and counsel the existing management, augmenting it where it is weak but leaving the previous management team intact until key processes have been successfully incorporated into the merged firm's operational infrastructure. Clearly, selecting the best managers for future organizational roles requires an understanding of the combined firm's operational processes going forward.

Just as you would not attempt to link financial systems without full knowledge of the intricacies of both the acquired firm's set up and yours, determining the appropriate power structure in specific departments requires a solid understanding of those units' technical workings and requirements. This is most effectively done by establishing joint planning sessions that include the managers of corresponding departments within each company. By involving both groups in planning for unification, you can generate momentum toward unification while gathering process-related information and input on individual people's skill sets and personalities for staffing-related decision making.

Management can make the best of a difficult situation by sharing the responsibility for decision making on who will fill managerial spots. Groups with common goals are best able to confront the harsh realities of the high-level staffing challenge and build for the future. Because every company is different, there is no one way to determine the perfect corporate structure. This adds to the difficulty of assigning roles and responsibilities because every decision is a journey into uncharted territory. However, decisions should ideally be team-based and must incorporate tact, patience, and understanding. And, of course, they must reinforce the new vision.

As you begin interacting with acquired employees, you will quickly identify their personalities and management traits. This assessment will determine whether they can effectively function in the merged firm's new cultural environment and, thus, play a role in achieving your strategic vision. Some cultural milieus require individuals with self-confidence, a results-oriented mind-set, and the ability to make difficult decisions. Other environments value intelligence, integrity, and vision. The various traits you identify in your acquired employees indicate the types of individuals you have gained and whether they have the potential to be key players in the merged company. A micromanaged company that is looking for managers to be the blind champions of an already-established, rigid vision will value an order-taker or "soldier" mentality over self-confidence, independence, and vision. Conversely, a company looking for its new employees to help take it into uncharted waters will place a high premium on the characteristics of entrepreneurial leadership and an orientation that favors risk taking.

Your organizational structure (whether centralized or decentralized) and specific corporate culture will determine the key management traits you value. So too will the strategic imperatives of the merged company. Defining the traits you need—and identifying the people who possess them—plays a large part in selecting the team that will lead you to the integration finish line and to your longer-term strategic objectives.

If you have already focused on dispelling the anxiety that accompanies any change of ownership, then the staffing battle is half won. The acquirer's plans for dealing with the acquired firm's management must be communicated up front. If the acquirer can assure its newly acquired management that it will remain intact, then avoiding weeks, if not months, of uncertainty will spare you from the inevitable drag on productivity and efficiency as managers await word on their fate. By the same token, if the plan is to clean house, then do it and move forward quickly and with candor. This will go a long way with those who are staying on as they observe the honest nature of your dealings. If you act disingenuously or without sensitivity, this will negatively impact the morale of those who stay.

It is wise to deal decently and generously with those who must be dismissed. But the acquisition's true measure of success is the commitment and effectiveness of those who remain. Deciding who will stay and who will go is a daunting process that takes into account input from both organizations. Some of the decisions will be clearly political, made to boost morale or maintain continuity. Others will be made to truly take the merged company to the next level. Both sets of decisions are equally important. Regardless of which decisions you make, they must be made as early in the integration process as possible. Every day that goes by without clarification being received by those who are wondering about their fate is a day spent moving in the wrong direction.

Effecting Teamwork and Cooperation

As two organizations are merged, there will initially be problems of cooperation and an unwillingness to share ideas. These obstacles are separate from the cultural hurdles that present themselves when two different corporate worlds collide. For cooperation to exist, there must be unconditional acceptance of the person on the other end of the phone or on the other side of the desk. The problems that prevent the free flow of ideas run deeper than basic cultural differences.

The foundation for teamwork and cooperation is trust. There must be a comfort level that shared ideas will not come back to haunt the new coworkers. Reward systems that focus on cooperation rather than competition will quickly break down barriers that might otherwise prevent trust and, in turn, honesty.

Trust will also be built by a steadily increasing level of communication throughout the organization. In addition to general merger communications, the acquirer should share information that was considered proprietary when the merger partners were market adversaries. For example, sharing product information, competitor intelligence, or past strategic plans with employees makes them feel as if the acquirer is offering them something without a quid pro quo. Doing so will quickly engender trust and provide a platform from which teamwork can spring.

Once you have established a foundation of trust between teams or individuals, the next step is to foster interdependence between them. By creating common goals and an agreed-upon game plan for accomplishing these objectives, understanding will grow. For example, this can by accomplished by eliciting input from acquired employees in creating new product or market strategies or by inviting managers to participate in meaningful strategy sessions. Involving all employees at their respective levels of interaction builds cooperation and strengthens the bonds of two-way trust that are critical for a successful integration.

INSIDER'S OUTLOOK

You start by asking the CEO, "What is the vision of your company?" to understand where he's coming from. It's not a matter of foisting your vision on him. If it's a company you want to buy, then the excellence that's there is something you want to protect. You become more of a vehicle to help them execute their vision than the other way around . . . particularly when you're attempting to penetrate new market sectors. For division acquisitions, where the division has something specific that it wants to achieve, its choice of target would be because it thought [the target] could help [the division] achieve it. But you'd still talk about the target's vision to make sure there's no disconnect. When you're trying to build your company by adding new sectors to your business, and you don't have a vested current way of doing something, you still need to determine what the target's vision is and how it's gone about realizing it. Have they thought about out-licensing? Have they thought about finding international partners? This is very iterative discussion. You want to hear back from them, "Gee, we can really use your organization to handle our products overseas." If you hear the target say, "We'd never want a parent company to distribute this," or "We're going to build our own organization" you start to see an inflexibility that indicates a vision mismatch or a culture mismatch or both. There's never a point in imposing a vision until you've heard, understood, and been able to react to the vision of the operation you're looking to acquire.

—Diane Harris, Hypotenuse Enterprises

Combining Corporate Functions and Internal Processes

Once the key managers have been identified and joint meetings have taken place among different departments, the cream will rise to the top. Those people willing to enthusiastically contribute and play on the new team will be differentiated from those who exhibit a nonproductive passive aggressiveness. But on an immediate and more fundamental level, corporate functions must be analyzed and integrated.

Each major department should be examined carefully to determine where coordination of efforts is necessary to maintain near-term operational continuity, as well as to pinpoint where cost savings may be attainable. The overriding goal, however, is identifying where individual capabilities (resident in either or both of the combining companies) can be harnessed to benefit the merged company as a whole.

In the accounting area, for example, most companies have adopted advanced information technology systems; smaller companies may not have equally sophisticated installations. In such cases, the acquired company's accounting operation can benefit from access to the advanced technology offered by the acquirer. This of course assumes that the acquired company's system will remain, as opposed to being subsumed into the acquiring company's process.

It is important to recognize that there are two basic mind-sets, or schools of thought, regarding integrating departments. We refer to these as the "democratic school" and the "autocratic school."

The democratic school is founded in the belief that combining the insights of both groups and focusing on a best-practice methodology will yield the best processes going forward. The benefit of this line of thought is that it forces two disparate units to cooperate and ultimately arrive at a process that combines the best elements of both companies so that in the end a better system will prevail. There are additional benefits to this approach. Rethinking processes in a democratic environment fosters teamwork, cooperation, and higher morale. It ensures that employees will not only intimately understand the new processes, but they will understand *why* they are the best processes. This will engender personal involvement and can increase the level of satisfaction that each employee has for his or her function.

There is a drawback to this approach, however, in that it requires a commitment to consensus-building, which takes longer and therefore may extend portions of the integration program beyond their anticipated time parameters. However, when performed with these issues in mind, democratized departmental integration has a much better chance of success than its philosophical antithesis, the autocratic school.

That school is rooted in the belief that the processes of the acquirer are already the best and therefore there is no need to incorporate those of the acquired firm. Adherents to this mode of thinking assert that the acquiring firm controls the power and, therefore, logically has the best ideas and processes. In essence, an up-front purely subjective value judgment is made that establishes the processes of the acquirer as more efficient and superior to that of the company it is acquiring.

There is a continuum of integration approaches under the autocratic school that drive staffing decisions. On one end of this continuum is the "shoot first" approach in which the acquirer aggressively and, often randomly, downsizes employees of the acquired department. Little or no thought is given to absorbing the skills those people possess or continuing the processes they support. The motivation is purely an economic one, and the savings celebrated by management are heralded until it is realized that the wrong people have been fired or that the sacrificed processes were, in fact, critical to the business.

After management shoots first, they typically start to ask the questions that rightfully should have preceded their actions. On realizing that the severed employees are central to continuing the acquired company's core processes, the acquirer may attempt to rehire the severed employees, luring them with stay-on bonuses or other incentives. Those that do agree to these ex post facto stay-on bonuses typically spend their time interviewing for new jobs, bad-mouthing the company to coworkers, or working in the least productive mode possible. Typically, the rehired employees maintain such animosity toward the acquirer that they do not last through the transition phase anyway.

Acquirers who shoot first initially view this strategy as cost-effective because of the obvious, readily attainable monetary savings. The reality is that since most of the severed employees are entitled to separation packages, management would be better off economically retaining those people for a period of time and paying them to work at transitioning various operational functions.

For example, a large investment company purchased another for approximately $1 billion and quickly set about firing the entire back-office staff. After a few weeks, management realized that they were unable to figure out the acquired firm's payroll system, delaying the weekly pay of over 600 acquired employees (and sparking widespread angst and animosity among them). After saving $75,000 in an abrupt downsizing, management was forced to pay over $300,000 in additional hiring costs and bonuses.

But, the intangible costs were far greater as many of the remaining employees lost confidence in the management of their acquirers and were slower to buy in to management's vision than they otherwise would have been. Normal postmerger attrition can run at 20% to 30%. There is no urgency to sever anyone except those people who demonstrate a poisonous reluctance to participate in the integration process and to play on the merged company's new team.

At the other end of the autocratic school spectrum is the "scorched earth" approach, in which all employees of the acquired firm are immediately severed. There is no attempt to import skills or to integrate operations. No value is placed on the people or the organizational processes of the acquired firm. They are all considered expendable.

The goal of growth-focused integration is harnessing and protecting existing skills and capabilities. It would seem that the democratic school of departmental and functional integration would better preserve skills and people's talents, in contrast to the autocratic approach, which is more cost reduction-oriented and diametrically opposed to integration based on transferring key skills between the merging firms.

Aligning Capabilities, Services, and Products

A capability is a skills-based phenomenon that exists as a result of individual and organizational processes. It can be a demonstrated strength in a particular subject area or a wealth of experience in specific tactical procedures. In either case, it is indelibly linked to the employees performing it whether they be engineers, lawyers, or assembly-line workers.

When a company is acquired so that its inherent capabilities or services can be expanded or applied to those of the acquirer, it must be remembered that people are the critical element to the successful transfer of that capability. More often than not, there are pivotal employees who have the skills and knowledge that collectively comprise the sought-after capabilities. For example, an R&D manager may be the visionary who drove the creation of a particular capability.

Invariably, individuals who played a part in the invention, design, or implementation of a capability are absolutely critical to its continued vitality and successful delivery after acquisition. Most recently, an old-line Wall Street firm merged with a boutique brokerage house that specialized in packaged investment products. In the transaction, the acquirer failed to retain most of the employees connected to this investment packaging capability. The acquirer mistakenly assumed that buying the capability without having the personnel to deliver it would still enable the company to offer that specialty in the marketplace. The company was dead wrong. Within weeks, sales of these products began to fall off and the capability weakened, as the methodology and insights of the acquired but not retained employees proved to be more critical to the success of this line of packaged investment products than the products themselves. A big part of the acquirer's merger investment had been thrown away.

Without question, the process of integrating a service capability is people-critical. Often there are many within a firm who are capable of selling or providing a particular service, yet there are probably only a select few who are responsible for the majority of its sales. Those people's importance cannot be overstated, as the standard 80/20 rule applies here. In most companies, 20% of the sales or service force is responsible for 80% of the revenues. Without the buy-in and support of that 20%, top-line revenues will falter—or vanish.

If the acquirer's goal is to replace those people with others in its own workforce, there may likely be customer resistance. In addition, the workers selected to absorb and deliver the service are bound to supplant tried-and-true methods (which made the service successful in the first place) with shortcuts and their own methods. Each individual uses his or her own personal roadmap to navigate the learning curve. If cloning a successful service is the goal, it must be taught by those already proficient in it, not learned from scratch by an uninformed employee. Those teachers must be preserved in the near term, even if they do not figure into your long-term staffing plans.

Integrating products requires an approach unto itself. In order to integrate the acquired company's products into your existing line of goods, in addition to a detailed comparative analysis of the merger partners' offerings, the people component must be addressed. For example, it should be a priority to educate the merged company's salespeople and customer service representatives so that they understand every aspect of a product's features, its customers, and its role in the overall product mix. In later chapters, a detailed examination of internal communications and training and development programs will provide additional guidance on the people-related aspects of unifying the merger partners' product-management efforts.

INSIDER'S OUTLOOK

Right after the letter of intent was signed, we set up a steering committee structure that had officers from our company and officers from [BC/BS] Delaware on it. We then formed 32 separate teams, each of which had a leader and five or so people on the team. Each team then started digging down into each functional area to see how things were historically done in each organization. "You do it this way; we do it that way. Can't we do it better if we move yours to ours? Can't we do it better if we move ours to yours? We market this way; you distribute that way. We have this product; you have that product. We have expertise in this area; we'll export it and implant it in your marketplace. You have expertise in your marketplace; we'll take that and implant in our marketplace." These were the types of questions we asked to determine ways to best integrate the two organizations . . . as well as to determine what market value the deal really has.

—Don Curry, Blue Cross and Blue Shield of New Jersey

Measuring Results

Effecting integration involves addressing a host of very intangible variables—things such as engendering teamwork and influencing attitudes. Still, any major organizational change program must have the inherent ability to be measured. You cannot gauge the success of a program if you cannot point to concrete accomplishments. More important, you cannot devise new and corrective measures for failing aspects of the program unless you can actually determine that those tactics are deficient. An integration program, therefore, must have measurable criteria to assess the progress of different aspects of the initiative.

Again, how do you truly measure teamwork? How do you really determine whether employees of the merging companies are now understanding and respecting each others' corporate pasts? Clearly, some aspects are not measurable. Other variables definitely are. You must strive to set forth measurement criteria wherever it is possible to do so, whether it is by setting time parameters by which certain integration tasks must be completed, by gauging attitude changes via employee research, or by tracking the number of people who stay with the merged company against expected levels of attrition.

Acknowledging the Two Levels of Integration

We stated earlier that postmerger integration is a long-term process that, in some cases, may never end. It is important to realize that there are two basic levels of integration. One is the prolonged initiative that relates to aligning cultures or effecting a new culture (from two disparate ones), a new corporate identity (the employees' psychological mind-set), and a new corporate image (that which the external market will perceive). The other level of integration relates to the imperative, immediate process of systematically integrating the functional departments of the merging firms.

Integration necessarily assumes that there are differences in the combining companies that need to be addressed. The historical perspective on integration has focused on these differences as the starting point for melding disparate organizations. Conversely, the growth planning approach to integration is based on a different orientation. That is, mergers and acquisitions can never succeed if those championing the integration process focus solely on the differences between the two companies. Rather, *the key to a prompt and effective integration launch is focusing on the similarities inherent in each organization and building on them.*

By isolating common factors and attempting to strengthen the bonds that can be forged from similarities, a successful integration strategy can be expeditiously set in motion. Once this platform for success has been built, all future integration issues can be addressed with a more aggressive mind-set. For example, it is less important to try to integrate the target firm's training and development process into yours when you do not have a training function. Therein lies a dissimilarity that does not necessarily merit consideration in the first level of integration planning. On the other hand, it is likely that both you and the acquired firm both have sales forces. Therein lies a distinct similarity that requires immediate attention. As we have discussed, an issue like this is central to the marketing due diligence process.

We know of a pharmaceutical company combination that exemplified a well-planned postmerger integration. The companies seemed to have done everything right in terms of aligning management teams, extensively communicating with workers worldwide, and bridging the cultural gap between employees. But the merged company failed in one important respect: It neglected to focus on the overlap of the similar function relative to the companies' two sales forces. For six months, while other exemplary integration activities were being carried out, the merged company had two separate sales forces competing with each other out in the marketplace. They were selling separate products and using their original brand names—and the sellers were calling on the same customers and prospects! The moral: There are so many facets of postmerger integration that it is operationally necessary—and, in the interest of expeditious realization of your initial growth strategies, beneficial—to channel your energies toward the all-important areas of commonality, as opposed to worrying about dissimilarities that can be focused on later in the process.

Maintaining Flexibility

No component of an integration program should ever be carved in stone. Maintaining a flexible mind-set is essential.

When the transaction is first envisioned, the creator of the deal has only a rough idea of what the new entity will look like. Certainly, he or she can envision the products, the basic organizational structure, and the image of a given employee working in a given job. But all that can change, and it frequently does. So many unforeseen influences shape and reshape the company along the integration path that the end result is rarely what the CEO or deal champion had first envisioned.

Maintaining a flexible mind-set and enacting procedural changes as necessary must be the goal of integration team members at every level of management. Often, a CEO or key member of the acquisition team is unwilling to allow an unexpected integration roadblock to alter the plan. The mistaken belief is that any change from the original program will derail the overall process. This is erroneous thinking. Changes in the marketplace, the political arena, and the social landscape will likely occur in the months and years after the merger is envisioned and consummated. Action plans will have to be modified. Timetables will have to be extended (rarely are they shortened). Additional expenses will surely be incurred. The integration process always takes longer than expected and often costs more than anticipated. With this in mind, accept the fact that integration requires foresight, patience, and a willingness to expect the unexpected. Remaining flexible will keep you on track—even when you are shifting directions. As long as your destination does not change, it really does not matter which route you take if it eventually gets you there.

Being humble is as important as being flexible. If you think you have all the answers or hold the copyright on the most effective way to address all the aspects of integration, think again. The most successful acquirers have made disastrous deals. In some cases, the finger of blame can be pointed at the failure to perform comprehensive due diligence. In others, failure can be blamed simply on poor timing. But the majority of acquisitions fail because the integration is neither smooth nor—in the worst-case scenario—recognized as being fundamental to the success of the acquisition. In the end, the merged company bears no resemblance to the vision that was in the champion's mind, and the strategic synergies sought are never actualized. Often, the only remedy is divestiture.

SUMMARY

No merger or acquisition can ever succeed if the integration process focuses solely on the differences between the two companies. Rather, the key to successful integration is identifying the similarities inherent in each organization and building on them while maintaining a disciplined yet flexible approach to what is, by all accounts, an arduous process. Isolating common factors and focusing on similarities provides the essence of the growth planning approach to devising and implementing a successful integration strategy.

Understanding the specific type of organizational structure you envision for the merged company will drive your specific integration strategies. All decisions will flow from the decision to enact a centralized or decentralized infrastructure. By examining the various components of these two bipolar infrastructures, and their inherent differences, you will be able to more easily craft an integration approach that leads to speedy realization of your strategic vision. Without this focus, your plan will flounder and chances are the integration program will fail, jeopardizing the ultimate success of the merger or acquisition.

The challenges you will face when attempting acquisition integration are myriad and will likely be different for each transaction. Most probably, however, they will contain the 12 challenges cited in this chapter. Focusing on these challenges will increase the likelihood of successful results. Miss one and your odds for a smooth and productive integration will decline precipitously.

It may be that mergers are like snowflakes in their distinct individuality. Yet identifying and acting on the general challenges to integration will help you keep from getting buried in an avalanche of avoidable problems that can hinder attainment of the strategic synergies you seek.

10

Analyzing and Aligning Corporate Cultures

When two companies merge, the usual claim is that there is a fit between them. Often that claim is based on the presumed "cultural compatibility" of the two organizations.

The notion that two disparate groups of separately trained employees, working in unique environments under varying circumstances, will automatically coexist as a merged workforce is tantamount to wishful thinking. Yet, long-term growth cannot be achieved unless the postmerger integration plan focuses strongly on aligning, as well as possible, the cultures of the combining companies.

How does one evaluate and then act upon something as intangible as corporate culture? The task seems insurmountable, especially when understanding not just one, but two, separate cultures is necessary to develop a comprehensive integration strategy. Nonetheless, a detailed analysis of the many process- and personnel-related variables that comprise an organization's culture must be conducted in order to avoid the proverbial "culture clashes" that have killed hundreds of otherwise strategically sound corporate combinations.

The first step is to identify the variables that collectively define the concept of corporate culture. Once understood, those areas of investigation can be examined further. In this sense, a systematic approach to cultural assessment becomes a useful tool both in the creation of acquisition candidate criteria and in crafting transaction-specific integration plans—the latter being the primary focus of this chapter.

Melding cultures is one of the most onerous challenges of postmerger integration. However, you must acknowledge the different levels of integration in terms of the activities that occur in the near-term integration program and those that occur in later months or years. Integration issues relative to formally aligning cultures clearly fall into the latter time frame.

Of all the aspects of integration, effecting cultural unity is arguably the most difficult and time-consuming one facing the merged firm's management. In one very important sense, aligning cultures may not even be viewed as a formal component of the postmerger integration program. Rather, the task facing management is to understand the merger partners' cultural characteristics in order to devise integration tactics that are appropriate to the merger situation—tactics that are appropriate for the companies being brought together. In other words, understanding each partner's corporate culture provides a general frame of reference that should influence and facilitate the planning and execution of specific integration activities.

There are many types of corporate cultures—all a function of their respective companies' strategic visions and the people who conceive and implement them. Yet, when two companies come together, only one strategic vision remains. And the stronger of the two cultures invariably takes over.

"But what about in a merger of equals?" some readers will ask. We are of the belief that there is virtually no such thing. There will nearly always be a stronger, more dominant partner in any merger. Of course, in a pure merger of equals (and, indeed, there are a scant few out there) two cultures combine to forge a completely new one. This occurs so infrequently, however, that it seems pointless to address this M&A rarity in any great detail.

Culture, in its most basic form, is a series of belief systems held by an employee base. The time it takes to fold the past belief systems of an acquired company into those of the acquiring firm is a function of how deeply embedded those belief systems truly are. When two companies come together to forge, essentially, a brand-new entity, a whole new set of beliefs will result.

Management can never assume that the development of a new belief system or overall cultural alignment will happen by itself. Belief systems must be built, learned, and reinforced. But before new beliefs can be created, old beliefs and attitudes must be gauged. Acquiring management that understands the belief systems that comprise the merging firms' cultures can better plan the integration of employee bases and move closer to achieving the transaction's underlying strategic vision. Therefore, before cultural alignment can occur, the employee mind-set of both companies must first be defined. Only after you understand how employees have come to think about their company and themselves can you fully understand the cultural environment that fostered that mind-set in the first place.

Once high-level compatibility between the merger partners has been established in the acquisition planning stage, then more in-depth analysis of the corporate culture must be conducted during the due diligence process. By first analyzing the people and the corporate environmental factors that impact them, a comprehensive diagnosis of the corporate culture can be garnered—and a framework for integration decision making will result. Moreover, identifying the strengths and weaknesses of the target's employee base and how they are linked to the corporate culture will offer valuable insight into how to leverage the positives and mitigate the negatives during the formal integration process.

DEFINING CORPORATE CULTURE

There has historically been much discussion of and disagreement over the ability to define an organization by cultural type. Management gurus have focused on organizational structure. The academic community has concentrated on the notion of the degree of risk in decision making with which management feels comfortable. Other observers have analyzed corporate culture by breaking it down into the various habits and customs of individual employees.

Too often, people attempt to define culture by saying that it defies definition. "Culture is simply how we do things around here," an executive might say. The criticality of cultural alignment to the eventual success of M&A transactions, however, means that you cannot take the definitional easy way out. Corporate culture *must* be defined in order to factor it into all aspects of your integration planning.

Our approach to defining corporate culture is based on viewing it on three levels, which include both internal and external variables:

- *Structural.* Culture as determined by such factors as company size, industry, and other readily identifiable characteristics.
- *Emotional.* Culture as influenced by the personal feelings individual employees hold toward the company, its policies, and the overall corporate context.
- *Political.* Culture as driven by the distribution of power throughout the organization and the primary modes of managerial decision making.

There is a clear interrelationship between each of these factors. Nonetheless, each needs to be examined individually before you attempt to understand them collectively.

The focus here will alternate between the analytical and the actionable. The insights offered relate both to evaluating a target company's attributes and to addressing those attributes in your postmerger integration and cultural alignment planning.

Culture: Structural Determinants

An organization's culture is determined in part by several factors that pertain to the physical composition of the firm and the industry and markets in which it operates. We call these the "structural determinants" of corporate culture; they include:

- Company size
- Company age
- Industry
- Geographic locale
- Level of diversification
- Genealogy

Company size. Size is the easiest to identify and one of the most influential of the structural determinants of culture. For example, the larger a company is (in terms of the size of its employee base), the more bureaucratic it is likely to be. This is not necessarily a criticism nor does it imply a shortcoming. It simply means that the challenge of managing a sizable employee population typically requires a multitude of administrative processes to track and provide managerial oversight of those workers.

The attribute of bureaucracy as engendered by company size directly contributes to the company's cultural composition. It speaks to the likelihood of there being firmwide rules, policies, and procedures that may spawn a rigid, almost governmental-like corporate context. Large companies, by nature, must be hierarchical. And with many layers of management, broad corporate decision making may tend to be slow—bogged down by numerous approval layers and corporate red tape in decisions ranging from purchasing paper clips to commercializing new products.

What about smaller companies? Typically, they exhibit less of the bureaucratic characteristics of their large-company counterparts. Decision making is usually quicker. The fewer levels of management (which is a result of there being fewer employees) means corporate strategies can be more quickly defined and altered as marketplace conditions require.

Admittedly, these are generalities. A large company may be less bureaucratic and more competitively agile than a given small company. Nevertheless, company size is usually a good indicator of how a company is oriented in terms of responding to its marketplace threats and opportunities—an attribute that, in part, helps characterize its culture.

Company age. Older people tend to be conservative and cautious. Younger people tend to be more progressive and less averse to risk taking. The same can often be said about companies; and each of these attributes, and their attendant operational mind-sets, help characterize their corporate cultures. Long-established firms may have long-established ways of doing business. Newer organizations are devising their modes of doing business as they go along.

Granted, older organizations change as their founders retire and new management takes the helm. Old ways of doing business may, as a consequence, change to become new ways as the organization competes in the marketplace. Nonetheless, the "old-timers' " legacy often lingers, as well as some well-entrenched policies, procedures, and organizational mores. Acquiring such a firm requires evaluating the extent to which this is the case and how, if it all, that cultural trait must be factored into your integration planning.

Industry. The industry in which a firm operates may influence its cultural character. Consider, for example, a company that functions in the moribund "smokestack" manufacturing sector, a low-growth segment that is not seeing much in the way of innovation or new market entrants. A company in that sector may have a culture that has been forged or is influenced by the slow-moving, conservative nature of its marketplace. Consider, on the other hand, the biotech or other high-tech industries—high-growth sectors where the successful firms competing within them are, by nature, aggressive and progressive.

Clearly, the competitive landscape varies industry by industry. Highly competitive industries require companies to continually be devising new products and marketing strategies in order to build and protect market share. Less competitive environments do not require the same level of aggressive product development and promotion. Competition, therefore, in part drives the way a company does business and determines the type of employees management needs to succeed in the marketplace. It is one of the factors that collectively contribute to corporate culture.

Geographic locale. Many people have observed how companies in different parts of the country do business differently from firms in other areas. People like to categorize individuals, and they do the same for companies; for instance, the so-called laid-back West Coast firm versus the "hyperaggressive" East Coast type.

The fact remains, however, that companies that serve a customer base in a given geographic area must craft their products, marketing, and customer service approaches to the buyers within those markets. Companies *must* do so in order to survive. It may be rightly assumed, therefore, that regional companies adopt the culture (or at least some of the salient traits) of the regional culture in which they compete. If you are examining a small or middle-market company that functions in one particular region, it is necessary see how the marketplace engenders or influences some of the company's own unique corporate cultural traits.

Level of diversification. Large, sprawling organizations that function in many markets and offer a multitude of products are likely to be much more culturally complex than smaller firms. The sheer geographic diffusion of a multidivisional organization—coupled with the many product lines that comprise its overall product mix—points up the likelihood of there being distinct heterogeneity among its employees.

The multitude of skill sets alone that are necessary for a large organization to offer numerous products in numerous markets spawns a complex patchwork of personalities. Even if the organization is deemed to have a strong cultural identity, the sheer breadth of the firm and the resultant diversity of its employee base suggest that there will be numerous subcultures, each of which must be identified and examined as part of the broader cultural evaluation process.

Genealogy. The focus of this book is on growth through mergers and acquisitions. Indeed, many companies have expanded by M&A so extensively over their corporate life spans that they, in fact, exist today as an amalgamation of different companies that were never effectively integrated into one corporate whole. (The insurance company example we cited in the previous chapter is a striking representation of just such a phenomenon.) Too often, acquisitive companies become simply a patchwork of companies—each one still representing a culture unto itself—that were never combined to forge one unified culture.

Consequently, when examining a company that has grown significantly through acquisition, it is necessary to study its corporate genealogy. Specifically, your culture-oriented investigation must evaluate the degree to which the target company has effectively integrated its own past acquisitions. The reality is that, if the firm has not done the job effectively, your integration challenge will be made dramatically more difficult. You will be forced ultimately to align not one, but multiple cultures. Caveat emptor!

Culture: Emotional Determinants

On a personal or emotional level, corporate culture may be defined as the collective thoughts, habits, and patterns of behavior of the people employed by the organization.

That, admittedly, is a somewhat academic-sounding definition. But it serves as an apt articulation of the basic components of corporate culture from the employee's individual perspective. Officially, therefore, a culture is made up of cognitive variables and attitudinal guidelines, which can be set forth in mission statements by management: "This is how our company is positioned and competes in the marketplace." "This is how we view our approach to serving our customers and communities." "These are the ways we run our business (operationally)." "This is how we interact with each other as coworkers (interpersonally)." These are the components of culture that can be written down on paper.

In fact, when an employee is hired into a given organization, that person buys into these cultural guidelines. In essence, that person is signing a "cultural contract" that dictates the employee's day-to-day activities and behavior. Management, therefore, establishes the framework of a culture by laying down the parameters of employee behavior. But, in reality, what ultimately results is a synthesis of personalities and environmental influences that, over a period of time, define themselves and comprise the true corporate culture. These are the attributes of the cultural contract that cannot be—or never are—written down.

INSIDER'S OUTLOOK

You have to think of culture as an iceberg. The visible part, like how the office is structured, whether it is formal or informal, is generally not as important as what lies beneath the surface. What you don't see are elements like the assumptions that a group holds. Assumptions about the nature of people, time, economics, business success, reality; fundamental assumptions that are seldom explicit, and less often elicited. Their significance doesn't really become apparent until they're juxtaposed against another culture. It's much like trying to combine two totally different automotive engines in an effort to make a bigger, better one. In fact, it won't work at all.

—Paul Cholak, SHL North America

There are 10 basic emotional factors that must be addressed as part of the cultural evaluation before the magnitude of the challenge of cultural alignment can be assessed. These factors represent the building blocks of the shared belief system, or the cultural contract, and represent the general attitudes and opinions that the employees hold toward themselves, their jobs, their company, and their overall work environment. Specifically, these issues relate to:

1. The company's leader
2. Management structure and style
3. Physical environment and atmospherics
4. Level of comfort and trust
5. Corporate definition of success
6. Level of autonomy desired
7. Level of commitment to superior, job, and company
8. Fairness of total compensation
9. Level of stress
10. Ultimate job satisfaction

By examining each of these 10 emotional factors in detail, we see a belief and value system begin to emerge that differs from company to company, and that contributes to employees' collective cultural orientations. The similarities and differences relative to these 10 factors will contribute to the creation of the backdrop for all attempts at integration planning and longer-term cultural alignment.

The company's leader. Employees may view the head of their company with respect, disdain, or neutrality. With every memo and in-person meeting, employees interpret the CEO's statements and actions as personality and character traits. Depending on management style, the CEO can be perceived as either an authoritative parent figure or an accessible "one of the guys" type.

How employees have come to view their leader has ramifications for how they see the role of a CEO in general. More specifically, how the target firm's CEO is perceived has implications for determining his or her role in the combined firm. If respect is the overall sentiment, will the acquired firm's employees follow their leader blindly and loyally in the postmerger environment? If the CEO is disdained or the object of disrespect, what does this say about how the CEO will be perceived by the combined employee base of the merged firm?

Management structure and style. Each employee has a very specific understanding of the hierarchical system of authority that defines the management style as a whole. Additionally, the mode of management—that is, whether it is dictatorial or consensus-driven—dictates such things as an employee's collective level of personal initiative and risk taking. Are employees encouraged to participate? And, if so, are there risks for "sticking one's neck out"? Are there rewards for making good suggestions?

Physical environment and atmospherics. The physical layout of the company and specific departments therein influence employee behavior and attitudes. For example, an open floor plan often engenders an atmosphere of sharing and personal openness. When senior managers and support staff share the same facilities (e.g., cafeteria, rest rooms, copy facilities), a more relaxed and collegial environment is internalized by employees.

Conversely, when senior and middle management work in their own ivory-tower quarters or behind closed doors, this physical separation creates a formality and interpersonal distance that becomes a part of all behavior and spawns an environment of secrecy and wariness.

Level of comfort and trust. People's opinions about comfort in the work environment most often relate to whether they sense a feeling of trust in the workplace. Workers are more productive when they are not questioning every decision they make nor looking over their shoulders for reproach.

Supervisors who micromanage often create an environment of distrust that inevitably leads to lessened productivity and a fear of making mistakes. An even bigger drawback to an environment of fear is when employees refuse to express their ideas lest their suggestions be their last.

Corporate definition of success. A part of each company's mission statement is its definition of success and how it is compensated. Typically, this emanates from the CEO's own personal definition. In general, success is defined in terms of the company's accomplishments, employees' individual accomplishments, and oftentimes both. Yet, if success is gauged only in bottom-line financial terms, then risk taking and new ideas that can fuel true growth will fall by the wayside as only safe and proven tactics that lead to achievable results are pursued. Conversely, overemphasizing personal growth in lieu of accomplishing the corporate goals will lead to a workforce that is selfish and ultimately incapable of furthering the corporate vision.

A company's concern for the personal growth of its employees is often manifested in the nature and breadth of its training and development programs. Ideally, management's focus on ensuring that every worker plays a role in securing customer satisfaction will allow employees to harness the necessary training to effect personal growth while, concurrently and collectively, working to effect corporate growth.

Level of autonomy desired. This attribute is determined by the mandates of the CEO. If power and/or control is withheld or granted at the highest level, very definitive employee attitudes and orientations result. An employee base with its collective head down waiting for the next directive from a superior adds little value. A workforce such as this stands in direct contrast to one that enjoys and desires greater decision making responsibilities. The former is reactive. The latter is proactive. These fundamental attributes have ramifications for integration planning, as discussed later on.

Level of commitment to superior, job, and company. Commitment differs from individual to individual in terms of its definition and ultimate actualization. Typically, the average and individual lengths of tenure with the firm would appear to provide the most accurate readings of the level of an acquired workforce's commitment. Understand, however, that this indicator is more of a rear-view gauge rather than a projection of commitment to come in the new combined company environment. Yet, managers who either exceed their personal performance objectives or display a strong work ethic are good bets to continue to show commitment.

Lower-level employees' commitment can be gauged by the level of praise they receive from their direct supervisors and coworkers, promptness in arriving to work, and willingness to stay until a specific task is completed (rather than watching the clock). Other indicators of commitment are an employee's desire to understand all technical aspects of a given business (beyond those that relate to one's specific job function) or an unyielding desire to go the extra mile in serving the customer in the best possible way.

Fairness of total compensation. Employees' perception of the fairness of their total compensation package is a key emotional component of culture. Those who feel dissatisfied with the way they are paid or rewarded for their efforts are likely to exist in any organization. Their negative sentiments, when voiced at the watercooler, can easily undermine the positive feelings of other employees. Those who feel they are fairly compensated will not dwell on reward issues in the daily performance of projects that may demand more than basic effort.

Disparities of pay between individuals from the merging companies who perform similar tasks or who serve in similar departments should be identified and rectified early in the integration process. This type of news travels quickly between merging organizations and will absolutely impact the intensified levels of commitment that will be required going forward.

Level of stress. Some companies foster notoriously more stressful environments than others. A high-pressure ad agency is going to exhibit pressure cooker tendencies significantly more often than a staid commercial bank. Some employees can survive—even thrive—in high-pressure or deadline-oriented milieus, while other workers cannot even think about operating in such environments. Determining the stress level of a company is important in the emotional realm of cultural analysis—whether that pressure is engendered by the industry, by the management, or by some other internal or external variable. (Keep in mind, too, that pressure levels vary on a department-by-department basis.) But, most important, realize that pressure levels dramatically vary when people are in the throes of a merger or acquisition.

Determining the level of stress that existed in a culture prior to the merger announcement is impossible after the fact. Once news of the impending transaction is disseminated, that organization and its level of stress will be forever and irrevocably altered. Behaviors in the workplace that were once considered a distinct part of the culture instantly change as people begin functioning in survival mode.

When viewing the culture in the aftermath of the announcement, be aware that there will be both a fear over loss of identity and a unification against the "common enemy" (the other merger partner). Work-related anxieties will overwhelm most individuals as they await the determination of their fate. The myriad responses to news of being acquired can run from initial anger, denial, and fear through the complex emotional gamut that typically accompanies any grieving process.

In short, normally stressful environments become incredibly more so. Low-stress environments experience pressure levels never before seen by the employee base. The stress factors will be clearer and not as impacted by people's short-term fixation on potential job loss and other sources of M&A-related anxieties, if one is fortunate enough to have the opportunity to analyze in detail the target firm's culture *prior* to news of the merger.

Ultimate job satisfaction. Many of the aforementioned emotional variables combine to comprise people's overall satisfaction with their jobs. But, again, immediately after the merger or acquisition has been announced, you will be unable to clearly interpret accurate levels of job satisfaction. Many employees' predominant emotion in the wake of the announcement will be survival. No one struggling to survive can rightfully claim to be, at that point, satisfied with one's job. Those who feel secure in their positions will appear satisfied, while those who are either uncertain or actually jeopardized will act in an understandably dissatisfied manner.

As roles and responsibilities change and managers are moved either up or down the corporate ladder, the workforce will become more inured to the changes around them. Those with better opportunities elsewhere will leave. Those who have been promoted to more visible or higher-paying positions will be more apt to accept the new culture. The balance will be torn between either retaining the core of their past roles or wanting to move forward with their professional lives.

Culture: Political Determinants

Of all the variables that contribute to defining a company's culture, none is more significant than its overall political climate.

By "political" we mean how power is distributed throughout the organization and how managerial decisions are made. But the political climate of a company has much broader ramifications. It sets the tone within an organization that directly impacts employees' day-to-day activities and contributes to the aforementioned emotional sentiments they hold toward the company and their roles within it.

From a political standpoint, corporate cultures move along a continuum that modulates from a dictatorial point of reference on one extreme to one of total employee empowerment on the other. Determining where a company stands on this "control continuum" is the starting point for a political-oriented evaluation of corporate culture.

Moreover, comparing where your company and the target firm are plotted along this range will offer the first insights into the likelihood of true cultural compatibility.

The control continuum transcends issues of company size and pertains to firms in all industries. Considering that the CEO is the starting point of all power in an organization, the first step in the political-oriented review of cultural composition is to determine the extent to which power is concentrated within the office of the CEO. Once this has been ascertained, you will be able to find where the organization fits on the control continuum.

The control continuum is characterized by different political contexts, each of which may be described as one of the following political culture types:

- Dictatorial
- Black knight
- Benevolent kingdom
- Rule book
- Enlightened
- Committee rule
- Consensus rule
- Autonomous

Examining the characteristics of each political cultural type will help you to more easily understand the control continuum.

Dictatorial culture. This political climate is characterized by a powerful leader who wields complete control. With the exception of major corporate decisions that require board approval, the dictatorial CEO rarely has to ask another's permission to do anything. In fact, the CEO typically carries such power that he or she can cede authority to any one person or group—and seize it back whenever desired.

The dictatorial culture is often seen in situations where one person has conceived the vision, possibly founded the company, made most of the financial investments, and taken the business risks to get the enterprise to its current stage. That person calls the shots—dictatorially. All decisions are made by this person or designees who are typically close friends, family members, or longtime, trusted associates. In fact, in this environment, trust and loyalty are the most valued of personal traits. Employees are often compensated and otherwise rewarded based on their loyalty and commitment to the personal goals posited by the dictator.

In a smaller company, employees are much more readily exposed to and influenced by the behavior of the CEO. That person's personality traits, as well as likes and dislikes, are well known. All determinations of what is and what is not appropriate behavior flow from this individual. Indeed, the dictatorial CEO will typically be surrounded with those who have learned to accept and, to a certain degree, adopt similar behavioral traits. As the dictator's personal and professional style trickles down to senior management, the leader's daily habits and philosophical beliefs are emulated. Those dealing with the CEO firsthand quickly find out what is important to that person and how he or she acts. If new ideas are neither tolerated nor rewarded by the CEO, they will never become a part of the organization's cultural fabric. If the head of the company is a martinet, then chances are that immediate subordinates down the chain of command will mimic this behavior. Essentially, the workforce slowly learns what is safe, what the boundaries are, and what works—as driven by the acts and attitudes of the CEO.

In larger companies with several locations and multiple managers, the direct influence of the dictatorial CEO becomes somewhat diffused. But employee behavior never strays too far from that which occurs in the home office. Subcultures may develop from the original culture. Geography and local market dynamics will alter the original corporate culture, maintaining the core culture yet personalizing it to the environment of the group at hand. As the local organization expands, the senior manager running the branch or region becomes the new source of cultural interpretation, and certain subcultural traits emerge. But since that person serves at the behest of the CEO, the dictatorial culture will never change too dramatically.

Black knight culture. One step removed from the radical extreme of the dictatorial control model is the "black knight" political culture (not to be confused with the old line M&A definition of an unfriendly acquirer drawn to a target once in-play). In this environment, power still flows directly from the CEO, but it can be seized by those willing to blindly enforce it. In a black knight culture, a select group of mercenarylike enforcers are the point of control, carrying out the will of the leader. The black knight never places his or her stamp over that of the leader. Instead, the black knight functions, almost robotlike, in carrying out corporate initiatives and in resolving issues and disputes. For example, the statements "That's how the CEO wants it to be" or "That's how it's always been done" suffice as a satisfactory reason for any decision leveled by a black knight.

Information is distributed only on a "need to know" basis. And, it is this secretiveness that alienates the workforce. Employees, in turn, are asked to blindly do their jobs without ever knowing any details or the strategic rationale of specific activities. This environment is characterized by low levels of morale and strong feelings of inequity in the areas of both workload and compensation.

Benevolent kingdom culture. Moving further away from the dictatorial control model, and closer to the center of the continuum, is the "benevolent kingdom" culture. Patriarchal in nature, this culture still enforces the will of the leader, who is treated as king. But, the difference between this and a black knight culture is one of personal involvement. Those carrying the will of the leader are not mercenaries. In contrast, they have a personal stake in the success of the company—and with that comes certain latitude in decision making. The control they wield is not blind, making them more than mechanical conduits of a higher vision.

In the benevolent kingdom, the will of the leader is humanized. Individual personalities of senior management are allowed to tint the mandates that are issued from on high. The personalized nature of the benevolent kingdom creates a greater sense of trust within the organization and a genuine feeling that all decisions are for the benefit of the company and the overall workforce.

Leaders of benevolent kingdoms can be generous to their workforces but on their own terms. There is typically not a lot of feedback sought from the workforce regarding benefits, compensation, and work conditions. But there is an effort on behalf of management to make the corporate climate a positive one for employees. The mood of the workforce is typically one of benign acceptance—no different than that of a child, making no decisions, and assuming Mom and Dad are taking care of everything.

INSIDER'S OUTLOOK

The number-one most important success factor is making the management culture work to the extent that there are differences between the two organizations. This is especially true in entertainment and media. They are very dependent upon quality personnel because of the type of services and products that media clients produce. Making the personnel cultural integration work is a key issue. The second most important success factor is realizing the expected synergies. Quite often the deal requires improved combined cash flow because of the synergies. And while cost cutting may be easy and quick to determine, the harder part is maximizing the revenue upside. Third, yet not least important, is minimizing the disruption in your existing business—in essence, making sure that you don't get so focused on the merger that you lose sight of your existing clients.

—Dudley Mendenhall, Bank of America

Rule book culture. Further along the continuum is the "rule book" culture, which focuses more on a set of conditions that have been established rather than on individual personalities. Employee behavior is dictated by a specific set of guidelines that ensures that everything is done by the book. The cultural contract that workers have with their employer is often guided by a rigid employee handbook or code of behavior such as a set of integrity guidelines. The answers to all questions seem to exist in some document, and management acts more as interpreters of the rules than sources of the directives themselves. Adherence to these fundamental guidelines creates a similarity of process and behavior that is often perceived as impersonal.

Senior management acts within very clearly articulated boundaries. The political channels and reporting relationships are specifically mapped out. Employees are rewarded when they heed these explicitly documented guidelines. In the rule book culture, staff promotions and visible status symbols (e.g., larger offices, designated parking spots, executive lounge access) indicate whether an employee knows the rules and plays by them.

Enlightened culture. The first point along the continuum in which we encounter any degree of employee empowerment is the "enlightened" culture. This model is one step removed from the rule book culture. In this environment, knowledge is power. Control still flows from the very top, but employees' awareness of the firm's corporate goals grants them power. The enlightened culture encourages individual contributions. Still a soldier carrying the leader's vision, the employee is free to interpret the vision and maximize one's own role within the context of the greater collective.

Management involves the employee in projects in which he or she has access to information usually reserved for those at the top. Those who understand and actively and publicly support the greater vision create the hierarchy. And, those willing to support and build upon the specific vision of the leader are rewarded with even greater access to information—and, consequently, greater involvement in progressively higher-level and higher-visibility projects. Absolute loyalty and adherence to the party line is insisted upon.

An enlightened culture prides itself in working for the greater good of the company within relatively tight constraints. But the flexibility to act within those boundaries and feelings that one is on the inside act as motivational tools. Morale is typically higher in enlightened cultures because even the lowest-level employee feels as if he or she is a part of the team and making a direct contribution to the furtherance of strategic initiatives.

Committee rule culture. The "committee rule" culture embodies a team mentality. The point of control is the committee, typically comprised of senior managers. They are usually given broad strategic mandates from the CEO and charged with developing action plans. The committee's strategies are then forwarded to selected middle managers for tactical implementation. In a committee rule environment, all major decisions are ultimately made at the top. But, buy-in is achieved by involving senior and middle managers in a limited consensus-building process. Because of the time involved in collecting input from various factions, decisions are made slowly.

Status is bestowed upon employees by virtue of their involvement in various strategic and tactical committees. Some organizations use committee appointments as forms of remuneration and reward for success in other projects. In committee rule, no one individual can ever take credit or blame for a specific action. Better and bolder ideas come from committee rule because of the encouragement to devise and share new approaches and practices. In a committee rule culture, involvement on—and association with—higher-level committees helps increase morale, but does not fuel the personal feelings of accomplishment that an individual may experience in a more autonomous setting.

Consensus rule culture. "Consensus rule" cultures take an even greater step towards employee empowerment. In this environment, the leader seeks the participation of senior management to actualize the broad strategic goals of the company. In fact, in a consensus rule environment, the vision of the company is conceived by committee. This openness of ideas and visions creates an environment in which the rules are not carved in stone but rather are developed continuously through mutual agreement.

The major drawback to this is that the direction of the company is not fixed and may, in fact, periodically shift. Meetings are held to sculpt and refine a group vision comprising all the members of senior management. This iterative process allows managers to have input into their own fate. Of course, if consensus cannot be reached, the leader must then make the final decision. This type of culture is similar to that of the U.S. Senate in which the vice president acts as tiebreaker in the event of a deadlocked vote. Morale is typically very high in consensus rule cultures because of the feeling of genuine involvement by management. But, as in committee rule environments, real change is often slow to occur because of the time it takes to make decisions. However, when change does occur, more often than not it is truly the will of the team. And the process of achieving group buy-in serves to further individual and collective commitment and productivity.

Each individual in a consensus rule culture feels that he or she is an integral part of setting the direction of the company. Since that is actually the case, consensus rule environments allow managers to forge their own roles and identities within the company.

Autonomous culture. The "autonomous" culture lies at the other end of the control continuum from the dictatorial culture. In this environment, informality is the rule, and the emphasis is on the individual employee completing individual tasks. The drawback is that as each employee focuses on individual activities, the direction of the company as a whole may flounder. The need to constantly create individual value often replaces concerns of accomplishing broader corporate objectives. As each employee strives to better one's personal standing within the company without an awareness of or sensitivity to the bigger picture, the company may find that it no longer serves the needs of the marketplace.

The focus on autonomy and personal decision making often relegates company management to a lesser role. The CEO acts more as a facilitator than a leader, the result being that he or she is perceived as a figurehead with no real power. This can lead to chaos and, in extreme cases, anarchy. (There have been a number of technology start-up companies that have fit this mold.) The drawback of the autonomous culture is an almost total lack of accountability. Who is in charge? Who is to blame when things go wrong? What is critically important, in such cases, is who will set the company back on the right track? Autonomous cultures often must be reined in and rebuilt at another point along the culture control continuum to survive the rigors of long-term business. Whether this occurs through a restructuring, acquisition, or merger, once it occurs, the employees who thrived in an autonomous culture will feel constrained in a more orderly context. Indeed, they may be totally unable to function in the more structured environment.

The political control continuum—coupled with the insights gleaned from examining the structural and emotional aspects of corporate culture—provides the basic input you need to begin the process of aligning corporate cultures. We are still, however, at the theoretical stage. In Part Three, strategies and guidelines are detailed to aid you in the task of formally melding diverse corporate contexts. For the purposes of cultural analysis, however, looking at how the aforementioned variables combine to result in discrete organizational attributes will help you better understand the guidance in that section.

ORGANIZATIONAL VALUES

As stated earlier, there is an inescapable interrelationship between cultural variables. Yet, separately and together, these intangible factors manifest themselves in very tangible ways.

Once the three corporate culture categories—structural, emotional, and political—have been evaluated in terms of their relevance to the M&A situation at hand, your investigation must move to a deeper level. Next, you must identify the characteristics that most accurately capture the essence of a company's cultural context. Exploring the following areas will lend additional insights into the shared understanding that employees have about the organization, how things are done in it, and the way workers are supposed to behave. In a phrase, the following comprise the company's "organizational values":

- Group versus individual performance measurement
- Competition between employees
- Reward systems
- Formality versus informality
- Communication protocol
- Departmental interaction
- Amenability to employee risk taking
- Commitment to individual growth
- Work-life orientation
- Conflict resolution

Group versus Individual Performance Measurement

Companies emphasize and reward performance based either on an employee's individual accomplishments or on that person's contribution to (and the success or failure of) the team to which he or she is assigned. Often, an organization's fundamental approach to measuring employee performance—and hiring—keys on the ability of employees to function in either a team- or individual-oriented environment. The extent to which company management is either team- or individual-oriented also determines the firm's overall stance on the level of intracompany competition it forges or tolerates, and the degree to which the firm fosters teamwork in general.

Competition between Employees

Some companies explicitly encourage competition among employees in the belief that making people strive to win out over coworkers will foster maximum individual productivity. Competition may be encouraged among teams or among the people within and outside of these teams. Clearly, this can be healthy or unhealthy. We are not making a value judgment here. But it is important to gauge the degree to which internal competition is fostered (and rewarded) in order to determine the orientation people will bring into the merged-firm environment.

Reward Systems

How are people rewarded? In terms of money (salary and bonuses)? Titles? Various and sundry corporate perks? Employees who are happy in a given company (and whose prolonged tenure reflects this) generally have grown accustomed to their company's reward system—both the provisions of those rewards and the time parameters within which they are granted (e.g., annual salary reviews).

Understanding a company's reward system, most importantly, requires knowing the criteria for performance evaluation. For instance, are employees rated on the basis of precise, quantitative measures that management has set for them? Or are people graded on more qualitative and subjective variables resulting, say, from input gleaned from "360° feedback" from supervisors, subordinates, and peers?

Formality versus Informality

This factor is a tone set at the top of an organization that filters down and throughout the company. For instance, does the CEO require subordinates (outside of his close circle of associates) to address him as "*Mr.* CEO"? Or is he greeted by his first name by coworkers at all strata of the corporate hierarchy? The level of formality or informality is manifested in many different ways within a company—from how people interact with each other in the corporate corridors, to how they can make suggestions on operational improvements, to whether or not the company Christmas party is a lampshade-on-the-head bash with blaring dance music or a staid, string-quartet affair with genteel conversation throughout.

Communication Protocol

Perhaps in no other area is the level of formality within a company more apparent than in its mode of internal communication. This transcends issues such as the style and tone of the company house organ. Rather, it has more to do with office communications between different levels of management. For example, we have seen organizations where any communiqué to a senior manager has to be in the official company memo format, with all the requisite cc:'s. We have also seen situations where a Post-it note stuck onto a photocopied news article was an eminently appropriate message format for a middle manager communicating with the company chairman!

The formality of communication protocol goes beyond the media employed for interoffice missives. Of perhaps even greater significance are hierarchical considerations and the channels through which messages may or may not go. Some extremely formal organizations allow communications to travel only one level at a time. That is, a manager may communicate only with an immediate supervisor, and not one level above that. Anthropologically, much can be learned about a society by the way its members communicate with each other. The same holds true for corporate cultures.

Departmental Interaction

A key to corporate success is close interaction between functional departments within a company. We discussed product development infrastructure in Chapter 5. In that context we cited the enhanced efficiency that results when the product development process is not relegated to the marketing organization. Rather, product development is greatly improved when there is regular, ongoing coordination between marketing, sales, manufacturing, and finance. The same holds true from a broader operational standpoint.

Effective organizations ensure that their various functional departments coordinate their activities. It is more than just making sure the right hand knows what the left hand is doing (which is largely a communication issue). The overall efficiency and cost-effectiveness of the entire enterprise results when all areas of the company pull toward a common goal and marshal the human and monetary resources necessary to do so. In the realm of departmental interaction, the connection to overall corporate teamwork is obvious.

Amenability to Employee Risk Taking

Our earlier look at the control continuum highlighted how the distribution of power within an organization dictates the level of autonomy employees enjoy in different political paradigms. An issue directly related to autonomy is employee risk taking. Employees who are afforded latitude in their own day-to-day decision making necessarily assume an element of risk taking. This orientation to risk is not one of personal volition. Rather, it comes with the autonomy territory. Consequently, employees' inclination to take decisional risks may either be thrust upon them by managerial mandate, or exist as an individual's personal inclination.

In either case, management has a say in the extent to which employees are risk-averse or risk-inclined. That is, management either fosters risk taking, condones it, or punishes it. Your investigative task then is twofold: determining the degree to which employee risk taking is prevalent in the target company's culture, and then assessing management's overall stance toward it.

Commitment to Individual Growth

Most large, progressive companies have formal training and development departments designed to effect employees' continuing education. Others, without in-house training capabilities and facilities, will finance educational training via outside resources. Irrespective of whether training is conducted inside or outside the organization, it is necessary to assess how committed management is to its workers' ongoing professional development.

Moreover, it is important to gauge what type of training management encourages its people to take—for example, skills related to technical aspects of the business, interpersonal training related to selling skills or verbal communications, or skills development in new or emerging office technologies. Understanding management's orientation to effecting individual employees' growth lends insights into its strategic imperatives (e.g., where there is an emphasis on selling or customer service skills) and the extent to which the firm is truly a "learning organization" committed to steadily increasing its market competitiveness and client focus.

Work-Life Orientation

There has been a major movement within American business relative to helping employees balance their professional and personal lives. Forward-thinking companies realize the importance of assisting employees in meeting their familial commitments in order to help them adequately and productively focus on their professional responsibilities. Flextime, telecommuting, and other corporate-imposed programs—coupled with governmental initiatives such as the Family Medical Leave Act (FMLA)—show society's increasing sensitivity to the importance of balancing the work-life equation.

Some companies clearly are more progressive in this regard than others. And their workforces are happier, more productive, and more loyal as a result. How does the company you are evaluating as a merger candidate stack up in this all-important regard? If it is high up on the progressiveness spectrum, its employees' expectations for similar work-life benefits will be equally high in the merged firm environment.

Conflict Resolution

Many companies encourage employees to openly air interpersonal conflicts and criticism. Just as many organizations do not. Identifying how a company handles the conflict resolution process is important in two key respects (one is negative; the other is positive). First, if the target company has broad, formalized conflict resolution procedures, that means it has had to institute them for a reason; the question becomes, "Is conflict so pervasive in the organization that it points up a potential problem area for the merged firm going forward?" Second, if the firm has learned to successfully handle conflicts, this represents an important skill that may be employed during the integration process, a time when interpersonal conflicts are typically at their highest and most intense levels.

GATHERING DATA ON CORPORATE CULTURE

Assessing a company's culture requires much more than walking the halls to get a "gut feel" for the defining characteristics of the environment. True, there is a distinctly subjective element to sizing up corporate culture. But it is more important to formally collect organizational data to enable you to assess the company based on the cultural variables we have identified.

When two companies are being merged, attempting to gather a detailed psychological profile of every single employee is neither practical nor necessary to ultimately integrate the firms. Nonetheless, it is necessary to examine the discrete components of the companies and assess the various departments comprising them.

An analysis of both companies' organization charts is a good starting point. Yet, simply placing names and titles in boxes provides sketchy information at best. A deeper look into such demographic issues as the age, years of service, and qualifications of senior and middle managers provides the first glimpse of the cultural makeup of each company. By further examining these people's experience prior to joining the firm, you can get a perspective on the industries and technical areas from which management has been hired. The answers to such questions as, "What is the average age of key personnel?" and "Do managers share a particular type of professional or academic background?" will offer some good basic information that can serve as a starting point from which to research larger cultural issues.

Beyond this staffing and demographic data, which is available in personnel files and departmental evaluation reports (and often housed in computerized human resources information systems), it is necessary to accumulate data relative to the employee base's psychometric composition. In Chapter 12, conducting employee attitude surveys as part of your postmerger internal communication planning is discussed. Chances are the target firm has conducted such studies. If so, reviewing the findings will provide helpful input on workers' beliefs regarding different aspects of the company, as well as on many of the emotional variables we discussed. Assumptions on the employee base's broader organizational values may also be made.

Of course, once the merger is finalized and formal integration tactics are set in motion, it is advisable to conduct employee surveys of your newly acquired workers regularly. Gauging their beliefs, attitudes, and sentiments—as well as those of people from your organization, whose outlooks may well have changed after the transaction—is necessary to begin planning out longer-term cultural change activities.

For instance, by performing focus groups in which the participants are asked such questions as, "What part of your job do you enjoy the most? The least?" and "What training did you find most valuable? Least valuable?" you can get a read on very broad or very specific attitudinal and functional issues. One such question area can relate to people's overall flexibility and orientation to change. Inquiring about the changes that have taken place in the merged organization and how people felt about them will reveal their attitudes toward the initial phases of the organizational realignment—input that is necessary to craft future cultural consolidation initiatives.

As is evident by virtue of the different types of data you should ideally collect, evaluating the culture of an organization is not an easy task. It takes time and extensive research. Unfortunately, the analysis must often be performed in a short period of time. By understanding what to look for and what questions to ask, and by accumulating as much data as you can from as many different people and sources as possible, the task will be smoother and the results will be more accurate and more actionable.

OBSERVATIONS ON ALIGNING CULTURES: SITUATIONAL FACTORS

The merged-company perspective holds that a company should be viewed from day one of your planning as an element of the future combined firm. Adopting this inherently comparative viewpoint is essential when assessing corporate culture. That is, the structural, emotional, and political aspects of your assessment—as well as the identification of organizational values—should be conducted both for the target company and for your own.

In general, where there are striking dissimilarities in terms of the cultural variables cited, the potential for a clash of cultures is heightened. Conversely, when broad similarities exist, the cultures can be more easily aligned and long-term integration more speedily attained. Other factors, such as company size, whether a company is in the service or manufacturing sector, whether the merger is a horizontal or vertical one, and whether the workforces are autonomous or closely managed, will either facilitate or complicate cultural alignment.

Company Size

It is obviously easier to align cultures when a smaller company is being absorbed into a larger one. More often than not, the smaller workforce is asked to fully and immediately adopt the cultural character of the acquirer. In the process, unfortunately, the managers and employees of the smaller firm may feel unimportant and overlooked, and may suffer from a complete loss of identity. Rather than being asked to integrate aspects of their culture into the acquirer's, they are asked to subjugate them. As a result, many employees will distance themselves from the acquiring company. This alienation may breed discontent and spawn future problems that can derail the integration process.

The key to aligning the culture of a smaller firm with that of a larger firm is allowing the former to maintain some of its uniqueness. Often, a domineering larger company will attempt to completely engulf the smaller firm's culture and eliminate it. This is a mistake. Within weeks, top-level management and key employees will leave. In the end, the acquisition will prove to be a failure, since all that you will have acquired is the skeleton of an operation, not the critical human assets that made the company a desirable acquisition target in the first place.

In acquisitions where there is a significant size disparity, it is critically important for the acquiring CEO to recognize that the top layer of management in the target firm is typically comprised of very entrepreneurial people. They will not be eager to toss away the culture they have built. It will be eminently beneficial to allow them to retain certain elements of it.

Service or Manufacturing Sector

Mergers that take place between companies in the manufacturing sector may be easier to integrate and culturally align than those in the service sector. This is not attributable as much to the makeup of the employee bases as it is to the presence of structured processes in a manufacturing environment. In manufacturing settings, there is a greater uniformity of procedures and behaviors, thus making outcomes somewhat more predictable. Raw materials are procured and goods are produced and delivered to the marketplace in very precise and regimented ways via established channels.

In service businesses (e.g., financial services, consulting), flexible behavior and processes are often the norm among many levels of workers. A service business, therefore, may have a wider range of acceptable employee mind-sets and procedures, which makes it more difficult to get those businesses and their people to adopt new modes of thinking and behavior.

Another issue relative to the manufacturing versus service industry dichotomy is one of pure geography and physical logistics. In the manufacturing sector, people function in specific identifiable areas such as distribution centers or manufacturing plants. Conversely, in the service sector, day-to-day business practices are often more geographically diffused. Service industry work often requires off-site business, conducted by a mobile professional staff, performing different functions in different places. The geographic dispersion and overall mobility of a company's people, therefore, contribute to its cultural orientation and to the ultimate challenge of cultural alignment.

Horizontal or Vertical Mergers

Horizontal mergers have a greater chance for facile cultural alignment because of the simple fact that the combining companies share a common business (or, at least, a majority of elements thereof). And, initially, cultural assessment is easier to perform when both companies, at least on a high level, understand each other's industry, products, and services, and the overall language of the enterprise. Essentially, if both companies sell the same products, compete in the same marketplace, or have some other area of commonality, there is a foundation for beginning the cultural alignment process.

Another advantage to a horizontal merger is that more often than not, the companies' managers have had a reason to interact with each other through professional associations, at industry trade shows, and the like. As competitive as they may be, many industries are notoriously close-knit; everybody seems to know everybody else. Thus, when merger discussions begin, people who have been playing in the same game may be more willing and amenable to *playing on the same team in the future*. The distinct element of familiarity among the people involved in a horizontal combination can facilitate many aspects of cultural evaluation and alignment.

Autonomous versus Closely Managed Workforces

The challenge of cultural alignment is directly influenced by the nature of the acquired firm's workforce as determined by where the company fits on the political control continuum. For instance, people in autonomous cultures may have greater difficulty accepting an acquirer's new culture if it is forcefully thrust upon them. A propensity towards defection and an unwillingness to relinquish authority to a new and unknown leadership are drawbacks that an autonomous culture poses to the integration process. That is the negative. The positive is that an autonomous culture is more likely to be able to transfer real value to the acquiring organization. An empowered workforce, though more difficult to integrate, often brings with it new ideas, a heightened focus on quality, and a more positive spirit than an otherwise dronelike culture.

OBSERVATIONS ON ALIGNING CULTURES: CRITICAL SUCCESS FACTORS

Taken together, the areas of guidance offered throughout this book will aid in effecting integration and eventual cultural alignment. Still, there are several critical success factors that merit citation here.

Establish a Vision, Not Just a "Mission"

The merged firm must be viewed as a corporate community that lives by certain standards and guidelines. It should not be ruled by them, but rather empowered by them. This starts with management very clearly articulating the corporate vision—not the platitude-ridden mission statements that adorn virtually every annual report, but a day-to-day "vision statement" that stresses the values of the company and the appropriate employee actions that will reinforce and support attainment of the corporate objectives underlying the vision message.

The vision must pervade all elements of the merged firm's operations and processes, from the human resources (HR) department to the company cafeteria. It must also be forcefully communicated in all media and forums. The rule in integration planning is not just to communicate with employees, but to overcommunicate! The merged firm's vision is arguably the most important message to trumpet loudly, broadly, and regularly.

Importance of Senior Management Buy-in and Involvement

Senior managers from the acquired firm must serve as the conduits of information being disseminated in support of the cultural alignment process. In essence, they are both the source and the delivery system of "the word" in their day-to-day interactions with members of their original employee base. The bottom line is that this group is central to helping effect cultural alignment, making their willingness to do so and their understanding of the obstacles to be encountered in the process the relevant issues. Their full and total commitment to meeting and overcoming the challenges of cultural consolidation clearly is fundamental. That is, if upper management is unwilling to enthusiastically participate in the process from the beginning, chances are that cultural alignment will never be effected and that the merger's long-term success will never ensue.

Effect Constant Employee Interaction

Integration planning requires forming teams of employees from the combining firms as a means of physically consolidating corporate functions. It is important to continue this over the long term to effect initial and enduring cultural alignment.

Only through strategically coordinated interaction among employees can people shed their emotional ties to their past company and begin to establish a bond with their new colleagues. If management and employees from once-separate firms are involved in various projects that promote the strategic vision, then when they all go home at night, not only will each feel and think the same things about the company's direction, but each will also take pride in his or her role. This is the true definition of cultural buy-in.

A once-radical, but recently more accepted, tool is the "social contract," which details (in writing) the roles of every member of a given department or division, including management. This not only concretizes the mutual responsibilities of all employees but alerts and binds them to everyone else's responsibility. This builds trust—an essential component of long-term integration. When employees can trust their new management and coworkers, they behave in a more positive way and also have a sense that a self-motivated contribution will neither be "unnoticed" nor punished despite the result. The existence of a social contract can also create a sense of willingness to contribute more regularly because each employee has management's commitment to them in writing.

The environment that centers around performance can more easily drive better performance on an individual as well as a group basis. This will create a social conscience that more readily understands when poor performance has occurred and focus on bringing better performance to the fore. Just as cross-training helps keep an athlete from becoming bored when performing a singular exercise such as running or biking, an organization that promotes cross-functional or trans-project work allows an employee to use additional skill sets in accomplishing a task.

Adding a strategic component to an employee's otherwise tactical job function not only promotes freer thinking and new ideas, but reinforces the belief in the employee. In a culture where individuals do not feel locked into a nine-to-five grind, they will tend to more consistently contribute to the organization in nontraditional ways while taking their primary task more seriously. The bottom line is profitability, and that can be simply derived from a cohesive, more productive workforce with stronger morale.

SUMMARY

When you acquire people via a merger or acquisition, you are gaining employees who bring with them an entirely different set of beliefs and values than your existing workforce. Either those people's former corporate culture will gel with yours and there can be an actualized alignment, or it will clash. But remember: *The merged organization's culture will ultimately define itself.*

When functioning in the throes of change wrought by a merger or acquisition, people's ability to embrace the combined company's values can spell the difference between having a productive and participatory workforce actively working toward a common goal or a robotic army of minions waiting for their next order. In essence, the real task of aligning the cultures of two organizations centers around a thoughtful and thorough analysis of the people you are acquiring. If you do not truly want them, do not go through with the transaction. If you want them to change, make sure that they are malleable. And if you want them to be a part of your vision, know that your vision must be inclusive and flexible.

Once a new cultural contract has been established, offered to the employee masses, and begun to be accepted, implementing instructive and motivational programs will help ensure the true consolidation of cultures—the tactics for which we detail in later chapters on communications, training, and reward and recognition strategies.

11

Aligning Products and Product Management Processes

For years the race was on between Matchbox cars and Hot Wheels. In what could be considered the quintessential "Brand Prix," the two product lines were locked in a heated competition for dominance of the miniature toy car market. Yet when Mattel Inc. merged with Tyco Toys Inc. in 1997, these two well-known product lines suddenly found themselves in the same pit stop. Each was competing in a new kind of contest—one that placed them on the same team and where, whichever brand won, the winnings would still go into the same corporate pot.

An important integration challenge arises when companies merge with or acquire firms offering essentially the same goods and services: product overlaps result. Decisions must be made regarding which items to invest in, or which to phase out, as the merged organization begins to compete in the marketplace anew.

Central to the marketing due diligence process is the evaluation of the products and services of a target company to assess the strength of those offerings and the degree to which they will help you strengthen or supplement your product mix. As discussed in Chapter 2, the strategic driver of obtaining a specific product or product-related technologies is often the core of a company's merger and acquisition program.

There are times, however, when acquiring product lines or capabilities is not an element of your M&A game plan. Still, any merger or acquisition necessarily brings new products and services into the fold. A key integration task then becomes determining if and how those items will have a place in the combined company's product mix going forward.

Acquisitions where the buyer intends to have the target function independently pose little challenge to the integrating of two firms' product offerings. Product-related integration becomes more of an issue in vertical integration scenarios, where the acquired firm serves a complementary role in the physical production or distribution of products. The greatest challenge, however, is the horizontal merger of companies in similar businesses, which creates a distinct challenge for the new organization's management: deciding what products and services will be offered to the marketplace in the wake of the transaction.

That there will be an overlap of companies' product offerings is a given. Determining which to market is one of the first and most significant challenges of the integration process—a challenge that is met by identifying the merged company's strategic growth priorities, as well as what attributes of the merging companies can be brought to bear to either enhance successful product and service offerings or to develop new ones.

The fact is, *one of the purest manifestations of strategic synergy resulting from a merger or acquisition is that of products and services whose ultimate marketability is bolstered as a direct result of the merger itself.*

Successfully realizing product-related synergies requires identifying the specific growth-oriented skills, capabilities, and processes resident in one or both of the merging organizations. Identifying where critical skills reside is a precursor to harnessing those capabilities to augment the merged company's competitiveness and overall marketing effectiveness.

The goal in strategic acquisitions should always be to identify capabilities resident in the acquirer or the target company in order to successfully transfer those skill sets into the merged organization. In the context of products, value is created when the skills of one company are transferred to its merger partner, thus creating products (or product improvements) that embody the strategic synergies that drove the deal in the first place.

For example, one company may have the technical expertise to develop a world-class product, while its merger partner brings the organizational brand power that can dramatically heighten that item's marketability. Or, one company has developed a unique new offering whose physical quality can be enhanced via its merger partner's advanced manufacturing capabilities. Mergers and acquisitions involve not only attaining new skills and capabilities, but also learning new ways of doing business. That is why Chapter 6 focuses on assessing not only a target's products but also its product development history and processes.

CHALLENGE OF PRODUCT ALIGNMENT

On finalization of the transaction, the integrated firm has a new array of products and services. Some items may be quite similar to each other. Some may be marginally similar. Some may be brand-new—that is, never before offered by one of the merger partners. Nonetheless, the collective of products points up the opportunity—indeed, the necessity—of assessing the complete product offering that the merged company will bring to the market.

A host of critical decisions must be expeditiously made relative to the organization's overall product mix and individual product lines. Additionally, questions must be asked regarding their production, pricing, promotion, and distribution.

(The nature of products and services is radically different and there are divergent ways to assess them. However, we tend to more frequently use the term "product," although it is not meant to give greater importance to manufactured offerings over intangible services. Where sharp differences exist, these distinctions are cited.)

The product-related decisions management must make after the deal's closing are relatively straightforward. Some products will be kept. Some will be discarded. Some products will be maintained, but then modified and strengthened as a result of specific skills one merger partner brings to the table in terms of manufacturing expertise, customer service, or sales and marketing support. This chapter addresses the strategies management should adopt when making decisions relative to forging the merged company's product mix, product lines, and individual product and service offerings. To readers experienced in strategic planning and business development, some of the guidance in the next section may sound familiar. If so, consider the following a refresher course. All readers, however, will find it helpful to understand basic product management concepts to better grasp the growth planning perspective on integration-focused product decision making.

A merger or major acquisition forces a company's management to reevaluate its overall product mix—the collective of all product lines and individual items the firm makes available to the marketplace. Although the focus of this book is on growth, not on cost cutting, the process of assessing the positives and negatives of individual products enables you to decide which offerings to phase out or eliminate to effect cost savings.

As detailed in Chapter 9, the growth perspective on integration requires that you determine if underperforming products can be quickly reenergized by injecting new skills and capabilities introduced by your merger partner. Therefore, the focus of your product assessment should be on ways to revitalize rather than summarily eliminate declining products and services. Before you look to make decisions on individual products, however, it is necessary to first understand the strategic thrust of the merged company's product and service offering.

UNDERSTANDING YOUR PRODUCT STRATEGY

Decisions relative to keeping, discarding, or revamping individual products and services can only be made after you have articulated the merged company's overall product strategy.

An organization's product strategy is determined by decisions made to its product mix, which—as discussed earlier—is generally characterized by its width and depth. Any time a company's products are brought into the fold via an acquisition, the acquiring firm's product mix will automatically be augmented. There will be additional products and services that either add new product lines (widening the product mix) or lengthen individual product lines (augmenting their depth).

Indeed, many of the strategic mergers discussed thus far were driven by the goal of supplementing or complementing individual product lines. Cited have been acquisitions that were designed to add a state-of-the-art new offering (e.g., the Lotus Notes groupware product joining IBM's software product category). Also chronicled were deals where an acquired product directly complemented an existing line (e.g., the Cordis Corporation's angioplasty surgical products, which dovetailed with Johnson & Johnson's "stent"). Identifying your product strategy should be a central component of your broader acquisition strategy. This, in turn, provides the perspective needed to evaluate product lines and, ultimately, the individual items within those lines.

For example, is your strategy to acquire new product lines to widen your product mix? Is it to add specific items to deepen one or more of your current product lines? Is it to add variations to individual products (e.g., in terms of product features or styling)? If yours is a well-defined product strategy, you naturally have the perspective and decision making criteria to ascertain whether acquired products and services fit into the new organization's total market offering, and where. (In other words, you knew what you needed productwise, and you went out and acquired it.)

INSIDER'S OUTLOOK

There are several fundamental things that determine the likelihood of long-term success of a merger. For instance, it's almost a necessity that the two companies serve many of the same types of customers, have little product overlap, and have the potential for synergies that strategically extend their individual product lines. Taken together, these contribute to the potential for earnings growth and enhanced predictability or stability of earnings.

—John Levinson, Westway Capital LLC

In situations where product attainment is not a strategic driver, such as in cases where new manufacturing processes or geographic territories are sought, you will still encounter the addition of the target's existing product lines. The product-related integration challenge then becomes, "What do you do with the new goods and services that came as part of the package?" You must determine a role for those new items in your product mix. Making that decision requires determining if those items fit strategically into the merged company's mission. The "keep or sweep" decision, therefore, must be based on your current priorities as driven by the merged company's guiding product strategy.

ANALYZING PRODUCT AND SERVICE LINES: STRATEGIC PLANNING ORIENTATION

Once you have identified the merged firm's product strategy, you are ready to begin assessing both the target's and your individual product lines. Sometimes the decisions are easy. For instance, if yours is an industrial customer base, and one of the ancillary product lines offered by the target is consumer-oriented, that product line probably does not mesh with your product market focus. Most likely you would opt to eliminate or try to sell off that line. But what happens when there is greater commonality between the target's and your product and service lines?

A strategic planning perspective is needed to determine which of your current product lines to *build*, *hold*, *harvest*, or *divest*—all terms that come from the infamous Growth-Share Matrix, a popular product planning paradigm.

The matrix is a diagram used in measuring the performance of a company's product lines, product portfolios, and strategic business units or SBUs. It is often referred to as the "Boston Box" in recognition of its creators, the Boston Consulting Group. The matrix contains four quadrants that are used to indicate the status of products in terms of market growth rate (the grid's vertical axis) and market share (its horizontal axis). Market share is a measurement of the product's share relative to that of its largest competitor. Company products and businesses fall into one of the four quadrants according to their positions on the two axes. The units are classified as follows:

- Question marks
- Stars
- Cash cows
- Dogs

Question marks are units that operate in high-growth markets but hold low market share. They require large amounts of financing to cover ongoing costs and to keep pace in the fast-growing market. Question marks are so named because they pose a quandary to management as to whether to continue supporting them.

Stars are market leaders in high-growth markets. Their high market standing does not necessarily correlate to positive cash flow for the company because significant financing is usually required to maintain market share, keep pace with market growth, and fend off competitors.

Cash cows are the most profitable units since they are market leaders in low-growth markets. Cash cows produce enough profit to financially support the company's other products. These units are profitable because the company need not finance capacity expansion (due to slowed market growth) and because they typically benefit from economies of scale.

Dogs are units with low market shares in low-growth markets. They require substantial financing and management time. Management must determine the fate of these underperforming units.

By identifying products' positions in the grid, you can decide whether to continue supporting them. Managers have four basic options:

1. *Build.* Short-term earnings can be given up in an attempt to build long-term market share. This strategy is appropriate for question marks that must grow if they have the potential to become stars.
2. *Hold.* Maintenance of existing market share is a strategy necessary for cash cows that must continue to generate positive cash flow.
3. *Harvest.* Short-term cash flow can be generated at the expense of long-term profits. It involves reducing expenses to increase profits. This strategy is appropriate for weak cash cows or question marks moving into the dog quadrant.
4. *Divest.* The decision to discontinue the product and reinvest resources into other products is appropriate for dogs and question marks that the company can no longer afford to finance.

Strategic planning requires that you employ the Growth-Share Matrix or another product-market evaluation model to periodically assess your own product lines. The merged company perspective of marketing due diligence requires that you view the target company's products using the same methodology.

Ideally, the product line assessment should be done up front in the search and screening process of evaluating different acquisition candidates. Unfortunately, the timing of a deal does not always permit an exhaustive review of every component of the target's product groups. When the deal is finalized, however, you then have the time (as well as complete access to the target's product information) to assess at length its various product and service offerings. The investigative goal is to gather information on the target's offerings, compare that data to your own firm's product attributes, and begin conceptualizing the composition of the merged company's ultimate product lines.

After you have evaluated the current value and future potential of the target's product and service lines using a tool like the Growth-Share Matrix, you are ready to begin deciding on the structure and composition of the merged organization's product lines.

INSIDER'S OUTLOOK

From a product planning standpoint, you must get as close to the market as you can. You have to work with the senior marketing and sales managers in your company to learn what they think is real . . . what products they think the market will actually buy. Too many people say the success of the transaction will be if "Company X will generate a 7% projected growth improvement in revenue per year." That's too vague. Your projections must be much more specific, based on such questions as, "How long will the life cycles of these (acquired) products be? What kind of price compression are we going to deal with in this particular aspect of the industry? What's going to happen to our cost structure?" There are just too many people out there who project a deal based on some far-fetched idea that sales will grow at some arbitrary figure over time. These people aren't thinking about such fundamental things as, "How many of what is each sales rep going to sell where?" Think about what you're going to sell, *then* figure out how much it's going to cost you to sell and what your profits will be.

—Terence Bentley, Siemens Corporation

MAKING PRODUCT AND SERVICE LINE DECISIONS

The process of devising specific product line strategies requires understanding the various ways that companies manage and modify their product lines. By focusing on your basic options, you can determine whether acquired products can play a role in strategically shaping the merged company's product group.

It has already been mentioned that you can deepen an individual product line by adding more products. Another tactic involves adding goods and services that take them out of the *range* the company's items have historically occupied. For instance, a company prices a particular product line at the medium price range. One strategic decision involves adding items to the product line that fall either above or below that range, a process known as "stretching" the product line. For instance, the acquired products can help you stretch your product line downward by adding products that serve the low end of the market (when you currently serve the high end). Or, products could be added to help you stretch upward—giving you high-end products when you currently serve the low end.

When should you consider stretching your product lines upward or downward? The latter is appropriate when you find slow growth hampering your products at the high end, or where competition is increasing and you need to counter with product introductions at the lower end of the spectrum.

Stretching upward is an appropriate strategy when—if the majority of your line is on the low end—you seek to position yourself as a full line provider or if your goal is to attain higher margins or growth potential. Another product line modification is the "two-way stretch," in which both high- and low-end items are added to a product line whose components are priced in the middle of the pack.

Moreover, the target's products can help you fill certain gaps that currently exist in your product lineup. So-called line-filling is a pervasive acquisition strategy. The Johnson & Johnson purchase of Cordis is, yet again, an example of an organization that saw a product line gap and sought to fill it with a complementary item or group of items offered by another company. Filling gaps is a viable strategic option when products are complementary and consistent with other items in the existing line.

Recall the earlier discussion in Chapter 5 on the concept of product line consistency, in which products are sold to the same end users, distributed to the market via the same distribution channels as your existing offerings, and manufactured in similar fashion to your current items. Ensuring consistency is important, but there is a danger of creating too much homogeneity when melding divergent product lines. It is imperative to ensure the products you ultimately include in a specific product line have a distinct element of "just noticeable difference" (JND) that distinguishes the various items you will offer in the postmerger environment.

This fundamental marketing concept JND relates to the theory that consumers assess products based not on the items' individual attributes, but rather in comparison to other products. When merging the target company's products with your own, you must make sure there are differences in product features that are readily perceptible to consumers. Not having a meaningful difference between products may cause customer confusion and, as a result, hinder sales.

A more detrimental end result is cannibalization, where the newly added products draw sales away from products in your original product line. Identifying situations where cannibalization may occur—or where JND may not—is important in determining which products should be retained or deleted in the merged company's eventual product lines.

Decisions on which products to continue offering are further complicated when there are overlapping product lines with distinct strengths. Sometimes the level of overlap is striking, such as in the aforementioned merger of Mattel and Tyco Toys. Both miniature car lines Hot Wheels (Mattel) and Matchbox (Tyco) have strong, steady sales and venerable brand names. Yet there is direct overlap and head-to-head competition between this market's top two players. Few merging companies have to contend with such an onerous product decision . . . although we are sure that many would like to!

The financial realities of business mean that merging companies cannot indiscriminately maintain each and every one of the products and services added in the wake of the transaction. Most companies face distinct financial and operational limitations. Product line additions generate new cost pressures resulting from expenses for inventory, increases to manufacturing capacity or changeovers, and additional distribution and promotion.

Invariably, decisions must be made as to which products to eliminate or gradually phase out. As stated, sometimes the decisions are easy. Products that are underperforming dogs in dying markets should be immediately scrapped. Products and services that do not fit into the merged company's strategic product mix and cannot be logically inserted to stretch specific product lines must also be eliminated. Typically, however, there will be marginal offerings that fall right on the line—the so-called question marks. A tool like the Growth-Share Matrix is a useful starting point for making product line decisions.

In growth-focused M&A planning, however, the evaluative process requires assessing each marginal item from the merged company perspective—the focus of which is on determining whether there are skills and capabilities of the merged company that can help underperforming products achieve desirable levels of profitability or, conversely, help high-performing products do even better in the marketplace.

MAKING PRODUCT ALIGNMENT DECISIONS: A SKILL-BASED PERSPECTIVE

Identifying and transferring critical skills and capabilities between merging organizations is central to growth-oriented M&A planning. It is particularly important in the context of product alignment planning, where the creative or managerial capabilities needed to help a particular product or product line succeed in the marketplace may be resident in the integrated resources of the combined firm.

The personnel-related aspect of product mix alignment relates to pinpointing which professionals in the buyer or seller organizations have the experience and talents needed to bolster each aspect of the product development and management process.

Our earlier discussions have cited the need to pay special attention to the target's marketing and sales team. People bring specific talents and skills to their positions. Critical skills, however, often reside not within one particular person, but rather in the target organization itself. Core capabilities are found within the fabric of a company residing in the day-to-day workings of and between individual departments and are typically the result of an interdependence among professionals whose respective talents are enhanced in an environment that fosters teamwork.

Aligning products and product-related processes requires assessing who in either (or both) of the merging organizations has the critical skills necessary to support the combined company's product development, marketing, and sales processes, as well as individual offerings.

Each of the following areas relates directly to the product development and marketing process and represents the skills inherent in any marketing-driven company—an array of transferable skills that constitutes a collective source of marketing intangible assets:

- Marketing planning
- Product management
- Marketing communications
- Test marketing
- Selling support
- Growth-related training
- Marketing research/competitive intelligence
- Sales forecasting
- Direct marketing
- Database marketing

INSIDER'S OUTLOOK

There are several key areas of analysis. First, you pull down the P&Ls; a company should have their P&Ls segmented by product and service. Next, you have to determine how much they have penetrated a given market . . . based on however the market has been segmented (e.g., by demographic categories). You then have to ask a number of questions: What's the structure of that product and service today? Is it a "new market" product and service or is it an "old market" product and service? If it's the latter, you have to determine what opportunities there are to retool that product and how much is it going to cost you to bring it up to market speed . . . and is it worth doing? There are always opportunities in gaining or shedding products. You don't need to have all products and services currently offered by the merging companies. You have to ask the question of your merger partner: "What products do we have that can allow you to shed a product or service? Or in what areas don't you have a product where we can implant a product that we have developed?" But, remember, you can't make these decisions in a vacuum. You have to focus on competitors. You have to understand what the competition is providing for product and service that will directly compete with your offering.

—Don Curry, Blue Cross and Blue Shield of New Jersey

Marketing Planning

Products often succeed or fail based on the strategies devised to support them over the span of their life cycle. Strategies are part of broader marketing plans. How plans are developed is an important skill that can directly support postmerger growth initiatives.

Effective marketing planning rarely is the result of just one person. Well-crafted plans require input from a host of internal and external people and sources. Internal sources include departments within the organization (e.g., engineering or finance) that provide data on their area of operation. External sources include such things as research of a primary or secondary nature, and the input of outside experts and business influencers. Marketing planning is a process, not a thing. And it is a process that requires timely, accurate information and the ability of a team of professionals to accumulate and analyze data to forge strategies that support the success of products and strategic initiatives.

Consequently, you must probe the process and efficacy of marketing planning so as to determine how those skills can be brought to bear in the merged company. During this process, key people will surface as being central to the process. Still, how those people work with personal and impersonal data sources to devise effective marketing strategies is a transferable skill that can and should be harnessed.

Product Management

Have any of your high-potential products failed in the past because of individual or organizational mismanagement? A distinct and transferable skill lies in the particular ways a company conducts product management responsibilities and ensures that the function is a corporate priority.

Product management expertise means being able to effectively introduce and provide ongoing oversight of product strategies in light of changing market conditions. Having skills in marketing intelligence relates directly to the product management process; data must be continually accumulated to aid in decision making on manipulating key marketing variables (e.g., pricing, promotion, distribution).

Another element of product management expertise is the effective interaction between product managers and other departments (e.g., sales, customer service) to continually monitor goods and services as they move through their different life cycles. Implicit in this is the ability to spot when corrective measures or shifts in strategy need to be effected. Determining how the product management function works within the target company—and what critical capabilities can be harnessed going forward—is useful in setting priorities and devising strategies for the overall product mix and for specific offerings.

Marketing Communications

This umbrella term refers to the various methods in which product and service information is delivered to the marketplace through advertising, public relations, sales promotion, and personal selling.

A company's skill in the area of marketing communications relates both to its development of key marketing messages and to the execution of communication strategies via one or more of the tactics cited. You must ascertain the target's skills in both of these respects from a process standpoint. In other words, you must gauge how the target approaches the message development process and, in turn, translates strategic concepts into impactive promotional communications. In-house staffers or outside agencies may be responsible for the actual execution. Even if the latter is the case, however, in-house expertise is usually required to manage and maximize the output of outside resources.

Why is marketing communications important from a product alignment standpoint? Possessing strong marketing communications skill is important for all products, but particularly for new items that require intensive building of name awareness and explanations of product features. It is also imperative in order to reposition existing products and services, as well as in the initial phases of corporate identity programs, where a new name for the merged company has been created and needs to be introduced to the market at large.

Test-Marketing

In Chapter 5 we emphasized the importance of exploring a target company's product development processes. Taken together, every methodological aspect of product development—how the function is structured, how concepts are devised and screened, the extent to which customer input is built into the process, and so on—represents a skill set that can be introduced into the merged company's infrastructure and into specific growth planning initiatives.

Yet, test-marketing is another key aspect of the product development process and represents an important competency unto itself. With heightened competitive intelligence activity, more and more companies are reluctant to test-market their new products as openly as they have done in the past (e.g., through advertising and promotional campaigns in selected geographic markets) for fear of alerting competitors to their new product strategies and sparking competitors' countermeasures. Test-marketing, however, is still essential.

Some firms, for example, now employ database marketing techniques to test new offerings by communicating product details to highly segmented groups of prospects via personalized communications. Adopting test-marketing skills is critical, especially if you plan a regular stream of new product introductions and require accurate projections to avoid losses resulting from ill-fated launches.

Selling Support

In examining a target company's sales force, you will identify high- and low-performing sellers. It is important to keep in mind that rarely are the successes, or failures, of salespeople solely attributable to individual talents and experience. This is due to salespeople's reliance on their organization's marketing infrastructure, which is designed to support and facilitate the sales process.

Identifying the strength and transferability of a company's sales support processes requires probing into several different areas. For example, how good are the company's lead-generation programs? How good are its promotional programs at raising market awareness and laying the groundwork for successful sales calls? How good are its marketing information systems in terms of arming sellers with the insights and market intelligence needed to highlight the target's competitive advantages and its competitors' weaknesses?

Effective selling support is based on an interrelated series of tools and processes that help individual salespeople either succeed or fail out in the proverbial trenches. You must identify how the target company provides the backup needed for successful selling as a precursor to transferring those skills and capabilities into the merged company's product and service marketing infrastructure.

INSIDER'S OUTLOOK

Compatibility of vision is essential. But the fact is, the managements of each of the two merger partners are likely going to have different opinions about some key issues. For example, the CEOs may not agree on the value-added attributes of the products or services customers want. In the utility industry, in particular, merging companies can be extremely different culturally, and therefore will have very different views of the things customers hold to be important. CEOs will have varying levels of marketing intelligence and information on which to base their views. Nonetheless, a successful merger begins with managements' agreement on the critical issues . . . including what value-added products customers feel are important and how the merged company should go about positioning those products postmerger.

—Rich Rudden, R. J. Rudden Associates

Growth-Related Training

Chapter 13 details the various types of training programs the merged company must develop to meld corporate cultures and facilitate postmerger integration. Of particular importance is sales and marketing training.

Marketing-driven companies regularly develop instructional programs to enhance their sellers' and other managers' skills. Progressive companies teach their salespeople about new and existing product and service offerings; provide refresher courses on basic sales techniques, such as identifying buying signals and overcoming objections; and instruct on oral, written, and interpersonal communications skills. Successful companies, however, do not relegate growth-oriented training to their sales and marketing professionals. True marketing-driven organizations design product-, sales-, and customer service–related courses for managers at all levels and in all divisions of the organization.

A company's ability to continually educate and train its employees to embrace a marketing orientation is a distinct marketing intangible asset. An important focus of product alignment planning, therefore, should be ascertaining the types of marketing-related training the target company has historically run to see if those programs can be adapted for the merged company's priority products and marketing initiatives. The actual course curricula will have to be modified in light of the new organization's products and markets. But well-designed training programs can provide a solid starting point for developing courses tailored to the merged company's specific offerings and strategic imperatives.

Marketing Research/Competitive Intelligence

Accumulating and disseminating marketing research is a core capability of growth-driven organizations. Much of the foregoing discussion of skills—such as product development, marketing planning, selling support—details capabilities that require ample information for sales and marketing decision making.

An increasingly important skill is that of gathering competitor intelligence. Specialized techniques for generating actionable data on competitors' activities are gaining prominence within the strategic planning divisions of major American companies. Ideally, the target company has processes in place to collect and analyze competitor intelligence data, which can and should be incorporated into the merged company's product management processes.

Of particular importance is the extent to which the target company has a comprehensive system of regularly accumulating customer and prospect information for inclusion in its customer database. Capabilities relative to regularly attaining and analyzing demographic and lifestyle-oriented information on customers for direct marketing purposes is a skill that can directly bolster the product development and management process.

Sales Forecasting

The ability to accurately project sales for short- and long-range planning is another important skill to seek out within the people and processes of the target company. Inherent in the technique of forecasting is accumulating and analyzing market and financial data. Ideally, there are employees in the merged organization who are skilled in using advanced forecasting models, such as econometric models, to project sales based on variations of marketing variables (e.g., the size of advertising budgets, sales force composition structures, distribution channels).

As with the skill of test-marketing, sales forecasting is a valuable talent needed to accurately project sales and revenues in new product launches, as well as in special initiatives for existing products that are being repositioned or redirected at new market segments.

Direct Marketing

The continuing move to highly segmented, individualized marketing and personalized communications necessitates having direct marketing expertise on the merged company's team. Businesses in all industries are channeling more and more dollars into direct marketing campaigns that employ print and computer-based media, direct mail, and telemarketing. The ever-increasing emphasis on direct marketing requires that, even if you plan to have outside vendors carry out most of your DM programs, there must still be managers on your team who understand and can guide the process to reap the maximum benefits.

Direct marketing's central characteristic, which distinguishes it from other forms of promotion, is that it is measurable in terms of consumer response. Voluminous statistics on customer demographics and buying patterns are generated via direct marketing programs—data that must be continually built into the merged company's database and used to forge new marketing and selling programs. People with the know-how to collect and manipulate data generated via direct marketing bring valuable skills to product- and service-specific promotional initiatives.

Database Marketing

Having marketing information is important, but knowing how to apply that data is essential. This is particularly true in the area of database marketing, which is becoming a central element of customer-focused marketing in all industries. Special analytical skills are necessary to review customer database information and effectively manipulate it to support existing sales and marketing programs, to devise new campaigns, and to test-market promising product concepts.

Specific skills comprise database marketing expertise. First and foremost is a strong direct-marketing orientation. Moreover, a level of technological proficiency is required to utilize computer-based data in crafting marketing segmentation schemes, buyer behavior analyses, and cross-selling programs based on customers' purchase histories and select demographic and psychographic criteria.

Skills-Based Orientation

Staffing decisions in the postmerger environment should never be made haphazardly. They should be based on a determination of your technical needs and your product marketing requirements, and then an assessment of the skills resident in the merging companies. This skills-based orientation is also important in cases where an acquired firm will operate as an independent subsidiary, since there will invariably be important skills possessed by its marketing and sales managers that can be imported into the parent company for selected projects or long-term initiatives.

Once you articulate the merged company's product strategy, evaluate the market standing of your various product lines. Then, determine what technical marketing skills are resident in the organization to help you identify which items should comprise your product mix going forward. In the evaluation process you may have discovered ways to shed certain products that either are duplicative or do not mesh with the merged firm's strategic direction. Ultimately, once product mix decisions have been made, you face the task of managing that mix to position the merged firm for immediate and long-term growth. In a phrase, you must enact your product strategy.

INSIDER'S OUTLOOK

Making your product line decisions is the obvious first step. You can't determine prices for products. You can't develop communications or collateral materials around them. You can't get your systems in place. You can't do any of those fundamental things until you know what products you're going to sell.

—Susan Schoon, Chase Manhattan Bank

PRODUCT MIX MANAGEMENT: CRITICAL FIRST STEPS

Bringing its new array of products to market is, arguably, the most essential high-priority undertaking confronting management of the combined company. Effective growth planning requires identifying the critical first steps the organization should take in a number of key strategic and operational areas. The following are the most important product-related areas that must be acted on immediately after the transaction's closing:

- Manufacturing
- Packaging
- Pricing
- Distribution
- Retailing and merchandising
- Physical distribution
- Marketing communications
- Branding
- Positioning
- Postsale service
- Customer relations

Manufacturing

The operations assessment of target company investigations involves determining how the company manufactures its products. Production installations are examined in terms of their locations and physical and technological infrastructures. The evaluation process focuses on what would be the most efficient and cost-effective way to produce the chosen array of goods to be offered by the merged company.

In the postmerger environment, plans may call for the acquired company to continue manufacturing in its existing facilities. Other times, production facilities will be consolidated. If the latter is the case, production-related variables require immediate attention. Failing to act quickly can spawn costly delays that result in products not getting to market, resulting in customer confusion and lost market share.

There is a distinct growth-oriented perspective on manufacturing. It is determining *which of the merging companies' production processes or facilities will produce products at the highest level of quality and design flexibility (in addition to the lowest level of cost).* Increased product quality is a powerful competitive differentiator. Moreover, effecting product redesign and improvement through flexible manufacturing systems also enhances an item's profit potential.

The importance of augmenting a product's quality is a given in product marketing. Determining how and if a product's physical properties can be improved via production changes—with the aim of enhancing its ultimate marketability—represents a significant growth-oriented variable to be explored in the realm of manufacturing facilities planning.

Packaging

A more fundamental issue relative to manufacturing involves product packaging. You may need to revise the packaging of products, say, if the item's features will be markedly upgraded. If so, this time-consuming task must also be planned expeditiously.

Keep in mind that the ancillary costs of packaging changes must be projected. Packaging alterations will have a direct impact on such operational areas as product preparation, technology, manufacturing changeover requirements, warehousing, and trade relations (e.g., retailers' reluctance or willingness to display newly packaged items).

Pricing

Many factors arising during the product alignment process may affect pricing decisions on goods and services offered by the merged company. For instance, greater manufacturing efficiencies may lower your fixed and variable costs and enable you to cut prices to garner higher market share. Or, changes in quality levels of individual products or enhanced service offerings may justify price increases. When raising prices, it is important to remember to gauge the acceptability of price increases with your key internal and external publics: customers, your sales force members, channel intermediaries, suppliers, and so forth.

Setting prices starts with setting the marketing objective for individual goods and services. For example, do you want to maximize sales, maximize profits, or just simply survive in the marketplace? Devising pricing schemes also requires determining demand levels for individual products at different price points, estimating the fixed and variable costs for manufacturing products at different output levels, and identifying competitors' pricing.

Bundled offerings of compatible products and/or services provided by the merging companies may influence pricing strategies for those items. Assume that two professional services firms merge; one is an audit firm, the other a management consultancy.

The combined firm may opt to bundle its tax, audit, payroll, and other services into a seamless offering to provide one-stop shopping for its clients. Consequently, the pricing of that joint service offering would have to be discounted to make it an alluring, cost-saving alternative for clients who would necessarily pay more for those services when purchased separately.

Distribution

For manufacturing concerns, distribution decisions must be made to determine where the merged company's goods will be made available. Distribution decisions involve selecting which channels of distribution to employ and the number of outlets in each distribution level. For example, the company must determine whether to employ:

- *Intensive distribution* (the company makes the product available in as many outlets as possible);
- *Exclusive distribution* (one particular outlet is used to carry the product in a particular market); or
- *Selective distribution* (the product is made available in just a few outlets in a given market area).

Distribution decisions are critical in that they affect myriad other marketing considerations, such as pricing, sales force management, and advertising and promotional expenditures.

Retailing and Merchandising

Devising product distribution strategies requires carefully selecting retailers. Your selections must be based on such factors as how *they* decide on their target markets, how *they* determine product assortments and attendant services, and how *they* price and promote the goods offered in their outlets. Understanding the dynamics of product distribution through retail outlets takes on even greater importance when the merged company will offer a wide variety of goods sold to different consumers in widely dispersed geographic locales.

The broader your distribution network the greater the likelihood of channel conflict (an issue addressed in Chapter 6). Of equal import in planning retail strategies is merchandising—the practice of determining which of the company's products will be offered in specific retail outlets, to which consumers, at what times, and in what quantities.

Physical Distribution

For manufacturers, decisions must also be made in the realm of physical distribution: coordinating the flow of materials used in manufacturing and in distributing finished goods to the market. Physical distribution requires decision making relative to procuring raw materials used in manufacturing and, ultimately, delivering finished goods to retailers, wholesalers, or other intermediaries. Included in this process is addressing the costs associated with such things as order processing, warehousing and inventory of stored goods, and the actual transportation of product through designated channels. The direct link between these decisions and the ultimate satisfaction of customers (e.g., in terms of timely delivery of undamaged goods) requires understanding the interdependence of the physical distribution function with other units within and outside the merged company.

INSIDER'S OUTLOOK

It's awfully hard to integrate a nonregulated business—or the products and services associated with a nonregulated business—with a regulated business. Any product or service that's being developed, marketed, and distributed by a regulated entity experiences some degree of public scrutiny. These will be managed quite differently in comparison to products that are not subject to regulatory oversight. The bottom line is this: If in the merged company there will be products and services that will continue to be sold by the regulated entity, and others that will be sold by the nonregulated entity, it makes the challenge of aligning and managing products in the postmerger environment even more difficult.

—Rich Rudden, R. J. Rudden Associates

Marketing Communications

A major failing of many mergers and acquisitions is a delay in getting out marketing communications to your key publics and the market at large. You must be prepared to launch advertising, public relations, sales promotion, and other marketing communication programs promptly after the merger is finalized (strategies for doing so are addressed in Chapter 15). This is the case for both corporate identity campaigns and promotional initiatives for individual products and services. Timing is one consideration. Content is another. That means that your branding and positioning strategies must be set as far in advance of the deal's consummation (or as soon after closing) as possible. Communications tied to your overall product mix may emphasize the acquired products' complementary nature with your existing items and the resultant, enhanced product offering available to customers.

Alternatively, communications may be designed to maintain a separate identity for those goods. In addition to the broad strategic approach, thought must be given to the critical communication tactics related to the products that will be featured in the merged company's overall product mix. A crucial consideration in your integration plan is the time needed to develop promotional strategies for specific products, as well as a timetable on which items will receive near-term promotional support and which will be promoted later on. Your goal must be to hit the ground running.

Branding

Branding is a critically important element of the product alignment process when you opt to forge new identities for all or some of the merged company's products. Again, branding is an issue when product lines are being formally combined. Conversely, if the target firm continues to operate autonomously, acquired products typically continue in their current configurations.

Branding decisions begin with an assessment of the strength of the merger partners' products' respective brand names. A powerful brand name owned by one of the partners provides an opportunity to bring the totality of the combining company's offerings under that venerable brand umbrella. Therefore, if Sears were to acquire a tool manufacturer, chances are the company would immediately brand those new items under its well-known Craftsman label. Although there are many other considerations, in general when similar products are being combined the stronger of the merger partner's brand names should be employed.

Positioning

Making substantive changes to selected products, in terms of new names, features, or characteristics, will likely necessitate rethinking how those items should be positioned in the marketplace. Positioning involves articulating a product's characteristics so that buyers understand and can appreciate products on their own merits, as well as in comparison to competitors' offerings.

For instance, adding significant new customer support services to a business machine product line will dictate changes in how that line is promoted in the marketplace. In fact, the products' new service attribute may represent a competitive differentiator that will become a key selling point in advertising and promotion. Remember that changes in product positioning also require making changes to other marketing mix variables. For example, a product that will be marketed and priced as an upscale item must be made available through higher-echelon retail outlets that foster the same sense of affluence.

Postsale Service

Another important product alignment activity relates to postsale service relationships with third-party companies. Consider an appliance manufacturer that makes much of its profit by offering a parts and service business while others rely on independent third-party firms. Your postmerger planning must determine who will provide postsale service after the merger is finalized. If a third-party company is involved, you will need to examine the contractual relationship between that company and the merged firm. Chances are you may not want to maintain that relationship and, as a consequence, you will need to begin looking at other providers. Conversely, if the target company has staff people who handle postsale service—such as repairs or customer training—those staffers may figure prominently in your efforts to retain key employees in the wake of the deal's closing.

Customer Relations

There are several key aspects of customer relations that must be finalized as the merged company begins to compete in the marketplace. For instance, you must establish procedures for answering customers' questions, solving their problems, and providing product-related information. This last aspect takes on tremendous significance when product features are being modified.

Other process-related considerations include forging policies for handling complaints and dealing with customer grievances; setting policies in which customer service representatives maintain regular contact with customers via periodic visits, telephone calls, or special media (e.g., customer newsletters); and devising programs that are designed to show appreciation toward customers while maintaining general goodwill between them and the company. Communicating with existing customers after a major merger or acquisition has been finalized is critical, and detailed strategies for doing so are offered in Chapter 15.

SUMMARY

Aligning products and product management processes in the merged company is a multistep process. The first task is focusing on the core product strategy that drove the merger or acquisition in the first place. Was the strategy to supplement a particular product line? Was it to broaden your overall product or service mix? By first determining how the acquired firm's products fit into your overall offering conceptually, you can then make practical decisions on which goods merit continued investment based on their future market potential and their consistency with the merged company's overall strategic direction.

Determining the fate of individual products requires looking at their current performance level and projected market demand based on such factors as their product life cycle stage and competitors' offerings. The merged-company perspective, however, provides a new decision making criterion: whether new skills and capabilities coming into the organization can boost the performance of "star" products or revive the fortunes of "dogs." Therefore, the product alignment process also depends on identifying where crucial product-marketing skills lie within the merged company—either in one or in both of the combining companies.

The search for skills begins with an identification of the organization's product strategies and marketing priorities. Your focus, initially, should be on the short term: harnessing the specific skills you need to launch your first wave of marketing initiatives. Other skills will be needed in the coming months and years as longer-term product and market strategies are devised and implemented.

The process of identifying available skills is also valuable in that it points up where gaps exist on your team that you need to fill by hiring people from outside the combined company.

If acquiring specific products or product-related technologies is not a primary driver of the transaction—or if the acquired firm will function independently—the integration challenges that exist differ from situations when products and product management processes must be combined. In such cases, management's focus should be on identifying the valuable product-marketing skills resident in the acquired firm that can be imported, when needed or appropriate, into the parent company's organizational infrastructure and management processes.

As is the case with all aspects of strategic acquisitions, the overriding goal is to harness the complementary skill sets of people in the merging organizations in order to forge a company that is greater than the sum of its individual parts. The surest way to realize the strategic synergies sought is to channel people's complementary capabilities toward the lifeblood of any commercial enterprise: its products, services, and overall program for corporate growth.

Getting ready to bring the combined company's products to the market with their new identities and configurations (if, indeed, that will be the case) is arguably the most pressing task facing the new management team. A number of critical areas must be addressed on finalization of the transaction vis-à-vis decisions on individual products and services. Speedy determinations must be made in such areas as product manufacturing, packaging, pricing, distribution, and customer service programs and processes, as well as more strategic areas relative to branding strategies, the positioning of individual products, and targeted marketing communications.

12

Employee and Organizational Communication Strategies

The memo was a tersely written, two-paragraph E-mail that was distributed to all employees of the recently acquired company. Weeks had gone by since word of the acquisition was first announced, and only a handful of memos providing general details on the transaction had been disseminated. Now, here was the first substantive communiqué: It announced that the CEO of the acquired firm was leaving.

Employee angst was rampant before the memorandum, and it skyrocketed in the days that followed. "If the CEO was just 'canned' what's going to happen to us?" was the prevailing question among the acquired firm's people—employees of a venerable, 100-year-old financial services firm that was about to vanish from the American business landscape. Already, the company had seen some defections by lower-level managers since the announcement. The vague and coldly worded memo announcing the CEO's "resignation" sparked additional departures. An organization's key asset is its people. Yet, just weeks after the transaction closed, many of the acquired firm's key personnel were rushing for the exits.

The rash of resignations and plummeting morale pointed up one of the key tasks facing a merged organization's management: that of developing timely, honest, and detailed internal communications in the days and weeks immediately following a merger announcement and the deal's eventual closing. Without both a well-conceived *and* well-executed communications program, tremendous sources of value inherent in the company's employee base stand to be lost. Moreover, the seeds of employee dissent may be planted to hinder both near- and long-term growth initiatives. Within the acquired organization, morale and productivity can be notoriously low after the transaction is announced: People fear for their jobs and are anxious about what the deal means to them personally.

Communications are, without question, the first and most important organizational activity that should be carried out after public pronouncement of the transaction. Too often, however, management thinks standardized communication materials and approaches will serve the purposes of informing and motivating employees in the wake of a transaction's announcement and closing. Too often, management is wrong. Devising employee communications in M&A situations requires a tremendous level of strategic forethought and skillful execution. A multiphased approach must be developed that commences as soon as the transaction is announced and carries over in the weeks and months thereafter.

It would have been an understatement to say that management of the aforementioned acquirer had given inadequate thought to employee communications in the wake of the transaction's closing. Although management had said it would make a concerted effort to quickly issue critical information of interest to the merged firm's populace, its memos were few and far between. The communiqués were empty, impersonal directives that provided little concrete information on the fate of the acquired company's employees, the particulars of the integration process, and how the merged company would ultimately take form.

In particular, management's communicative ineptitude was typified by the aforementioned memo announcing the CEO's departure. First, there was the content. Here was a man who, a few years earlier, had single-handedly turned the organization around, bringing it from the brink of financial collapse to a position of enduring profitability. This was a man who was loved and respected by his employees. Yet the memo contained trite and clichéd phrases like "thanks for his years of service," which were viewed as empty platitudes that worsened an environment already characterized by mistrust and doubt.

The second problem with the communiqué was its form: an E-mail. The immediacy of the medium is one of its valuable attributes, yet the cold impersonality of it is one of its distinct drawbacks. The third problem related to the memo's source. The announcement came from the assistant to the CEO of the acquiring company—a stranger to the acquired firm's staffers. "Who is this person?" employees asked. "And who is she to be telling us this?" Many employees felt that the news of the CEO's departure should have come from the CEO himself.

Timing was yet another problem with the memo. The announcement of all senior management appointments in the new organization was scheduled for the following week. Management should have waited until then to release word of the CEO's departure in the context of other managerial shifts. Allowing it to be released earlier made the message stand out. In fact, had the news been of a positive nature, it might well have been beneficial to employee morale. That it was a negative missive served only to heighten employee incertitude.

This chapter explores the distinct internal communication challenges posed by major mergers and acquisitions, and the strategies and tactics necessary to address them. Communication activities are viewed from several different standpoints. First, near-term tactics are discussed: the communications that must be disseminated immediately on announcement of the merger. Second, communications to the merging firms' respective employee bases are addressed.

Next, long-term communication programs are discussed: The merged organization requires new means of communicating new messages through new channels to what is, essentially, a new organization. Extensive research is required to devise impactive communications that directly support the integration process. Consequently, the "why's" and "how to's" of conducting employee "attitude surveys" and an all-important "communications audit" are addressed.

PRECLOSING COMMUNICATION STRATEGIES: THE FIRST WAVE

The merger is about to be announced. Press materials have been written. Advertisements may have been designed and the media space secured. Most important, internally directed information must be ready for distribution to employees of the combining firms who are the most significant and first audience to be reached with communications on finalization of the merger or acquisition.

Chapter 15 emphasizes the importance of never letting customers and other key stakeholders learn about the transaction in the press. Yet, there is no greater M&A-related communication error than allowing employees to hear about the transaction first from the media or other outside sources such as competitors. Employees must always learn about it directly from the merged company's management. The first emotion that employees feel should not be one of resentment because they were not directly informed of their collective fate.

In the initial stages, timing may be more important than content. Each company must be ready to make the announcement to its respective employees at the same time. The initial announcement need not be overly elaborate. It should provide the basic details, which are based on the five W's of journalistic reportage:

- Statement that the merger or acquisition is taking place (the "what")
- Background on the company being acquired or merged with (the "who")
- Projected timing on the transaction's closing (the "when")
- The strategic rationale (the "why")—pointing out the multiple benefits to the employee base
- When appropriate, the location of the merger partner vis-à-vis the markets in which it operates (the "where")

Time does not always permit the creation of a comprehensive package of information on the transaction. Ideally, however, a kit should be produced for distribution to employees on the day the deal is announced. At a minimum, the kit should contain the following elements:

- A basic statement on the merger that details the strategic rationale and the particulars of the transaction (the aforementioned five W's). This statement should take the form of a memo or letter (not an E-mail) signed jointly by the merger partners' CEOs.
- Fact sheets on each company detailing the firms' histories, their fundamental corporate missions, their products and services, and the customers they serve.
- A list of managers employees can call for additional information (managers from both organizations should be listed, along with their office locations and phone/fax numbers).
- An announcement that integration teams will be formed and require the input of all employees.

Mergers have the most immediate and dramatic impact on the people who serve the combining firms. Many of them have invested years of their lives to these organizations, which will soon be radically redefined. It has been aptly observed that the first two letters of "merger" are "me." People want to know what the deal portends for their current positions and their future professional prospects.

For this reason, information released immediately on the deal's announcement should focus on the projected impact on the two firms' employee bases in addition to the strategic rationale for the combination. You must anticipate employees' questions and be prepared to respond to them as well as possible.

What are the most frequently asked employee questions? There are several categories that characterize employees' initial informational requirements. The basic question areas are:

- Will there be job cuts?
- What benefit and health insurance programs will there be?
- Will job responsibilities and status levels change? (In other words, even if people keep their jobs will their positions and levels of power remain the same?)
- Will work locations change? (Will there be employee relocations?)
- How will the merger affect accrued pension benefits?
- What happens to employees' investments in company stock?
- Will there be a new schedule for performance reviews and salary increases?
- What will the new policy be for personal time off and sick pay?

Logically, the preponderance of questions employees have relate to themselves. People generally understand that organizational changes are a long-term certainty, but want assurances that their near-term livelihoods will be unaffected. It is only after the initial shock of the merger wears off that employees begin to ask questions of a more strategic nature, such as, "What will the new company name be?", "Will we continue to use our company logo?", "Will we continue to offer the same products and services?"

Management often thinks that the employee rank and file will have the same business- and strategy-oriented questions that they would have. The simple fact is, most employees really just want to be sure of such issues as whether or not dental coverage will continue under the merged company's new benefit plan.

Management, of course, is not always sure what the precise effect of the transaction will be on all employees. In terms of job cuts, for example, there may be terminations as the combined firm strives to increase efficiencies by eliminating duplicative operations and personnel. Yet with more and more acquisitions focusing on growth opportunities, the prospect of necessarily losing one's job is becoming less of a certainty. But management may still not know who or how many workers will actually be let go.

The time between the merger's announcement and its closing is, ideally, when organizational assessments are conducted and personnel decisions are made. Management of the merging firms must acknowledge that potential may indeed exist for job cuts, but that not enough information may be available to make that determination. In strategic acquisitions, the focus is on growth. Consequently, management should say with all sincerity that the deal's rationale is to make the combined company bigger, not smaller. That is a key message to impart to anxious employees: that their old jobs may indeed be eliminated, but that the emphasis on growth means that new jobs may ultimately be created.

Delivering Initial Internal Communications: Media and Forums

A combination of print memorandums, electronic mail messages, companywide voice mail announcements, and special editions of company publications should all be employed as the media for initial merger announcements to the combining firms' employee bases. These one-way communications are important, but two-way communication media are even more so.

For example, immediately following the initial announcement, meetings should be held between company managers and employees. These forums should begin with management reiterating the basic messages imparted in the initial announcements. The meeting agenda should then move to question-and-answer sessions where employee issues are addressed.

Again, communications may not contain much specific information on the "how will this affect me?" concerns of employees. Nonetheless, these forums should be open exchanges of information. Company representatives must be extremely well-prepared for these sessions. Indeed, the spokespeople should prepare the same way they would for a major media interview. That is, the presenters must be skilled at delivering carefully worded messages, and they must anticipate the negative questions that may be asked and know how to effectively respond to them.

Other forms of two-way communications should be set up within each organization. For instance, consider establishing a hot line telephone number that employees can call. If, in fact, the telephone cannot be manned continually, you may want to set it up as a voice mail–driven system where employees leave their questions on the machine and a company representative responds to those queries within 24 or 48 hours. If the call back takes any longer, then a message of nonresponsiveness will be sent. Another two-way medium might involve a special fax number that is set up to receive questions. In this case, you should develop a standard form on which employees indicate their questions. As with the voice mail system, make sure the fax hot line is manned with a complement of people who can promptly respond to queries.

Another two-way communication medium is that of teleconferencing. Teleconferencing is valuable when management needs to communicate with a widely dispersed employee population located in multiple offices. There are two main drawbacks of teleconferencing. First is the cost. Teleconferencing is a tremendous logistical undertaking that typically involves scores of technicians and complex telecommunications hookups, which dramatically add to your bottom-line costs.

The second drawback is that teleconferencing is a limited two-way communication medium. It is possible, via the installation of TV cameras at each downlink site, to give viewers the opportunity to pose questions of speakers at the host location. Invariably, however, the exorbitant cost of satellite air time limits opportunities for detailed Q&A. Nonetheless, if immediacy, impact, and geographic reach are important to your merger announcement, teleconferencing may be worth the investment.

Importance of Senior Management's Involvement

Senior management's active participation in all phases of the preclosing communications effort is critical.

The communications planning process begins with management's input into the formulation of the key messages to be imparted—the basic story management wants to tell. The merger partners' officers will most probably not actually write the initial round of internal communications materials. Therefore, they must be readily available to work with the people doing so to finalize the message and to approve the precise language being used to express it.

Most importantly, the timing of preclosing communications must be impeccably planned. No delays should ever result from differences between managers in the creative expression of the message or because the CEO or the lawyers could not make time to review and approve draft text. In the preclosing stages it is imperative to devise and finalize the message, then get it out swiftly and broadly.

If the first wave of communications is designed to announce the general details of the merger or acquisition, the second wave is intended to initiate the critical long-term process of bridging the two organizations. Before delving into the strategies for the next phases of your internal communication planning, it will help to examine some of the unique obstacles and challenges to organizational communication inherent in the M&A process.

COMMUNICATION CHALLENGES PRESENTED BY MERGERS AND ACQUISITIONS

The challenges of effective employee communications in merger and acquisition scenarios are enormous. Decisions have not yet been made or information is not available or ready to be released. Yet employees with deep, emotional interest in the specifics of the corporate combination are desperately seeking input.

By their very nature, mergers engender feelings of uncertainty, secrecy, and mistrust among employees. Oftentimes, however, circumstances prevent you from devising and executing communication programs to confront these negatives head-on. Unfortunately, failing to do so can set the merged organization back before it even gets a chance to begin moving forward. Yet the criticality of comprehensive and well-timed communications—as a means of preserving the merger partners' collective human assets—cannot be overstated.

In Chapter 15 we cite the necessity of prompt communications issued to the merged company's external publics relative to the timing and provisions of the transaction. These external communications are designed in large part to protect the assets represented by the merging companies' respective customer bases. Conversely, internal communications are aimed at protecting the assets comprised of the merging companies' collective employee base.

Protecting human assets is the immediate goal of your communications program. The longer-term aim relates to achieving swift postmerger integration. Both objectives are complicated by several inherent challenges of M&A-related organizational communications:

- Overcoming employee fears
- Communicating with no information
- Learning how to communicate with new audiences
- Having to deliver bad news

Each of these factors poses an obstacle to communication planning and implementation. In the following pages, each one is briefly examined and strategies are cited to help you address them.

INSIDER'S OUTLOOK

If you don't do the communication planning during the deal process, it makes the integration process much more difficult later on. In a sense, focusing on communications during the deal process tees it up for the people who have to do the implementation. Preclosing communications facilitate postclosing communications.

—Diane Harris, Hypotenuse Enterprises

Overcoming Employee Fears

Safeguarding human assets requires first acknowledging the fragility of the human psyche in merger and acquisition situations. History has shown that such psychological protective measures are imperative. The tremendous level of vulnerability employees feel when a merger is announced is justified as a result of it having been so well-documented.

Numerous articles have been written that chronicle the victims of merger-driven downsizings. It is no wonder then that people directly affected by major mergers and acquisitions immediately fear for their corporate lives.

Workers worldwide have been conditioned to sense instant peril upon learning that their firm is about to engage in a merger. The fact is, the first act of the management of many acquiring companies is to eliminate duplicative positions. Cost reductions have been the historical driver of many corporate mergers and there is, indeed, a justifiable rationale for eliminating wasteful or overlapping functions.

Basic business sense tells us that you do not need two accounting departments, two human resource directors, or two managers of a corporate subsidiary. Cost cutting will always be a fact of life in mergers and acquisitions. And since people are a company's greatest cost, they are often the first to be sacrificed when management seeks a discernible way of showing bottom-line financial results to shareholders and the investment community. That will not change. Consequently, neither will employees' fears toward mergers and acquisitions.

Employee anxiety is exacerbated in acquisitions where a larger, more dominant organization subsumes a smaller, weaker firm. In general, employees of the acquiring company generally do not experience as much fear as those in the firm being acquired. Some employees, of course, may be apprehensive about possibly losing their positions to newcomers from the acquired firm. But it is the people within the target company who tend to feel they are at significantly greater risk. Still, it is safe to say that employee anxiety is even present in so-called mergers of equals. And rightly so, since there are very few such combinations, and most times a distinctly dominant culture ultimately emerges. For instance, in 1989, two of the world's largest accounting firms—Arthur Young and Ernst & Whinney—combined in what was billed as the quintessential merger of equals. The new firm was called Ernst & Young, but Ernst got more than top billing. It got "top dog" status in a merger that effectively signaled the demise of a major player (Arthur Young) and the first scaling-back of the Big Eight accounting firms.

Ultimately, it was the partners at Ernst & Whinney who became the merged firm's seniormost officers. Layoffs were significant, with most of them coming from the Arthur Young ranks. The indisputable disparity between the acquired and the acquirer in virtually every corporate combination necessitates a carefully segmented approach to communications when the transaction is announced.

Communicating with No Information

Clearly, personnel and organizational changes are an inevitability. Thus, it is how and when you ultimately communicate those changes that determines whether you serve the long-term interests of the merged company by safeguarding its prized human assets.

This fact points up the central communications goal of M&A planning and integration. Employees need to be told what the deal means to them: what kind of changes will occur, how their roles will change, who their new boss will be, and when all the organizational changes on the horizon will be enacted. Questions abound, and employees need and deserve answers.

The truth is, however, that answers are not always available at the time people want them. Yet problems arise when management hides behind a veil of secrecy. There is a severe danger in keeping silent. Employees need information, and when there is a lack of it, people tend to create it themselves. Delays and gaps in communication are filled by rumors. The grapevine flourishes with negative prognostications on the fate of people and positions. When management does not communicate, employees speculate. And their speculation is not likely to be positive. If information is not available, it is important to admit that this is truthfully the case, while giving time parameters as to when it will be.

Learning How to Communicate with New Audiences

By its very nature, the merged organization is comprised of a collective of new employee groups. Each segment brings its own attitudes, beliefs, and unique perspective. As members of defined organizational environments, their past experiences and thoughts about their individual futures as employees of a new merged corporation have molded them into a distinct culture. Therefore, each employee segment represents, in effect, a new audience that has to be communicated with via new ways and means of disseminating information. Your planning, therefore, must focus on forging new communications media through which carefully crafted messages are delivered.

Addressing the key steps involved in creating these communicative mechanisms and strategies will help to lay the groundwork for a detailed communications program. This will involve conducting a review of information channels used in the past (with an eye toward developing new ones for the future) and gauging employees' current attitudes and mind-sets (in order to devise persuasive communication messages that engender belief systems to help facilitate the integration process).

Learning how to effectively identify and communicate with the new audiences that make up the merged company is a longer-term communication task. More immediate attention must be paid to dealing with the inevitability of delivering news about the merger-driven changes that will adversely affect selected employees of the combined company.

Having to Deliver Bad News

The massive organizational changes wrought by mergers and acquisitions typically carry with them bad news of both an actual and a perceived nature for many employees. Consequently, your internal communications program must include a component that deals specifically with imparting information on situations that will adversely affect employees.

Communication strategies must be formulated to address the specific types of merger-related bad news, which may involve one or more of the following issues:

- Terminations
- Changes in roles
- Shifts in lines of reporting and decision making
- Relocations
- Decreased resources

Terminations. Employees in the target firm, as well as some within the acquiring organization, will lose their positions when duplicative functions are eliminated, facilities are closed, product or service offerings are discontinued, or any number of other organizational or operational shifts are effected. Entire departments or divisions may be scrapped, or selected employees within those units will be let go. Indeed, terminations are bad news for the people receiving them. They are also bad news, in a sense, for the managers who have to communicate them to coworkers.

Changes in roles. People whose positions are unaffected may nonetheless experience a shift in responsibility. An increase in one's responsibility is generally viewed as good news. A decrease in responsibility, as well as a formal demotion in title, clearly represents bad news. Changes in roles may be negative from a psychological standpoint, but they are also organizationally problematic in that they create an adjustment period in which workers must embrace new skills and responsibilities. Declines in productivity and emotional commitment may well arise as a result.

Shifts in lines of reporting and decision making. People who remain may experience shifts in reporting relationships and/or in the ways corporate or departmental decisions are made. A change of one's boss is not necessarily good or bad news in and of itself. But even if the change is viewed as beneficial, it represents a significant shift that will take some getting used to. Workers need to adjust to a new boss's way of operating, how he or she makes decisions, and the extent to which the new supervisor involves employees in day-to-day decision making.

Relocations. Employees may have to relocate as a result of changes in the merged company's organizational structure. Being asked to uproot one's family is one of the more stressful changes an employee will ever have to make. Being asked to relocate in the context of a major merger may exacerbate the situation. That is because employees may still fear the prospect of losing their position or having to endure additional organizational changes even after they have relocated.

Decreased resources. Downsizing and shifts in organizational structure and priorities drive changes in manpower and capital allocations. As a result, some department heads who were used to having a given complement of people and budgetary dollars will now have to "do more with less." It is often little consolation that a person has been able to keep his or her job when that position has been made so much more difficult because of severe cutbacks in human and monetary resources.

Keys to Communicating Bad News

Bad news is never easy to deliver; nonetheless, it is management's obligation to impart it in a way that is as minimally hurtful as possible. Here are four keys to imparting bad news relative to the aforementioned types of merger-related organizational change:

1. *Always communicate in person.* Never rely on impersonal means of communication when delivering bad news to employees. Sending a memo with the proverbial "pink slip" is the easy way out, but the most impersonal and painful. The fact is, people should be dealt with on a one-to-one basis. If memorandums are the means by which bad news is initially communicated, make sure to follow up those written communiqués with personal phone calls or face-to-face meetings. But do not let too much time elapse.

2. *Provide a reason "why."* People have a right to know why decisions are being made. Sending out a message that cites the "what" (the changes being enacted) without providing the "why" (the reasons for those changes) is unfair to the people being impacted by those negative developments.

Also, try to avoid "corporate speak." Managers often tend to use vague, empty terms that fill today's business vernacular (e.g., "downsizings to streamline operations," or to make the company "lean and mean") so as to make the bad news palatable to recipients. People deserve direct information and straight answers to the inevitable questions of "why me?" in the case of terminations or significant downward changes in responsibility.

3. *Detail what is "in it for them."* When communicating a termination, you must be immediately prepared to discuss the terms of the severance agreement. The package that people will take with them is typically the only cushion to the blow of termination. Those terms need to be communicated in the same conversation as the person's dismissal—not days, or even hours, later. The provisions of relocations must also be addressed in communications detailing the physical moves of people and departments. For instance, if a suburban-based employee will now be required to commute into the city, any additional salary or commuting expenses being offered should be detailed to the affected worker.

4. *Focus communications on all audiences.* Bad news affects selected employees. For their benefit, it is important that you heed the above communications recommendations. Particularly in situations where downsizings are involved, it is important to recognize that the entire organization is ultimately affected.

The people receiving bad news are the friends, bosses, and subordinates of the employees who will remain in the merged corporate fold. The anxiety and distress that the "survivors" indirectly experience can potentially linger long after their coworkers have officially left. You must maintain an open-door policy to field questions and address the concerns of these people. Dealing ineffectively with the remaining workers from a communications standpoint may engender enduring resentment that can hinder productivity, morale, and your ongoing integration efforts.

POSTCLOSING COMMUNICATION STRATEGIES: THE SECOND WAVE

Internal communications, in the weeks and months following the closing, take on a broad new level of importance as the critical integration task moves from communicating relatively straightforward messages to two separate companies, to communicating more complex and instructive information to employees that now work for the same organization.

The first goal of postclosing communications is effecting a reciprocal understanding by employees of the merging companies' respective personalities and cultures. Employees must gain an intimate understanding of the combining firms' unique values, history, and organizational processes. Until that occurs, the integration process cannot commence. Once a level of mutual appreciation and respect has been achieved, the long-term act of transferring skills and capabilities can expeditiously occur.

Extensive communications research should be conducted prior to developing the second wave of internal communications. In general, employees' information needs must be ascertained. Prevailing attitudes must be gauged. And the best means of communicating to the merged company's audiences must be determined.

Postclosing communications research takes two forms: a "communications audit" and an "attitude survey." It is necessary to gauge how the merging organizations have historically disseminated information internally in terms of messages, channels, and media. A new set of beliefs and attitudes is created when a new company is forged through a merger. Consequently, those attitudes must be effectively measured in order to devise impactive communications strategies that facilitate, expedite, and help shape the longer-term integration process.

Communications Audit

Prior to the merger, the combining firms communicated in certain ways. It is necessary to assess how those communications took place in terms of their frequency, content, and media employed. New communication procedures can only be developed once the old procedures have been ascertained. These insights are gained through a comprehensive communications audit.

The audit is a detailed study that identifies historical patterns and modes of organizational communication. In M&A situations, an audit should rightfully be conducted on both firms' communication processes and procedures. Ideally, you have done some kind of assessment of your own organization's communication practices and are in a position to identify similarities and dissimilarities between yours and that of the firm with which you are merging.

If not, you should conduct a high-level audit of your own communications infrastructure before doing a comparative assessment of that of your merger partner. The following guidance details the process of conducting a communications audit, and describes as well how to use the data collected to create near- and long-term communications strategies.

The communications audit is an integral part of any organizational change initiative, particularly that of a merger or acquisition. The audit yields the input necessary to effect shifts in organizational practices, as well as to ultimately help employees gain a sense of the merged firm's new identity. In essence, a communications audit is a broad-based assessment of an organization's internal communications effectiveness.

The audit focuses on communication processes and how well they are working, and evaluates existing media and communication channels. What is more, the phase of the audit that analyzes the content of communications reveals what the key issues are within the firm, how they have been communicated, and how well they have been received by the intended audiences.

An audit has several key characteristics and benefits:

- It reveals what employees think about downward, upward, and horizontal communications—that is, how workers perceive the ways they communicate with subordinates, superiors, and peers.
- It allows direct audience participation in the integration process.
- It sends a powerful signal into the employee ranks that management is interested in devising communications policies that are beneficial to the merged company, and therefore understands the employee's information needs.
- It provides the basic research necessary to enable the merged firm to modify existing communication practices and/or to devise new ones to support the integration process. Well-functioning communication practices can be continued and strengthened; weak practices can be corrected or eliminated. Moreover, new and effective communication processes will likely be revealed in the course of your research.

Research techniques. A combination of research techniques comprise the communications audit process. First, qualitative research should be generated via interviews with the firm's senior executives, as well as one-on-one and focus group interviews with representatives from the firm's different employee subgroups (i.e., division managers, middle managers, field employees, supervisors, etc.).

Next, quantitative data should be culled from survey instruments such as printed or electronically disseminated questionnaires, soliciting data from representative samples of each employee subgroup. Questionnaires should always allow for anonymity, since more candid feedback is garnered when respondents know their identities will not be revealed.

The data collected should relate to employees' likes and dislikes toward existing communications media; employees' philosophy of effective organizational communication; and their view of the firm's mission, vision, and values (insofar as how well these are communicated via existing media and channels). Additionally, input should be sought from employees in the area of overall media effectiveness: frequency, timeliness, content, relevance, comprehension, aesthetic considerations, and so on. Finally, subjective data should be collected via professional evaluations. Consultants with expertise in organizational communication practices should be retained to assess media as to content, appearance, and collective impact on their intended audiences. Additionally, these outside experts should review the findings of your internal research (if, in fact, they were not involved in that process).

In short, the communications audit should examine the physical ways a company sends messages to its employees (media and channels of communication), the desired communication effects of those messages (content), and actions taken by the organization's employees as a result of those communications (response).

Ideally, the communications audit should compare the combining firms' communications infrastructures and processes. The comparison will reveal differences and similarities in how, and how well, the two companies have historically communicated. By gauging the quality and effectiveness of individual media and communication processes, you can identify those methods that will best support the merged firm's near-term communication challenges and long-term integration initiatives.

INSIDER'S OUTLOOK

You don't do it all. Your employees do it all. If you create the right attitude and the right morale, they'll run through fires for you. You need to make them feel that they're part of the group.

—CEO of Fortune 1000 industrial management company

Next steps. It is difficult to speculate about what the precise results of a communications audit will be. There are, however, several action items that typically surface from the investigative process. For example, the audit should first and foremost point up what key messages and overall communication themes should be developed to reinforce senior management's vision for the merged organization (e.g., how to communicate the new company's mission and strategic direction).

Second, the likes and dislikes employees voice regarding communications media—such as the preferred sources for receiving company information—will aid in deciding what channels should be employed in the future. Next, the audit should identify where there are gaps in information in terms of both channels and content. For instance, gaps in channels may be typified by a company that has a firmwide E-mail system that may not, but should be, employed more broadly for corporate communication purposes (as opposed to simply for horizontal communications between coworkers). Information gaps in content typically relate to educational issues that point up the need for formal training and development programs that teach employees about customer needs, industry trends, and so forth.

Perhaps the most significant element of your communications research, however, involves assessing prevailing attitudes throughout the merged company's employee base. Only after you identify people's beliefs, sentiments, desires, and fears can you begin to influence them in support of the integration process. Gauging the employee base's collective psyche requires conducting an attitude survey. This is a process that should be continued at regular intervals over the course of the year following the deal's consummation. Attitudes will evolve, and as they do, you will more specifically have identified both the message that needs to be sent and the communications media that will carry that message.

Attitude Surveys

Communications create, dispel, or reinforce people's attitudes. Periodically determining how workers feel toward their company and its policies is important in any organization. Determining how employees feel toward the newly forged company is essential in merger situations as you begin the process of devising communication, training, and other informational programs to support the integration process.

Attitude surveys are designed to measure employee opinions at a time of massive organizational change. Conducting attitude research helps identify the prevailing sentiments, both positive and negative, that employees hold toward the corporate combination. Gauging what those sentiments are and the degree to which they exist is the first step toward developing communication activities that effect unity and address employee concerns. Only then can you effectively espouse the firm's new corporate mission and strategy to its diverse new employee base.

Identifying and evaluating employees' attitudes requires soliciting input from people at all levels and in all units of the merged firm. Companies with a small number of employees should strive to query every person. Conversely, it may be difficult in larger organizations to survey everyone. In such cases, it is necessary to draw samples from various geographic and political strata throughout the overall employee population.

Sampling strategies. Sampling is the process of selecting members from a given population in such a way that the input from those members is representative of the population as a whole. Sampling is necessary to help assure accurate, valid results in the research process, but it is also needed to effect logistical and cost savings. For instance, it would be very costly and difficult to survey every member of a 20,000-employee organization.

Sampling allows a select number of people to be surveyed, the theory being that the sample would tend to have the same characteristics and yield data in the same proportions as the total population. Samples in research studies are either probability or nonprobability samples.

Probability samples are those in which every member of the total universe of respondents has an equal and known chance of being selected. Assume, for example, that a survey is being conducted on people's feelings about the food service in the company cafeteria. If the cafeteria is filled to its capacity of five hundred people on a given day, and the probability sample being sought is one hundred, each person would have one chance in five of being selected. There are three types of probability samples:

1. *Simple random sample*. This process typically involves assigning numbers to units of the population. A set of random numbers is then generated and the units having those numbers are selected for the sample. Thus, numbers would be assigned to the five hundred people present in the cafeteria, then one hundred would be selected based on the preassigned numbers.

2. *Stratified random sample.* The population is divided into mutually exclusive groups (such as gender or department), and samples are drawn from each. Thus, the cafeteria users could be divided into males and females or plant workers and supervisors, and then samples would be drawn accordingly.
3. *Cluster sample.* The population is divided in arbitrary groups based on their location (e.g., cafeteria users in different company locations), and the researcher draws a sample from the designated groups.

Nonprobability samples, on the other hand, are based on criteria that ensure that some members of the population have a higher probability of being sampled than others. There are three kinds of nonprobability samples:

1. *Judgment samples.* The researcher subjectively selects survey respondents whom the researcher feels will yield accurate information. For example, the researcher chooses those cafeteria users waiting in line at a particular service area within the dining facility.
2. *Convenience samples.* The researcher interviews those people who are accessible to the researcher (such as employees in the cafeteria location where the researcher is also based).
3. *Quota samples.* The researcher interviews a select number of people from a given category (e.g., men, women, people from different company divisions or based in different office locations).

There are three main advantages to probability sampling. First, such samples rule out human biases that might be involved in subjectively selecting people to be interviewed, as in judgment sampling. Second, probability samples increase the likelihood that the sample drawn is truly representative of the broader population. Third, probability sampling is the only sampling method that offers measurable estimates of accuracy.

Therefore, sampling error can be determined by computational methods that estimate the degree of error to be expected in a given sample. Sampling error ties to the fact that no probability sample can ever represent the exact characteristics of the total population. It is important to note that sampling error decreases as the size of your sample increases.

Respondents identified through sampling must represent the different groups that comprise the new merged company. Employee groups can be identified based on such variables as title (e.g., manager, supervisor, line worker, administrator); tenure (long-term employees versus those who joined the organization recently); or geography (in multioffice companies, employees from different parts of the country).

Of paramount importance is drawing samples of employees from both sides of the merged organization. As stated, there may be notable differences in how employees from the acquiring organization feel about merger-related issues in comparison to employees from the acquired firm. In multidivision firms, samples of employees might also need to be drawn from the different organizational components of the merging firms.

Need for customization. Attitude surveys must be customized in every situation since organizations vary widely in terms of their size, product offerings, geographic locations, and scores of other variables. Moreover, the organizational issues that arise throughout the first year will necessarily vary based on the particulars of the corporation combination. Still, there are a number of basic issues that typically arise even months after the acquisition that can be assessed through attitudinal research. The following are some of the areas employees of the merged firm might be queried on, as well as the general nature of the questions that should be posed:

- *Job security.* Do they feel they are in jeopardy of losing their jobs? If so, why?
- *Job satisfaction.* Are they basically happy in their current and potential new roles? If so, why? If not, why not?
- *Compensation.* Do they feel they are being adequately paid in light of their job function, tenure, performance, and so on? Do they feel their compensation is commensurate with that of their peers?
- *Management relationships.* How would they characterize their relationships with their new supervisors? Formal? Informal? Cooperative? Adversarial? How would they characterize the difference between their relationship with their new supervisor and their former supervisor?
- *Values.* Do employees understand the new organization's concept of corporate values? If so, how would they characterize them?
- *Motivation.* Do they feel they are being properly motivated by their managers, as well as by the organization's overall compensation and reward structure?
- *Working conditions.* How do they feel about the quality of their physical working conditions? What improvements, if any, would they make?
- *Training and development.* Do they feel they have a distinct career track that is being advanced through ongoing professional development?
- *Performance appraisals.* (If and when they have been conducted) do they feel appraisals are accurately assessing their abilities and contributions? Are job evaluations being conducted frequently enough?
- *Mission.* Do they know what the merged company's mission is? How do they feel about the firm's mission statement in terms of its being relevant and understandable?
- *Productivity.* Do they understand the indicators and measures of productivity? Do they feel management helps or hinders their efforts to maximize their individual productivity?
- *Benefits.* How do they feel about their corporate benefits program? Are they happy with their benefits? If not, what changes would they make?
- *Diversity.* Do they feel diversity is important in the merged organization? If so, do they agree or disagree with the steps management is taking to promote diversity?
- *Ethics.* Do they believe the merged company is an ethical organization? If ethics guidelines are in place, are they understandable and relevant?
- *Policies and practices.* Do they feel general corporate policies are rigid? Flexible? Conservative? Liberal?

- *Working relationships.* How do they assess their relationships with new coworkers and how important are harmonious relations to individual employees' overall job satisfaction?
- *Safety.* Do they feel they are employed in a safe workplace? If not, what can be done to increase safety?
- *Company image.* Do they have a sense of whether the merged company is perceived positively or negatively in the market? What would they do to strengthen or improve the company's image?

Management must ascertain the sentiments employees from the merging organizations hold toward these and other critical issues. Even though there will likely be distinct differences between the two employee camps, the key is to identify areas of common concern.

For example, if diversity issues are important to both representative groups, therein lies a similar issue that must be acted on. Integration occurs when people share beliefs, are committed to working toward common goals, and are able to do so. Be sure to emphasize in subsequent communications the importance management is placing on the core issues facing the merged company and the steps it is taking to address them. This last point raises an issue about attitude surveys: *Always publish the findings.* Management's communication of the results sends the message that it has been open to employees' concerns. Not publishing the results creates the impression that management is one-way–oriented, simply taking information without giving any back.

However, it is also important to emphasize at the outset of attitude research projects that management may not necessarily act on each and every recommendation voiced by employees. It is not problematic to not respond to every area of employee concern provided that explanations are given for inaction. Consequently, if management fails to communicate a survey's results—or shares the results without offering a rationale for why certain suggested changes were not enacted—management's credibility is weakened.

The results of attitude research are beneficial for the purposes of developing communication and training and development programs. Attitude research is also beneficial in and of itself. Conducting an attitude study demonstrates management's interest in involving all employees in the integration process. The research also sensitizes employees to the topics being covered, thus helping raise awareness and expectations in a constructive manner.

For instance, querying employees about their feelings toward changing the new company's logo sends a message that management is considering making changes to the company's corporate image. Management may indeed never change anything. But the act of asking people's feelings about doing so sends a message that this is an issue on which management is soliciting individuals' input. If, in fact, change does occur, the employee base will not have been caught by surprise. If no change occurs, workers will likely appreciate the fact that their collective voice had at least been heard.

Firmwide productivity and motivation are secured when employees share the strategy and values of the newly merged organization. Effecting that unity over the short and longer term requires pinpointing attitudes that may need to be changed or reinforced to move the merged company forward.

LONG-TERM COMMUNICATION STRATEGIES: THE THIRD WAVE

Internal communications and the integration process go hand in hand. It is through communication that employees of the merging organizations gain an appreciation and understanding of each other's products and services, cultures, and general ways of doing business. The communications audit lends insights into how, when, and what a given company communicates to its employees—information that is a necessary starting point in forging new communication approaches for the merged organization. The attitude survey unearths employees' fears and concerns, as well as gaps in information, that must be addressed in postclosing communication initiatives.

Some managers think that communications stop after the closing. On the contrary. Finalization of the transaction represents the time when long-term communications must be articulated and planned out over a multimonth timetable.

There is a key difference between the first and second waves of communications. First-wave information is largely news-oriented. It provides, essentially, the "what, why, and when" of the transaction. Second-wave communications take on much more of an instructive nature. They must educate, motivate, inculcate, and coordinate. That is, employees must first be educated about the firm with which their company is merging. Next, they must be motivated to enthusiastically embrace the inevitable changes that will come with the merger. Next, workers must learn and appreciate the merged company's evolving new culture (indeed, they must help shape that culture). Ultimately, the third wave of communications must provide the foundation on which groups within the company coordinate with each other and, thus, are allowed to function effectively on a day-to-day basis.

The motivational and educational aspects of postclosing communications lay the groundwork for creating the new company's identity and facilitating formal integration initiatives. Preclosing research, as well as information collected during the marketing due diligence process, generates important insights for use in crafting postclosing internal communications. Additionally, observations resulting from communications audits and attitude surveys are also directly applicable in devising communications strategies.

Every merger situation is different, so precise communication objectives will necessarily vary. Nonetheless, there are several basic goals that mark all postmerger communication efforts. These include:

- Creating a sense of shared purpose
- Effecting teamwork
- Imparting administrative information
- Detailing product-service information

Creating a Sense of Shared Purpose

Employees of the merged company must feel they are all striving toward a common goal. They must understand that the rationale for the merger is attaining a sought-after end that the merger partners could not have achieved separately, but which they can achieve by working together.

The overriding purpose of the corporate combination must be articulated and forcefully communicated. It may be that the merged firm will now be able to develop new products that, individually, the merger partners were unable to create. Or, it may be that the merger will enable the firms to penetrate new domestic or global markets. Whatever the aim, it should be communicated from the standpoint of how the merging firms *together* can attain it.

Effecting Teamwork

Once the strategic rationale for the merger has been communicated to employees, the process of forging true teamwork between the organizations commences. This is obviously very easy to say, but very difficult to achieve. Many employees will cling to long-standing ways of doing business. Some will resist working with people from the other side. An "us versus them" mentality may persist. This mind-set is the single greatest barrier to effective integration, and the communication process is the central way of overcoming that obstacle.

Teamwork must not only be talked about, it must be formally engendered—for example, via the formation of functional integration teams, wherein representatives from the merging organizations are assigned to those groups. Teamwork needs to be identified and rewarded. It is only through recognizing acts of true teamwork that workers can embrace the concept as being real and necessary, as opposed to their viewing it simply as an empty phrase uttered by management. For instance, we have developed for clients internal house organs whose central editorial focus is reporting on postmerger functional teams. Many of the articles in these internal media key on the positive interactions of representatives from the merger partners as they plan and carry out a variety of integration-related activities and share success stories. Teamwork is reported on—and unabashedly applauded.

INSIDER'S OUTLOOK

When our company was smaller, I played a pretty big role because I was very active and I did a lot of the acquisitions myself and a lot of the due diligence. I wrote my own letters and welcomed everybody [in the acquired companies]. As you grow, you've got to bring people in and get them to handle that responsibility. We developed a system that we use to welcome people and stay in contact with them. On every anniversary date, we write them a letter and congratulate them on their first, second, third, fourth, and fifth anniversaries.

—CEO of Fortune 1000 health care services company

Imparting Administrative Information

Effecting a sense of shared purpose and teamwork is reinforced in the process of disseminating information that is administrative in nature. For example, employees need to know about the new organizational structure; the roles and responsibilities of the new management team; and policies, procedures, and benefits information.

There is a sense of comfort when management is able to provide this information, since doing so tells employees that the merging organizations have truly begun to function as one. Releasing administrative information is the first tangible example of integration, and the information, in and of itself, tells employees how the merged firm will conduct business going forward.

From a timing standpoint, it is important to release details on administrative matters as they are finalized. For instance, some companies make the mistake of waiting until the official benefits materials have been designed, written, and produced. In reality, the fancy four-color brochures can wait. Information—even if it takes the form of simply produced internal memorandums—should be released as soon as possible.

Detailing Product-Service Information

Effective growth planning requires communicating details on the products, services, and sales and marketing strategies of the merged company. Whereas the first postmerger communication challenge addresses the employee motivation issues that facilitate integration, firmwide growth initiatives can only be launched successfully when workers understand what the merged company is selling.

Moreover, employees need to know about the company's competitive differentiators, its advertising and marketing communication strategies, its distribution game plan, and the key executives leading the business development charge. Disseminating product-related information may be considered a strictly practical exercise because employees need to know it. However, promptly communicating marketing-related details also supports the aforementioned objectives of effecting teamwork and a shared sense of purpose.

Without question, specifically crafted product-related communications are important in and of themselves. But they are also beneficial when combined with motivational and administrative messages, since they collectively help move disparate employee bases in the same strategic direction.

MEDIA SELECTION AND DEVELOPMENT

Postmerger communication planning involves both crafting messages to further the integration process and developing media through which those messages will be delivered to your internal audiences.

As your integration program moves forward, new media should be created to impart organizational information. For the first phase of your communication program, however, it is advisable to use existing communication vehicles (e.g., newsletters used in the past by both organizations). To start employing new communications media in the early phases of the communication process may make anxious employees even more so. Many people are resistant to change. Therefore, change should not be introduced too quickly. Using an unknown channel communicates a change that people may not be ready for. *Although the integration needs to occur expeditiously, employees must be eased through it.*

The easier approach is to modify existing media. For example, you can retain the company newsletter's name, but add a subhead to reflect the merger. Another way to alter a medium's look without fully abandoning its overall identity is to keep the publication's name, but slightly modify its logo or layout. Using the names of both newsletters for a few issues will help the transition if one name is to be kept. But, these are short-term measures. Ultimately, new media with new names and looks should be created.

It is when the second wave of communications—those disseminated after the transaction's closing—commences that new communication vehicles should be phased in. At this point, the merged company is indeed a new organization that requires new ways of communicating. New print and electronic media should be developed, although they may, in effect, be visually or editorially derived from predecessor publications.

Devising new firmwide media is just one element of the broader postclosing communications program. It is at this point that specially tailored communications materials should also be considered. A research-driven approach must be taken to devising messages to different audience segments within the merged company.

There will be many pieces of company information that must be disseminated to all employees. But there will also be instances where information must be tailored in terms of language, content, and presentation. For example, the level of detail on certain issues that is imparted to senior managers may be quite different from that which is disseminated to the rank and file. Moreover, different communication techniques may be required to reach workers in different geographic locales, especially global locations where verbiage may need to be translated.

The need for customization is critical; different employees need different information delivered to them in different ways and at different intervals. Ideally, the analysis that drove the sampling phase of your communications research will indicate the different audience groups that must be reached going forward. In addition, the findings of your communications audit and attitude survey—particularly from the standpoint of preferred media and the prevailing issues and concerns of different audience segments—will provide additional insights that can be factored into both your ongoing communications planning and long-term programs.

As important as it is to use varied, yet integrated media during the first wave of your *external* communications, the same holds true for your *internal* communications efforts. Even if a striking new publication is developed, one vehicle should never be the sole source of critical integration-related information. That medium may be the lead vehicle for important merger-related information, but it should be used in concert with other means of communication.

The goal is always to ensure that employees receive information from whatever sources they prefer, on an ongoing basis. Never assume that even though a major article in the new corporate house organ was devoted to important integration developments that everybody in the company absorbed that information. It may never have been seen. Or it may have been seen but not read.

SUMMARY

Achieving the synergies that comprise the strategic foundation of a merger requires devising a comprehensive approach to integrating two disparate organizations. Without effective organizational communications, the process of effecting integration can be delayed and made even more complex. Management of the acquiring firm stands to lose valuable time, money, and human resources when employee communications are ineptly handled.

A communications program is one of the most important steps management can take toward expeditiously melding two companies. Communications are also one of the integration-related activities that have historically received less than adequate attention in the process of forging the newly combined corporate entity.

Your communications strategy should always involve extensive research and the employment of multiple media that appear at regular intervals and which reach all key employee segments. There may be tremendous variety in the media used for your postmerger communications. There should never be, however, any variation in the most important aspect of your communication efforts: crafting and regularly disseminating the central messages to your employees.

13

Training: Catalyst of Integration and Skills Transfer

So many aspects of postmerger integration relate to theoretical concepts and efforts to influence organizational intangibles—employee attitudes and corporate culture being chief among them. Eventually, the time comes to address these issues and the challenges they present head-on in order to get the merged company moving in the right strategic direction.

The postmerger internal communication program enables you to begin the process of actualizing the strategic drivers that lie at the heart of the transaction. Yet communication, as valuable and necessary as it is, is mostly passive: The employee base receives messages that are designed to inform and motivate. But true *action* is required to start people thinking and functioning in ways that will allow the merged firm to harness its collective capabilities and forcefully begin competing in the marketplace.

People need to think and act differently in order to perform more effectively. That is why a comprehensive training program is needed to effect behavioral change as a means of expediting integration, transferring critical skills, and, ultimately, aligning corporate cultures.

In the postmerger environment, unification springs from education.

As soon as a merger is announced, people from each organization will have a voracious need to know everything about the other. An informational void has been created, as has a cultural gap that needs to be bridged. Neither situation can be addressed solely by management memos or other forms of internal communication. An entirely new way of doing business cannot be imparted via management missives. As a result, training looms large as a critical component of unifying the combined companies in order to actualize the strategic synergies you seek.

More immediately, however, employees need to be taught about the newly merged company, revamped processes need to be methodically explained, accepted and desired behaviors need to be demonstrated and reinforced. Training provides for the enlightenment of the workforce, the involvement of the individual employee, and the reinforcement of productive work styles by enhancing workers' technical, personal, and problem-solving capabilities. Training is also central to articulating the new vision of the company.

Clearly, there is also an attitudinal modification aspect to training. In the wake of any major merger or acquisition, both positive and negative sentiments will spread throughout the merging organizations. Anti-acquirer propaganda will begin to flow from those who either do not approve of the transaction or fear being deemed unnecessary and expendable. But even those with a positive mind-set require something to fill the cultural void that most likely has been created. They have lost something and in many cases do not know precisely what it is. Management now has the opportunity—indeed the responsibility—not only to fill that cultural and informational chasm, but to reinforce specific behaviors and ways of doing business.

Acquisitions have a potentially negative human impact, which is manifested in the form of job insecurity and a lack of productivity. The root cause of this negative and undesirable behavior is uncertainty. Management must quickly recognize this pervasive employee sentiment and move to mitigate it via educational measures. Proactive training strategies can help employees cope with the emotional upheavals accompanying a merger or acquisition.

Training is the tactical delivery system of all behavior modification that can breed success at both the corporate level and the personal level. By focusing on training that directly supports individual growth, management will be laying the foundation for corporate growth. Basic skills learning and transfer can bring employee know-how and capability to a higher level through confidence building and knowledge sharing. Moreover, subsequent reinforcement techniques linked to performance can establish a strong platform from which growth initiatives can spring.

Training programs are necessary in all companies at all stages of development. The event of a merger, however, often requires a radical redesign of training curricula to retool the workforce with new skills that will support the new corporate vision. Training is particularly important for an acquired firm's workforce. Management must acknowledge that something has been "taken" from the acquired company's culture and, therefore, something must be put back. In many cases, this is not only expected by the employees, but greatly appreciated. Increasing the skill sets of all employees while concurrently integrating them into the broader culture can be accomplished via an ongoing training initiative. Without question, education expedites integration.

INSIDER'S OUTLOOK

Training and development issues to be addressed in a merger or acquisition center around clarifying roles and taking a close look at the jobs that need to be done and who is doing them. In the size-driven merger, large company A will shove its systems down the throat of small company B. The smart merger will look at both organizations to identify best practices in every aspect of operations and develop them across the board. This way it's not "know-it-all" A teaching the "unlearned" company B. It's A and B as a new organization making sure everyone is trained to go forward as the new "we."

—Paul Cholak, SHL North America

The postmerger training program must identify the specific courses necessary to educate, motivate and improve the collective skills of the employee base. And, there are several types of training courses that must typically be offered by management, at least in the first phases of the training initiative. By viewing the various types, you will gain a strong understanding of what types of information truly need to be conveyed.

COURSE SUBJECT MATTER

Each merged organization will have specific training requirements based on the company's product and service mix, its strategic imperatives, and a host of other factors. However, there are several basic categories that should comprise the framework of every postmerger training program. These include:

- Corporate vision
- Merger partners' company history
- Product and service offerings
- Customer characteristics and requirements
- Marketplace conditions
- Administrative procedures
- Information technology
- Interpersonal and group communications
- Conflict resolution
- Benefits and retirement education
- Career development

Precise topics within each of these courses would be dictated necessarily by the particulars of the combining companies' people, products, and processes. In general, however, designing your course work should begin with an understanding of the basic function of each curriculum element.

Corporate Vision

One of the first aspects of training must tie to articulating the merged company's corporate vision. The values of the company must be stressed and imparted to all levels of the employee base. When everyone from the CEO on down has the same sense of direction, then the integration process can commence and the groundwork for subsequent cultural alignment can be laid.

Management can successfully communicate the vision by explicitly detailing the strategies that will be undertaken to realize it. Moreover, the greatest impact will be made when the vision is personalized—where each employee understands his or her role in achieving it. By avoiding broad terms and vague directives, strategies can be translated into clear objectives and practical action plans that are more easily embraced by the rank and file. Once the workforce believes in and is ready to act on their marching orders, employees will more quickly understand and adopt the new systems and processes being instituted to actualize the new vision.

Training curricula that focus specifically on imparting the new vision are important. Yet continually articulating and reinforcing the vision is necessary in virtually all other informational initiatives. That is, this common message must run through all aspects of both formal and informal training and be present in all major communication programs launched after the deal's closing.

Merger Partners' Company History

It is necessary that both communications and modules within your training curricula address the merger partners' respective company histories. This, in effect, represents the most basic orientation that all employees should go through.

In high-level terms, all employees must learn about their new partner's beginnings and the key chronological events that led to the organization's current-day composition. Who were its founders? In what businesses did it originally operate? How has it grown? What acquisitions or mergers has it engaged in? Particular emphasis should be placed on the company's specific accomplishments and the strategic and competitive differentiators that made it an alluring merger partner in the first place.

In most cases, when a company is acquired, its entire workforce is asked to give up its corporate history and embrace another. Showing respect toward its past by addressing it now in training will go a long way in getting employees from the acquired organization to work together with yours in the future.

Product and Service Offerings

Part of explaining the history of each merger partner is explaining its products and services. This topic, however, is too important to cover in an ancillary way during a general orientation training. The products and services of the merging companies should be discussed in all courses for all levels of the employee base. However, sales and marketing and customer service employees must be extensively trained in all aspects of the merged company's current and future product mix (product features, pricing, promotion, etc.).

A company's product history is important as well. If there was a failed product or service in the past, all should be made aware of it. Now is not the time for keeping skeletons in the closet. New employees will appreciate an honest accounting of what worked and what did not. More important, if product failure information is withheld, and somehow your sellers wind up in an awkward situation with a customer or prospect, that negative news will travel very quickly within the organization. Discussing past product failures is also significant in the all-important respect of putting people in a position to learn from past mistakes.

Product-related training should be ongoing. Yet, sales and marketing people are not the only employees who should be schooled regularly and comprehensively in the merged company's evolving product offerings. All employees must be continually updated on new goods and services—either through internal communications or, where necessary, through revised training courses. An effective way to teach all employees about the products and services offered by the new firm is to hold a resource fair. In this environment, each product manager, practice reader, or divisional head can showcase the capabilities resident in their respective area. This is a compelling step toward interdependence and cross-selling.

Customer Characteristics and Requirements

Regardless of a company's industry or its product and service line, all employees must understand who the firm's customers are, what needs buyers have, and how the merged company will strive to meet those needs.

Employees must recognize that without the customer, there is no company. And they must understand that every employee exists to ultimately serve the customer. Moreover, understanding the customer will help employees more easily understand the business. It is shocking how many nonmanagement employees in many American companies have a shallow understanding of their company's services and products. More profound is workers' lack of knowledge about the customer. Postmerger training provides you with the opportunity to ensure this is not the case with the combined employee base going forward.

The interrelationship among training on products, markets, and customers is obvious. Training in each of these subject areas will create a more involved workforce and higher levels of customer focus in all aspects of the merged company's operations. Personalizing an employee's individual role in serving the customer can generate an honest concern for the success of the business and enhance people's collective focus on quality.

Limiting this type of training to the customer service department misses the point. True customer service is not a separate corporate function. It is a philosophy that should pervade the workplace and permeate all employee activities. A customer focus must be taught and reinforced. Regardless of whether employees actually deal directly with a customer, they should all embrace the same principles that apply to customer-contact personnel—such as maintaining a positive attitude, solving problems, and striving for continuous improvement and quality.

Marketplace Conditions

Most employees should be made to understand the prevailing dynamics of the marketplace and the merged company's approach to addressing those conditions.

Your people should learn about the external market forces that will impact the merged company's current initiatives and future profitability (e.g., the macroenvironmental forces discussed earlier). Again, these issues may be covered in high-level terms with the broad employee base, but must be treated in extensive detail in training your sales, marketing, and customer service professionals.

Of course, no discussion of marketplace conditions is complete without a detailed look at the competitive climate. Employees must understand both the direct and indirect competitors of the merged company. Information should be provided on competitors' offerings, the strategic differentiators thereof, and other particulars relative to such things as their distribution strategies, promotion, and pricing.

There is also a psychological benefit of analyzing and addressing the competition—one that will also directly support your integration efforts. By placing a strong focus on the competition, employees will feel as if they are on the same side. Focusing on competitors unites employees against a "common enemy." As each of the members of the organization rallies behind this common cause, the workforce becomes more cohesive and integration accelerates.

Administrative Procedures

In acquisition situations, the acquired firm's employees must learn how the acquiring company handles its day-to-day administrative activities. In those rare merger-of-equals situations, where it ostensibly follows that brand-new administrative procedures will be developed (or at least select ones from each of the combining companies will be adopted to varying degrees), all employees must learn new administrative practices. Regardless, administrative activities typically must be taught to those people who will be responsible for complying with them.

What are these administrative processes? Completing purchase orders, filling out time sheets, and making requisitions from the company supply department are just some of the many administrative tasks for which employees will be responsible. Many such processes are central to any company's day-to-day activities. Consequently, it is important to educate those who need to know as soon as it is practicable. Delays in teaching employees these basic processes can create internal confusion, cause costly errors, and hinder many of the purely mechanical aspects of effecting departmental integration.

Information Technology

With the exception of basic word processing and spreadsheets, many companies have technology applications that are unique to those organizations. Such tools include customer databases, computerized accounting systems, and warehousing and inventory tracking protocols, to name just a few. It is necessary to examine information technology (IT) differences carefully from an organizational process perspective. That is, some IT applications are immediately critical to the combined company's operations. Other applications need not be addressed until later in the integration process. For example, information technology employed for financial and accounting controls is more important in the near term than computer-based systems used to collect and disseminate market research. Both are important. Yet priorities must be set from a training standpoint.

There is another important nuance to IT-related training. Different departments employ different types of information technology. Consequently, training course work may well have to be more tailored and specialized than other companywide educational initiatives.

Interpersonal and Group Communications

Many companies have regular training to improve employees' verbal (both speaking and writing), interpersonal, and group communication skills. Effective communication takes on even greater urgency in the postmerger environment in light of the obvious challenges of integration and aligning corporate cultures. Generic communication training is important. Yet specialized instruction may be necessary in merger situations where there are significant language barriers (the reference here is not to foreign language barriers as much as to differences resulting from the companies having historically operated in divergent businesses). Employees from the merging companies may need to understand new terms, frequently used acronyms, and even slang expressions unique to one or both of the merger partner companies. Keep in mind that both communication content and communication setting are important in planning training in this area. For instance, if one of the merger partners frequently asks its people to function in small-group settings—or to present at auditorium-sized gatherings—it may be necessary to offer public-speaking and presentation skills to employees who may not be used to communicating in those types of forums.

Conflict Resolution

An issue related to interpersonal communication is that of conflict resolution. In the wake of any merger or acquisition, tension is typically at its highest level. As employees, regardless of their status, begin to operate in survival mode, their business demeanor changes. They often become fearful, paranoid, defensive, and aggressive. Conflicts between new coworkers are bound to flare up. And people must know how to recognize and deal with them.

For example, postmerger conflicts arise frequently in the following scenario: When employees first learn that they have been acquired, they may feel that their chances of survival will be better if they follow one of two courses of action. Actually, the first is a course of inaction. This behavior manifests itself by lying low, choosing to be invisible, and essentially hoping that no one will notice them. This work vacuum forces coworkers to pick up the slack in those persons' productivity. As the coworkers' workload increases, morale and efficiency decline. At the other extreme is the employee who starts doing everyone else's job in hopes of being noticed by the new management. Unfortunately, in the process, he or she often steps on coworkers' toes. The less qualified worker soon is overwhelmed and underperforming. Those with greater competencies become underutilized and frustrated that they are not being recognized for their efforts.

If not quickly resolved, conflicts can leave lasting scars. Training must, therefore, be designed to help people understand how to minimize conflict between themselves and their new colleagues. Training is also necessary for group managers who are asked to intervene in disputes arising between people within their departments.

INSIDER'S OUTLOOK

I have always believed very heavily in training in all aspects of the business. You have to train in marketing, management, accounting . . . and you can never train too much. For example, we just finished training every one of our sales managers for four solid days. You must invest in all your people . . . especially sales people who are on the front lines. They must be trained how to sell the service, how to approach the customer, and how to handle the customer. We have even trained our salespeople on how to evaluate a customer in terms of whether he's even listening to you or not. So many employees in America have never been trained in anything, yet it's so important.

—CEO of Fortune 100 telecommunications company

Benefits and Retirement Education

Educating employees on the provisions of their new benefits plan is largely an internal communications function. At the same time, certain administrative aspects of employee benefits—such as knowing how to complete and process medical claims forms—fall into the aforementioned training category of administrative processes. There is, however, another element of benefits-related training that has become almost mandatory in American business today: retirement planning.

Devising a comprehensive retirement education program can serve three purposes:

1. The program will provide employees of the merged firm with critical information on the specific provisions of their new retirement plan (e.g., informing people about their different asset allocation options) and the best ways to invest in it based on individuals' investment objectives and future financial needs.
2. Greater understanding and awareness of their retirement planning options will likely increase participation in the merged company's 401(k) or other defined-contribution plan.
3. Implementing a retirement education training program will engender goodwill from employees toward the merged firm's management and, consequently, aid in employee retention.

Career Development

The merged organization will most likely have new requirements for employees' personal advancement in terms of both status and compensation. One of the merger partners may have promoted people based solely on tenure. The other may have granted promotions based exclusively on the employee's attainment of rigorous performance objectives. Employees need clarification and direction.

Career development may also be viewed as a topic best covered as part of your internal communications program. Indeed, it should be covered in this "mass medium." But it should also be addressed in one-on-one sessions between employees and their managers. Still, there is a role for training in educating people on the ways to advance in the new organization.

Employees can learn about different staff levels and what continuous education they must undergo to qualify for them. (In this sense, they participate in training to learn what other training they will need to get ahead.) The bottom line is, the merged company's people must have a clear understanding of what it will take to advance up the ranks of the new organization. Only then can they take the steps necessary to do so. And, only then can ambitious employees help further the productivity and market competitiveness of the company itself.

Ideally, all employees of the merged company should undergo some type of training, albeit to varying degrees and in different subject areas. Clearly, the courses an assembly-line worker takes are quite different from those that a middle manager would take. Having looked at the basic types of training subject areas, you can now address how you would plan educational programs for different levels of the merged organization's corporate hierarchy.

TRAINING: A STAFF CLASSIFICATIONS PERSPECTIVE

Determining who should be trained, when, and in what subject areas is central to designing an effective postmerger training program. Planning the initiative requires understanding the different subject areas that would be appropriate for:

- Senior management
- Middle management
- Broad employee base
- All levels

In general, the higher an employee's staff level, the more strategic the training received will be. The lower the person's staff level, the more the training will be tactical or administrative. At the same time, there will usually be some overlap in terms of the training course work offered; that is, some of the same courses (or variations thereof) may be appropriate for two or more levels of employees.

A practical way of articulating the relationship of the subject areas and the appropriate employees who will attend is the "training triangle"—a tool that resembles a pyramid with four horizontal layers, the top being senior management, the bottom being all levels of employee. It indicates the training subject matter that is appropriate for a merged company's different levels of management, as well as the rank and file. This topical breakdown is largely applicable in virtually any corporate setting irrespective of whether the organization is engaged in a major merger or acquisition. It is a particularly helpful paradigm, however, in structuring postmerger training initiatives.

Senior Management

The highest-ranking executives in the merged firm require training in the highest-level issues facing the merged company. For instance, these officers should undergo training in understanding the merged firm's strategic plan and the specific tactics that will be employed, as well as the human and monetary resources that will be allocated. Large, diversified companies may find the need to train their senior executives on the organizational structure of the combined company, particularly the management and the major programs being orchestrated by different divisions or subsidiaries.

Even if your senior executives will not be directly responsible or get involved in the company's financial and accounting systems, they should nevertheless be trained in the general characteristics of those setups. Senior management may also find beneficial training that relates to the merged company's key outside relationships—such as those with law firms, accounting firms, advertising and public relations agencies—as well as the specific responsibilities those vendors have or will have in the months ahead. This level of management would be placed at the top of the training triangle.

Middle Management

Training for middle managers combines strategic- and tactical-oriented subject matter. Middle managers, for example, must be aware of the merged firm's strategic plan and major market initiatives. Such descriptions, however, may have to be somewhat more vague than information provided on the same subject to the company's senior officers; there may be some information relative to the firm's strategic plan that is inappropriate for managers below the organization's upper ranks (e.g., financial investments being made in certain operational areas, ongoing discussions with a potential joint-venture partner). Still, middle managers must be trained in understanding the company's strategic goals if they are to contribute to reaching them. This level of management requires training in some topics of a semiadministrative nature. For instance, it may be necessary to instruct middle managers on such things as the merged firm's recruiting and promotion policies, procedures for procuring supplies, and other topics related to managing individual departments or teams.

Earlier, communication-related training was discussed. For middle managers, group presentation and public speaking skills may be more apropos than courses on improving one's interpersonal or written communications (although everybody can generally benefit from practice or refresher courses in these areas). Another topic referenced earlier related to conflict resolution. Again, given the stress and tension levels that typically result in the integration process, conflicts between coworkers almost always arise, albeit to various degrees under many different scenarios. Invariably, middle managers will be asked to mediate disputes between coworkers. Consequently, managers must be trained in the ways to identify and promptly defuse such encounters. Within the training triangle paradigm, this group is placed beneath senior managers.

Broad Employee Base

At the broadest level of the employee base, training becomes almost purely administrative in nature. Workers will require training on basic forms processing, general computer skills, and interpersonal and verbal communications. Conflict resolution may also be appropriate for workers at this level. Yet this may take the form of a "do it yourself" approach to defusing coworker conflicts, as opposed to the more supervisory-oriented training middle managers would receive on the same topic.

Clearly, this category represents the largest group of employees who need to be trained. And that is why this group fills out an area just above the base of the training triangle. As a result, there will be more standardization in the subject matter and training approach. This contrasts the training designed for higher levels of management. Many times, sessions for senior managers will have to be structured more flexibly in terms of timing and content. There are two main reasons. Company officers tend to have more demanding time constraints, so they cannot always be certain they will attend scheduled sessions. Second, senior people may be less amenable to training to begin with, and flexibility will be needed to garner their participation (if not their full and enthusiastic commitment).

All Levels

There are certain topics that comprise training subjects for employees at all levels of the merged company. (And therefore this group runs across the base of the training triangle.) The depth of detail will necessarily vary by level. Nonetheless, all people must undergo some form of training in order to understand such areas as corporate vision, products and services, and organizational structure.

Corporate vision. The underlying strategic goals and objectives of the merged firm, its philosophies regarding customer focus and service, and its approach to serving its other markets and communities can be presented in a format that more than simply disseminates a mission statement. Again, training suggests that specific tactical information be provided on how the merged company will realize its vision.

Products and services. Training sessions can cover the full range of offerings the merged company will bring to the marketplace, including the key features and attributes of those offerings and their competitive differentiating characteristics. As stated, training on the merged firm's product offering must be handled in significantly greater detail with sales, marketing, and customer-contact personnel than in higher-level orientations for rank-and-file employees.

Organizational structure. The various components of the organization can be covered in terms of its regional offices, divisions, subsidiaries, and so forth. The larger and more strategically and geographically diversified the combined company is, the greater the need for training that educates workers on what the corporate pieces are and how they fit together. Personalizing departments and divisions, with the names of their heads, will help new employees better relate to the organization's functionality.

Every company's training needs will be different. By creating your own training triangle and designating the skill sets in which employees at different levels must be trained, you will be able to design a training program that meets many of the educational requirements of the merged firm's workforce.

TRAINING METHODS AND APPROACHES

Today, companies employ a variety of techniques in the realm of corporate training. One or more of these training formats may be appropriate for your organization, depending on existing resources, timing, and corporate preferences; that is, certain companies have found particular training techniques more successful than others. There are five basic training approaches that you should consider:

1. Classroom teaching
2. Train the trainer
3. Facilitation
4. Self-study
5. Coaching and mentoring

Let's explore the nature of each training approach, as well as the specific benefits and drawbacks of each in the postmerger environment.

Classroom Teaching

This is the most traditional and common approach to corporate training. A course leader or instructor is designated. Workbook materials are distributed or computer terminals are provided. The instructive communication is largely one-way (teacher to student), although two-way communication in which attendees ask questions or seek clarification on the instructor's points is encouraged.

There are several shortcomings to the classroom style approach to training. Employees must spend time away from the office, which can be a drain on their individual productivity. Second, if internal facilities are not suitable for the size of the group being trained, costly off-site locations (e.g., hotel conference rooms) must be rented. Third, prolonged sessions tend to overload students with significantly more information than they can realistically absorb—although take-home course materials are intended to be reviewed subsequently for detailed examination or as a memory-jogger.

There is one extremely important benefit, however, that offsets these negatives: interaction. In this sense, interaction does not refer to that which occurs between instructor and student. Rather, it refers to the ability for interaction between coworkers from the merging firms. Putting people together in forums in which the subject matter is designed to move them toward a common goal fosters mutual understanding and unification. The interaction helps you achieve incremental levels of integration.

You can increase the likelihood of this occurring. Whether the training occurs in large groups or small "breakout sessions," always seat and convene people who work in teams or the same department together. These groups will learn simultaneously and therefore be indoctrinated en masse. Once the training ends, these teams can continue to support each other's efforts and reinforce what they have learned.

Train the Trainer

Cost considerations often preclude training programs in which large groups of geographically dispersed employees are able to attend, say, a nationally organized session. Travel and hotel costs could be exorbitant. And entire departments might have to be shut down as the people assigned to them go off for multiday educational retreats. One way to minimize the cost of having to train large numbers of employees from many different locations is to employ a "train the trainer" approach. This involves assembling a group of managers who will receive training and then, in turn, go back to their home offices to train others.

The cost-saving aspect of this approach is obvious, and more and more companies are adopting it to increase the leverage and scope of their training initiatives. Care must be taken, however, when structuring such an approach. There are two critical issues that you must address: One is germane to any corporate setting; the other is specific to merger and acquisition situations.

First, whether or not you are engaged in an integration initiative, it is necessary to select as your trainers people who truly have the ability to train others. Not everyone can teach, regardless of how strong a command of the subject matter that person may have. Consequently, make sure the people you select for this role have the intellectual and personality traits that make teachers effective: enthusiasm, strong communication skills, and the ability to explain complex concepts in simplified terms.

Second, apply great sensitivity to determining who will be teaching the course. You do not want to have a manager from Merger Partner A instructing employees from that company on the particulars of Merger Partner B's operations. This might serve to promote, rather than dispel, the proverbial "us versus them" mentality. Moreover, it leaves open the possibility of there being (consciously or unconsciously) errors and misrepresentations in the information imparted. Ideally, your instructors should be people from both sides of the merger equation. In fact, team teaching—with one instructor from each of the merger partner companies—may be appropriate for certain forums and subject areas.

Facilitation

An increasingly popular alternative to traditional classroom learning is having key managers lead the process of facilitation.

Facilitation is a quasi-training technique that has as its centerpiece an individual who is proficient in a given subject area. Rather than teaching large groups of employees in a formal training atmosphere, the facilitator leads a small group through a kind of self-discovery meeting in which approaches to solving specific problems or gaining new skills are addressed. One of the more effective facilitation sessions we directed involved helping a Fortune 100 technology company integrate a newly acquired telecommunications firm. In three, day-long sessions, senior managers from both companies learned about each other's motivations, competencies, and attitudes. We unearthed critical information (e.g., competitor intelligence, potential internal conflicts, and roadblocks to integration) and ultimately forged a framework for melding the two companies. The results of these types of sessions can be a strong foundation for a multitude of integration initiatives.

Consider, for example, the process of developing divisional business plans. A facilitation approach can be used in which a facilitator leads a given divisional manager and his core staff through a strategy session. In this forum, the facilitator would ask the group questions such as, "What capabilities does the firm have?", "Who is the competition?", "What business do we want to be in?", "What are our budgetary constraints?", and "What are our strengths and weaknesses?" The members of the group already know the answers to the questions, but they do not know the right questions to ask. The process of discovery that each group member goes through is in itself training. At the end of the session, the answers have been arrived at, each member of the group now understands how to develop a business plan, and the document itself will have been developed. In this capacity, the facilitator serves as a trainer, yet those being trained are in essence training themselves.

Self-Study

Training books, audio tapes, videos, and multimedia CD-ROM products are increasingly being used for corporate training purposes. The benefits of this approach include giving people the ability to learn at their own pace, minimizing time away from the office, and saving money on travel and hotel expenses for off-site training sessions. The primary drawback of self-study tools is the absence of interaction between student and teacher—specifically, the former's inability to ask questions and seek clarification from the latter.

In M&A situations, there is another shortcoming to the absence of student-teacher interaction in self-study training: This approach is based on an independent orientation to learning, yet an environment that fosters interaction between trainees from the merging organizations will more directly support other integration activities.

Coaching and Mentoring

The foregoing training techniques involve either group instructional settings or independent study. There is, however, a middle ground. That involves assigning a coach or mentor to a given employee. In this scenario, the employee—usually a person who demonstrates an especially high level of professional potential—is assigned a coach, who is senior to that person in terms of skills and experience. The employee benefits from learning directly from a person whose knowledge is relevant to that person's professional development. Moreover, a bond forms between teacher and student that engenders trust. This, in turn, can expedite the successful transfer of technical skills.

In addition to skills development, coaching and mentoring is also beneficial in helping employees cope with the personal and professional difficulties that often arise during the integration process. At a stage so fraught with uncertainty and political stumbling blocks, an employee can benefit greatly from the personal guidance and counsel rendered by a respected member of the combined company's managerial ranks.

Coaching and mentoring is a form of individualized instruction. There is a particular benefit to this form of training: namely, the ability to more quickly cultivate an employee's specific skills and thereby maximize that person's near- and long-term contributions. Next, you should focus on how individualized training can play a role in your broader, postmerger educational initiatives.

INDIVIDUALIZED TRAINING

Too often in the corporate world, the wrong individuals come to hold the wrong positions. Sometimes this happens when employees are pigeonholed in roles that prevent them from broadening their skill base and assuming responsibilities more in line with their true talents and interests. Over time, these individuals get locked into the career path they originally sought or which was imposed on them by former managers. Their real competencies are never assessed, nor mined. This creates a twofold negative effect. The employee never actualizes his or her potential in the areas that person is best suited for, and the company never benefits from an individual who could better serve the organization in a different capacity.

Remember, though, that you are starting with a veritable clean slate after a merger. Management can eradicate this problem by proactively exploring the skill competencies of key employees within the combined workforce. By assessing the strengths of selected managers and key employees, and then exploring where those people's interests and aspirations lie, the company can link both the employees' talents and preferences to positions that support the company's business goals.

This type of interaction between employer and employee is often considered radical. It is not. It is eminently logical to have the best person in the organization performing the task that individual does best and likes most. Herein lies the framework for individualized training and career development.

The process of devising individualized training begins with an identification of the traits that are held to be important in your particular organization. Such traits may include skills in:

- Learning
- Entrepreneurism
- Leadership
- Teaching
- Interpersonal interaction

- Quantitative analysis
- Teamwork
- Conflict resolution
- Communication

You can probably identify people in your organization right now who have skills that could be better utilized in other areas. Conversely, there are likely to be other employees who have obvious skill weaknesses that can be strengthened through appropriate training. Identifying employees' technical and personality-related strengths and weaknesses should be conducted as empirically as possible in order to generate valid and actionable results. Objective, fact-based insights—those that help you identify the individuals whose skills and interests are most closely aligned, as well as those whose capabilities are not—are necessary for decision making regarding new roles in the combined company. Again, using the integration process as an opportunity to evaluate and reassess every employee gives you the chance to pinpoint the totality of skills resident in the newly combined employee base.

It is not necessary to perform this aspect of your training initiative immediately (although a high-level assessment of the workforce's skill base should ideally be done during the due diligence process). By identifying those people with strengths or weaknesses in critical skills areas, the company can be more effectively tooled as employees gain a greater sense of self-worth and make progressively greater contributions to the organization.

Analyzing employees' skills and aspirations is a precursor to another form of training: career counseling.

When an acquisition first occurs and the buyer is analyzing the resumes and backgrounds of newly acquired employees, management is in a position to identify the most appropriate candidates for new or existing job functions. Among the acquired workforce are individuals who possess capabilities needed in many positions within the acquiring company or in the merged firm's new organizational structure. Identifying these individuals is the first step to placing them in the right positions now and in devising dedicated career counseling for them to benefit the combined company further down the road.

Key employees should ultimately receive training in the form of guidance on career opportunities vis-à-vis the future skill requirements of the merged company. For instance, a training methodology known as "career pathing" trains employees in long-term career development. The most qualified individuals are able to advance through the ranks of the organization by getting the most broad and well-planned job experiences. They are marked as being on the fast track within the new organization and are included in all internal training programs that will support their continuing personal development.

Moreover, companies may send these promising employees through external training programs. These can take the form of seminars, workshops, industry trade conferences, and even degree programs such as those for an MBA or PhD. There is a greater cost to an outsourced training approach. Yet, the fact that a company believes in their employees enough to subsidize or totally finance this cost can often ensure the participants' commitment and enthusiasm, as well as their long-term loyalty and tenure.

The bottom line on individualized training is this: Group training is a mass market approach to skills-related education. That is not necessarily a criticism. Yet many companies are finding that more personalized training curricula are appropriate for given employees. Courses can now be readily developed that comprise a structured approach to fostering managers' development via highly individualized, experiential curricula. This approach typically provides a format and timetable allowing minimal disruption of a key employee's day-to-day business responsibilities. Employing techniques such as these has been shown to increase job satisfaction, while helping employees more quickly gain the technical skills they require—in comparison to traditional classroom learning.

In sum, individualized training may be more welcome and beneficial to certain employees. And it may be more beneficial to *you* if it directly benefits the career development of your most promising people.

TRAINING: TIMING CONSIDERATIONS

When do you train?

Ideally, training should commence immediately on closing of the transaction. Realistically, however, there are likely to be many other integration activities that will take higher priority. Nonetheless, training program design is not something that should be kept on the back burner too long.

Every day that passes without firmwide training adds to the information vacuum. An informed workforce is a more capable workforce. If training programs are not in place at the earliest possible juncture, employee confusion and uncertainty will be maximized and the effectiveness of your other integration tactics will be minimized.

The most basic and inclusive training addresses the merged firm's workforce as if they were all new employees. They are entitled to the same initial orientation that a new hire would receive within the first week of employment. In that basic training, critical questions on the new employee's mind are addressed. Remember that a merger or acquisition raises critical questions in existing employees—queries that must also be addressed expeditiously.

SUMMARY

Training must be the focus of every company whose management seeks quality and productivity in its employees, excellence in its products and services, and growth in its bottom line, especially in the postmerger environment. In M&A situations, training can link the critical components of disparate organizational infrastructures.

In addition to tightening the weave of the cultural fabric, training helps facilitate the transfer of skills from employee to employee and, more importantly, from merger partner to merger partner. Buttressing this transfer of skills, training ensures that the most qualified people are developed and motivated to take the merged company to its desired next level.

A newly merged workforce that can focus on business issues instead of personal issues and petty distractions can best actualize the company's vision. What is more, a workforce that is well-trained in the skills needed to realize that vision will take the shortest path in achieving it. From a more practical standpoint, if issues such as administrative procedures and departmental policies are quickly understood by employees, valuable time will not be wasted at the watercooler or on the phone discussing details with coworkers or friends.

Each of these benefits of training contributes to increased productivity, morale, and feelings of personal growth and positive self-worth. In turn, higher levels of employee retention typically result. Training is, in essence, the delivery system of change. The benefits of this change will continue to grow as they build on each other by reinforcement and people's continual involvement and interaction.

In the postmerger environment, implementing a training program must be viewed not as an option, but rather as an obligation by management to create and control the technical and motivational information that must be shared by all employees of the merged company. Since training is the tactical delivery system of all behavior modification that can breed success at the corporate level, it should be recognized as a key tool in the long-term integration process. Training programs are essential in both aligning cultures and imparting the merged firm's new vision to all employees.

The event of a merger or major acquisition represents a time when your workforce must be reevaluated and retooled. Training will help you in both critical areas while, at the same time, ensuring the smoothest integration possible. With the appropriate tools and a workforce willing and committed to training, management can help the merged company begin realizing its fullest potential.

14

Reward and Recognition Programs and Employee Motivational Techniques

Behavioral psychologists tell us that people do things, both in and out of the workplace, to satisfy their own needs. Usually their actions are motivated by some kind of payoff or reward. Interestingly, one of the reasons so many postmerger integration efforts either stall or fail outright is because they lack a critical component: a formal reward and recognition program that promotes and reinforces employee actions that facilitate or expedite the integration process.

An effective reward program can be the glue of successful integration. When properly designed, it can fuse the corporate vision and business focus of a company with the merging employee workforces. This linkage of people, strategy, and business—whose catalyst is a meaningful reward system—ensures employee retention, reinforces the new vision, and motivates employees individually and collectively.

In order to attain the merged firm's corporate objectives, management will require very specific behaviors of the combined employee base, including all senior managers. As discussed, the most effective method of influencing postmerger organizational behavior is through key members of the management team. If managers are motivated to endorse the new vision and assist with effecting a comparable level of support by their people, the integration process will proceed more smoothly and the merger or acquisition will have a greater likelihood of success.

The building blocks of organizational motivation are laid by providing employees with challenging and specific performance objectives. You can then build on this foundation by rewarding the accomplishments of individual and group achievements at different staffing and divisional levels of the firm.

Behavior is influenced and reinforced by how the organization evaluates performance and what personal actions it rewards. This is the case in any organization at any point in its corporate life cycle. However, employee rewards take on a new dimension in M&A situations. They are eminently necessary, since if employees are informed of the new corporate vision and direction but denied a reason to endorse both of them (beyond the threat of termination), why should they?

Simply announcing that the new era has arrived will do little to sell its importance to people throughout the organization. A far-reaching reward system must be established to motivate employees to accept new ideas and effect an immediate and positive attitudinal shift. Without these proactive measures, the merged organization can neither swiftly nor effectively bring about the necessary structural and cultural changes that will ensure attainment of the strategic and financial gains sought via the transaction.

The types of integration-related rewards that an organization should offer its newly combined workforce include direct compensation, indirect compensation and incentives, and nonfinancial rewards. Rewards can be distributed on an individual, group, or companywide basis. By exploring the various types of reward systems, you will be able to determine those most appropriate for your company's specific integration program or general cultural environment. First, however, you need to explore the precise benefits of a reward and recognition program (beyond the obvious advantages).

GOALS OF REWARD AND RECOGNITION PROGRAMS

Almost every company has some kind of reward and recognition program. Some include provisions as basic as allowing employees to take additional days off ("comp" time beyond official vacation days allotted) or honoring an employee's tenure or dedication with a plaque. However, when a company is involved in a merger or acquisition, the implementation of a substantive, firmwide reward and recognition program tailored specifically to the integration program is necessary. Formal reward campaigns are a vital part of ensuring integration success for five main reasons. Specifically, they:

1. Reinforce the new vision
2. Instruct people on valued behavior
3. Effect employee retention
4. Motivate employees individually and collectively
5. Offset compensation imbalances between companies

Before detailing the ways to realize them, it is important to examine each of these basic benefits.

Reinforce the New Vision

Employees will have a host of perceptions about the direction their lives will take now that they carry the flag of a "new" company. If they can be made to feel necessary or even vital to the success of the merged firm in their new roles, then they will likely embrace the vision of the combined organization. Building consensus among employees is not an easy task. It requires clearly laying out the importance of their new roles, recognizing and monitoring behavior for effectiveness and then, most importantly, reinforcing that behavior through rewards.

Of course, employees need to understand specifically what the new vision is and what precise strategic steps are being taken to actualize it. Reward programs must be designed to acknowledge specific activities, goals, or objectives. Collectively, these milestones must tie to the broader vision and relate directly to the merged firm's tactical initiatives. As employees work to support these efforts in the hope of attaining tangible rewards, they will increasingly gain an understanding of the vision and, consequently, begin to formally take personal ownership of it.

Instruct People on Valued Behavior

A well-managed and well-promoted reward program also serves an educational purpose. By identifying the activities that employees will be recognized for—and then subsequently communicating those individual or team successes throughout the organization—workers will learn which behaviors will support the integration process and, in turn, will qualify them for the attendant rewards.

Over time, this will prove motivating to the point where more and more workers will seek recognition. Additionally, promoting people's specific accomplishments will spark ideas in others. Thus, a snowball effect will be created with more people devising ideas that will likely become increasingly more diverse and sophisticated.

It is necessary to address, at least briefly, the flip side of a reward program: the punitive measures that must be taken against those disgruntled employees who threaten to poison the integration process. Committed employees should be recognized and rewarded for doing the right thing. Conversely, those who do not must be dealt with quickly and decisively. Individuals who either overtly or by passive aggressive behavior refuse to participate must be differentiated from those who are simply afraid or unsure. By recognizing antimerger sentiments and addressing them early on, management can more effectively bring about behavior that engenders collegiality and productivity.

In general, employees with bad attitudes who are just unwilling to participate in the integration process will never be won over. Thus, there will never be a role for them, and they must be cut loose. The impact of severing non-team players sends a dual message to others who might otherwise attempt to undermine the integration process. In the post-merger environment, job security is a very motivating reward. The lesson can be simple: Those who maintain negative attitudes and espouse them to others will face possible termination; those who make honest efforts to adapt to change have the security of a job.

Effect Employee Retention

Integration-oriented reward and recognition campaigns are valuable ways to encourage employees to remain with the merged firm at a time when organizational uncertainties may be prompting key people to consider moving to greener, more stable pastures.

As was discussed earlier, key employees of the acquired firm should be identified and possibly paid stay-on bonuses immediately after the acquisition, regardless of whether they will ultimately be retained for the long haul. This move buys time for the acquiring management to make the appropriate long-term staffing decisions while displaying goodwill to employees in the near term. However, often acquiring management forgets about its own key employees. It is critical to psychologically assure and equally reward top performers in your own organization before they too begin experiencing uncertainty regarding their future job prospects—the same feelings acquired employees experience.

All employees who you have determined will play a role in the merged company need to know that they are safe and being asked to support the cause. Recognizing the important contributions of your human assets from both of the merging companies through basic acknowledgment and rewards will reinforce their current behavior and limit the organizational distractions swirling around them.

Rewarding employees with bonuses and other awards will assure them that they will continue to be counted on. Moreover, it will redirect their focus away from the vagaries of the integration process and toward the strategic imperatives of the merged firm.

Motivate Employees Individually and Collectively

As we will see, reward and recognition programs can be implemented at either the individual or the group level—and, ideally, at both levels concurrently. Through reward initiatives, employees can be motivated to augment their individual contributions. Similarly, formal groups or teams of employees from the merging companies can be motivated to pull together and use their collective strengths to meet or exceed departmental or divisional objectives that support the broader integration program.

Organizational success requires the efforts of both individuals and teams. Devising reward systems that encourage and recognize the efforts of employees and groups will serve to get all people moving in the right direction. As a consequence, so too will the newly merged organization.

Offset Compensation Imbalances between Companies

Invariably, there will be employees within the merging companies who perform the same function but who are compensated differently (e.g., individuals who have the same title, perform the same job, yet have different compensation levels and terms). By first recognizing who these individuals are and then attempting to "level the playing field," you will quickly eliminate a major obstacle to smooth integration.

We have seen this inequity persist in companies years after an acquisition. If it is not addressed promptly in the weeks or months following the closing, you run the risk of spawning employee resentment and animosity as word spreads of people's similar duties but dissimilar salaries.

Obviously, management cannot immediately double the salary of one employee or halve that of another. One near-term solution to this problem—while companywide compensation issues are being ironed out—is to develop a reward program that grants incentives based on integration-oriented objectives. Thus, underpaid employees in one of the merging companies can be given the chance to receive bonuses and rewards that bring their total compensation in line with counterparts in the other merging firm. This not only solves a compensation inequity, but offers the new employees greater professional enrichment. When these expanded responsibilities include goals based on furthering the integration process, the results will more than pay for themselves. Moreover, if the incentive scheme is instituted on a long-term basis, bonuses and other financial rewards can avoid the fixed expense of permanent salary boosts.

CORE STRATEGY: BUILDING WIDESPREAD EMPLOYEE COMMITMENT

Performance-based reward and recognition programs are a vital part of integration for the five reasons we have just discussed. In short, however, such incentive programs are designed to do one key thing: build commitment among all employees of the combined company. But what is commitment?

Commitment is characterized by three traits:

1. A strong belief in and acceptance of the organization's goals and values
2. A willingness to exert considerable effort on behalf of the organization
3. A strong desire to maintain membership in that collective

Yet, people's commitment is a fragile thing in the M&A context. During the integration period, not only will management question the commitment of some of its employees, but the acquired firm's employees themselves will consistently assess their own level of commitment as well. If people are unsure about their roles going forward, they can never form a bond with the organization, let alone develop any sense of obligation to its success.

Commitment can be engendered and reinforced by the proper use of incentives. By strengthening each of the three traits of commitment via recognition and rewards, you can ensure that all employees not only develop a sense of loyalty to the merged company, but also take steps to actively help move the new organization forward.

All three traits of commitment suggest an active relationship between employee and management in which there is some type of quid pro quo. It is the nature of these core traits that is the foundation for devising a meaningful reward system. That is, if you can foster a strong belief in and acceptance of the organization's goals and values within your new employees, then dictating specific managerial actions will come more easily.

The action most desired by management is employees' willingness to exert effort on behalf of the organization, and this requires motivating employees to truly care about the merged organization. From this will flow the desire to belong. If an employee believes, is willing to exert effort to support that belief, and desires to belong, then he or she will be a valuable and productive asset in the merged company going forward.

ACTIONS MERITING REWARD AND RECOGNITION

Before looking at the types of rewards to bestow on people, it is necessary to address some of the activities that might merit formal recognition.

There will necessarily be acts and activities specific to your company's strategic initiatives or to the provisions of the integration program. Yet, here are some generic actions that typically deserve to be acknowledged:

- Meeting or bettering an activity-based deadline
- Achieving sales goals/new business objectives
- Effecting cross-selling opportunities
- Identifying new marketing or revenue enhancement opportunities
- Devising new integration techniques
- Making suggestions that lead to operational improvements or productivity gains

It is critical to examine each one in the hope that doing so will spark ideas on specific personnel actions that can be encouraged and rewarded to facilitate your integration program.

Meeting or Bettering an Activity-Based Deadline

The best-laid plans and best-managed projects can be severely delayed—or completely derailed—in the context of postmerger integration. A market analysis involving the work of different departments, a feasibility study being conducted by multiple units, consolidating the computer files that will comprise the merged firm's new HR information system—these and scores of other assignments collectively comprise the integration program. And all require the close-knit interaction of people who have never worked together before and/or who have yet to adopt the collegiality and trust so necessary to sparking effective teamwork and generating bottom-line results.

It is necessary to acknowledge the inherent difficulties integration poses to the completion of critical tasks. More important, it is advantageous to reward both individuals and groups who successfully meet and exceed the deadline for specific projects. Of course, simple activities with eminently attainable deadlines do not merit any unusual fanfare. And meeting a deadline is irrelevant if the end product is lacking. Use your discretion, needless to say. When the results are there on or before the date they were supposed to be, consider rewarding the individuals or teams behind the success.

INSIDER'S OUTLOOK

Sometimes there are select employees who provide the value or intellectual capital you're seeking. In those cases, you have to say to yourself, "If we're talking about getting 100 people in this company, of which 15 are the key players, then why not pay them each $1 million instead of spending $35 million for the whole company?" Even when that's not the case, it's imperative to make sure key employees stay on after the deal closes. The major mistake many companies make is when they realize they want a bunch of key people, buy the whole company, but then don't do anything to keep them around. It's essential that you consider making the deal contingent on stay-in-place contracts with these people . . . or devise their eventual payout to be based on certain performance and timing requirements.

—Carolyn Chin, IBM

Achieving Sales Goals/New Business Objectives

Members of the merged company sales force will be assigned specific sales targets based on whatever criteria the firm adopts: revenues generated, units sold, number of new accounts opened, and so on. Establishing sales goals is a given for any organization's sellers. In the context of postmerger integration, however, sales goals that merit special recognition might tie to interdependence or the merged company's new product mix.

A salesperson's ability to sell his or her own firm's offerings is expected. But the seller's ability to understand, promote, and successfully close business on a merger partner's products—quickly—is deserving of additional recognition and reward. Yet another criterion for sales-related awards might be the salesperson's ability to expeditiously penetrate new markets—product categories or geographic territories that opened up as a result of the corporate combination.

There is invariably start-up time before a seller of unfamiliar products is able to forge new contacts and close business. Sellers who are adept at doing so promptly and effectively merit rewards that transcend those granted for achieving or exceeding their standard sales bogeys.

Effecting Cross-Selling Opportunities

Many mergers and acquisitions have as an underlying strategic driver the goal of cross-selling products and services to the merged firm's collective new customer base. Issues of territoriality and protecting one's own customer relationships are typical roadblocks to cross-selling in any organization.

Those roadblocks tend to get even more insurmountable when cross-selling is requested of sellers, who may historically have been arch-enemy competitors, but are now playing on the same team as a result of a merger or acquisition. Meeting or exceeding goals relative to cross-selling merit acknowledgment for a purely quantitative, sales target perspective.

Of greater significance is what successful cross-selling truly represents: teamwork, an openness to share, and an orientation to break down internal barriers that are certain to exist in an organization—especially one newly forged as a result of a corporate combination. It is for this reason alone that effective cross-selling will be difficult to engender and, therefore, particularly deserving of tangible rewards for these employees who enthusiastically embrace interdependence.

Identifying New Marketing or Revenue Enhancement Opportunities

Related to successes in cross-selling and formal sales target achievement are employee gains in the broader area of marketing, customer service, and overall revenue enhancement. Again, no management team or business development department has all the ideas on the best ways to promote and market the merged firm's goods and services. Some of your best marketing ideas will come from nonmarketers working in different sectors of the combined company.

Reward structures and provisions will obviously vary based on the source of new marketing or customer service ideas. That is, people whose job it is to devise and implement marketing strategies are necessarily compensated for doing so. And those who quickly meet or far exceed their expected objectives in this area should naturally be rewarded. But a different reward scheme should be devised for rank-and-file employees who conceive ways to intensify your marketing efforts, identify or increase revenue sources, or craft new techniques of strengthening the bond with your most important external audience—your customers.

Devising New Integration Techniques

This entire volume is filled with guidance relative to integration planning. You and your best people from both merger partner companies will map out a series of integration techniques. But nobody has a monopoly on ideas. Inevitably, the people who are the pawns of the integration chess game (no derogatory connotation intended) will come up with ideas to further the integration program. Although great ideas merit acknowledgment and reward, not so great ones do as well.

Any employee showing the interest and initiative to devise ways to better or more quickly effect integration is deserving of the proverbial pat on the back—and then some. Such people are demonstrating an admirable ethic of wanting to make the merger work. Thus, their gesture is deserving of recognition, irrespective of its level of creativity or its practical feasibility. Some employees will come up with suggestions on their own. Still, it may be worthwhile to formally solicit ideas from the employee base as a means of both collecting usable tactics and further engendering and promoting an integration and teamwork mind-set.

Making Suggestions That Lead to Operational Improvements or Productivity Gains

Suggestions relative to integration strategies are obvious in their intrinsic and applied value. Other suggestions employees may make regarding operational processes are valuable as well. And just as integration-specific recommendations highlight an employee's commitment to the merged organization, so too do suggestions relating to other aspects of the combined company's broader organizational activities.

Of particular import are recommendations that lead directly to enhanced efficiencies, cost savings, and overall lifts in individual or group productivity. Ideas may relate to newly detected ways of effecting economies of scale or scope. Or they may tie to just a better way of handling administrative chores. Such quantifiable improvements should be met with quantifiable or other tangible forms of reward.

DESIGNING REWARD AND RECOGNITION PROGRAMS

There are a variety of ways to structure a rewards program, each featuring different types of incentives for various individuals and/or teams. Before assembling this program, you will need to examine the various ways you can design it and the specific provisions that would comprise it.

Rewards can be as simple as a memo of commendation or as grandiose as a generous raise and the corner office. The reward continuum stretches wide and includes these and scores of other options. But, there are essentially only two types of rewards: extrinsic (tangible) rewards and intrinsic (intangible) rewards.

Extrinsic Rewards

"Money talks," so the saying goes. And the fact is, no reward and recognition program will ever succeed if the only awards management is willing to bestow on employees are empty platitudes, as opposed to tangible things with real value. This is not to say intangible rewards are totally worthless. Indeed, they are very important to many people in many types of situations, but they have to be complemented by something that can be touched or felt. Nonetheless, the successful integration-focused reward program must have as its foundation significant tangible awards that will motivate employees to attain them.

Examples of such extrinsic awards are:

- Monetary rewards
- Status symbols
- Flexible hours
- Additional vacation time
- Choice work assignments

These awards can be granted individually or in combination, and there are specific provisions that can be offered in each category.

Monetary rewards. All employees understand and expect direct compensation comprised of a basic wage or salary. Above and beyond the base, most companies offer lower-level workers standard overtime and holiday premium pay. Employees rightfully do not consider these forms of compensation as rewards. That is why it is so important to link pay with performance, especially in the realm of monetary rewards tied to integration program accomplishments.

The forms of monetary rewards that can be offered to employees in M&A-related reward programs essentially mirror those provided to employees in any progressive, performance-based corporate milieu. These include:

- *Individual incentive programs*, where payment is directly related to meeting individualized goals. With regard to managers, so-called management incentive plans are an example of how achieving goals is rewarded with a tangible, monetary benefit—typically a cash or stock bonus. This focus on measurable objectives and results has replaced the traditional evaluation system that gauged such traits as technical proficiency in one's subject area, punctuality, and interpersonal relations. In an M&A environment, importance should be placed on behaviors such as interacting with employees from the "other side," or contributing to an integration initiative. By focusing on the tangible results of these behaviors and quantifying in advance what rewards their accomplishment will bring, the core of an entire monetary reward system can be created.
- *A lump-sum payment*, which is a onetime reward based on individual performance. This type of formal extrinsic reward can also be linked to the employee's standard management incentive. However, these types of payments are often project- or action-specific. For example, a payment can be granted as a finder's fee to an employee who sources a strategic alliance or revenue enhancement opportunity for the merged firm.
- *Exceptional stock options*, which are grants of stock or stock options to nonmanagement employees. These rewards are typically tenure-related and send a very strong message to the workforce that loyalty and longevity are valued in the new environment.

More than a motivational tool, the granting of exceptional stock options can act as a strong retention incentive to a midlevel employee. Since the integration period will likely last several years, and you will want to retain these employees during the transition period, it is imperative that these stock awards have a vesting schedule that extends beyond the end of the anticipated integration period. This vesting schedule can help ensure that the midlevel employee maintains a longer-term focus and remains committed to the merged firm over the long haul.

- *Profit sharing*, which is a uniform payment given to all or most employees based on corporate earnings. This type of payment is often linked to management incentive plans as the determinant of whether a bonus will be received. The typical arrangement structures one half of the expected reward to be contingent on earnings, and the other half on personal achievement of objectives. In most companies, if corporate earnings reach their target, then every manager linked to the incentive program will receive at least the portion of the bonus that is contingent on corporate performance.

An important point on financial incentives: Most companies link receiving a bonus for accomplishing personal objectives to the success of the corporation, region, unit, or department. In many instances, if a manager achieves goals but the company does not reach its own earnings target, he or she will not receive a bonus. Yet in the context of a merger or acquisition, a manager who accomplishes integration-oriented objectives must be rewarded in some way. Obviously, if there are no profits in the year or years following a merger, there will be no profit pool from which the manager can be rewarded. Some other reward and recognition program must compensate the individual who has worked toward integration regardless of whether corporate profit objectives have been met.

If employees feel that their hard efforts have not been rewarded, they will quickly begin to develop a negative attitude toward the policies and practices of senior management. It is critical that determined efforts toward integration and demonstrated commitment to the corporate vision always be rewarded—in both good years and bad. Remember: It is not the employee who made the decision to merge or acquire. Therefore, the individual cannot be held accountable for the profitability (or lack thereof) of the endeavor. By the same token, all employees have been asked to dedicate themselves and make sacrifices toward the integration initiative. If they do their part, irrespective of the merged firm's bottom-line financial results, they should be compensated.

Status symbols. In every organization, there are people who are extremely status-conscious. To them, pure status symbols are more important awards than monetary remuneration. For such people, a large office with a view and beautiful office furnishings, a private secretary, or a choice parking spot will all serve as substantive, desirable awards for exemplary behavior. We know of one senior manager who, in order to be coaxed to stay with a newly merged firm, insisted on being able to fly first-class. His hectic travel schedule was such that he practically lived on airplanes. So, in one sense, his was a practical demand. To the people who knew him, however, it seemed more of an ego-driven ultimatum.

Flexible hours. Senior managers do not punch a clock, and enjoy significantly greater flexibility in setting work hours than their lower-level colleagues. Allowing flexible work schedules, therefore, is rarely a compelling gesture for upper management. It may be, however, for the rank-and-file employee.

Some workers value being able to take their lunch at a particular time, which may be different from the company's official lunch hour. Others might prefer to come in at 8:30 A.M. and leave at 4:30 P.M. rather than the conventional nine-to-five routine. A note of caution: Granting flexible hours to certain employees—irrespective of the meritorious reason for doing so—can spawn resentment among a lower-level worker's immediate coworkers, not to mention that person's counterparts from the merger partner company. Care should be taken when juggling work schedules, unless of course the shift in hours granted as an award carries a particular time frame (e.g., the awarded employee can only modify his or her hours for a set period of weeks or months).

Additional vacation time. Granting employees vacation days above and beyond those officially allocated to them is an alluring incentive. And it is alluring to people at *all* levels of any organization. Vacation time is one of the truly cherished and time-honored aspects of a worker's overall compensation package. Awarding an employee, say, a week off as recompense for model behavior will heighten that person's organizational commitment (the goal of each of the awards we are discussing), as well as serve to reenergize that person (the goal of vacation time in general) to scale ever-greater heights.

Choice work assignments. There are "plum" assignments in every corporate department or company: serving on a special committee or task force; attending a major trade show (e.g., one that takes place in Miami in February); representing the company as a speaker at an important symposium; and so forth. Assigning an employee to participate in these and other types of desirable initiatives can serve as a valuable reward. Of course, it is important to first ascertain that these initiatives are, in fact, things the employee would want to do. What you think may be exciting or fascinating for someone may actually seem like an additional chore to that person. Consequently, if you feel a particular work assignment would serve as a desirable reward, check with the intended recipient. If it is, in fact, *not* something the employee would want to do, ask for suggestions. Yes, it is the thought that counts. Just make sure it is the right one.

Intrinsic Rewards

Intrinsic rewards are those that relate to an employee's satisfaction with his or her job. They are intangible by nature and include such things as:

- Title increases
- Commendations
- Increased involvement

Intrinsic awards are not necessarily less effective than their tangible, extrinsic counterparts. Ideally, the integration-focused reward program should combine both types of awards. It is important to become familiar with the essence of each of these intrinsic award types.

INSIDER'S OUTLOOK

For key employees, I try to assess what their likelihood of staying would be. Then I try to identify what it would take to motivate them in the future. I probably do more of this than others because I place such a high priority on people. And not only do you want key people to stay, you want them to stay and be committed. You have to determine if there's something you can bring to the table that will really excite them and motivate them in order to get the best out of them. Is there something you can do to structure this person's compensation package or give them a chance to do something they couldn't do in the past? Something for personal growth as well as for financial growth. I try to give a lot of thought to these things because there's always a lot of turmoil after the deal closes, and you have to spend a lot of time building a trust relationship.

—Carolyn Chin, IBM

Title increases. One of the most welcome rewards to bestow on a contributing employee—especially one from the acquired company—is an increase in title. Even without a boost in pay, granting a vice president the new title of senior vice president will raise that individual's feelings of personal self-worth, power, and influence. Not only will that person instantly feel like an accepted member of the new order, but he or she will be more likely to champion the new vision with greater zeal because of being now publicly identified with it. In essence, that person will feel personally obliged to support the goals of the merged company.

Invariably, when people's titles are raised they tend to assume direct responsibility for helping to support the new company's mission. There is a danger of increasing people's titles too widely, however, and creating so-called title inflation, in which so many people gain lofty titles that those monikers in effect become meaningless.

Commendations. These take the form of congratulatory memos from management, acknowledgment in company meetings or group forums, and other means of publicly thanking employees for their efforts or accomplishments. In most cases, commendations do not compare to hard-dollar or other tangible forms of reward. But they can go a very long way toward making people feel their efforts in support of the integration process are being noticed and enthusiastically embraced.

Commendations may exist as any of the aforementioned public citations. That is, they may be issued in existing company media or forums. Another way to provide commendations is to create official new materials—for example, specially produced plaques or certificates—that are developed specifically to reward activities that comprise the integration reward plan. Commendations may be offered as stand-alone gestures. They of course may also be proffered in conjunction with tangible rewards (e.g., the monetary award an employee receives is then cited in a company newsletter, thus giving the worker both a tangible and an intangible form of reward). Publicly acknowledging exemplary accomplishments is a key element of an effective reward and recognition program.

Increased involvement. Recently, managers have used the reward of "involvement." This is actually a combination of formal recognition and an intrinsic reward. It works this way: The employee who is intrinsically rewarded for positive behavior is elevated to a higher level of group belonging. As a sense of belonging builds and is strengthened through further involvement, the employee becomes more empowered. The employee not only feels more motivated, but ideally becomes a model for others and can help champion integration causes to those both below and above in the hierarchy. The ultimate reward: more involvement.

What are some ways to increase employees' involvement? A manager can do so by having workers participate in departmental goal setting and planning. Other ways are to include employees in group problem solving—ideally, addressing issues that relate to specific challenges of the integration program. Those sessions, in turn, can be followed up with group decision making initiatives. This is a subtle way to foster acceptance of the decisions, since each employee has had enough involvement to deem the decision of their own formulation. If you have built your intrinsic reward program around involvement, then all team members will have participated in planning, problem solving, and decision making.

By recognizing an employee's desire to participate in the integration process, and rewarding it with additional involvement, you will not only build a more dedicated workforce but will accomplish particular integration tasks more quickly and effectively. Caveat: The increased involvement will require that the employee work more hours and harder. Be prepared to financially bonus or otherwise reward the employee if this is the case.

TEAM-BASED AND GROUP REWARDS

When merging firms are being integrated, it is individuals, particularly those in the management ranks, who must ultimately be recognized for their contributions and rewarded accordingly. However, as you move down the corporate ladder, you will find that most initiatives and projects are performed by groups. Accordingly, there should be team-based recognition provisions as part of the overall organizational reward paradigm.

When you design a reward system for group initiatives, you can set the performance measurements at a higher level. That is because you can demand greater output and more efficiency from a group-based project or task. Since groups, in contrast to individuals, will typically consider more alternative solutions to problems because of their broader perspective, you can focus the reward criterion on results that would not normally come as easily to a group. For example, since quick decisions are not a characteristic of group efforts, the reward could be based on the group completing its assignment by an aggressive deadline. Just as effective is a reward granted when the group's suggestions are formally adopted or implemented.

There are two basic types of reward systems for group-based activities: "gain sharing" and "small-group incentives."

Gain Sharing

Gain sharing rewards are shared equally by employees for productivity and efficiency gains in a particular organizational unit. They offer the work group, team, or department the opportunity to share in corporate increases in productivity. This can be a very effective reward method because it recognizes operational effectiveness and efficiency, not necessarily monetary profits (which are impacted by a wide range of other variables beyond the individual group's control). For example, each group participating in the gain sharing plan establishes specific quantitative measurements that are unanimously agreed on. Members of the team then receive a bonus based upon the level of cost savings realized during a given time period. Gain sharing encourages teamwork and cooperation as the group strives to maximize its productivity and, consequently, reap the maximum rewards for its collective efforts.

Small-Group Incentives

These are onetime awards to all members of a group for achieving predetermined goals. Similar to gain sharing arrangements, small-group incentives are specifically linked to team performance. These types of extrinsic rewards are separate and distinct from any individual-based incentive reward program and often are project- or task-specific. For example, members of a joint transition committee may be awarded a group bonus for establishing an interfirm cross-selling initiative or for exceeding the number of integration-related tasks on their original agenda.

In the postmerger environment, however, it is groups that can most expeditiously forge a true corporate consolidation. This is because small groups—ideally comprised of people from both merger partner organizations—must function as teams. They, therefore, represent microcosms of the broader organizational teamwork you are trying to effect via the overall integration effort. Thus, when small groups function effectively as teams, they set an example for other teams, as well as for the merged company as a whole.

KEYS TO AN EFFECTIVE REWARD PROGRAM

We have addressed the importance of reward and recognition programs in the realm of facilitating postmerger integration and discussed what employee behaviors to reward and the different ways of doing so. There are four keys, however, to devising and executing a successful reward program:

1. Educate people on what will be rewarded.
2. Promote/publicly acknowledge those being rewarded.
3. Standardize reward criteria across the organization.
4. Establish measurable criteria.

Each of these factors is important in and of itself, as well as in direct relation to one another.

Educate People on What Will Be Rewarded

People must understand that rewards will be granted to people who further the integration initiative. More important, they need to know specifically what actions will be acknowledged and how people will be remunerated. This is important for two reasons.

First, it gives people clarification on the types of behaviors and initiatives management holds to be important; thus, people can actively focus on precise tasks that management has indicated will augment the overall integration effort.

Second, from a broader standpoint, the act of announcing a formal rewards program serves to promote the overall concept and importance of teamwork to achieving integration objectives.

Formal internal communications programs should be devised to internally market the reward program criteria. It may, however, be necessary to instruct people on how to embody the behaviors that will be rewarded. In other words, if an award criterion involves devising new ways to better serve the merged company's customer base, formalized training may be necessary to educate employees on customer needs and how the combined company can best meet them.

Promote/Publicly Acknowledge Those Being Rewarded

Just as the reward program must be publicized up front, the recipients of those awards must be publicly commended for their accomplishments. Award winners should be cited in company publications, memorandums from management, and public forums such as meetings and company conferences. These acknowledgments should be as detailed as possible in the sense that communicating *how* a person garnered the award provides instructive guidance to others who may be motivated to do the same. That is, announcing that an employee is being recognized for playing an important role in the integration program is not as impactive as detailing how specifically that person did so. Publicly promoting people's exemplary acts gives those workers the recognition they deserve and, more importantly, further communicates the importance of that employee's act, thus encouraging others to do the same.

Standardize Reward Criteria across the Organization

There is no greater threat to the success of the reward and recognition program than to have different criteria for awards for employees from the merging organizations. Measurements must be standard across the board. Having different criteria sends the signal that borders still separate the combining companies. Sending this message runs counter to the broader integrative steps you will be taking to dismantle the psychological barriers that prevent true corporate unification. Even if the standards are comparable, any perceived discrepancy will be interpreted by employees as such. Thus, it will foster the dreaded "us versus them" mentality at a time when you are attempting to dispel that pejorative mind-set.

That having been said, it is advisable, where possible, to craft your nonfinancial awards around those things that individuals within the organization find important or desirable. Since the purpose of a reward is to motivate and reinforce specific behavior, it can have the anticipated effect only if it is truly desired by the recipient. Simply giving someone a reward that the person does not desire serves no purpose and can undermine what would otherwise have been a strong motivational incentive to another employee. What one employee views as highly desirable another can find irrelevant. For example, offering the corner office to an individual who prefers being situated in a high-traffic smaller venue closer to the water fountain serves no purpose. In fact, the reward of that corner office could have been an effective motivational reward for another employee who would find that a valuable expression of your appreciation. Financial reward levels should never vary. Conversely, nonfinancial rewards can and should be tailored to the individual recipients as much as practicable.

Establish Measurable Criteria

Effectively recognizing and rewarding behavior cannot exist without very specific, understandable measurements. Establishing mutually agreed on measurement criteria must start at the highest level of the merged firm. Management must set and acknowledge the corporate objectives, designate responsibility for their accomplishment, determine the role of the individual in attaining them, and ascertain how to reward employees accordingly.

Measurement is important not only as the basis for granting tangible rewards, but also in continually motivating employees as they strive to meet or exceed specific targets or performance milestones. Another important point is that feedback must be directly linked to performance and be instructive. That is, it must teach employees methods of being more productive. This will benefit employees by arming them with important knowledge about themselves (particularly where they fit into the scheme of the company as a whole), while helping them gain a greater understanding of the consequences of their actions on a personal as well as an organizational level.

SUMMARY

This chapter has emphasized the criticality of a recognition and reward program to a successful integration plan. In the postmerger environment, the focus must be on making integration work. The reward system should relate to activities that support this basic goal and to objectives that are directly linked to those activities' ultimate success.

Central to devising any reward program is determining and designing measurement or performance appraisal criteria for specific actions deemed worthy by management of advancing the integration process. Once this has occurred and an appraisal system has been implemented, you will have a foundation from which to provide adequate feedback to employees on their results. After that, the next step is to consider how to tie the available corporate rewards to the outcome of the appraisal. Irrespective of the specific provisions, performance rewards must be focused on individuals and teams pulling toward the common goal of effecting true corporate unification.

In the wake of a merger or acquisition, you require the right people, a focused vision, and a compelling message. And, even then, there is no guarantee that pro-integration behavior will catch on and spread widely throughout the organization. But if all parties involved—all levels of management, as well as the rank and file—agree on a reward system that is results-oriented, then there will be a common goal: embracing and motivating behavior that advances the integration process.

Incentives can be used to motivate, retain, reinforce, or level the playing field. A well-thought-out and -designed reward and recognition program can bring results in all four of these areas. Without rewards, an environment characterized by a lack of direction and sinking morale can result. Without the important element of commitment, your workforce will be unfocused and uncaring.

By recognizing behavior that directly supports the integration process and rewarding employee actions both extrinsically and intrinsically, you will dramatically increase the chances for success of the merger itself.

15

Postmerger External Communication Strategies Supporting the Merger's Launch

The discussions leading up to a major merger or acquisition are strictly internal. A select few senior executives from the combining companies, along with their attorneys and financial advisers, are the sole people aware of the evolving transaction. Secrecy prevails. Ultimately, after both sides are satisfied with the terms, a letter of intent is signed and the deal is made public. Weeks or months (and in some cases, years) may elapse, however, before regulatory approvals are secured and all the paperwork is signed and sealed.

Eventually, the day comes when the transaction is finalized and growth planning shifts into growth realization. It is at this point that a comprehensive communications initiative must be executed not only to announce the deal's completion, but also to signal to the merged firm's key audiences that it is ready to compete as a formidable new concern.

Devising the postclosing communications program requires the same rigorous planning and execution as any major marketing communications campaign—but even more so. Your key publics must be identified. Your messages to those audiences must be articulated. The media and communications channels you select must effectively carry those messages to their intended targets.

Therefore, your postmerger communications strategy involves determining what to say, when to say it, to whom, how you communicate it, and how often you do so. It sounds straightforward. But communications developed in the wake of a merger take on an added dimension in light of the volatility inherent in a corporate combination.

There is volatility in terms of organizational policies and processes prior to the time when the merger partners effect true integration. This volatility often breeds uncertainty on the part of customers, prospects, stockholders, the financial community, labor union leaders, and the market at large. (Employees, in particular, represent a key audience that must be reached with carefully crafted communications, which is why the issue of employee and organizational communications is treated in detail in Chapter 12.)

Without question, poorly planned and executed external communications in the weeks and months following a major merger will spawn negative conditions for the merged company that can hinder the creation of its new market image and the attainment of its ultimate growth objectives.

This chapter focuses on all the key elements of formulating the postclosing external communications program. After differentiating your audience segments and setting communications objectives, the first element, message development, keys on the educational and promotional information that needs to be imparted to the various external audiences and the different ways that information should be tailored to those different audience segments. Next are insights on how and through what channels communications should be issued to maximize their individual and collective impact. These are followed up with the timing issues—specifically, when to communicate those messages to your divergent audiences.

DIFFERENTIATING AUDIENCE SEGMENTS

External communications planning first requires identifying the audiences you need to reach. There are certain common messages management needs to impart. Yet, those messages typically need to be modified to meet the informational needs of your different audience segments, which include customers, shareholders and the investment community, labor unions, prospects, channel intermediaries, suppliers and vendors, and influencers.

Customers

A company's current and future value is inextricably linked to its customer base. Of all the groups that must be reached during the first stage of your external communications efforts, customers are arguably the most important. The volatility that typically characterizes the business environment in which the merged company initially operates necessitates a carefully planned program to reach customers with timely, benefit-oriented information. The specific approaches you must take to effect customer protection and customer development in the wake of the merger's closing are examined in detail.

Shareholders and the Investment Community

Shareholders of the merging organizations are the companies' true owners. Professionals operating in the investment community (e.g., analysts, portfolio managers) are the people who either make investment decisions or influence and advise individual and institutional investors. Both segments represent critically important groups that must be targeted with information early in the communication process. With shareholders of public companies, issuing specific information is required to meet the fiduciary responsibility of the merging partners' management.

On closing, it is imperative to secure shareholder buy-in. You should attempt to generate investor enthusiasm for the company's shares via investor relations programs, encouraging them to take on an even larger financial stake in the merged company. Perhaps more importantly, gaining investors' enthusiastic support is necessary to keep them from selling off their current shares (if they feel the corporate combination will not be strategically or fiscally sound in the long run).

Additionally, analysts must be aggressively reassured that the merger or acquisition is a positive event. An analyst who feels pertinent information is being withheld can change his or her rating on a company. Even worse, a wary portfolio manager can unload a position in a company if he or she thinks the company's shares' upside has been capped by the transaction. This can send a message that other shareholders should follow suit.

Labor Unions

When acquiring or merging with a company whose workers are represented by unions, the leaders of those groups become critically important audiences with which to communicate. The unwavering support of union leaders is central to the long-term success of the transaction. Effective preliminary communications lay the groundwork for smooth negotiations.

As the new owner of a union-represented company, you will have to negotiate such issues as wage rates, employee benefits and incentive plans, grievance and arbitration procedures, and overall collective bargaining agreements. Failing to adequately and regularly communicate with labor representatives during all phases of the transaction's evolution can spark negative sentiments by them toward the deal. In many cases, a merger can be derailed without labor's unequivocal support and commitment.

Prospects and the Market at Large

Prospects represent the valid, qualified potential buyers of the goods and services offered by the merged company. These people contrast other consumers in the market at large who may not initially be viewed as potential buyers, but who may be important to the merged company's long-term viability. Prospects comprise those in your market who have not purchased goods from either of the merging companies, or have, yet so infrequently that they are considered veritable noncustomers. The new product offerings of the merged company or its newly enhanced attributes augmented by product quality or delivery represent an opportunity to win over prospects that in the past may have been reluctant to deal with either or both of the merging companies.

Channel Intermediaries

Wholesalers, retailers, and others in the consumer or industrial product delivery chain represent a crucial audience segment, particularly if these organizations are a distinct component of the merged company's customer base. Therefore, when the combined firm ultimately markets its products to resellers, effective postmerger communications take on greater significance than when those agents are solely conduits in the chain of moving products from manufacturer to end user.

Suppliers and Vendors

Companies that provide support services or materials for product manufacturing may or may not figure in the merged company's plans. For instance, two suppliers that serviced the individual merger partners in the past may not both serve the merged organization in the future.

Decisions relative to the sources from which the combined company will procure its raw materials and other ancillary services are typically not made until after the company has begun to integrate its operations. Consequently, before such decisions are made, key vendors and suppliers should be treated as groups that *will* serve the new company. Therefore, they merit inclusion in your initial communications program, even though they may never actually play a role in your long-term plans.

Influencers

Influencers are the people and institutions who directly or indirectly convince others of the need for a product or the choice of a particular provider. In the context of a merger or acquisition, influencers can play a valuable role in promoting the strategic viability and potential of the transaction to other audience segments. For example, influencers may be prominent members of trade associations, business and industry groups, or the financial community.

Influencers may also be companies. For instance, having a particularly well-known company as a customer represents a relationship that can be leveraged to procure clients who are operating in the same industry. Each corporate combination has different influencers. You must determine which are the most important to help you engender positive market response to your transaction.

SETTING COMMUNICATION OBJECTIVES

Messages to be imparted to your target audiences must be tailored to meet the precise informational needs of each group, as well as to further your various promotional objectives. Most likely, there will be specific messages for each audience segment. At the same time, there will be certain recurring themes that will be sounded to all groups. The first step in devising messages is to recognize the basic communication objectives that virtually every acquirer has.

Create General Awareness

Obviously, no major merger or acquisition worth doing should go unannounced to the world. When the transaction is consummated it signals the time to start building market awareness of the merged firm's broad new capabilities. In mergers of public companies, it is management's fiduciary responsibility to communicate the details of the transaction to shareholders and to the financial community.

No legal responsibility exists for having to communicate the transaction to your other external publics. Good business sense, however, dictates that you should. People central to a company's current operations and future success should not hear about things after the fact—especially the monumental occasion of a merger or acquisition. It is therefore necessary to promptly announce that the transaction has closed, even though there may be a distinct lack of concrete details to explicitly promote at that point.

Generate Enthusiasm and Secure Buy-In

Strategic mergers and acquisitions, by definition, portend good things for the people and groups holding a stake in the merging companies. Specific information on the resultant benefits of the merger will be communicated as they occur over time. Initially, however, the task is to build upon the benefit-oriented messages contained in the initial announcements of the corporate union.

You must reinforce the strategic drivers of the merger to build momentum and engender market enthusiasm for the combination. All external audiences should be favorably disposed to the merger or acquisition. Of course, the support of some of those groups is more important than others. Nonetheless, all publics should be given a reason to maintain positive—or at least neutral—sentiments toward the transaction.

What happens when one group is particularly averse to the deal? It is possible that its negative feelings can influence another constituency (assuming, of course, that the group feels strongly enough to aggressively attempt to sway others' beliefs).

Consider, for example, that a group of labor representatives is against the merger because they feel the transaction will lessen the number of union jobs in the new firm. This group might communicate its dissatisfaction to other publics or the press. The resultant negativism can potentially create problems in your relations with those other groups—which, collectively, can hinder your efforts to achieve your strategic goals. By and large, broad buy-in and enthusiasm by all of your external publics is necessary, and every effort should be made to secure the maximum level of acceptance as quickly as possible.

Communicate the Potential for Imminent Change

Specific changes resulting from a merger are not always easy to predict. Some changes are immediately foreseeable, such as a move of the company's corporate headquarters. Others are more difficult to forecast. In the absence of finalized information about such shifts in the merged company's day-to-day operations, it is necessary to alert key publics that some changes will likely be enacted.

Rarely are things exactly as they were before a major corporate combination; even a company that has been acquired to function as a stand-alone subsidiary may still experience shifts in certain operational areas. Thus, it is important to communicate that there *will* be changes even though you may not know precisely what changes may occur. Your external publics need to be alerted to the potential for change with a positive spin, even if none ever actually occurs.

Allay Fears

Each segment of your external audience may experience some trepidation toward the merger. Customers may fear changes in product availability or pricing; shareholders may fear a short- or long-term dip in the stock price; labor leaders may fear job losses; vendors and suppliers may fear that postmerger instability will jeopardize their relationship with one of the merger partners.

It is important that your initial communications build in tactics to allay any fears that your key constituencies may hold. Again, specific information on the ramifications of the merger is often unavailable in the early stages after the transaction's closing. And although messages might have to be general, continuous yet vague messages are always better than none.

Begin the Corporate Identity Building Process

Your initial external communications begin the arduous process of forging the merged firm's new identity. This is particularly significant in situations where the merged company will take on a new name. For example, Ciba-Geigy and Sandoz's announcement in

1996 of their merger stated from the outset that the combined company would carry a new moniker: Novartis. That the organizations had developed their new corporate name indicates that their growth planning work had commenced—as it should—very early in the merger process. (No multibillion-dollar company devises a new corporate name without months of extensive research and testing!) The companies realized the corporate brand-building challenge ahead of them. And they began taking steps to address it even before the transaction was announced.

MESSAGE DEVELOPMENT

Every merger is different. Situational factors vary. The groups you must communicate with require different types and amounts of information relative to the transaction. There are, however, several relatively standard messages that should be communicated to the critical external audience segments.

INSIDER'S OUTLOOK

Very early in the process [of intergrating Chemical Bank and Chase Manhattan Bank] we started with brand positioning both at the retail bank level and at the corporate level. The challenge to the marketing department was to come up with the new personality before the personality has formed. It had been decided that the new company name would be "Chase." That's something the marketing department obviously did not have to decide. But everything else from a branding standpoint we *did* have to decide. It was a challenge to come up with the look and feel—both external and internal communication-wise—before the personality had been formed. The first thing we did was implement a strong brand positioning statement, which the senior people at the retail bank level had to agree to. We then had to translate that into, "Okay, what does that really mean in terms of what our customers are expecting?" We then had a template against which we could judge all the pieces of information that had to go out to our customers. The benefit was that you could develop something that had a consistent look and feel across TV advertising, print, signage, collateral . . . everything that touched the customer.

—Susan Schoon, Chase Manhattan Bank

Customers

Information initially directed at customers should be a combination of sales and administrative data. Sales information includes facts and figures on new products and services resulting from the merger; enhanced capabilities and increased product quality levels; and other details on how the merged company will be better able to serve buyers, perhaps with greater cost-effectiveness or efficiency. Administrative information relates to changes that may occur in the wake of the transaction, such as shifts in prices, delivery schedules, or payment terms. It is most important that your internal sales and service representatives be well-versed in these changes, since they will more than likely be the first to impart this information to customers.

Shareholders and the Investment Community

Information initially directed at these groups typically relates to financial matters and the final terms of the transaction (e.g., the value of shares being exchanged, any provisions that may have changed in the time between the announcement and closing). Beyond the purely financial details, shareholder communications should espouse the strategic benefits of the transaction insofar as they will augment the merged company's current assets and future value. Data should be provided on the synergies that will emerge from the combined company, new products and services to be offered, and new markets to be served. Financial stakeholders also require information on how the merged company will take form. Consequently, details on the organization's integration activities and timetable should be provided as soon as they are available, and then delivered on an ongoing basis during the integration process either directly or via public communications.

Prospects

Many of the communication messages imparted to customers should also be directed at prospects. The specific ways the merged company will be better able to serve buyers should be emphasized. Any organization typically has key prospects that it has been courting. Finalizing the merger gives the partnering companies the opportunity to call on their respective prospects—this time with specific information that might help convert those potential buyers into actual customers. In this sense, communications may have to be crafted on a company-by-company basis. Communications should be developed to address the specific objections prospects may have held in the past, while keying on how the merged company's strengthened capabilities will effectively mitigate any prior concerns.

Channel Intermediaries

The companies serving as middlemen in the distribution chain represent key relationships held by the merging organizations. They are, however, an audience that generally requires less information than others on the particulars of the transaction, the reason being that wholesalers and retailers do not really care who the owner is of the company providing them with product. They care about two things: first, that the branded products they stock will be unchanged or improved after the merger, and second, that there will not be any significant shifts in pricing or deliveries.

From a branding standpoint, intermediaries want to know that there will be no downward change in a product's quality and that the overall brand image of that item will be safeguarded. The ways that the merged company will protect or enhance a product's brand image should be communicated—the plans management has for long-term advertising, publicity, and sales promotion campaigns.

There are, however, some situations where intermediaries become one of the most critical groups to communicate with on consummation of the merger or acquisition. These cases involve changes being made to the overall product distribution paradigm. For instance, earlier Quaker Oats's doomed acquisition of Snapple was addressed. In that situation, the company planned to totally revamp Snapple's distribution procedures, utilizing the mass market channels it had employed for its Gatorade beverage, and forsaking the small retail outlets through which Snapple had historically been sold. Quaker Oats failed to promptly alert its distributors to its change in strategy. The initial losses in market share that Snapple suffered were attributable, in large part, to Quaker Oats's failure to both communicate its significant shift in distribution mechanics to distributors early on and also gain their buy-in.

Suppliers and Vendors

The companies that provide raw materials or ancillary services to the merging companies also have issues that need to be addressed via your external communications. A supplier's first concern is whether it will still have a customer. It is a justifiable concern, but one that you may not be able to address immediately, since vendor decisions are generally made weeks or months after the deal's closing.

Assume, however, that the merged company will continue to use that vendor. That information should be imparted promptly, but you must then be prepared to address the next round of concerns that a supplier may have. Namely, will the merged company be financially stable enough in the near term to pay its bills? Will suppliers have new purchasing agent contacts at the merged company? Will suppliers be forced to interface with new managers at the merged organization's new production facilities? Vendors will be happy to learn they will still have the merged company as a customer. Nonetheless, the particulars of that relationship may be a source of concern.

Influencers

Companies seek to communicate with influencers as opinion leaders who, by virtue of their support of the company, can spur others to support the new organization as well. Consequently, communications to influencers require somewhat less product-specific information, but more details on issues relative to the company's future role in the business and financial community. For example, information should underscore the merged company's commitment to the local markets in which it will function, its measures to support public service initiatives, and the like.

A case in point: There was a merger some years back involving a company that employed some 40% of a small town's population. There were widespread fears that the merged company would relocate, taking those jobs with it. In announcing the transaction's close, senior management held a town hall meeting with local officials to allay their fears regarding the company's rumored flight. These local influencers were assured of the company's commitment to the community, and ultimately, they served as unofficial spokesmen for the merged firm, spreading positive sentiments about the transaction to different economic and social constituencies.

Once you secure the support of influencers, it is advisable to then leverage their collective buy-in via subsequent marketing communications. For example, in the megamerger that brought Nynex and Bell Atlantic together as a telecommunications powerhouse, full-page ads were developed to carry the testimonials of influencers from different segments of the civic and business communities. Specifically, the viability and social and economic benefits of the merger were touted by spokespeople from such diverse groups as the Business Council of New York State, the Communication Workers of America, the United Cerebral Palsy Associations, and the NAACP.

Having addressed the basic strategies in the realm of message development, you must now turn to considerations relative to selecting mass media channels and timing your marketing communications activities.

SELECTING COMMUNICATION CHANNELS

A combination of personal and nonpersonal channels should be employed in your external communications program. Personal channels include face-to-face meetings, correspondence, and telephone calls. Nonpersonal channels include the mass media (print vehicles such as newspapers, magazines, and newsletters, and broadcast vehicles, including TV and radio) and electronic media, such as the Internet and videotapes. In selecting communication channels, keep in mind that the degree of personalization decreases as you move from communications with your most important publics to the broader market at large. There are communication channels that are appropriate for each audience segment.

Customers

Reaching major customers requires using highly personal communication channels. Communications must be delivered by phone call, personal letter, or other one-on-one types of communiqués. We will detail later on how, when, and why to communicate with customers to protect and ultimately grow those relationships. However, in the context of communication channels to employ, here is an apt example on how *not* to deliver merger-related news to your current buyers.

A company we know opted to communicate news of its recent acquisition via letter, which is fine. Unfortunately, the letter issued was a terse and impersonal "Dear Customer" form letter. What made matters worse was that management never alerted its sales force to the mailing. Many of those sales representatives were extremely embarrassed when they were told by their own customers that management had sent them a form letter announcing the merger. There were two problems with that approach: first, the communications were impersonal; second, they were not delivered by people with whom the customers had a direct relationship.

Shareholders and the Investment Community

Investor relations departments typically have standard channels through which they issue news to shareholders. These include newsletters, regularly issued letters from the company's CEO or senior financial executives, inbound 800 numbers, Internet sites, and annual shareholder meetings. Each of these channels should be employed in the first stages of the external communications program. In addition, these channels—as well as mass media advertising and publicity—should be used to reach important leaders in the broader investment community.

Prospects and the Market at Large

Broadly defined, prospects are all qualified buyers of a company's goods or services who have never purchased those items before. Narrowly defined, prospects are selected potential buyers whom a company has targeted and, in fact, may have previously contacted in some way. These distinctions are important to keep in mind as you select channels to reach prospects, who vary in terms of their past dealings with either or both of the merger partners. Nonpersonal media should be employed in reaching low-potential prospects and those in the market at large. On the other hand, personal channels should be utilized to reach high-potential prospects whom you have been actively courting. In the latter case, it is advisable to have the salespeople who have been working those prospects contact them on finalization of the transaction to impart the news.

Channel Intermediaries

In general, the corporate managers in charge of trade relations should serve as the communication conduits for merger-related information to channel intermediaries. Particular provisions of the transaction, as stated earlier, may not be of tremendous significance to intermediaries. In general, that is true. A reminder, though: When the merger will significantly alter a company's distribution system (such as in the Snapple deal), the ramifications of the merger take on greater significance.

The bearers or channels of communication to middlemen may vary. Therefore, it should be the responsibility of the intermediary's regular contact to impart relevant news about the merger and any significant developments that will arise. When communications are particularly sensitive, it is advisable to have a member of senior management—in conjunction with the intermediary's regular contact—deliver information to those important publics.

Suppliers and Vendors

The existing contacts at both merger partners should also deliver merger-related news to their respective suppliers and vendors. Important suppliers should be contacted via personal channels. Subsequently, impersonal channels can be employed to impart any messages that are not deemed time-sensitive.

On the deal's closing, it may be advisable to hold a meeting specifically for suppliers and vendors. One manufacturing industry client coordinated such a session, which involved formal presentations by the merged company's management, Q&A, and a buffet luncheon. The meeting was beneficial in two key respects. First, it served as an eminently personal communications forum at which important details of the merged firm's operations were provided to the vendor community. Secondly, the lavish surroundings and celebratory atmosphere served to strengthen the bonds between the company and its suppliers—which, collectively, represented the lifeblood of its manufacturing enterprise.

Influencers

Influencers are, by nature, high-ranking professionals or leaders in the business, financial, or governmental community. People at this level should receive merger-related communications from those of the same stratum—namely, senior executives from one or both of the merger partner organizations.

The channels through which those communications should be disseminated include both personal and nonpersonal means. The rule of thumb is this: The more local the communications message, the more personal the channel should be. Recall our earlier example of a town hall meeting held to assuage a community's fears that a merger would rob that town of thousands of jobs. That was a local event that required highly personalized communications with senior company management presented at the public forum. Subsequent communications to influencers at the national level—specifically, professionals within the financial community and major trade associations—were generally handled through nonpersonal, mass media channels (in addition to some personal contacts made by senior management to portfolio managers and influential analysts).

TIMING YOUR COMMUNICATIONS ROLLOUT

Audience Considerations

Once you have looked at different audience segments, message content, and the means through which communications to those audiences should be delivered, you can turn to timing considerations.

Without question, external communications must be carefully timed to ensure that your different audience segments receive the first waves of merger-related news at strategic intervals. In general, the more important the audience, the sooner that segment should be reached as part of the communications rollout. Communications must be issued immediately to some groups. Other segments can and should be targeted over a longer time horizon.

Immediate. Certain communications should be disseminated within days of the merger's finalization. Issuing a news release will generate publicity that provides general details on the close of the transaction. Next, more focused communications should be issued to provide additional details on provisions that will be of interest to specific groups of stakeholders. For example, shareholders, brokerage firm analysts, major customers, labor leaders, and your banks and primary lenders all will have questions—the answers to which have likely been sketchy at best since the initial announcement of the deal. Proactive communications will slow and possibly reverse the natural avalanche of uncertainty and speculation that the investment community may have. If yours is a publicly traded company, it is important to keep the lines of communication open to all influencers in the financial markets. If at any point analysts or portfolio managers are unable to contact you in the days following the announcement, they will assume that there is a problem.

Medium-Term. The medium-term time frame refers to the several weeks after the merger's close. Communications to companies with which the merged company has integral working relationships should be issued during this time window.

INSIDER'S OUTLOOK

Our goal is always to retain the mark, because the Blue Cross name has tremendous brand value to it. Our brand is second to Coca-Cola. It's strong with the elderly population, the "X" generation, and still very, very strong with the Baby Boomers. Our market research shows that the name is strong on both ends of the spectrum. Consequently, it's necessary to maintain the integrity of the Blue Cross brand and leverage it, wherever and however possible, in our postmerger marketing communications.

—Don Curry, Blue Cross and Blue Shield of New Jersey

Specifically, a company's suppliers, vendors, and channel intermediaries are among the groups to reach with information in the medium term. In some cases, communications to intermediaries can ostensibly wait a little longer unless there is the potential for major alterations in the merged company's distribution strategy, which would increase the urgency of communicating with these publics. Still, you may not have your formal distribution strategy in place so soon after a merger's completion. Nonetheless, the communication process must commence even if the information you have is light on the particular details.

As we have said, vague information is better than no information. The moral: Never let any of your key audiences be caught off-guard. Feed them whatever information you have, regardless of the lack of specificity. Then, provide progressively more details as they become available.

Longer-Term. The longer-term time period refers to several weeks to a few months. That may seem like a long time. But, rest assured, the communications program to your primary external audiences will likely take up plenty of time in the period right after the transaction's close.

The groups that should be included in your longer-term communications rollout include prospects and influencers. Again, there are exceptions. Prospects who are close to being turned into customers merit faster communications. Also, influencers whose support can help win over other important audience segments should also be considered for earlier contact.

The other audience that falls into the longer-term communications time frame is the market at large. Here we move into the task of reaching mass audiences. From a message development standpoint, marketing- and investor relations–oriented communications comprise the message platform in which the merged organization's augmented offerings to the marketplace are highlighted.

Media Planning Considerations

Communications to your primary external audiences have been developed. Now comes the task of devising and placing marketing communications in a strategic sequence to ensure that these and other audiences are reached with the messages that will further the merged firm's specific growth initiatives.

Effective media planning is required to reinforce the messages initially imparted to your external audiences. You now need to build on those messages with a coordinated series of advertising, direct mail, publicity- and sales promotion–oriented communications that run in the medium to long term. By this time frame we mean the period from the point at which the merger is finalized to roughly six months later.

Once you know who the merged firm's primary audiences are, and some of the primary communications objectives that merging companies typically have when announcing a corporate combination, you will have a firm grip of the who and what of M&A-driven marketing communications planning. It is now crucial that you continue the process and turn to three other variables that are typically addressed in the context of media planning:

1. *When* to schedule communications
2. *What* media to employ
3. *Where* your audiences are located

Volumes have been written on the topic of media planning and the issues of audience analysis, reach, impact, and frequency. The subject is beyond the scope of this book, but some basic considerations and strategies are advised when planning communications that launch the combined company's growth initiatives. The following subsections provide a general overview.

When to schedule communications. Your formal marketing communications program should be revealed on the day of the merger's completion. An example is that of the Ciba-Geigy/Sandoz merger referenced earlier—the deal that formed the company Novartis. Novartis's management had its marketing communications eminently well-planned. The day the merger was finalized, full-page ads ran in business media in major markets across the United States. These were much more than tombstone ads. They were well-designed and carefully written display ads that began the corporate identity building process. The new company's logo was introduced in a print campaign whose rhetorical emphasis was on the organization's core businesses and the broader synergies resulting from the merger.

It was evident how extensive planning and creative work went into having the print campaign ready to break on the deal's closing. Not every transaction, of course, evolves with enough time to prepare creatively designed and perfectly timed advertising insertions, since some deals are announced and close within a few weeks. Still, it is advisable to at least develop simply designed ads that carry basic marketing themes, and which provide a contact point for interested parties to obtain additional information (e.g., the name and phone number of a representative in the PR, sales, or investor relations department).

Over the ensuing weeks, communication activities—such as direct mail, telemarketing, and feature-story publicity placements—should be issued in a coordinated series of waves that broadly reach all external audience segments. Advertisements should be placed in longer lead time publications. Direct marketing materials should also be readied for distribution along with your other promotional tools.

Particularly important audience members—key clients and prospects, labor union officials, and members of the investment community—should be contacted as soon as the merger or acquisition is finalized. For these people, consider sending informational materials via overnight delivery, timed for receipt on the day or day after the transaction is consummated. The package could include a personalized letter from the appropriate company contact, as well as news releases being issued and any ad slicks of the media insertions scheduled to run in the subsequent days or weeks.

It is always important to coordinate your marketing communications in terms of their timing and content. In recent years, marketers have embraced the concept of "integrated marketing" as a means of ensuring that people receive thematically consistent communications, on a regular basis, in a wide variety of media to which target audiences are exposed. Strategic and budgetary considerations will dictate which media you select for your postclosing communications.

But regardless of the marketing mix chosen, you should be cognizant of the need to ensure all media carry the same messages and to coordinate when they will appear, especially if they refer to one another. For example, if your advertising promotes the availability of marketing literature on the merged company, make sure that material is actually available at the time it is promoted.

People responding to the offer of information will be frustrated if it is, in fact, unattainable—a situation that suggests a lack of coordination and belies the message of stability the merged company may be attempting to proclaim. Such a situation occurred in the otherwise well-planned Novartis communication rollout. On the day the company's national ad campaign broke, Novartis's communications instructed readers to visit the merged company's new Web site. Unfortunately, when you accessed the site, there was no information to be found. Several days later the site was up and running. But, the ads were no longer running to direct readers there.

What media to employ. While the mass media will reach a cross-section of your external audiences, different media must be employed to effectively hit specific segments. Communications to customers and prospects should be targeted for the same media you will ultimately select for product-specific or institutional (corporate image-building) advertising and publicity.

Shareholders and the broader investment community will be reached through financial print and broadcast media and the business and personal-finance pages of daily newspapers. Trade publications and newsletters serving suppliers, vendors, and channel intermediaries should be tapped to reach those audiences. Influencers should be reached through a combination of personalized direct mail and telephone calls (not impersonal telemarketing), as well as through upper-echelon business media targeted to carry institutional advertising.

Product line and branding strategies often are forged over a prolonged period of time. As soon as practicable, however, the merged company should begin running product-related marketing communications, even if detailed strategies have yet to be finalized. Consider, for example, a pharmaceutical company that combines with a food manufacturer to create a new line of nutritional products. Even though the products, brand names, and specific positioning strategies have not yet been determined, the company should begin planning product line–oriented ads in vehicles such as food and health media to announce the organization's plans to develop those offerings.

Where your audiences are located. The audiences you will want to reach are often geographically dispersed. This means that, from a media planning standpoint, certain local publications and broadcast media may have to be employed in your communications rollout. For example, it is important to alert audiences in the communities in which an acquired firm currently operates. Therefore, it may be necessary to place news and advertising in media in the headquarters location(s), as well as in markets where the company has major offices, divisions, or subsidiaries.

The same geographic-oriented planning is necessary for other communications tactics you plan to use. For instance, if seminars or town hall meetings are envisioned, they should be held in those local communities via a road show approach (in which the speakers, presentations, and handout materials are standard for each meeting location).

Reaching geographically dispersed audiences is a problem eliminated by purchasing insertions in national media. But advertising buys in national print and broadcast vehicles may not be possible if budgetary constraints exist. However, the quintessential national and international medium today is the Internet. Placing announcements and merger news on one or both of the merging companies' Web sites provides a speedy, inexpensive, and broad platform to reach worldwide audiences. Remember, though, that getting people to log into your Internet address requires ample promotion unto itself.

CUSTOMER PROTECTION: KEY COMMUNICATION STRATEGIES

The different target audiences you need to reach in your postclosing communication program have been cited. In many respects, existing customers are the most important of those segments. The criticality of the merged company's current customer base necessitates that special attention be devoted to the content and timing of communications aimed at this critical group of stakeholders. Why?

It is an all-too-common scenario: The deal is announced in the press and employees from the acquired company begin to receive their internal communications—yet customers, the lifeblood of the business, receive nothing. Major customer relationships are often jeopardized in the wake of a merger or acquisition due to inadequate or delayed communications by management regarding the timing or provisions of the transaction. Customers are either not informed of the deal promptly, or the information imparted to them fails to allay their fears over potential service disruptions that often impact operations during the integration period.

There are traces of blood in the water, and the sharks are moving in. Most competitors know that the best time to aggressively court your clients is when you are going through a merger. The distractions are limitless, and as management attempts to quell the organizational chaos that often occurs internally, they lose sight of the most important factor—the customer.

Your competition knows that it is far from "business as usual" leading up to and immediately following the deal's closing, and that customer service frequently suffers. Competitors sense vulnerability and blatantly attempt to exploit it. Immediately on learning of the deal, competitors will begin contacting your customers to fan the flames of uncertainty that all customers feel when a company that provides important services to them is engaged in a major corporate combination. Unfortunately, customers' fears are well-founded. The time preceding and immediately following a merger is typically characterized by employee uncertainty, low levels of morale and productivity, and a lack of direction by company management. Volatile business environments spawn operational glitches that can negatively affect many aspects of day-to-day dealings with customers.

By nature, there is always organizational upheaval in the aftermath of a major merger or acquisition. The people, products, and processes of combining companies must be melded—an undertaking that historically takes an average of 18 months and, conceivably, may take years. That is a long time to go without the unconditional loyalty of your customer base. The need for a broad-based integration plan that commences immediately on consummation of the deal has never been more important. But the ever-increasing competitive environment dictates that, even before the integration planning process begins, a customer retention program must be set in motion. Its goal: to ensure that customers are kept apprised of the transaction and understand what it means to them, and that their expectations are exceeded so they are happier doing business with you than before.

Service disruptions during a merger may be completely unavoidable. But a sound communications strategy can lessen any customer damage that may result.

Customer Communications: Content and Delivery

The timing of communications aimed at customers is critical. Of equal significance are the content of those communications and the channels through which they are disseminated. There are some key strategies to keep in mind.

Identify profitable and potentially loyal customers. The merger is the perfect time for you to assess your book of business. Your profitable customers are, first and foremost, your company's most important asset. Cost-cutting initiatives mean little if they are offset by the loss of your most profitable customers or a decline in their loyalty. Conversely, if there are clients that are not profitable or even cost you money, now is the time to mitigate that aspect of the relationship or even eliminate it. In the wake of the merger, view your customers in terms of their loyalty and profitability. Make efforts to preserve and enhance both through a marketing campaign that stresses customer service, gives the customer an incentive to stay with you, and offers a special product or service because of the merger or acquisition.

INSIDER'S OUTLOOK

We took a look at the direct-mail function. The merchandising and promotion function. The classic advertising function. The database management function. We also looked at the contact management function—identifying what the history with that customer was, what's been sent to him so that one area of the bank is aware of and understands all the communications that somebody has sent to that customer in the past.

—Susan Schoon, Chase Manhattan Bank

Alert key customers as soon as the deal is announced. Prompt notification is imperative. The goal is tell the story of the merger to your customers before your competitors do. Make sure all customers are contacted. This cardinal rule of customer relations may sound obvious, but some companies do not tell their clients when they have engaged in a significant corporate combination; they wait for them to ask. Such a scenario was cited in an article a few years back in *Mergers & Acquisitions* magazine.

A company was about to merge with a major competitor. One of the company's key accounts was IBM, with which it had a long-term relationship that generated a seven-figure annual revenue. But the acquirer never informed IBM of its merger plans and that big buyer, in self-protection, suddenly cut back its orders because it was uncertain how deliveries would be affected by the combination. Millions of dollars were lost over an inexcusable oversight.

Identify specific customer concerns. It is necessary to anticipate the negative sentiments and fears that customers may potentially have regarding the merger. Make sure to identify all possible concerns and build your communications platform to directly address them. Indeed, this may need to be done on an account-by-account basis. To do so, ask your sales, marketing, and account reps for their insights on possible customer concerns and what messages will effectively allay them. In fact, the introduction of a small-sample customer survey that includes questions about service- and merger-related issues may offer hints about how to proceed with the rest of your customers. If you have not instituted these feedback mechanisms previously, employ a focus group or telephone survey at the first hint of a deal. It will help you better understand your market within the context of all the change that is about to occur. Here are some of the more common customer issues, and retention strategies to address them:

- *What impact will the merger have on prices and delivery schedules?* Customers may have to contend with price changes, differences in product delivery times, or payment terms. A more beneficial price or delivery schedule should be forcefully communicated as a benefit of change. Conversely, be prepared to explicitly detail changes that will negatively impact the customer, and have good reasons why those changes are being enacted.
- *Who will be handling my account?* Customers generally want to be assured that the people they have been dealing with will continue to service their accounts. Customers can get uncomfortable at the prospect of having to work with strangers after the merger. Continuity of the account manager can minimize the impact of the transaction on an individual customer. On the other hand, if new representatives are to be assigned to the account, they should meet with customer management as soon as possible.
- *How long will it take for things to get back to normal?* Customers realize that changes in a company's ownership can create unforeseen complications that manifest themselves at the product or service delivery level. In your communications, emphasize stability. Many customers want to know that you have plans in place to quickly meld operations in order to minimize service disruptions. Of course, it is advisable to actually have your integration plan developed as opposed to simply talking in sketchy terms about your plans to ultimately combine operations.

While a customer may ask for the intimate details of a merger, the customer can best be served by your presenting the acquisition in a low-key manner. The customer would rather hear about continuity rather than change, which can be unsettling for everyone involved in the process.

Segment your communications delivery system. After you have articulated your communications strategy, devise a timetable and determine how and by whom your messages should be delivered. All customers are important, but some are more important than others. Major accounts should be afforded special treatment when communicating details of the merger. Consider having senior management—along with the account people who service the customer—make in-person visits to the customer as soon as possible after the deal's announcement.

Make sure to emphasize the specific benefits the customer will reap as a result of the merger. Avoid citing empty clichés about synergies. Customers do not really care that the merged company will be able to save millions through operational cost cutting, unless those cuts will lessen the prices they, in turn, pay for goods or services. That message that should be trumpeted loudly.

Customers are unconcerned with the heightened competitiveness you will achieve through the deal, unless your enhanced capabilities will augment the quality of your offerings. That, too, must be explicitly communicated. Personal visits need not be made to all customer accounts. But make sure to have a mailing and/or telephone calling program planned to sound your new messages to companies on the lower range of the customer spectrum.

Different customers require different messages. Unless you are a single-product company that sells one product or service to a homogenous market, different messages must be crafted for each product and for the various target markets in which you operate. The various demographic groups comprising your customer base must be approached with acute sensitivity to their individual needs. This is particularly true in consumer services such as health care and banking. For example, a customer base comprised of older individuals should be communicated with differently than a Generation X customer base.

Younger customers are more exposed to current technology, and are therefore more used to receiving important communiqués via computer, while older customers, in general, are more comfortable with in-person or telephone contacts. Similarly, a customer used to dealing with your company on a daily basis as opposed to less frequently would expect to be treated more as an integral part of the daily operations, and feel entitled to more information.

Remember: Do not minimize the people factor either internally or externally. Companies can often be viewed as faceless monoliths or entries on a computer screen. In reality, they are people relating to other people. The same behavior that helped build customer affinity in the first place should be employed to maintain and strengthen it after the deal.

This is especially true in industries undergoing deregulation and restructuring which, in themselves, are catalysts to increased competition. For example, as the deregulating utility industry becomes a hotbed of M&A activity, energy executives are seeing a larger part of their efforts being focused on customer retention strategies in merger situations.

Helping merging or acquiring clients avoid customer cherry picking by competitors is a big part of the work we have done in the energy industry with an alliance partner, R. J. Rudden Associates, Inc. Today, utility customers must be courted with a renewed vigor as they are being offered the possibility of choice for the first time.

Use the plan as the foundation for a broader communications strategy. Devising a communications platform that heralds the benefits of the merger to the customer is a helpful starting point in crafting communications aimed at the merged company's other stakeholders. Employees, shareholders, vendors and suppliers, distributors, and the market at large are all groups that must be reached with information on how the merger will affect the organization's strength and strategic posture. Yet, many of the benefit-oriented communications directed at customers are the same as those that should be imparted to your other key publics. For example, such benefits as higher quality levels and broader product variety are customer selling points that also represent profitability improvement opportunities sought by all those with a stake in the merged company.

Minimize Competitive Threats, Maximize Marketing Opportunities

Without a customer retention plan, management is at the mercy of competitors who will attempt to exploit customers' collective apprehension. Clearly, there is a defensive element to this strategy. At the same time, there are distinct marketing benefits of a well-executed customer communications campaign.

For example, we provided marketing due diligence and integration services to a company that was acquiring a medium-sized consulting organization. The closing on the transaction was expected to be a few days away from a major industry trade show at which our client and the acquiree were both set to exhibit. It was an important venue where clients and prospects of the respective firms would be in attendance. Ideally, from a marketing standpoint, the deal could be announced at the trade show. But the actual transaction closing date was uncertain. After analyzing the situation, our firm designed a communications program. It featured two sets of high-quality yet inexpensively produced marketing materials, each carrying a separate message: one announcing that our client had in fact made the acquisition, the other that it was a *strategic alliance* that had been formed between the two organizations. Additionally, two sets of trade show signage were developed for the firms' exhibit booths announcing the two separate scenarios. The promotional materials were to be displayed at both locations.

As it turned out, the acquisition was not closed before the trade show, so the "strategic alliance" message was disseminated. As part of the communications plan, our client sponsored an on-site reception at which the alliance was announced to more than 50 clients, prospects, and trade media representatives. Executives from the two companies highlighted the strategic synergies that resulted from their alliance and which significantly enhanced their service capabilities to clients. Many new contacts were made. Ultimately, eight new business opportunities for the merged firm resulted from relationships forged at the client reception.

The customer retention plan also mapped out the activities that should commence immediately after the transaction closed. For instance, a series of personalized direct mailings and telemarketing programs were planned to announce the acquisition to the firm's newly combined customer base, as well as to attendees of the recent trade show. All communications hit the street as soon as it was possible to do so—leaving no time for competitors to reach clients with disruptive, propagandistic messages of their own. Customer concerns were preemptively assuaged.

SUMMARY

Acquisition integration planning should commence as early as possible—even before the merger or acquisition is finalized. Yet, the first phase of any integration program necessarily involves a marketing-driven communications program that promptly informs the merged company's key stakeholders—particularly its customers—of the benefits they will realize through the transaction. By focusing on the critical issues that affect the groups in the wake of a merger, you can ensure their loyalty and build on it.

A central tenet of marketing is that it is much harder and more costly to find new customers than to keep existing ones. An effectively designed and executed communications program can stave off competitors' advances and help effect customer protection, which is arguably more important than customer development when you consider that a company's value is directly tied to the breadth and quality of its customer base. Lose key customers and you lose the key components of a company's current and future worth.

Getting on track to execute growth programs after a merger is difficult enough. Management would do well to make sure the job is not made any harder by having to deal with customer and key stakeholder defections that can set the merged company back before it takes even its first strategic steps forward.

16

Designing the Merged Firm's Organizational Structure: A Framework for Decision Making

The transaction closes and, immediately, two organizations must become one. Dual workforces that were hired based on separate criteria and trained to perform tasks in different ways must now be functionally aligned to create one fine-tuned, smooth-running machine.

Earlier discussions about postmerger integration and cultural alignment showed why combining two companies' multitude of processes, personalities, and capabilities is a monumentally difficult task. Crafting a new organizational structure serves as an important means of launching that process. By proceeding with patience and a strict adherence to the strategic intent of the merger itself, a strong organizational architecture for the new company can be forged.

The merged firm must be structured to include elements of both the acquirer and the acquired firm and their conceptual synergies in the most effective design. Above all, organizational design flows from the organization's guiding vision. A link must be created between the effective execution of the company's strategies, the actual work processes required to achieve those strategies, and the people who will perform the requisite tasks.

The difficulty of this effort is compounded by the fact that a typical organization is made up of hundreds of groups as well as interpersonal and interdepartmental relationships. In theory, each should somehow be assessed and linked to both the strategic vision and the actual business. In reality, that is often impractical. Nonetheless, only by drafting a blueprint based on underlying business objectives first, and then designing processes to address them, can the new organization be effectively constructed.

For many in management, the starting point for devising an operational paradigm is the organization chart—small boxes cascading down from larger boxes that cite the names of managers at all levels. The "org chart" is useful for initially understanding the hierarchy of the company and the various lines of reporting. But a new company cannot be designed solely by plopping the names and titles of people down on paper. *Organizations must be designed based on a systematic approach that links employees, the combined mix of products and services, the processes that support them, and key business issues to the company's strategic imperatives.*

ITERATIVE PROCESS OF MERGING STRATEGY AND DESIGN

Major external changes affecting a company at any stage of its growth require that organization to modify its strategies to respond to the new environment. These changes, in turn, often create the need to modify the organizational design, to varying degrees, so that it is consistent with the revised strategy. In essence, strategy must always be the foundation of organizational structure.

In mergers and acquisitions, growth results from an awareness of the opportunities and needs created by the strategic synergies envisioned for the new company. There must be a focus on employing the existing or expanding resources more profitably. Implementing a new strategy requires a new, or at least a significantly refashioned, structure if the combined firm is to operate efficiently and ultimately live up to its profit potential.

Even if the initial postmerger results are successful, moving too far without adjusting the structural makeup of the merged company can lead to long-term inefficiencies and failure in realizing the synergies that were the initial drivers of the strategy. For example, merging the products of one company with the broader distribution capabilities of another company is a perfect conceptual synergy and one that can yield quick gains. However, if the marketing systems that initially supported the sale of that product are not revamped to reflect the new distribution capabilities, then, more than likely, sales will not increase to the maximum levels possible. In fact, if the strategy is not fully supported by the requisite shift in organizational and procedural design, the result can be actually be a drop in sales. If these negative results continue for an extended period of time, the long-term results can be so disastrous as to lead to a downward spiral of continued losses and ultimate divestiture.

Often, the failure to change organizational structure and key processes not only prevents a merged company from realizing its new vision, but also sparks detrimental developments that can severely impact profits and market share. Such was the case in the Snapple acquisition, where dramatic early market share losses and lost revenues resulted from the acquirer's failure to revamp its distribution infrastructure.

The lesson is that for every merger to succeed on the most basic of levels, management must properly understand its market opportunities, make functional decisions on the basis of those opportunities, and then—organizationally—deploy its resources to capitalize on them.

This chapter addresses the key considerations in postmerger organizational redesign. Clearly, it is impossible to offer a one-size-fits-all approach to devising organizational structure. There are just too many variables that are unique to each merged company, its strategic drivers, and the resources it has at its disposal. It is possible, however, to offer our *perspective* on interorganizational design decision making. That is our goal here.

ORGANIZATIONAL DESIGN: TRADITIONAL VERSUS STRATEGIC APPROACHES

In order to understand how to approach postmerger organizational design, let's start by looking at the two basic options for devising a corporate structure in the wake of an M&A transaction.

The first is the traditional approach, in which an acquiring company simply folds the acquired company's people, products, and processes into the buyer's existing organizational paradigm. The other, which is based acutely on the belief that a new company is being formed as a result of any sizable combination, is more strategic in nature and more complex in its execution. In this latter scenario, a completely new structure emerges.

Most acquirers approach organizational design in the traditional way. That is, they organize the merged company into some version of their own. As a result, the merged company's tangible characteristics mimic or parallel those of the acquirer. The decision to design the company this way is often born out of management's inexperience, ego, and belief that it knows the best way to do things—not out of any true expertise or acknowledgment of the potential inherent in a new structural framework.

Strategic acquirers must, instead, embrace the notion that the transaction's close presents an opportunity to build a better company from scratch. It is the chance to start over. Few acquirers recognize and seize this opportunity. Rather, they venture forth with too much old baggage when they should rightfully be viewing this situation as a chance to enter a brave new world with progressive and exciting, albeit challenging, opportunities.

As is evident, traditional postmerger organization design is the most expedient methodology because it is using an understood paradigm. All decisions are made from the acquirer's viewpoint and are based on the belief that the acquirer's current organization structure is not only the dominant one, but also one that contains the best and most desirable traits that will be needed going forward.

Unfortunately, an "our way is the only way" mentality pervades too many postmerger planning sessions that involve determining the combined company's organizational design. This closed-minded orientation inhibits decision making that is based on a true best-practices methodology. Consequently, the major drawbacks of this approach are an aversion to new ideas and a rigid mind-set whose core is complete and utter subjectivity.

Certainly, managerial hubris is not always behind the decision to take the traditional route. Sometimes, the failure to attempt to redesign a new internal structure is attributable to an overemphasis on operational activities by the executives responsible for integrating the two companies. Other times, it stems from management's inability to develop an entrepreneurial outlook. And, even other times, inaction is driven by a fear of political repercussions.

In a worst-case scenario, when a larger company acquires a smaller one, the acquired employees are viewed as second-rate citizens. As such, they are deemed to be less important, and are typically excluded from the planning process. This creates an environment where the new structure is designed without consideration for the special traits, capabilities, and sources of value resident in the acquired firm.

In this instance, the new organization is redesigned using the acquiring organization as both the foundation and the framework for the vision. The acquired organization is, at best, an afterthought. In such cases, the acquired organization is simply absorbed, and the acquired employees are forced to adapt or leave. The merged firm then typically retains the most flexible employees, but not necessarily the best.

Conversely, a strategic approach to organization design attempts to preserve the special or value-added characteristics of the acquired organization—and much of the foregoing guidance in Part Two of this book was geared to pinpointing those sources of value. Maintaining a strategic orientation assumes that these sources of value will be evaluated in comparison to the acquirer's capabilities.

In most acquisitions, it is an understatement to say that the organizational design process has not been well thought out. Many transactions have been characterized by an environment in which the acquirer's dominant orientation drove all organizational decisions. By all accounts, this attitude has left the new design of the merged companies pigeonholed and misdirected.

What is needed today is a mind-set focused more on flexibility than on ego, one that leaves the greatest number of possibilities available to the planning committee and which enables it to focus on the organization-related critical success factors that tie directly to the new entity's strategic vision.

INTERORGANIZATIONAL DESIGN: THE STRATEGIC APPROACH

We refer to the strategic approach to devising the postmerger corporate structure as "interorganizational design" (IOD). Though more complex than traditional methods of design and requiring more up-front planning, this perspective should drive the organizational structure of every strategic merger or acquisition. In transactions where a new corporate vision is being forged—as is the case in most deals today—an IOD perspective is the way to increase the likelihood that the merged firm's long-range goals will be actualized.

Approaching IOD is based on addressing three levels of different, yet interrelated, considerations:

1. Products, market coverage, and technological infrastructure
2. Roles and relationships
3. Strategic driver requirements

Together, these areas should provide a focus to help you craft an organizational structure that is based on both your long-term strategic needs and the physical, financial, and human assets available to you on the transaction's close.

Products, Market Coverage, and Technological Infrastructure

There are three fundamental considerations that must be addressed as you begin the IOD process. Each differs in the focus of its orientation, concentrating on either the product and service requirements of the company, variables relating to market coverage (e.g., the physical markets in which the merged company will operate), or its technological infrastructure.

By examining each of these key variables, you will be able to determine the ones that are most consistent with your strategic needs and other critical issues, such as the financial resources available to you and such intangible yet critical issues as corporate culture. Above all, focusing on these considerations will help you determine the specific job functions (and the interrelationships thereof) you will immediately need in the combined company.

Products. Interorganizational design may be approached based on the goods and services to be offered by the merged firm. A product-service orientation is based on structuring the company to most efficiently and cost-effectively develop and distribute those offerings to the marketplace. For instance, a product-service perspective will drive decisions on what staffers are needed to handle manufacturing, physical distribution, and other managerial functions relative to the creation and promotion of the merged company's goods.

In a service company, organizational decisions are based on the professionals charged with creating and providing those services to clients. These professionals are the ones who must deliver existing offerings, as well as possess the ability to create new and enhanced services to clients.

Market coverage. IOD decisions based on market variables relate to the physical deployment of people and facilities. The overriding goal is ensuring that the organizational structure provides the company with a presence in the markets where it will compete.

In a manufacturing organization, IOD decisions will impact the situation of production, distribution, and warehousing sites. In a service company, the location of key service providers will be determined based on where the company's clients are located, or where the combined firm hopes to attract new buyers. Clearly, there is a direct link between a product-service approach to organizational design and that of a market-focused orientation. Both have ramifications for staffing requirements, as well as for the physical deployment of people and facilities needed to furnish the company's goods to current and prospective buyers.

Technological Infrastructure. Today, technology pervades virtually all aspects of a company's operations. Technology is applied to either enhance the efforts of human resources or to make those human resources obsolete. It is clear, therefore, how technological applications in the merged company will drive many decisions relative to both process- and personnel-related issues.

As the technological wave has swept across the business landscape worldwide, compressing the time required to perform most tasks, the consistent upgrading and improvement of commonly used technology is leading to more efficient operations, increased productivity, and improved working conditions. Companies' back offices have been the major recipient of this technological boom as it has accelerated or eliminated the traditional clerical functions such as filing, word processing, and data entry via the use of computer-based systems.

In a sense, technology should not be viewed as a sidebar or an ancillary issue, but rather as a full-blown approach to organizational redesign. Typical impacts of technological applications include:

- Altering the processes used for doing work in order to change the relationships between the employee and his or her machine
- Upgrading or altering the equipment used in day-to-day work, ideally moving to a completely high-tech environment
- Modifying production or service delivery methods
- Changing design and engineering processes to replace old, cumbersome, or less reliable mechanical equipment and systems

In mergers, many times one company will have a greater level of technological sophistication than the other. Forward-thinking organizational design initiatives must take technology into account and incorporate it into procedural- as well as people-focused decision making.

In the context of technological changes to the company's organizational structure, it is important not to lose sight of the bigger picture. Technology rarely exists purely by itself. There are almost always ramifications from a staffing and broader procedural standpoint.

For example, the management of a newly merged company was performing a technological approach to the redesign of its organization. Management's initial intent was to upgrade the facilities throughout the acquired company to be on a par with those of the acquirer. The goal was to integrate the systems of the acquired into those of the acquirer. Yet, after performing extensive data collection on the acquired company, it was determined that its R&D department was the driving force behind its five-year growth spurt (which is what initially attracted the acquirer to this target in the first place). To redesign the R&D department and change the technology currently in use would have undermined a very effective process and could have possibly destroyed the growth engine of the company.

Of equal import was the director of the R&D department himself. He had developed very efficient and effective processes by which the R&D department operated. And, he managed those processes very closely to ensure quality and cost controls. To impose new processes or tamper with such a successful operation would have undermined one of the true sources of value inherent in the target company.

It is important to note that the product-service, market coverage, and technological infrastructure considerations relative to interorganizational design are not mutually exclusive. One area may exist as the primary focus of your organizational decision making. However, IOD must take into account each of these three fundamental variables. One may represent the dominant focus of your planning. Yet, more likely, the final organizational architecture will embody traits of all three (not to mention others that are specific to your particular situation).

In order for the architecture of the combined organization to be successfully developed via an IOD approach, you must address its creation from the merged-company perspective. Focusing your efforts on revamping the structure of one merger partner first and then the other will lead to shortsighted and possibly one-sided decisions. Clearly, this approach—although actually pursued by some acquirers—is completely contradictory to strategic M&A organizational planning.

INSIDER'S OUTLOOK

In any merger or major acquisition, the combining companies—in my view—are really starting all over from scratch. After the deal closes, you have a whole new group of people and, most times, a whole new lineup of products. Consequently, it's a chance to forge entirely new ways of doing business in a way that brings all these diverse yet complementary elements together and moves them toward a common goal.

—Corporate development officer, Fortune 1000 electronics manufacturing company

Roles and Relationships

Next, it is necessary to understand the second level of organizational design issues that will guide decision making on how to structure the merged company:

- Job descriptions
- Command
- Control
- Communication flow

In general, these factors relate to determining what functional skill sets will be needed, how managerial oversight will be deployed throughout the organization, what managerial levels will be instituted to monitor ongoing progress toward achieving business objectives, and the channels and flow of information to maintain and enhance operational efficiency.

Job descriptions. Once the product, market, and technology infrastructure issues have been addressed, you must focus on a linkage to occupations and roles needed to meet your stated requirements. Determining the skill sets you need is a precursor to determining the complement of people required to provide those skills.

It is clear how the initial considerations of IOD will influence the job functions you define. For instance, considerations vis-à-vis products and services will drive decision making regarding the design, production, promotion, and distribution of those offerings. Job function issues relative to geographical markets may dictate skills that are necessary in light of a person's ability to understand or operate in a given locale (e.g., the job classification may have as a requirement particular language skills or the ability to interact with customers of a given socioeconomic category). In the realm of technological applications, job definitions will likely include the ability to employ particular computer-based or advanced mechanical systems (e.g., such as for manufacturing or facilities management).

INSIDER'S OUTLOOK

The smart merger will develop assessment and selection processes based on strategic goals, not on the power of one company over the other. Identify the skills, abilities and competencies you'll need going forward and, based on that, assess and select the people who can fulfill those functions. Ending up with the right people depends on how well you develop the criteria on which you will base your judgments and how fair your measuring standard is. It is a good idea to involve your employees in developing the criteria and having them represented on an interview board that will review all candidates.

—Paul Cholak, SHL North America

It is rather straightforward to determine, for example, that the merged firm will need a manager in charge of distribution in the northeast region. Yet, factoring in IOD considerations will help you determine the extent to which that person must be able to intimately understand the nuances of your product and service offerings, grasp the particular dynamics of the geographic locale in which the employee will operate, and/or be able to apply technological tools the new company plans to use in executing this particular function.

Command. Once the basic job classifications are defined, managerial levels must be created to oversee day-to-day activities. These positions of command must manage the people in specific roles who will actualize the merged company's strategic goals on a tactical basis. Not only is it necessary to determine who will occupy these command positions, but you must also decide the merged firm's overall command structure.

The problem that many large organizations have immediately on merging is that there are multiple layers of commanders and extensive duplication at each level. This situation is exacerbated when an organization with a regional command structure merges with an organization that has more of a matrix structure. Confusion reigns when an employee is not sure whether to report to a regional manager or a divisional superior—or when forced to report to both.

Clear lines of command must be drawn, but there is the danger of too steep a hierarchy. It is important to keep in mind that closeness to the decision making authority—or at least a perception of closeness—gives a sense of clarity to the employees implementing a given directive or the broader vision of the company.

Chapter 9 addressed the characteristics of centralized and decentralized management structures. Each, you will recall, has its distinct benefits and drawbacks. For instance, a decentralized structure creates an environment where empowerment is granted at the local level and thereby brings tactical implementation closer to the source of the directive. An added benefit of a decentralized command structure is that local units can more quickly change and react to important shifts in the marketplace.

The inherent flexibility of a decentralized structure allows decisions to be made expeditiously and more in sync with local capabilities. Pronouncements emanating from a distant management source that is too far removed from local operations often fall on deaf ears or can be misinterpreted, leading to the possibility of flawed implementation.

Obviously, if your company is one with a centralized command structure and a steep hierarchy, the stage has already been set. However, an awareness of the problems that may present themselves in this environment and a willingness to take proactive steps to reduce or eliminate any managerial roadblocks that exist will help you in deciding if this command structure is appropriate going forward.

Control. As an organizational consideration, control relates specifically to the number of managerial layers you will create and the size of the employee groups to be assigned under each. In general, control relates to your ability to monitor and evaluate people's performance against specific goals and objectives.

Managers at the highest levels of an organization typically deal with more strategic and operationally focused issues and, therefore, have fewer employees that fall under their control. As the hierarchy descends, the span of critical issues narrows and the number of employees falling under the direct control of lower-level managers increases. An organization that has more layers, yet fewer employees in each layer, is run quite differently than a company with fewer layers but more individuals in each stratum.

When two organizations combine, span-of-control issues should be addressed early on. An interesting note: Companies that have more effectively trained their employees generally require fewer levels of supervision. The more training and experience subordinates have, the less direct supervision they need. Moreover, well-trained and flatter organizations tend to be more efficient than companies with multiple layers.

This should be factored into your premerger review of a target company, as well as when you decide on personnel and resource allocations postmerger. Take, for example, a situation in which you are assessing two companies of equal size. Assume that one firm has an annual training budget of $300,000, while the other has no training program but 14 more managers, each with annual compensation of $50,000. In this scenario, the second company is spending $400,000 more for "untrained" management (14 × $50,000 = $700,000; $700,000 – $300,000 = $400,000) and probably has an undertrained workforce. Whichever of these two firms you were to acquire would pose different considerations and approaches to determining span-of-control issues in the merged company.

Communication flow. Much has been discussed thus far on the importance of communication as a tool in melding organizations—first as a necessary tactic to alert employees to the particulars of the merger and then, subsequently, as means of expediting integration and facilitating the alignment or corporate cultures.

From the standpoint of organizational design, communications represent not a means to an end, but rather an end in itself: devising how and through how many layers communications must travel throughout the merged company in order to maximize productivity and operational efficiencies. In this context, communication is viewed not in terms of its content, but rather in how it should flow to and between the corporate strata that comprise the new organization.

Rigidly structured companies tend to formalize communication flow (e.g., communications may only move vertically between managerial layers one level at a time). More loosely structured firms allow more of a free flow of information across the corporate hierarchy. Keep in mind that information flow in the former scenario can lead to misinformation. Multiple layers of information flow may create situations akin to the game of "telephone." By the time a message from on high reaches the rank and file, it has gone through so many permutations that it is rarely what was articulated in the first place. By the same token, senior management can rarely get timely and accurate feedback from lower levels of the organization when the official communication pathways are overly steep.

Employees in traditional hierarchies are often overwhelmed by the multiple messages they receive from the top down and the responses they are required to send back up. At best, conflicting information is received at both ends, requiring extensive interpretive sensitivity. At worst, the garbage in/garbage out adage will wreak havoc on the merged company, spelling disaster for near-term integration programs and longer-term growth initiatives.

Strategic Driver Requirements

Of all the considerations you must key on when designing the merged firm's organizational structure, none is more important than the strategic drivers of the merger or acquisition itself.

Chapter 2 cited the 10 basic drivers of strategic mergers. Some will figure prominently in decisions regarding how to organize the merged firm. Others will not. For instance, the strategic driver of "effecting organizational growth" does not have a direct link to the merged company's structure. That is, when the goal is growing the size of your company, your intent is adding on to that which you already have. Consequently, the structure of the new firm is not altered as much as it is augmented. This does not eliminate the need for a careful approach to reformulating the personnel and procedural sources of value you have attained. It just means that if your sole goal was to add to existing resources in order to achieve critical mass, you may be less in need of modifying the organizational structure in contrast to other types of strategic drivers.

In particular, however, four of the strategic drivers cited will likely have direct bearing on the organizational design you adopt for the merged organization. These are:

- Gaining entrée into new markets and access to distribution channels
- Obtaining new products
- Pursuing innovations/discoveries in products or technologies
- Strengthening reputation and credibility

Let's now see how each of these drivers will pose certain requirements that will likely influence your organizational decision making. Organizational design decisions may necessitate deploying people, channeling resources, or establishing facilities, all of which are components of the merged company's overall corporate structure.

Gaining entrée into new markets and access to distribution channels. If your goal is to gain a presence in geographic markets where you have not competed before, the organizational structure must provide both a corporate presence and delivery system in those locales. Thus, if the intent of an acquisition was to penetrate markets with discrete physical boundaries, you will need to deploy resources in those sectors. Offices may need to be opened in these new markets, or facilities that have historically operated there may need to be staffed with a greater complement of people to support your enhanced activities. For instance, sales and marketing resources will also have to be deployed. Moreover, new vendor relationships—such as those involving material suppliers or outside service support agencies (e.g., local marketing, public relations, or selling agents)—may be needed if an intimate knowledge of those markets is required. Consequently, from an organizational standpoint, you may need managers assigned to those areas who have expertise in guiding the work of those outside vendors.

Obtaining new products. Securing new products through a merger or acquisition will likely have a significant bearing on staffing decisions. Managers responsible for those offerings will need to be retained. This is important in terms of both the physical production of those goods and their delivery and promotion in the marketplace. And as with the previous driver of penetrating new markets, physical delivery systems must also be developed to ensure the timely provision of those offerings to consumers—delivery systems that will require both in-house staff and outside resources to support them.

For service firms, the people in the target company who manage key client relationships will most likely also have to be factored into your organizational paradigm. These people's physical location becomes critical in your efforts to protect the client relationships they have forged, since buyers will most probably require that their account managers continue to be based nearby to maximize their service delivery capability.

Pursuing innovations/discoveries in products and technologies. In this realm, a sought-after source of value may be the target company's R&D function. Indeed, there may be very sophisticated laboratories and testing sites in which R&D teams work, which cannot be moved lest you dismantle the physical facilities in which innovations are conceived, tested, and produced.

Key R&D workers are another critical consideration. Not only may you not be able to easily uproot R&D facilities, you may not be able to persuade your R&D stars to relocate from their home bases or move to new installations. Thus, the merged company's organizational structure may be driven in part on where product- and technology-related innovations are devised. Consequently, there are immensely important physical and personnel-related considerations that will influence organizational design decisions.

Strengthening reputation and credibility. Augmenting your company's reputation and credibility via acquiring a company held in high regard requires protecting those intangible attributes of the target company. Doing so may influence the merged firm's organizational structure. Consider, for example, the case where a Midwest-based publishing house seeks to position itself as a provider of Internet-related content. The company acquires a New York–based firm specializing in this area. The so-called Silicon Alley in New York has emerged as a veritable Mecca of companies with expertise in developing Internet content.

The acquiring firm, in order to effectively position itself in this product market, would likely have to maintain the acquired firm's presence in New York as opposed to folding its operations into the acquirer's Midwest operations. Granted, reputation and credibility are eminently portable qualities. But they are intangibles that, in business, are very often linked to the very tangible variable of where a company operates.

INSIDER'S OUTLOOK

In a sense, the merger is an opportunity to start over again. It's a chance to see what you've done right . . . and what your merger partner's done right in order to share best practices. In another, perhaps more important sense, it's a chance to look at what you may have done wrong in the past and devise ways to avoid those mistakes in the future—with the help of a merger partner that makes your organization stronger than it ever was before.

—Chief financial officer, business services and document management company

FINAL THOUGHTS ON ORGANIZATIONAL DESIGN

Effecting postmerger organizational design signals to the combined workforce the realization of massive change that had been anticipated since the transaction's announcement. Management is advised to proceed with caution in two key respects:

1. Preserving value
2. Providing ongoing employee communication and training

Preserving Value

Interorganizational design is predicated on the strategic drivers of the M&A transaction and devising roles and responsibilities of people to ensure attainment of the underlying strategic objectives. Keep in mind, however, that there may be particular sources of value inherent in the company you are requiring that, although are not directly related to your near-term goals, may well be important to the company in the future.

For instance, these highlights can take the form of a department or group of managers whose particular functional skills are not needed today, but which may play a role in the new organization further down the road. In other words, both actual and potential sources of value must be preserved and nurtured for their possible leverage in the combined organization. Identifying these highlights is critical to putting the merged company in a position to respond to future, as yet unforeseen needs.

For example, an acquirer with a national focus may have no use for a regional marketing unit that was very effective in the acquired's organization. However, recognizing the quality of skills inherent in the group, the acquirer can add this group to the national marketing function, develop adjunct marketing teams throughout the rest of the organization, or even use it as the model for future marketing functions. Your advance planning will help you determine the best route for accomplishing that goal.

We reiterate: It is important to remember not to shoot first and ask questions later. Too many acquirers have eliminated effective functions and personnel because they did not take the time to understand what they actually did or to consider what role they could potentially play in the future.

Providing Ongoing Communication and Training

The importance of regular internal communications and specially designed training and development programs cannot be overstated. Their significance is particularly noteworthy as you begin actually reorganizing the merged company.

Few companies are in a position to make massive organizational changes immediately on the transaction's close. The reality is, time is needed to go through the investigative and analytical exercises detailed in this chapter and elsewhere in the book. As your planning and decision making continues, it is necessary to keep the merged company's workforce abreast of developments. This not to suggest that you reveal organizational design and managerial decisions before you are ready to. It means that employees should at least be alerted to the fact that organizational shifts are imminent. The rule of thumb in effective postmerger integration is to minimize surprises. In general, people do not like them. In M&A situations in particular, surprises exacerbate an already volatile and fearful environment.

Internal communications are necessary to prepare the merged company's employees for imminent change. They are imperative to announce and, ultimately, detail the particulars of the merged firm's new structure. Moreover, communications are necessary to explain the significance and strategic rationale of the new organizational paradigm.

If, as expected, the structural redesign will create new roles, responsibilities, and procedural changes, training and development programs should be devised to work hand in hand with your communications to help employees quickly understand and embrace the new ways of doing business.

Employees presented with a new structure and unaccustomed patterns of behavior must accept the new order. The route to organizational redesign is not necessarily a smooth one. And, the most important determinant is whether the change in employee behavior that supports the new design is voluntary or involuntary. Voluntary change is when an employee learns new attitudes by identifying with and emulating some other person who holds those same attitudes. Involuntary change is when the employee adopts new behaviors by being placed in a situation where new attitudes are *demanded* as a way of solving unavoidable problems. Voluntary change tends to build more committed employees because the decision to adapt is not made under duress. It is a freethinking and conscious decision that has behind it a spiritual motivation as opposed to one of convenience or circumstance. However, regardless of whether change is voluntary or involuntary, once an employee accepts the platform for redesign, he or she stands ready to incorporate whatever changes management presents. Communications, training, and development programs can help make this happen.

The important point is that when two companies are being combined, all employees must recognize the need to change the organization's design. They must be willing to accept the new design ideas regardless of the extent of the change. And they must be willing to implement the most effective change strategy to support this design. Without this broad level of acceptance, an organization's ability to respond to both internal and external lack of stability and continuity is greatly diminished. This, in turn, reduces the merged organization's ability to operate effectively in the short term, which necessarily weakens its chances of succeeding over the long haul.

SUMMARY

In postmerger organizational planning, the lesson is an important one: When combining multiple processes, personalities, and capabilities of two distinct companies, you must proceed first with patience and, second, with a steady focus on the merger's strategic drivers.

As the merged company takes form, the shape of that enterprise going forward must include pieces of both merger partners, regardless of which company is calling the shots. The organizational design must be inclusive enough to bend to the merged organization's strategic intent and vision. Once the basic design has been agreed on, it must be linked to the company's strategies, the work processes required to achieve those strategies, and the people who will perform that work.

As we have stressed throughout this book, all efforts must connect back to a business issue–focused blueprint that sets the stage for all future design initiatives. Once this blueprint is forged, the strategic vision and the processes needed to accomplish that vision will flow.

Objectivity is of the utmost importance. In the event that headquarters will be directing the organizational design, it is critical that it break away from the "dictatorial" or "black knight" mind-set for the purposes of crafting an all-inclusive architecture. Management must accept that there will likely be people, products, and processes resident in the acquired company that are better than those in place in the acquiring company. If management can adopt an "enlightened" approach and embrace the concept of IOD, then developing a blueprint for a successful organizational architecture will not be impeded by politics or ego.

Organizations in a postmerger environment require a structure that facilitates the new vision and promotes its advancement over both the short and longer term. Work processes that are effective and supportive of best practices must be recognized and maintained. If they do not currently exist, they should be developed in a triage fashion ensuring that the organization continues to run while they are being crafted. This often requires bringing in one or more outside consultants to help develop the effective fusion of new or revised processes while current management does what it needs to do: manage. It is virtually impossible to design new processes and effectively manage current ones simultaneously. Attempts at this will lead to the burnout of key managers, who will seek shortcuts when in actuality taking the long way around will be most beneficial to the long-term viability of the new entity.

Many companies are reluctant to allow outsiders to assume full responsibility for defining the processes of the new organization. Yet outside assistance is usually necessary to support internal resources and to provide an all-important element of objectivity. Consultants should work side by side with management to forge the best of the old and the new and let the strategy dictate the structure.

The IOD viewpoint approaches the organizational design process with an open mind and a blank slate. There should be only one preconception—that of the new corporate vision, which should be pursued as an ideal. Yet, an understanding that achieving the ideal is a utopian accomplishment should not discourage you from attempting to attain it anyway. In fact, if in the earliest stages of articulating the strategic vision your attention is also focused on designing the organization, the steps that make up the IOD process will smoothly follow.

The success of interorganizational design rests not only on accurately identifying the strategic thrust of the merged firm, but also on the challenges that will arise in melding the products and processes of both companies and in successfully reducing people's resistance to change. The organizational design must be strategically sound and be one that addresses all critical issues. Needless to say, it must also make good business sense in the process.

Whether you choose the traditional approach to organizational design or the more complex and strategic interorganizational approach, you must remember that the day following the transaction's close should be viewed as the first day of the rest of the merged company's life. On that day, nothing is carved in stone. Fresh ideas, a new direction, and a whole new company will emerge. Take the time to recognize this and the chances of attaining enduring success will be greater.

Appendix

Researching Acquisition Candidates: Information Requirements, Sources, and Data-Collection Techniques

Marketing due diligence provides both a perspective and a starting point for merger and acquisition planning. Once your strategic goals have been articulated, you are ready to begin identifying and gathering data on potential acquisition candidates that will help you achieve your corporate growth objectives.

Evaluating candidates requires gathering particular types of data needed to size up those different potential partners. The research techniques discussed in this section should be employed in the initial phase of your acquisition program when you are first scouting out the market landscape for viable candidates with the attributes you seek. Ultimately, however, the information culled on the most promising prospects will be useful when making contact with those companies, as well as when the formal investigative process begins as both parties agree to explore the corporate combination.

The data-gathering techniques described herein are meant to provide both background and detailed competitive information on potential targets. Yet, investment bankers and business brokers that you may have hired typically have extensive financial research on companies that are formally "in play." Sometimes that information takes the form of a specially produced compendium of data—"the book" prepared by the company itself or by strategic or financial advisers working on its behalf—that provides all critical details on the firm's business, finances, and operations.

Of course, "the book" is essentially a promotional piece that puts a positive spin on all aspects of the organization. Negatives about the company are not cited or are significantly downplayed. Moreover, there are likely to be some pieces of information that are not contained in such materials produced by the company. Consequently, research-gathering techniques may be more helpful in filling these informational gaps or in verifying overly self-promoting claims made by a prospective seller.

Data collection strategies are pertinent before and up to the point where formal negotiations with a given acquisition candidate commence. You will ultimately have complete access to the company data you need when the acquisition candidate opens up its books for your review. Still, the data you have collected up to that point will highlight organizational strengths and weaknesses that merit detailed review when company records are made available to you and your initial research findings can either be confirmed or refuted.

IDENTIFYING ACQUISITION CANDIDATES: LONG LISTS, SHORT LISTS

The search for acquisition candidates begins with assembling a universe of companies that may provide one or more of the strategic attributes you seek. Your goal is to create a "long list" of potential candidates, conduct a preliminary assessment of those organizations, and then pare down the grouping to a manageable number of candidates that will eventually be subjected to a more rigorous review.

The first phase of this activity involves generating a list of companies that meet your general strategic criteria. Today, electronic databases available in CD-ROM offerings by selected companies or via the Internet contain literally millions of company names. These listings provide basic information on such areas as products and services, company size by revenues or employees, industries served, geographic locations of the headquarters and key divisional offices, and major subsidiaries and corporate affiliations.

Beyond electronic databases, other sources include trade associations, trade publications, industry observers, industry analysts, and business leaders. Keep in mind that some of the same sources of information you initially review to find candidates will be the same sources you revisit when you more deeply probe the most promising candidates.

A beneficial by-product of your preliminary research is that you gain important insights into industry trends, conditions, and the best performing companies in the particular business segment under review. Although those organizations may not be viable candidates (their size may place them outside your price range), it is valuable to see how and why they are successful. Some of the traits that make them high-performing companies may be attributes that are exhibited by other organizations. Overall, the insights gained in this phase of your research will be useful when your investigation moves to deeper levels of exploration.

It is likely that your first compilation of company names will be quite extensive. Your task is then to winnow the list down by assessing companies against your criteria: the specific strategic drivers you seek. Thus, your short list will be comprised of the most promising candidates that merit further investigation.

There are various methods to generate comprehensive information on these priority candidates. This is the critical first step before determining which of those organizations will be formally approached to begin merger or acquisition discussions.

Determining Your Information Needs

Depending on the organization, company-specific data may be extraordinarily easy or extraordinarily difficult to accumulate. Data collection, for example, is a straightforward exercise when the company under review is publicly traded. Volumes of data can be tapped into via a host of electronic and print information sources. On the other hand, when the target company under investigation is a private concern, information on that firm is significantly less attainable.

The guidance in this section, though useful in both instances, will help you in situations where data relative to the target's people, products, and processes—and in some cases, financial performance—must be unearthed through meticulous investigative measures.

Gathering data on specific companies begins with identifying your data requirements. Most likely your organization has, or can readily access, market data on specific companies or markets. Thus, the dual task becomes defining the information that you already have and determining what information you will have to actively seek out for M&A planning purposes. Your information needs are typically driven by the strategic goals you hope to achieve through a corporate combination. Chapter 2 discussed the drivers underlying strategic mergers and acquisitions. Identifying the drivers that motivate *your* acquisition provides a focus for the information-gathering process.

To help you chart your research work, it is advisable to construct a matrix that identifies both the strategic drivers sought and the individual companies' attributes relative to those expedient characteristics. When constructing such a matrix, the vertical axis indicates the strategic drivers relative to your specific corporate goals. (Your own company's primary strategic drivers may be different, and these should be listed in order of their importance.)

The horizontal axis will indicate boxes or cells that represent different target companies. At the outset of your research the cells will simply be empty boxes. Initially, you should check off the boxes that identify which target companies offer which strategic benefits. As data is collected—and your long list of targets narrows to a smaller group of candidates—the goal is to incorporate progressively more qualitative and quantitative information into each cell.

The objective of this exercise is to generate additional information that distinguishes candidates and identifies the degree to which they are stronger or weaker in different strategic respects. As additional information on the targets is accumulated, you should develop a revised matrix. The horizontal axis of target companies will become narrower as a result of there being a smaller list of candidates, and the cells will necessarily become bigger, thus enabling you to accommodate addition information. Eventually, you will be able to determine which handful of candidates will merit deeper exploration and, possibly, contact by senior management to begin preliminary merger or acquisition discussions.

A disciplined approach to information collection facilitates all phases of the acquisition planning and decision making process. Amassing data on different companies helps you ascertain which of them are viable candidates and merit your initial consideration. As the information collection process continues and you learn more about those organizations, you are able to winnow out the companies not offering the strategic characteristics you seek.

At this point you will know which firms deserve closer review and what pieces of information you still need to collect on those organizations. Understanding a framework for cataloging the collected information is important, but even more so are the ways to actually compile the data and critical company-specific intelligence you require.

RESEARCH TECHNIQUES: A "COMPETITOR ANALYSIS" APPROACH

The information you need to help create your long list of initial target company investigations is readily found through publicly available data sources. As your research progresses—and your list becomes a short one—you need data of greater breadth and depth. Such information gets progressively harder to obtain, and requires a more comprehensive and professional approach to data collection: research techniques that fall into the category of "competitor analysis."

Competitor analysis is similar to market research in that it involves culling information from public and private sources. The burgeoning field of competitor analysis is different from traditional market research in one key respect. The data accumulated in competitor analysis is designed to provide the basis for discrete actions. Specifically, the nature and scope of the information collected is designed to enable you to respond to the findings with specific tactics or long-term strategies. Competitor analysis is futuristic and predictive.

The data itself may amount to a snapshot in time, but it is how that data is analyzed and applied that differentiates this intelligence from that which is collected in traditional market research. In fact, competitor analysis professionals draw a harsh distinction between information and intelligence, the former referring to the result of traditional research approaches and the latter suggesting a much more comprehensive product for use in business decision making. In short, competitor analysis strives to transform information into actionable intelligence for the purpose of devising and implementing corporate strategies.

Competitor analysis techniques are eminently applicable to M&A planning. Interestingly, the same data-gathering techniques employed in competitor analysis are those that can be used in conducting research on acquisition candidates. Many of the things an acquirer wants to find out about a target company are identical to the variables that any company would study when conducting competitor analysis. These include information on the target's products and markets, its organizational composition, and its near- and long-term strategic initiatives.

Competitor analysis can unearth critical information on a target company's people, products, and processes—the three critical areas of integration that marketing due diligence studies. Clearly, the value of competitor analysis techniques to the M&A planning process increases as the amount of attainable information on a given company diminishes.

The Process of Intelligence Gathering

Before addressing the sources of competitor analysis information, it is helpful to understand how to organize the data-gathering process. Your first step is conducting a "gap analysis" that ascertains the information you have in hand and that which you need to collect, with the aforementioned matrix being the tool to graphically chart and organize the data you accumulate.

Where do you start to look for data? The answer is, right in your own corporate backyard.

Many times valuable information is resident within your own company. For instance, company documents such as marketing and business plans (particularly those developed by corporate divisions other than your own) contain important insights on specific companies and markets. Next, you will want to read up on a target company by obtaining a copy of its annual report (if a public company), and by conducting an article search via Internet research. Today, personal computers (PCs) connected to the Internet link users to volumes of company- and market-specific data.

Sometimes, however, the inclination of managers assigned to the research task is to immediately jump onto the Web to see what is out there on a given company. Generally, that is advisable. Conducting a simple database search, for example, of recently published articles on the target provides a good foundation for subsequent research. The danger lies in the tendency to spend too much time scouring one particular research source without first establishing your basic research needs. Valuable time and money can be spent collecting data that you already have in hand or that you simply don't need.

The next phase of your preliminary data collection is talking to your own colleagues. Sales and marketing managers, division heads, and other executives generally have important insights on specific companies. Other colleagues you should speak with include customer service representatives, product and purchasing managers, engineering and R&D people, finance and treasury executives, corporate counsel, and members of senior management.

A helpful exercise at the completion of the first phase of research is to write a profile of the target company. Taking the information you have accumulated and drafting a dossier on that organization will point up the information you need. It is often said that writing is one of the best forms of learning. Developing a written profile of the target forces you to summarize the most critical information you have been able to amass. As you tell the story, you will discover the key details you are missing. This will lend direction to the next steps in the information-gathering process.

For instance, data may have been easy to collect on the target's promotional campaigns for existing products, but not about its new product plans. Or data may have been readily available on the target's CEO and other senior managers, but not about the key operating managers responsible for executing strategic initiatives. The information you deem important, but which you have been unable to collect in the first phase of your research, constitutes the gap you need to fill. The next stage is accessing sources that will help you amass the deeper levels of intelligence you require.

The following sources are neither comprehensive nor exclusive to each area of investigation. For example, accessing a Dun & Bradstreet report will render input (albeit very general data) on both a company's financial performance and its senior officers. There will likely be overlap in that you may find data on different areas of examination by tapping one data source. As you begin your research you will find which sources provide which types of information. Subsequent exploration will always be speedier and more cost-effective as your research learning curve increases and you spend less time scouring sources that offer little valuable intelligence. Nonetheless, your initial efforts lay the groundwork for a more detailed approach to data collection that involves the following five steps:

1. *Access industry information.* Collecting data on the industry in which the target company operates is essential. It is important to be as specific as possible in identifying industry segments. The example cited earlier, the high-tech industry, can be subdivided into such areas as hardware, software, and semiconductors. Continue to drill down deeper into each subsector until you arrive at your desired area. Generally, the place to start is with trade periodicals and specialized industry newsletters, which should include citations and articles on the firm under review.

Next are industry trade associations. Although these groups are generally reluctant to provide company-specific data (except to members), they can usually highlight important trends and market data that may point you in the direction of the company information you seek. Most major trade groups publish annual studies or reports that provide ample industry statistics, including market share levels of the major industry players. A valuable source of trade association information is the *Encyclopedia of Associations*, published by Gale Research. This directory provides names, addresses, and phone numbers of all major trade groups in the United States, along with information on the groups' officers and publications, and the dates and locations of their national and regional meetings.

2. *Interview key outsiders.* Interviews with your colleagues and close business contacts should be followed by discussions with well-regarded industry observers. Consultants, journalists, academicians such as business professors, and investment analysts all may be able to offer insights on given companies. Additional input can be culled from discussions with other industry players such as suppliers, distributors, agents, and customers (both yours and those of the target company).

3. *Use the "endless chain" to link up with other interviewees.* The name of one source usually leads to the names of others. In sales, the endless chain refers to the method of asking for the names of new prospects from existing customers and other contacts. In competitor analysis, for example, the people cited or quoted in articles reviewed in your database research represent other potential interviewees. Contact those people, indicating where you saw their names, and ask if they would be willing to provide insights on the company- or industry-specific topics you are exploring. After you have interviewed them, ask if they can refer you to additional people they know who would be willing to be interviewed.

4. *Review government filings.* In both public- and private-company research there is generally ready access to governmental materials that provide worthwhile financial and operational information. For example, government filings include such documents as annual reports and proxy statements on public companies; securities filings (such as 10-Ks); Occupational Safety and Health Act (OSHA) filings; Environmental Protection Act (EPA) filings; and other submissions that must be furnished to agencies such as the Department of Labor and federal and state departments of commerce. Other materials that fall into the public domain, and which may provide helpful background, are local tax and zoning filings, as well as court papers relative to lawsuits and bankruptcy proceedings in which the company or its subsidiaries may be involved.

5. *Access information from the target company itself.* All companies issue information that is designed for public consumption. Such materials include advertising, press releases, sales brochures and other promotional literature, coupons, in-store displays, technical papers delivered by company executives at professional conferences and trade shows, and other materials. As discussed earlier, many companies today have Web sites on the Internet. Accessing information directly from this electronic source typically provides the most up-to-date background on the organization, including current press releases issued by the company.

COLLECTING DATA ON PEOPLE, PRODUCTS, AND PROCESSES

Competitor analysis techniques produce data on all aspects of a company's operations. Of particular importance in the realm of M&A growth planning is information tied to the "three Ps of marketing due diligence": people, products, and processes. Eventually, when you are formally studying a company with which you are negotiating, you will delve into all aspects of the target's operational infrastructure. Nonetheless, it is advisable to begin collecting this information in the early stages of your research.

Each of the aforementioned sources (e.g., database searches) will provide data relating directly or indirectly to these critical areas. Still, there are some specific data sources that can be tapped to collect deeper levels of information.

People

It is relatively easy to find information on an organization's senior-level officers, particularly those serving public companies. It is generally more difficult to gather intelligence on divisional heads and line managers. A good place to start is the *Who's Who* directories (*Who's Who in America*, *Who's Who in Business and Finance*), which provide biographical information on leading professionals. These sources, however, are by no means comprehensive. The people cited are generally invited to submit biographical information, and screening committees determine which professionals ultimately merit inclusion.

Another source of personnel information is the executive recruiter. Many such professionals specialize in a given industry. Speaking with headhunters who work with managers, say, in the banking industry, can provide input on individuals working in that segment. Naturally, as you get the names of particular managers you can then generate additional input on those people via the data-gathering techniques already discussed. Headhunters may either be able to tell you who the key people are at a given company, or they can point you in the direction of former employees at the target who may be willing to speak to you. Headhunters may also be able to give you insights on a company's organizational structure in terms of people's titles and reporting relationships.

Yet another source of personnel information is the display employment ads in major national newspapers such as the *Wall Street Journal* and *The New York Times*, as well as in leading trade journals serving different fields. Interestingly, more and more companies are advertising available positions within recruitment modules of their Web sites.

INSIDER'S OUTLOOK

Competitor analysis etiquette suggests you offer to repay your sources for the information they provide. Your research will likely entail interviewing busy, hard-to-reach professionals who, by right, owe you nothing and will likely be hesitant to furnish information. Consequently, it's necessary to be able to offer something in return for the information they provide. Money isn't the answer. An *informational quid pro quo* may be. Identify what data you can provide in return for the data people give you. For instance, you may have access to special, nonproprietary research materials that may be of interest to them. Or you can offer to let them call you if and when they need information on a particular topic *they're* researching. The bottom line is to have something you can offer. You may never be asked for anything in return, but you should have something in mind if and when the request for a return favor is made.

—Tim Powell, T. W. Powell Company; former director,
Society of Competitive Intelligence Professionals (SCIP)

By studying the positions that target companies are currently seeking to fill, you can often glean information on the strategic initiatives driving the need for the professionals sought. For instance, a company seeking professionals with fluency in a particular language may be attempting to penetrate foreign markets in which that tongue is spoken.

Products

Information on a company's existing products is relatively easy to procure via such sources as company Web sites, print and broadcast advertising, in-store displays, and other forms of promotional media. Print clipping services also are valuable as a means of tracking product-related advertising. Video monitoring bureaus, the electronic counterpart of print clipping services, can supply tapes of radio and TV spots.

Other valuable sources of product information include retailers, wholesalers, and other intermediaries who move products manufactured by both the target company and its competitors. Not only can they provide details on current offerings, they may also be privy to details on soon-to-be-marketed goods and services or those currently under development.

Processes

Data on a company's core processes, such as manufacturing, R&D, production, finance, budgeting, and planning, is also worthwhile as you accumulate progressively more background on your priority M&A candidates. Many of the foregoing data sources will provide pieces of process-related information. For instance, article searches can be focused on articles written by company managers for technical publications and scholarly journals. Industry trade associations, as mentioned earlier, may also provide process-related information from an industry standpoint—data that can potentially lend insight into industry practices that the target company likely embraces.

Some process- and operations-related information is also contained in a company's annual report. Usually this relates to major new R&D investments and operating strategies. Financial data, needless to say, is also detailed in the annual report. Unfortunately, the wealth of operational and financial information contained in these publications is not attainable for private companies, which do not produce them. Compiling financial information on private companies requires constructing estimated financial statements, whose basis is data collected via the competitor analysis process. We will discuss how to construct a financial statement in a moment.

Customers

Included under "people" in the three P's of marketing due diligence-focused target company examinations is the category of "customers." At the outset of your acquisition candidate research it is important to begin assembling preliminary data on a target's buyers. Your initial task is to identify who the major ones are. Often the company itself actively promotes its buyers by "name dropping" the major companies it serves. Many of the promotional materials you would review to cull product-related information are likely to also contain information on major customers. If those sources do not provide this information, vendors and suppliers serving the industry segment in which the target operates should be able to cite some of the company's key purchasers. It is also important, if possible, to learn how big the existing accounts are.

Beware of companies that cite the names of major customers but have actually done only a small amount of work with them. You will also want to gauge whether or not the customer relationship is current. Many companies loudly trumpet their relationship with a given customer while, in reality, the work done for the customer was performed 10 years ago! Next, it is important to ascertain the extent to which the customer deals with the target in comparison to the target's competitors. For instance, if the target is one of 20 firms the customer does business with in procuring the same goods or services, that is vastly different than if the customer is a longtime buyer who deals with the target exclusively.

CONSTRUCTING A FINANCIAL STATEMENT

A specialized area of competitor analysis involves accumulating information that allows you to build an estimated financial statement for a given company. Divining fiscal information is important in cases where the target company under review is either a privately held concern or the subsidiary of a large corporation.

Financial performance information of public companies is required based on SEC regulations and rules of disclosure. However, private firms do not generally make their finances public, and the financial data of corporate subsidiaries is typically buried within the broader fiscal statistics of their parent companies. Still, private companies and corporate subsidiaries may be among the array of your primary acquisition candidates, and unearthing information on their financial performance becomes an important part of the screening process.

Constructing a financial statement involves tapping two readily accessible sources of information: credit reports and financial ratios.

Credit reports are among the first pieces of company-specific intelligence you should gather. These are relatively easy to attain. Credit reports provide such basic information as a company's sales and net worth, its primary line(s) of business, and SIC classification. Additional information is provided on the firm's past financial difficulties, legal actions brought against the company, and any court cases that are currently outstanding. The emphasis of a credit report is on a company's debt levels and payment history. Rarely do these reports contain specific information on the firm's income or operating expenses.

Besides the emphasis on debt levels, there are some other drawbacks to the information contained in credit reports. The first is that the data may be old. Typically, the credit agency does not have the company's latest financials. Second, the breadth of information covered in credit reports varies widely based on the credit source used and the amount of information it has been able to collect. The data presented may range from comprehensive financial statistics to merely a general rating as determined by the credit bureau's own analytical methodology. The third and most significant drawback is that many small private companies are not tracked.

Even though the information may be old, sketchy, or incomplete, it is still advisable to obtain a credit report for whatever financial data it does provide, either to supplement statistics you have been able to collect from other sources or to confirm or refute other information you have amassed.

The next step in assembling fiscal data on a target involves reviewing financial ratios of publicly traded companies of the same general size as the target. Ratios such as return on equity (ROE), return on assets (ROA), and current ratio (current assets divided by current liabilities) should be collected from multiple sources. For example, financial ratios are attainable from major trade groups, which track statistical data on companies operating in their particular industry segments. Ratio data is also available from leading banks, which track data on companies in hundreds of industries for the purpose of making lending decisions.

There are also publications produced by private concerns and governmental agencies that chronicle industry-specific financial data. These include volumes such as the *Annual Statement Studies* source, produced by Robert Morris Associates of Philadelphia, and the *Quarterly Financial Report for Manufacturing, Mining and Trade Corporations*, produced jointly by the U.S. Federal Trade Commission and the Securities and Exchange Commission.

It is important to emphasize that the process of constructing financial statements carries a large element of estimation. The goal is to compile as much statistical information on critical financial variables and to project its applicability to the target company. As we have seen, collecting financial information involves studying general industry averages culled largely from public-company filings and business and governmental information sources. The financial statement you ultimately construct should be reviewed by objective third parties. Earlier we cited consultants, journalists, and academicians as being sources of company and industry information. These are the same people you should turn to assess the accuracy of financial data you have compiled. You should maintain a reporter's sense of skepticism when gathering quantitative and qualitative data; never fully believe that which you discover without having confirmed it. Always check the information you have collected against other data to spot inconsistencies that may require additional investigation.

Although the accuracy and completeness of the financial data you collect may be extraordinarily suspect, the process of accumulating it is beneficial in and of itself. Conducting finance-oriented research helps you broaden your understanding of industry trends and dynamics and the performance of major industry players. Collectively, this data can be used to compare the target company against both its peers and other firms in the industry. In addition, financial research will give you many important quantitative benchmarks you can use when studying the target's actual financial performance when its books are eventually open for your review in the due diligence process.

Information-gathering relative to constructing financial statements may be the most difficult and time-consuming aspect of your research. It should come in the latter stages of your inquiry, after you have assembled as much qualitative data as possible. And considering the time and effort involved, it is advisable that this be reserved for the high-priority acquisition candidates on your final short list.

THE IMPORTANCE OF FACT-CHECKING

Conducting competitor analysis research is a lot like being a newspaper reporter. You dig for information. You see where that information leads. And you unearth other sources of data. Thinking like a reporter requires another important skill: fact-checking.

Not all information you uncover will be timely or accurate, so your findings must always be verified. Those findings even include information you obtained from ostensibly authoritative journalistic sources. Keep in mind that articles on a given topic may, in fact, be based on articles that were written by others. Information that was accurate in one news account may become inaccurate after it has been recycled in the creation of subsequent stories. Remember, research of any kind requires accumulating facts and ascertaining the currency and veracity of that information. Do so by checking your information against other sources, as well as with business leaders and industry analysts you will be interviewing.

A word of caution is in order relative to data collection via competitor analysis techniques: The information-gathering process must always be kept legal and ethical.

Acquisition candidate research involves exhaustive investigative analysis that invariably touches on highly proprietary, sensitive information. Yet, honesty and openness are the watchwords when employing competitor analysis techniques. That may seem to be at odds with the M&A planning process, an exercise that is typically characterized by secrecy and confidentiality. Using outside consultants, who can identify themselves without necessarily having to identify you, is advisable in situations where data is needed yet where protecting your corporate identity is imperative.

OTHER APPLICATIONS OF THE DATA COLLECTED

The information-gathering strategies we have discussed are valuable at various stages of a company's ongoing mergers and acquisitions program. Collecting company- and industry-specific information is useful during the initial planning phases when the organization is just considering an M&A transaction, through to the time when company officers are preparing to enact formal discussions with one or more target companies. Moreover, information collection and analysis is valuable in the following ways:

- Assessing various corporate growth options
- Modifying strategies and acquisition criteria
- Determining potential for strategic fit
- Spotting areas that would merit closer examination in later stages of investigation and due diligence
- Supplementing your marketing information system
- Showcasing knowledge of the target's strategic requirements
- Calculating the proposed purchase price

Assessing various corporate growth options. Information collection is invariably preceded by some kind of strategic self-assessment. Management identifies what its strategic needs are and begins to seek out market information to determine its various internal and external growth options. By determining what strategic or operational gaps need to be filled, the information-gathering process produces input for decision making on whether or not the sought-after attributes are attainable by merging with or acquiring another company. In essence, the company determines whether an acquisition is the appropriate growth strategy. It may be that a strategic alliance, joint venture, or equity investment is the more viable and cost-effective growth option at that particular point in time.

Modifying strategies and acquisition criteria. Information collection is central to compiling lists of potential acquisition candidates. As information is collected, the list of companies grows. As more data is accumulated, and companies are subjected to closer scrutiny, the target list often shrinks. When the list is narrowed down, additional information is collected on those remaining organizations. However, once ample information has been accumulated, it usually becomes apparent whether there are companies in the marketplace that can adequately meet your acquisition criteria. Chances are there are no companies that can, or that there are firms that would offer the attributes you seek but which would not be amenable to a corporate combination. At that point it may be necessary to modify your strategic parameters. In other words, you may have to redefine your acquisition criteria to make them more realistic in terms of the actual availability of viable M&A candidates.

Determining potential for strategic fit. The more data you collect and the deeper you probe into a given company, the more you will be able to gauge its potential strategic fit (or lack thereof) with your organization. The information you gather will indicate where a company is, where it is heading, what it stands for, and how compatible or incompatible that organization is with your own, both operationally and culturally.

You may discover that the company is similar enough to yours in certain critical respects that a true fit can most certainly be achieved. On the other hand, you may discover that nothing short of a complete revamping of the target's organizational and cultural composition can ever enable the melding of the two organizations. Obviously, if the latter is the case, that company would get scratched from your target list. Conversely, there may be differences that are significant but which would not pose insurmountable obstacles to a successful union.

Spotting areas that would merit closer examination in later stages of investigation and due diligence. Differences in operations and strategic philosophy do not necessarily mean that a merger with a particular company would be disastrous. Marked differences may, however, raise red flags that should be addressed if and when you enter into formal merger discussions. That you have done your homework allows you to probe into issues and concerns when the actual negotiations commence. In other words, you know what potential problems exist and you are prepared to actively address them. Many times what appears to be an onerous situation may actually be less problematic once the issue is put on the table and the target's management has had a chance to respond to it.

Supplementing your marketing information system. Even if you ultimately decide not to pursue an acquisition, the data-collection process serves to supplement your ongoing marketing information systems. Data you collect on companies operating in a given market or industry segment constitutes a repository of timely intelligence that can be used for other business development applications. Growth planning strategies key on the collection and analysis of product- and market-related information. But, the fact is many corporate functions directly align with sales and marketing management (e.g., R&D and manufacturing). It is likely, therefore, that generating marketing-related information via acquisition research will necessarily yield additional data useful for other business development purposes or for ongoing competitor analysis and tracking.

Showcasing knowledge of the target's strategic requirements. Understanding your strategic drivers helps focus your search for likely acquisition candidates. Understanding a *target's* strategic requirements helps determine the viability of the potential fit between you and the target company, and assists you in "selling" the conceptual transaction to that merger candidate. In other words, your company-specific research will unearth information on a candidate's strategic drivers. Showcasing that knowledge at the point where you formally approach the target will significantly strengthen your solicitation and lay the foundation for focused and substantive discussions. Your credibility is greatly enhanced when you can showcase an intimate understanding of that firm's business and strategy and articulate specific potential growth synergies. Detailed and accurate intelligence will give you the powerful insights needed to make the most compelling and persuasive solicitation possible.

Calculating the proposed purchase price. Gathering detailed data on a target company will assist you in determining the ultimate value of that organization. When negotiations commence, there will be an asking price set forth by the seller based on a combination of financial indicators on current performance and future projections. The data you have collected on fiscal, operational, and business development characteristics of the target company will be useful in assessing the initial asking price and in subsequent negotiations relative to calculating the final deal premium.

Arming yourself with information to identify and preliminary assess acquisition candidates helps makes your M&A efforts more efficient. Good research will pinpoint worthwhile candidates that merit further investigation, and will provide you with much of the background you need to determine what company or companies you plan to ultimately approach. Conversely, research will quickly spot those target companies that will never serve your strategic objectives.

Once you have made contact with the target organization, hammered out the basic terms of the transaction, and detailed those provisions in the letter of intent, the marketing due diligence process commences. Now let's turn to the analytical techniques that must be employed in assessing the precise areas of growth potential offered by the target company, and the planning steps necessary to devise actions plan that will enable you to realize top-line revenue enhancement.

INDEX

Printed in the United States
114500LV00002B/6/A

9 780471 190561